Q161.2 .E94 2019 Gr.6
Elevate Science

Course 1

D1476899

elevate science

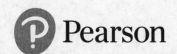 Pearson

Boston, Massachusetts **Chandler, Arizona**
Glenview, Illinois **New York, New York**

MURDOCK LEARNING RESOURCE CENTER
GEORGE FOX UNIVERSITY
NEWBERG, OR 97132

You're an author!

As you write in this science book, your answers and personal discoveries will be recorded for you to keep, making this book unique to you. That is why you are one of the primary authors of this book.

✏ **In the space below, print your name, school, town, and state. Then write a short autobiography that includes your interests and accomplishments.**

YOUR NAME ....

SCHOOL ....

TOWN, STATE ....

AUTOBIOGRAPHY ....

....

....

....

....

....

....

Your Photo

The cover photo shows lava entering the sea from an active volcano in Kilauea, Hawaii.

Pearson Education, Inc. 330 Hudson Street, New York, NY 10013

Copyright © 2019 Pearson Education, Inc., or its affiliates. All Rights Reserved. Printed in the United States of America.

This publication is protected by copyright, and permission should be obtained from the publisher prior to any prohibited reproduction, storage in a retrieval system, or transmission in any form or by any means, electronic, mechanical, photocopying, recording, or otherwise. For information regarding permissions, request forms, and the appropriate contacts within the Pearson Education Global Rights & Permissions Department, please visit www.pearsoned.com/permissions/.

Attributions of third-party content appear on pages 528–530, which constitute an extension of this copyright page.

PEARSON and ALWAYS LEARNING are exclusive trademarks owned by Pearson Education, Inc. or its affiliates in the United States and/or other countries.

littleBits, littleBits logo and Bits are trademarks of littleBits Electronics Inc. All rights reserved.

Unless otherwise indicated herein, any third-party trademarks that may appear in this work are the property of their respective owners and any references to third-party trademarks, logos, or other trade dress are for demonstrative or descriptive purposes only. Such references are not intended to imply any sponsorship, endorsement, authorization, or promotion of Pearson's products by the owners of such marks, or any relationship between the owner and Pearson Education, Inc. or its affiliates, authors, licensees, or its affiliates, authors, licensees or distributors.

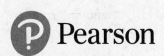

ISBN-13: 978-0-328-92506-3
ISBN-10: 0-328-92506-3

1   17

Program Authors

ZIPPORAH MILLER, Ed.D.
Coordinator for K-12 Science Programs, Anne Arundel County Public Schools
Dr. Zipporah Miller currently serves as the Senior Manager for Organizational Learning with the Anne Arundel County Public School System. Prior to that she served as the K-12 Coordinator for science in Anne Arundel County. She conducts national training to science stakeholders on the Next Generation Science Standards. Dr. Miller also served as the Associate Executive Director for Professional Development Programs and conferences at the National Science Teachers Association (NSTA) and served as a reviewer during the development of Next Generation Science Standards. Dr. Miller holds a doctoral degree from the University of Maryland College Park, a master's degree in school administration and supervision from Bowie State University and a bachelor's degree from Chadron State College.

MICHAEL J. PADILLA, Ph.D.
Professor Emeritus, Eugene P. Moore School of Education, Clemson University, Clemson, South Carolina
Michael J. Padilla taught science in middle and secondary schools, has more than 30 years of experience educating middle-school science teachers, and served as one of the writers of the 1996 U.S. National Science Education Standards. In recent years Mike has focused on teaching science to English Language Learners. His extensive experience as Principal Investigator on numerous National Science Foundation and U.S. Department of Education grants resulted in more than $35 million in funding to improve science education. He served as president of the National Science Teachers Association, the world's largest science teaching organization, in 2005–6.

MICHAEL E. WYSESSION, Ph.D
Professor of Earth and Planetary Sciences, Washington University, St. Louis, Missouri
Author of more than 100 science and science education publications, Dr. Wysession was awarded the prestigious National Science Foundation Presidential Faculty Fellowship and Packard Foundation Fellowship for his research in geophysics, primarily focused on using seismic tomography to determine the forces driving plate tectonics. Dr. Wysession is also a leader in geoscience literacy and education; he is the chair of the Earth Science Literacy Initiative, the author of several popular video lectures on geology in the *Great Courses* series, and a lead writer of the *Next Generation Science Standards**.

*Next Generation Science Standards is a registered trademark of Achieve. Neither Achieve nor the lead states and partners that developed the Next Generation Science Standards were involved in the production of this product, and do not endorse it. NGSS Lead States. 2013. *Next Generation Science Standards: For States, By States.* Washington, DC: The National Academies Press.

REVIEWERS

Program Consultants

Carol Baker
Science Curriculum

Dr. Carol K. Baker is superintendent for Lyons Elementary K-8 School District in Lyons, Illinois. Prior to this, she was Director of Curriculum for Science and Music in Oak Lawn, Illinois. Before this she taught Physics and Earth Science for 18 years. In the recent past, Dr. Baker also wrote assessment questions for ACT (EXPLORE and PLAN), was elected president of the Illinois Science Teachers Association from 2011–2013, and served as a member of the Museum of Science and Industry (Chicago) advisory board. Dr. Baker received her B.S. in Physics and a science teaching certification. She completed her master's of Educational Administration (K-12) and earned her doctorate in Educational Leadership.

Jim Cummins
ELL

Dr. Cummins's research focuses on literacy development in multilingual schools and the role technology plays in learning across the curriculum. *Elevate Science* incorporates research-based principles for integrating language with the teaching of academic content based on Dr. Cummins's work.

Elfrieda Hiebert
Literacy

Dr. Hiebert, a former primary-school teacher, is President and CEO of TextProject, a non-profit aimed at providing open-access resources for instruction of beginning and struggling readers, She is also a research associate at the University of California Santa Cruz. Her research addresses how fluency, vocabulary, and knowledge can be fostered through appropriate texts, and her contributions have been recognized through awards such as the Oscar Causey Award for Outstanding Contributions to Reading Research (Literacy Research Association, 2015), Research to Practice award (American Educational Research Association, 2013), and the William S. Gray Citation of Merit Award for Outstanding Contributions to Reading Research (International Reading Association, 2008).

Content Reviewers

Alex Blom, Ph.D.
Associate Professor
Department Of Physical Sciences
Alverno College
Milwaukee, Wisconsin

Joy Branlund, Ph.D.
Department of Physical Science
Southwestern Illinois College
Granite City, Illinois

Judy Calhoun
Associate Professor
Physical Sciences
Alverno College
Milwaukee, Wisconsin

Stefan Debbert
Associate Professor of Chemistry
Lawrence University
Appleton, Wisconsin

Diane Doser
Professor
Department of Geological Sciences
University of Texas at El Paso
El Paso, Texas

Rick Duhrkopf, Ph.D.
Department of Biology
Baylor University
Waco, Texas

Jennifer Liang
University of Minnesota Duluth
Duluth, Minnesota

Heather Mernitz, Ph.D.
Associate Professor of Physical Sciences
Alverno College
Milwaukee, Wisconsin

Joseph McCullough, Ph.D.
Cabrillo College
Aptos, California

Katie M. Nemeth, Ph.D.
Assistant Professor
College of Science and Engineering
University of Minnesota Duluth
Duluth, Minnesota

Maik Pertermann
Department of Geology
Western Wyoming Community College
Rock Springs, Wyoming

Scott Rochette
Department of the Earth Sciences
The College at Brockport
 State University of New York
Brockport, New York

David Schuster
Washington University in St Louis
St. Louis, Missouri

Shannon Stevenson
Department of Biology
University of Minnesota Duluth
Duluth, Minnesota

Paul Stoddard, Ph.D.
Department of Geology and
 Environmental Geosciences
Northern Illinois University
DeKalb, Illinois

Nancy Taylor
American Public University
Charles Town, West Virginia

Teacher Reviewers

Jennifer Bennett, M.A.
Memorial Middle School
Tampa, Florida

Sonia Blackstone
Lake County Schools
Howey In the Hills, Florida

Teresa Bode
Roosevelt Elementary
Tampa, Florida

Tyler C. Britt, Ed.S.
Curriculum & Instructional
 Practice Coordinator
Raytown Quality Schools
Raytown, Missouri

A. Colleen Campos
Grandview High School
Aurora, Colorado

Ronald Davis
Riverview Elementary
Riverview, Florida

Coleen Doulk
Challenger School
Spring Hill, Florida

Mary D. Dube
Burnett Middle School
Seffner, Florida

Sandra Galpin
Adams Middle School
Tampa, Florida

Margaret Henry
Lebanon Junior High School
Lebanon, Ohio

Christina Hill
Beth Shields Middle School
Ruskin, Florida

Judy Johnis
Gorden Burnett Middle School
Seffner, Florida

Karen Y. Johnson
Beth Shields Middle School
Ruskin, Florida

Jane Kemp
Lockhart Elementary School
Tampa, Florida

Denise Kuhling
Adams Middle School
Tampa, Florida

Esther Leonard, M.Ed. and L.M.T.
Gifted and talented Implementation Specialist
San Antonio Independent School District
San Antonio, Texas

Kelly Maharaj
Challenger K–8 School of Science
 and Mathematics
Spring Hill, Florida

Kevin J. Maser, Ed.D.
H. Frank Carey Jr/Sr High School
Franklin Square, New York

Angie L. Matamoros, Ph.D.
ALM Science Consultant
Weston, Florida

Corey Mayle
Brogden Middle School
Durham, North Carolina

Keith McCarthy
George Washington Middle School
Wayne, New Jersey

Yolanda O. Peña
John F. Kennedy Junior High School
West Valley City, Utah

Kathleen M. Poe
Jacksonville Beach Elementary School
Jacksonville Beach, Florida

Wendy Rauld
Monroe Middle School
Tampa, Florida

Anne Rice
Woodland Middle School
Gurnee, Illinois

Bryna Selig
Gaithersburg Middle School
Gaithersburg, Maryland

Pat (Patricia) Shane, Ph.D.
STEM & ELA Education Consultant
Chapel Hill, North Carolina

Diana Shelton
Burnett Middle School
Seffner, Florida

Nakia Sturrup
Jennings Middle School
Seffner, Florida

Melissa Triebwasser
Walden Lake Elementary
Plant City, Florida

Michele Bubley Wiehagen
Science Coach
Miles Elementary School
Tampa, Florida

Pauline Wilcox
Instructional Science Coach
Fox Chapel Middle School
Spring Hill, Florida

Safety Reviewers

Douglas Mandt, M.S.
Science Education Consultant
Edgewood, Washington

Juliana Textley, Ph.D.
Author, NSTA books on school science safety
Adjunct Professor
Lesley University
Cambridge, Massachusetts

Go to PearsonRealize.com
to access your digital course.

▶ **VIDEO**
• Museum Technician

👆 **INTERACTIVITY**
• What Makes Up Matter?
• Molecules and Extended Structures
• Calculating Density
• Weight on the Moon
• Properties of Matter

📱 **VIRTUAL LAB**

☑ **ASSESSMENT**

📖 **eTEXT**

📱 **APP**

HANDS-ON LABS

Connect The Nuts and Bolts of Formulas

Investigate
• Models of Atoms and Molecules
• Observing Physical Properties
• Physical and Chemical Changes

Demonstrate
Help Out the Wildlife

TOPIC 2

Solids, Liquids, and Gases

The Essential Question What causes matter to change from one state to another?

Quest KICKOFF Getting a Lift

MS-PS1-4

Go to PearsonRealize.com
to access your digital course.

▶ **VIDEO**
• Materials Scientist

👆 **INTERACTIVITY**
• Particles and States of Matter
• Properties of Solids, Liquids, and Gases
• A Matter of Printing
• Particle Motion and States of Matter
• States of Matter
• Thermal Energy and Changes of State
• Gas Laws
• Hot Air Balloon Ride

📱 **VIRTUAL LAB**

☑ **ASSESSMENT**

📖 **eTEXT**

📱 **APP**

HANDS-ON LABS

иConnect Solid, Liquid, or Gas?

иInvestigate
• Properties of Matter
• Mirror, Mirror
• Testing Charles's and Boyle's Laws

иDemonstrate
Melting Ice

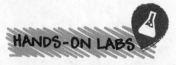
Go to PearsonRealize.com
to access your digital course.

▶ **VIDEO**
  • Energy Engineer

INTERACTIVITY
  • Get the Ball Rolling • Understanding Machines • Levers • Force and Energy • Interpret Kinetic Energy Graphs • Racing for Kinetic Energy • Roller Coasters and Potential Energy • Prosthetics in Motion • Types of Energy • Forms of Energy • Energy Transformations • Take It to the Extreme

VIRTUAL LAB

ASSESSMENT

eTEXT

APP

HANDS-ON LABS

иConnect What Would Make a Card Jump?

иInvestigate
  • What Work Is
  • Mass, Velocity, and Kinetic Energy
  • Energy, Magnetism, and Electricity
  • Making a Flashlight Shine
  • Law of Conservation of Energy

иDemonstrate
3, 2, 1... Liftoff!

▶ **VIDEO**
• Firefighter

● **INTERACTIVITY**
• Flow of Thermal Energy
• A Rising Thermometer
• Methods of Thermal Energy Transfer
• Heat and Reheat
• A Day at the Beach
• Solar Oven Design
• Matter and Thermal Energy Transfer

▯ **VIRTUAL LAB**

☑ **ASSESSMENT**

▥ **eTEXT**

▯ **APP**

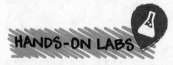

HANDS-ON LABS

Connect How Cold Is the Water?

Investigate
• Temperature and Thermal Energy
• Visualizing Convection Currents
• In Hot Water

Demonstrate
Testing Thermal Conductivity

TOPIC

5

Introduction to Earth's Systems 174

The Essential Question How do matter and energy cycle through Earth's systems?

Quest KICKOFF Forest Fires 176

MS-ESS2-1, MS-ESS2-4

Go to PearsonRealize.com to access your digital course.

VIDEO
- Aquaculture Manager

INTERACTIVITY
- Describing Systems
- Thermal Energy and the Cycling of Matter
- Maps and Methods
- Constructive and Destructive Forces
- The Water Cycle
- Siting a Fish Farm
- Floridan Aquifer System

VIRTUAL LAB

ASSESSMENT

eTEXT

APP

HANDS-ON LABS

Connect What Interactions Occur Within the Earth System?

Investigate
- Where Heat Flows
- Surface Features
- Water on Earth

Demonstrate
Modeling a Watershed

TOPIC 6 Weather in the Atmosphere ... 218

The **Essential Question** What determines weather on Earth?

Quest KICKOFF Preparing a Plan 220

MS-ESS2-4, MS-ESS2-5, MS-ESS2-6, MS-ESS3-2, MS-PS1-4

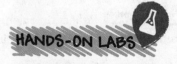

Go to PearsonRealize.com to access your digital course.

▶ **VIDEO**
  • Meteorologist

👆 **INTERACTIVITY**
  • Layers in the Atmosphere • Patterns in the Wind • Ways That Water Moves • Water Cycle • Interruptions in the Water Cycle • Clean Drinking Water • When Air Masses Collide • Mapping Out the Weather • Using Air Masses to Predict Weather • Weather Predicting • Not in Kansas Anymore • Tinkering with Technology

📱 **VIRTUAL LAB**

☑ **ASSESSMENT**

📖 **eTEXT**

📱 **APP**

HANDS-ON LABS

иConnect Puddle Befuddlement

иInvestigate
  • Effects of Altitude on the Atmosphere
  • How Clouds and Fog Form
  • Weather Fronts
  • Tracking Weather
  • Predicting Hurricanes

иDemonstrate
Water from Trees

TOPIC 7

Minerals and Rocks in the Geosphere 276

 The Essential Question What events form Earth's rocks?

 **Quest KICKOFF** Science in the Movies 278

MS-ESS2-1

 **Go to PearsonRealize.com to access your digital course.**

▶ **VIDEO**
• Product Engineer

☝ **INTERACTIVITY**
• Hot on the Inside
• Earth's Layers
• Comparing Earth and the Moon
• Designing Satellites
• So Many, Many Minerals
• Mineral Management
• Don't Take it for Granite
• Is There a Geologist in the House?
• Rocky Changes
• Rock Cycle
• Rocks on the Move

▣ **VIRTUAL LAB**

☑ **ASSESSMENT**

▥ **eTEXT**

▢ **APP**

HANDS-ON LABS

u**Connect** Build a Model of Earth

u**Investigate**
• Heat and Motion in a Liquid
• Mineral Mash-Up
• Growing a Crystal Garden
• A Sequined Rock
• Ages of Rocks

u**Demonstrate**
The Rock Cycle in Action

TOPIC
8

Plate Tectonics 326

The Essential Question How do geological processes change Earth's surface?

Quest KICKOFF To Hike or Not to Hike 328

Go to PearsonRealize.com
to access your digital course.

▶ **VIDEO**
• Volcanologist

👆 **INTERACTIVITY**
• Land and Seafloor Patterns
• Slow and Steady
• By No Fault of Their Own
• Relative Plate Motion
• Stressed to a Fault
• Earthquake Engineering
• Locating an Earthquake
• Placing a Bay Area Stadium
• Landforms from Volcanic Activity
• Volcanoes Changing Earth's Surface

📱 **VIRTUAL LAB**

☑ **ASSESSMENT**

📖 **eTEXT**

📱 **APP**

HANDS-ON LABS

uConnect How Are Earth's Continents Linked Together?

uInvestigate
• Piecing Together a Supercontinent
• Plate Interactions
• Analyze Earthquake Data to Identify Patterns
• Moving Volcanoes

uDemonstrate
Model Sea-Floor Spreading

TOPIC 9 Earth's Surface Systems

The Essential Question What processes change Earth's surface?

MS-ESS2-2, MS-ESS3-2

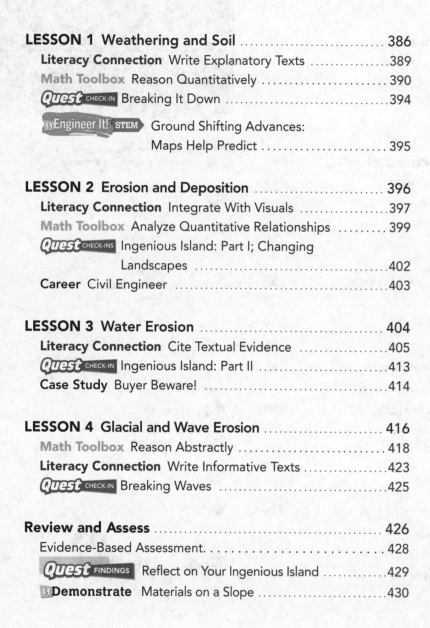

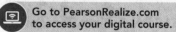
Go to PearsonRealize.com
to access your digital course.

▶ VIDEO
- Civil Engineer

👆 INTERACTIVITY
- Colors of the Sand
- Dating Using Weathering Rates
- Classify the Force of Weathering
- Predicting Disasters
- Material Slope Angle
- Changing Landscapes
- Karst Topography
- Carving a Canyon
- Mammoth Caves
- Effects of Glaciers
- Glacial Ice
- Coastline Management

📱 VIRTUAL LAB

☑ ASSESSMENT

📖 eTEXT

📱 APP

HANDS-ON LABS

uConnect How Does Gravity
Affect Materials on a Slope?

uInvestigate
- Freezing and Thawing
- Small, Medium, and Large
- Raindrops Falling
- Changing Coastlines

uDemonstrate
Materials on a Slope

 Go to PearsonRealize.com
to access your digital course.

VIDEO
• Public Health Advisor

INTERACTIVITY
• What All Living Things Have in Common
• Mom's Car Must Be Alive
• Classify It
• Life as a Single Cell
• Viruses by the Numbers
• Vaccines and Populations
• There's Something Going Around
• Modifying a Virus
• Different Cells, Different Jobs
• Identifying an Organism
• Organization of Organisms

VIRTUAL LAB

ASSESSMENT

eTEXT

APP

HANDS-ON LABS

uConnect Is It an Animal?

uInvestigate
• Cheek Cells
• Living Mysteries
• A Mystery Organism No More!
• Life In a Drop of Pond Water
• Algae and Other Plants

uDemonstrate
It's Alive!

Elevate your thinking!

Elevate Science takes science to a whole new level and lets you take ownership of your learning. Explore science in the world around you. Investigate how things work. Think critically and solve problems! *Elevate Science* helps you think like a scientist, so you're ready for a world of discoveries.

Explore Your World

Explore real-life scenarios with engaging Quests that dig into science topics around the world. You can:

- Solve real-world problems
- Apply skills and knowledge
- Communicate solutions

Make Connections

Elevate Science connects science to other subjects and shows you how to better understand the world through:

- Mathematics
- Reading and Writing
- Literacy

Quest KICKOFF

What do you think is causing Pleasant Pond to turn green?

In 2016, algal blooms turned bodies of water green and slimy in Florida, Utah, California, and 17 other states. These blooms put people and ecosystems in danger. Scientists, such as limnologists, are working to predict and prevent future algal blooms. In this problem-based Quest activity, you will investigate an algal bloom at a lake and determine its cause. In labs and digital activities, you will apply what you learn in each lesson to help you gather evidence to solve the mystery. With enough evidence, you will be able to identify what you believe is the cause of the algal bloom and present a solution in the Findings activity.

Math Toolbox

Graphing Population Changes

Ohio's Deer Population

Changes in a population over time, such as white-tailed deer in Ohio, can be displayed in a graph.

Deer Population Trends, 2000–2010

Year	Population (estimated)	Year	Population (estimated)
2000	525,000	2006	770,000
2001	560,000	2007	725,000
2002	620,000	2008	745,000
2003	670,000	2009	750,000
2004	715,000	2010	710,000
2005	720,000		

Relationships Use the data

READING CHECK **Determine Central ideas**
What adaptations might the giraffe have that help it survive in its environment?

Academic Vocabulary

Relate the term *decomposer* to the verb *compose*. What does it mean to compose something?

Build Skills for the Future

- Master the Engineering Design Process
- Apply critical thinking and analytical skills
- Learn about STEM careers

Focus on Inquiry

Case studies put you in the shoes of a scientist to solve real-world mysteries using real data. You will be able to:

- Analyze Data
- Test a hypothesis
- Solve the Case

Case Study

MS-LS2-1

THE CASE OF THE DISAPPEARING

Cerulean Warbler

The cerulean warbler is a small, migratory songbird named for its blue color. Cerulean warblers breed in eastern North America during the spring and summer. The war blers spend the winter months in the Andes Mountains of Colombia, Venezuela, Ecuador, and Peru in northern South America.

Enter the Lab

Hands-on experiments and virtual labs help you test ideas and show what you know in performance-based assessments. Scaffolded labs include:

- STEM Labs
- Design Your Own
- Open-ended Labs

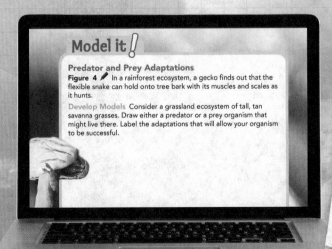

Model it!

Predator and Prey Adaptations
Figure 4 In a rainforest ecosystem, a gecko finds out that the flexible snake can hold onto tree bark with its muscles and scales as it hunts.

Develop Models Consider a grassland ecosystem of tall, tan savanna grasses. Draw either a predator or a prey organism that might live there. Label the adaptations that will allow your organism to be successful.

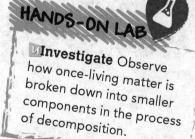

HANDS-ON LAB

Investigate Observe how once-living matter is broken down into smaller components in the process of decomposition.

NGSS PERFORMANCE EXPECTATIONS

MS-PS1-1 Develop models to describe the atomic composition of simple molecules and extended structures.

MS-PS1-2 Analyze and interpret data on the properties of substances before and after the substances interact to determine if a chemical reaction has occurred.

GO ONLINE
to access your
digital course

 VIDEO

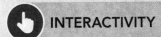 INTERACTIVITY

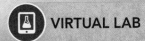 VIRTUAL LAB

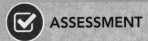 ASSESSMENT

 eTEXT

 APP

How did this ice form?

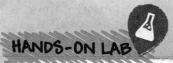

HANDS-ON LAB

и**Connect** See how you can model particles that are so small you can't see them.

The Essential Question

How can we observe, measure, and use matter?

If you step outside when the temperature is well below freezing, you can bet it will not be raining. You are more likely to see snow if there is any precipitation at all. Water in the clouds is so cold that it turns into ice crystals. What are some of the physical differences between rain water and ice crystals such as snow?

....

....

....

....

....

Quest KICKOFF

How can you use science to make special effects?

Phenomenon A special effects company would like to be chosen to develop the special effects for a new movie. But first, the movie director wants to check out the company's capabilities. In this problem-based Quest activity, you will develop a movie scene that uses some amazing special effects. You will write the script and the storyboards. As you develop the special effects, you will explore different types of substances that are used to make special effects. You will understand the role that physical and chemical properties of matter play in the special effects. Finally, you will present your scene, along with an explanation of the special effects and the properties of matter behind them.

 INTERACTIVITY

Lights! Camera! Action!

MS-PS1-2 Analyze and interpret data on the properties of substances before and after the substances interact to determine if a chemical reaction has occurred.

NBC LEARN ▶ VIDEO

After watching the Quest Kickoff video about special effects, complete the sentences about special effects you have seen in movies. Then discuss your answers with a partner.

1 One special effect I have seen is

....

....

....

2 It added to the scene because

....

....

....

Quest CHECK-IN

IN LESSON 1
How can substance changes play a role in special effects? Think about how you can take advantage of physical and chemical changes to create special effects.

 INTERACTIVITY

The Science of Special Effects

IN LESSON 2
How will the amounts of substances affect physical and chemical changes? Consider the amounts of substances you will need to create the special effects you want.

Quest CHECK-INS

IN LESSON 3
How do substances interact? Explore substances and how they interact. Collect and analyze data to help develop your special effects.

 INTERACTIVITY

Mysterious Movie Fog

HANDS-ON LAB

Cinematic Science

Smoke in movie scenes can be eye-catching and dramatic, but it is never accidental. Directors carefully manage the production and movement of the smoke to create the desired effect.

Quest FINDINGS

Complete the Quest!

Present your scene and storyboard, and include an explanation of the physical and chemical changes involved in your special effects.

👆 **INTERACTIVITY**

Reflect on Your Scene

3

1 Describing and Classifying Matter

Guiding Questions

- What is matter made of?
- What properties describe matter?
- How can you classify different types of matter?

Connection

Literacy Integrate With Visuals

MS-PS1-1

Vocabulary

matter
substance
physical property
chemical property
atom
element
molecule
compound
mixture

Academic Vocabulary

distill

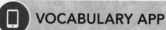 **VOCABULARY APP**

Practice vocabulary on a mobile device.

Quest CONNECTION

As you learn to describe and classify matter, think about what types of properties you would want your special effects to provide for the scene in the movie.

Connect It !

✎ **Several substances are shown in Figure 1. Two of the substances are in two different forms. Label these substances and each of their forms on the image.**

Identify Is there any matter in **Figure 1** that you cannot see?

....

Form a Hypothesis What substance might impact the formation of volcanic rock?

....

Matter

Anything that has mass and takes up space is **matter**. Wood, metal, paper, glass, cloth, plastic, and air are all matter. In fact, you are made of matter, too. We classify different types of matter by their properties. Some matter is visible, some is not. Some types of matter are usually found in liquid form, and others are usually solid. Chemistry is the study of matter and how it changes.

One of the first steps in classifying matter is to determine whether something is a **substance**—a single kind of matter that always has a specific makeup, or composition. For example, sodium chloride is a substance that we know as table salt. It is considered a pure substance because its composition is the same whether you're looking at a single grain of salt or a boulder of salt taken from a salt mine. Sea salt, on the other hand, which is formed when seawater evaporates, is not a pure substance. There are many other substances in seawater, and those substances are left behind with sodium chloride when the water evaporates.

Matter on Earth
Figure 1 Hot lava cools in the ocean to form this volcanic island.

VIDEO

Learn more about physical and chemical properties.

Physical Properties

Whether you have a pure substance, such as gold, or a mixture, such as seawater, how it behaves and interacts with other substances depends on its properties. A **physical property** is a characteristic that can be observed without changing the matter into another type of matter. For example, gold melts at 1,064°C and boils at 2,856°C. It is an excellent conductor, meaning electricity moves through it very easily. Gold also has a high luster, or shininess, and a distinctive color. All of these characteristics are physical properties. They can be observed without changing the gold into something else.

Physical and Chemical Properties

Figure 2 Can you tell physical and chemical properties apart?

1. Synthesize Information Analyze the photos and read their captions. Write "physical" or "chemical" next to "Property".

2. Cite Evidence Below each photo, cite evidence that guided you to classify the properties as physical or chemical.

Water and carbon dioxide in the leaves of the coconut palm tree are converted to oxygen and sugar, thanks to the energy provided by the sun.

Oxygen is a substance that dissolves in water. Fish absorb oxygen from the water. When dissolved oxygen levels are low, it can be hard for organisms to survive.

Property

Evidence

....

....

....

Property

Evidence

....

....

....

Chemical Properties Other properties can only be observed by combining or breaking apart substances. These are **chemical properties**—characteristics that describe something's ability to become something else. For example, if you inject carbon dioxide gas into liquid water, some of the water will react with the carbon dioxide to produce carbonic acid. This ability to react is a chemical property of water. Likewise, the ability of carbon dioxide to combine with water and become carbonic acid is a chemical property.

Look at the images in **Figure 2** and read their captions. The images and captions will help you determine whether chemical or physical properties are being described.

✓READING CHECK **Infer** Flammability is a measure of how easily something burns. Is this a physical or chemical property? Explain, using an example.

....

....

....

....

Literacy Connection

Integrate With Visuals As you determine whether the images and descriptions involve physical or chemical properties, set up a two-column table in your notebook in which you can record and classify examples of physical and chemical properties.

📓**Reflect** Think of two substances that aren't mentioned on these pages. Name a physical and chemical property for each one.

If iron is exposed to air and water, it can rust.

Property

Evidence

....

....

....

Wood tends to be hard and relatively inflexible, especially when it's been dried. This is why wood is an excellent building material.

Property

Evidence

....

....

....

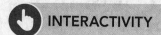
Components of Matter

There are a lot of tiny particles we can see, such as grains of sand. Have you ever wondered whether these tiny grains have even smaller particles inside? They do! The particle theory of matter explains that all matter is made up of very tiny particles called atoms.

Atoms An **atom** is the basic unit from which all matter is made. Different substances are made up of different types of atoms. But all atoms have the same basic structure. An atom has a positively charged center, or nucleus, containing smaller particles. Negatively charged particles circle around the nucleus and form a cloud of negative charge.

Elements Substances that are made up of only one type of atom are called **elements**. For instance, the element aluminum is made of only aluminum atoms, and no other pure substance has atoms like aluminum's atoms. Each element can be identified by its specific physical and chemical properties. You may already be familiar with some elements such as gold, oxygen, and carbon (**Figure 3**). These cannot be broken down into different substances. Elements are represented by one- or two-letter symbols, such as O for oxygen and Al for aluminum.

Atoms Combining

Figure 3 Diamond and graphite are extended structures of the same element: carbon. Diamond, the hardest natural substance, forms under intense pressure, with atoms packed tightly together. Carbon atoms form layers in graphite which easily slide and break off.

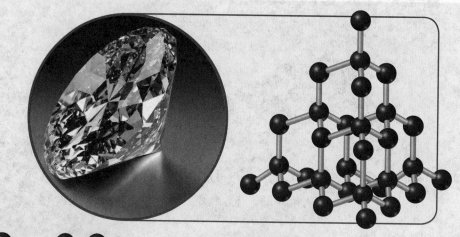

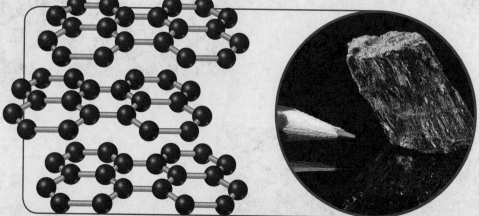

Molecules Most atoms can combine with other atoms. When this happens, a chemical bond forms. A chemical bond is a force of attraction between two or more atoms. Sometimes, atoms combine to form extended structures. One type of extended structure is a molecule. A **molecule** is a group of two or more atoms held together by chemical bonds. A molecule of carbon dioxide, as shown in Figure 4 for example, is made up of a carbon atom chemically bonded to two oxygen atoms. Two atoms of the same element can also combine to form a molecule. For example, a hydrogen molecule is made up of two hydrogen atoms. Some large molecules are made of thousands of atoms!

HANDS-ON LAB

☑**Investigate** Develop your own models of atoms and molecules.

Model It !

Molecules and Atoms

Figure 4 The four molecules shown here are made of different combinations of carbon, oxygen, or hydrogen atoms. Below each molecule, list the types of atoms in it and how many atoms there are of each type. The first answer is completed as an example.

Water	Oxygen	Carbon dioxide	Methane

1 oxygen atom,
....
2 hydrogen atoms
....

Develop Models ✎
Draw a model of a two-atom molecule of hydrogen and label the atoms.

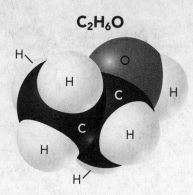

C₂H₆O

Compound From Corn

Figure 5 Ethanol is a chemical compound made from sugars in corn and other plants. It can be burned to power engines.

👆 **INTERACTIVITY**

Develop models of extended structures including molecules.

Compounds When a molecule contains more than one element, it is called a compound. A **compound** is a substance made of two or more elements that are chemically combined in a set ratio. A compound is represented by a chemical formula, which shows the elements in the compound and the ratio of atoms. For example, the chemical formula for carbon dioxide is CO_2. The subscript *2* tells you that every molecule of carbon dioxide contains two oxygen atoms. If there is no number after an element's symbol, it is understood that the number is 1. In CO_2, there is one carbon atom. The ratio of carbon to oxygen is 1 to 2.

When elements chemically combine, they form compounds with properties different from those of the individual elements. Ethanol, shown in **Figure 5**, is a compound that contains carbon, but because it also contains hydrogen and oxygen, and the molecule has a particular shape, it has different properties than the pure forms of carbon, hydrogen, and oxygen. There are many different compounds made of different combinations and configurations of those three elements.

☑ READING CHECK **Integrate With Visuals** How are pure carbon, oxygen, and hydrogen different from the compound ethanol which contains all three of those elements?

....

....

....

....

Types of Mixtures

You have learned that elements and compounds are substances. Most of the things found in nature, however, are not simple elements or compounds—they are mixtures. A **mixture** is made up of two or more substances that are together in the same place, but their atoms are not chemically bonded.

Mixtures differ from compounds. Each substance in a mixture keeps its own properties. Also, the parts of a mixture are not necessarily combined in a set ratio. Look at **Figure 6A**, which shows a bowl of mixed nuts. They are mixed together, but they are not chemically bonded to each other. This type of mixture is known as a heterogeneous mixture.

A homogeneous mixture is different from a heterogeneous mixture. In a homogeneous mixture, it is difficult or impossible to see the different parts. Combining dry ingredients for baking results in a homogeneous mixture, as shown in **Figure 6B**. Air is another homogeneous mixture, made of gases rather than solids. You know that oxygen is present in the air because you are able to breathe, but you cannot pinpoint exactly where the oxygen is in the air. A solution is a liquid example of a homogeneous mixture. Salt water is an example of a solution.

If you want to separate a mixture, you need to divide its parts according to their properties. This is possible because the substances in a mixture retain their own properties. The methods you can use to separate the parts of a mixture include distillation, evaporation, filtration, and magnetic attraction.

Magnetic attraction involves holding a magnet near a mixture to pull out anything that is attracted to the magnet, such as a metal. Evaporation is a good way to separate dissolved or suspended substances from water. This is how sea salt is harvested from the ocean. In filtration, a substance is passed through some kind of filter that allows fine particles, such as molecules of water, to pass through while filtering out larger particles. **Distillation** involves separating liquids by boiling them. The liquid with the lower boiling point will vaporize first, leaving the other liquid behind.

✓ **READING CHECK** **Apply Scientific Reasoning** Think about a lake. Would you describe it as a homogeneous mixture, a heterogeneous mixture, or both? Explain.

....

....

....

A

B

Heterogeneous and Homogeneous Mixtures

Figure 6 A bowl of mixed nuts is a heterogeneous mixture. You could easily separate the nuts by type. A bowl of cake mix is a homogeneous mixture. You could not easily separate the flour in the mix from the other dry ingredients.

Academic Vocabulary

Someone may ask you to distill a complicated idea into a brief summary that gets right to the point. How does this relate to distillation in chemistry?

....

....

....

MS-PS1-1

Ammonia

Key

○ Hydrogen

● Nitrogen

1. Interpret Data Which term or terms can be used to describe this model: element, compound, or molecule? Explain.

....

....

....

....

2. Identify What is the chemical formula for the molecule shown?

....

....

3. Evaluate Claims Suppose you find a website that describes the rusting of a nail as a change to only the physical properties of iron. Would that be accurate? Explain.

....

....

....

....

4. Classify Think about different mixtures that are in a kitchen. Name and describe two homogeneous mixtures and two heterogeneous mixtures.

....

....

....

....

....

....

....

5. Construct Explanations What is the difference between a molecule and a compound?

....

....

....

....

....

....

....

....

....

Quest CHECK-IN

In this lesson, you learned about the properties that are used to describe matter. You also learned about mixtures and how they are classified as well as how their components can be separated.

Evaluate Why is it important to know what substances you have available to work with, and how they might change, when developing special effects?

....

....

....

INTERACTIVITY

The Science of Special Effects

Go online to learn about how different substances can be combined in various ways to achieve different outcomes.

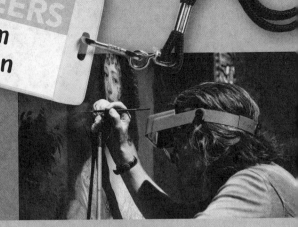

Saving the World's Art

The world is full of works of art, from the delicate to the majestic, from the ancient to the new. Many are made of organic materials, such as paint, wood, and some stone. These materials are sensitive to changes in temperature and humidity. They break down as they age, just as living creatures do. This is where the museum technicians come in! It's their job to restore works of art.

If you are strongly interested in both science and art, a career as a museum technician might be perfect for you! It combines an appreciation of art, architecture, and sculpture with a detailed knowledge of the chemistry that breaks down artwork so that it can be restored to its original beauty.

 VIDEO

Learn how a museum technician restores pieces of art.

MY CAREER

Type "museum technician" into an online search engine to learn more about this career.

Before

After

This is a painting on the ceiling on the Sistine Chapel after restoration. The inset shows what it looked like before.

13

2 Measuring Matter

Guiding Questions

- How can matter be measured?
- What properties of matter can be determined through measurement?

Connections

Literacy Cite Textual Evidence

Math Draw Comparative Inferences

MS-PS1-2

Vocabulary

mass
volume
weight
density

Academic Vocabulary

convert

 VOCABULARY APP

Practice vocabulary on a mobile device.

Quest CONNECTION

Consider how you would measure matter in coming up with your special effects.

Connect It!

✎ **In the fruit market photo, outline three things that have mass.**

Hypothesize How much do you think an apple weighs?

....

Infer How do you think an object's mass relates to its weight?

....

....

Expressing Weight, Mass, and Volume

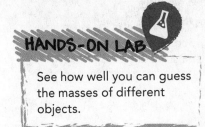

HANDS-ON LAB

See how well you can guess the masses of different objects.

Recall that matter is anything that has mass and takes up space. **Mass** is the amount of matter in an object. An object's mass does not change even if the force of gravity upon the object changes. The amount of space that matter occupies is called its **volume**. All forms of matter—solids, liquids, and gases—have volume. If we want to measure matter, such as the fruit in **Figure 1**, we need to measure both mass and volume.

Weight First, consider weight. **Weight** is a measure of the force of gravity on an object. The force of gravity depends on the mass of the planet or moon where the object is being weighed. Because the moon has much less mass than Earth, on the moon you would weigh about one sixth of what you weigh on Earth. Jupiter has much more mass than Earth. On Jupiter, you would weigh more than twice what you weigh on Earth.

To find the weight of an object, you could place it on a scale like the ones shown in **Figure 2**. The object's weight pulls down on mechanisms inside the scale. These mechanisms cause beams or springs inside the scale to move. These movements are calibrated in such a way that the object's weight is displayed on the face of the scale.

Fruit Matter

Figure 1 At a fruit market, you can buy fruit by the pound. Pounds are a unit of weight.

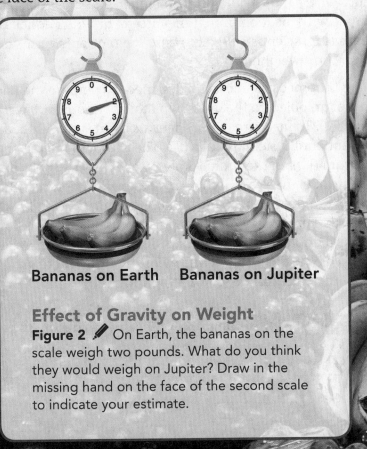

Bananas on Earth   Bananas on Jupiter

Effect of Gravity on Weight

Figure 2 🖊 On Earth, the bananas on the scale weigh two pounds. What do you think they would weigh on Jupiter? Draw in the missing hand on the face of the second scale to indicate your estimate.

VIDEO

See what your weight and mass would be on Mars.

Triple-Beam Balance Scale

Figure 3 A mechanical scale is like a see-saw. An object of unknown mass is put on one side of the scale, and then weighted tabs are moved on the other side of the fulcrum until the two sides are in balance. Gravity is acting on both sides with equal force, so it is not a factor in measuring mass this way.

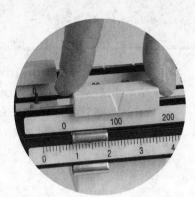

Literacy Connection

Cite Textual Evidence
Underline the text that explains why we cannot rely on measurements of weight to measure mass.

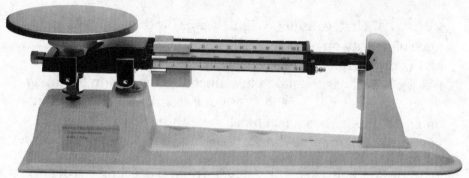

Mass Weight changes as the force of gravity changes. Even between different places on Earth, the force of gravity has slight variation, so your weight would as well. This means we need a measure of matter that is not affected by gravity. That's where mass comes in. Remember that mass does not change with location even if the force of gravity changes. For this reason, scientists prefer to describe matter in terms of mass rather than weight.

Academic Vocabulary

In this context, how is the term *convert* different from the term *change*? Can you think of another example that captures the difference?

....

....

....

....

....

....

....

Scales that measure mass are designed to compare the known mass of an object to the unknown mass of another object (**Figure 3**). To measure mass, scientists use a system called the International System of Units (SI). The SI unit of mass is the kilogram (kg). In the United States, we tend to use pounds to measure weight. We can **convert** pounds to kilograms when the force of gravity at a location is known. If you weigh 130 pounds on Earth, your mass is about 60 kilograms, because a kilogram is equivalent to about 2.2 pounds. Sometimes, a smaller unit known as a gram (g) is used to measure mass. There are 1,000 grams in a kilogram, or 0.001 kilograms in a gram.

✓ **READING CHECK** **Summarize** What are weight, mass, and volume?

....

....

....

Volume Volume is the amount of space that matter takes up. We generally measure the volume of solids in the SI units of cubic meters (m^3), cubic centimeters (cm^3), or cubic millimeters (mm^3). We measure the volume of liquids in liters (L) and milliliters (mL). A milliliter is 1/1,000 of a liter and has the same volume as 1 cubic centimeter. Gases do not have a definite volume of their own because their particles move to fill their containers. So the volume of a gas is measured by the units of its container.

Math Toolbox

Calculating Volume

Objects of Regular Shape

The volume of an object of regular shape can be calculated by measuring the object's dimensions. For example, the volume of a boxlike piece of carry-on luggage that is 20 cm deep, 30 cm wide, and 45 cm long can be calculated by using this formula:
Volume = Length × Width × Height

1. **Calculate** What is the volume of the bag?

   ....

2. **Apply Mathematics** Large numbers can be rewritten by multiplying a number times a power of ten. For example, because 10^4 is equal to 10,000, you can rewrite 30,000 as 3×10^4. Rewrite your answer to Question 1 in this form.

   ....

Objects of Irregular Shape

One way to find the volume of an irregularly shaped object is by submerging it in a volume of water that is known. The volume of water that is displaced equals the volume of the object.

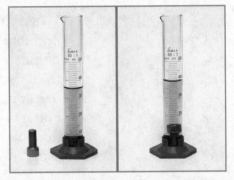

3. **Design a Solution** Suppose the irregularly shaped object is a massive whale shark that is about to be moved into a cube-shaped aquarium tank. How might you combine the "Length × Width × Height" formula with the displacement method to determine the shark's volume? Explain.

....

....

....

....

....

....

Density and Water

Figure 4 When people throw coins into a fountain, the coins drop to the bottom. Why do the coins drop to the bottom of the fountain?

....

....

....

Determining Density

A kilogram of sand takes up much less space than a kilogram of feathers. The volumes differ because sand and feathers have different densities—another important property of matter. **Density** is a measure of the mass of a material in a given volume.

Calculating Density
Density can be expressed as the number of grams in one cubic centimeter (g/cm^3). For example, the density of water at room temperature is stated as "one gram per cubic centimeter" ($1 \ g/cm^3$). Recall that volume can also be measured in milliliters. So the density of water can also be expressed as 1 g/mL. You can determine the density of a sample of matter by dividing its mass by its volume.

$$\text{Density} = \frac{\text{Mass}}{\text{Volume}}$$

When you drop things into bodies of water, some things sink and some things float. What determines this? You know the density of fresh water is $1 \ g/cm^3$. Objects with densities greater than that of water, such as a rock, will sink. Objects with lesser densities, such as a piece of wood, will float. If you shake a bottle of oil and vinegar, you will see the oil slowly separate to float above the vinegar. This happens because oil is less dense than vinegar.

Model It!

Liquid Layers

This beaker shows five layers of liquids of various densities. The liquids are listed in the table below.

Liquid	Density
vegetable oil	0.91 g/mL
honey	1.36 g/mL
corn syrup	1.33 g/mL
water	1.00 g/mL
dish soap	1.03 g/mL

Develop Models ✏ Complete the model by using different shading for each layer shown, according to the densities in the table. Then, label each of the substances.

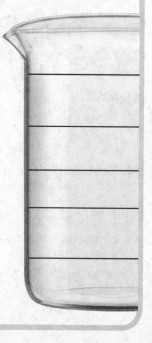

Density and Temperature You know that mass is a physical property. Density is a function of mass and volume, so it too is a physical property. Note that increasing or decreasing the total amount of a given substance won't change its density. If you have 5 or 75 cubic centimeters of silver, they will both have the same density because they are both made of the exact same substance.

One factor that does affect density is temperature. In general, most substances become less dense as temperature increases and more dense as temperature decreases. This is why warm masses of air rise up from Earth's surface and cold air masses sink toward Earth's surface. Water also follows this general rule, but not always. Liquid water does expand, or get less dense, when it gets warmer. It condenses, or gets denser, as it gets colder. But when water cools below 4°C, its density actually begins to decrease again, as you can see in the Math Toolbox.

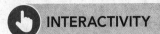

INTERACTIVITY

Investigate density using various materials including solid and liquid water.

HANDS-ON LAB

Investigate Explore the physical properties of mass, volume, and density.

Math Toolbox

Temperature and Density of Water

Although the density of water is usually considered to be 1 g/cm³, the true density of water varies with temperature, as shown in the table and graph.

1. **Analyze Data** At what temperature is water densest? Circle that point on the graph and record your answer here.

....

2. **Draw Comparative Inferences** Explain the sudden decrease in density when water is at 0°C as shown on the graph.

....

....

....

3. **Apply Concepts** If ice were, like most other substances, more dense than its liquid form, what would this mean for bodies of water that freeze in the winter? What would happen to the organisms that live in them?

....

....

....

....

....

Density of Water vs. Temperature	
Temperature (°C)	Density (g/cm³)
0 (ice)	0.9168
0 (water)	0.9998
4	1.0000
10	0.9997
25	0.9977

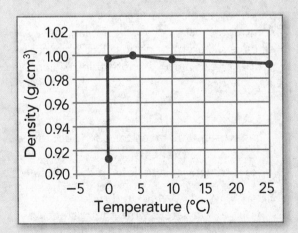

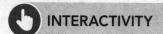
INTERACTIVITY

Compare the weights, masses, and densities of objects on Earth versus on the moon.

Using Density

Because density is an intrinsic property of matter, meaning that it does not change with the shape of an object, density can be used to identify substances. Imagine that you are looking for gold in stream beds in Alaska. You find an area where the gravelly streambed seems to be flecked with gold. First, you sort the gold-colored pieces from the other parts of the sediment. You set aside four of the largest pieces, hoping at least one of them will be valuable gold. You use a small digital scale and a graduated cylinder filled with water to measure the masses and volumes of each sample. Those data are shown below each sample in the Math Toolbox. If one of the samples has a density of 19.3 g/cm^3, then you've found gold!

Math Toolbox

Densities of Unknown Substances

2.8 g/cm^3

19.3 g/cm^3

5.0g/cm^3

3.0 g/cm^3

	Gold	Muscovite	Biotite	Pyrite
Mass	284 g	67.2 g	60 g	120 g
Volume	14.7 cm^3	24 cm^3	20 cm^3	24 cm^3
Density				

Although these rocks look similar, they all have different densities. This physical property can help you determine which is really gold.

1. Calculate ✏ Use the mass and volume measurements given for each substance to calculate the density of each sample. Record your calculations in the table.

2. Identify ✏ Based on the densities you've calculated, write the correct names of the substances in the labels by the rocks.

3. Plan an Investigation Besides density, what other physical property can you use to confirm that the gold is indeed real gold? Describe how you would conduct a test to confirm the sample's identity.

....

....

....

....

....

....

☑ LESSON 2 Check

1. **Calculate** What is the mass of a sample of a substance with a volume of 120 mL and a density of 0.75 g/mL?

....

2. **Explain** If density usually increases with decreasing temperature, why does ice float on liquid water?

....
....
....

3. **Evaluate** Why is mass a better unit for measuring matter than weight?

....
....
....

4. **Calculate** ✏ The force of gravity on the moon is only 16.6% the force of gravity on Earth. For each item listed in the table below, fill in what its weight would be on the moon.

Weights on Earth and the Moon		
Item	Weight on Earth	Weight on the Moon
Apple	150 g	
Hammer	1.5 lbs	
Person	180 lbs	
Blue whale	200 tons	

5. **Use Mathematical Thinking** A small bar of pure gold, whose density is 19.3 g/cm^3, displaces 80 cm^3 of water when dropped into a beaker. What is the mass of the bar of gold?

....

6. **Cause and Effect** What might happen if a large cloud in the sky suddenly encountered a colder air mass with a temperature of 5°C?

....
....
....
....

7. **Connect to Society** In much of the world, SI units are used in everyday life and not just in science. Why would it make sense for people in the United States to use SI units in everyday life, too? Explain using math terms such as *calculate* and *convert*.

....
....
....
....
....
....
....
....
....
....
....
....
....

An EPIC DISASTER

On April 20, 2010, an explosion took place on an oil rig called Deepwater Horizon in the Gulf of Mexico. Within two days the rig had sunk to the ocean floor. Crude oil then leaked from the underwater oil well. The spill lasted 87 days and dumped millions of gallons of oil into the Gulf waters.

Because oil is less dense than water, it floats on the water's surface. The oil in the Gulf disaster, however, did not all float. Scientists estimate that about 10% of it sank to the sea floor. How could a less dense substance sink in a substance of higher density?

Three factors contributed to this phenomenon. First, some oil mixed with natural gas and seawater, causing it to become more dense. The second factor was the climate. Wind currents, ocean waves, and evaporation all acted on the oil and affected its density. The third factor was microorganisms called phytoplankton. They released a sticky substance when exposed to the oil. The substance stuck to bits of algae and other items, causing them to mix with oil and sink.

The Deepwater Horizon oil rig exploded in the Gulf of Mexico on April 20, 2010.

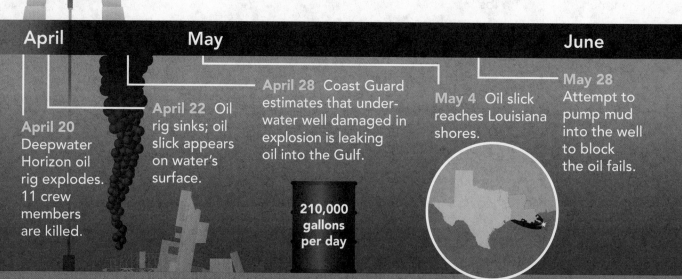

April   **May**   **June**

April 20 Deepwater Horizon oil rig explodes. 11 crew members are killed.

April 22 Oil rig sinks; oil slick appears on water's surface.

April 28 Coast Guard estimates that underwater well damaged in explosion is leaking oil into the Gulf.

210,000 gallons per day

May 4 Oil slick reaches Louisiana shores.

May 28 Attempt to pump mud into the well to block the oil fails.

Use the timeline to answer questions 1–2.

1. **Calculate** Approximately how much oil may have spilled into the water between April 20th and July 12th?

....

2. **Construct Explanations** Why do you think it took so long for the workers to stop the flow of oil from the underground well?

....

....

3. **Solve Problems** How might a team of engineers solve the problem of access to an underwater oil well for necessary repairs?

....

....

....

....

....

4. **Predict** What do you think the nations of the world should do to prevent disasters such as Deepwater Horizon from happening in the future?

....

....

....

July   **August**

July 5 Oil slick reaches Texas shores.

July 12 New containment cap is installed.

July 15 Oil has ceased to flow from the well.

August 5 The well is permanently sealed.

July 10 Broken containment cap is removed from well; oil now flows without any restrictions.

3 Changes in Matter

Guiding Questions

- How are changes in matter related to changes in energy?
- What is the difference between a physical change and a chemical change?

Connections

Literacy Write Explanatory Texts

Math Use Ratio Reasoning

MS-PS1-2

Vocabulary

physical change
chemical change

Academic Vocabulary

conservation

 VOCABULARY APP

Practice vocabulary on a mobile device.

Quest CONNECTION

Your special effects must include physical changes and chemical changes. As you read this lesson, think about how to recognize and describe these two types of changes in matter.

Connect It!

✏ **Circle at least two things in the photo that are undergoing the process of changing matter.**

Explain What is causing the marshmallows to change their state of matter?

....

....

Form a Hypothesis Why do you think matter changes state when outside forces act upon it?

....

....

....

Physical Changes in Matter

A **physical change** alters the form or appearance of matter but does not turn any substance in the matter into a different substance. If you accidentally drop a glass onto a hard floor, the glass may shatter. However, the chemical composition of the broken glass is still the same. A substance that undergoes a physical change is still the same substance after the change.

Changes of State You have learned that most matter exists in three different states—solids, liquids, and gases. Suppose you leave an ice cube in a glass and forget about it. When you come back, there is a small amount of water in the glass. The ice cube has undergone a physical change. The solid water that made up the ice cube has melted into liquid water. A change in state, such as from a solid to a liquid or from a liquid to a gas, is an example of a physical change.

HANDS-ON LAB

Use chalk to distinguish between physical and chemical changes.

Reflect As you read this lesson, record examples of physical and chemical changes that you encounter, as well as examples that you think of from your own life. Categorize them in a two-column chart.

Changing States
Figure 1 Fire is a useful tool for causing changes in states of matter.

Sculpting Ice

Figure 2 An ice scultpor breaks ice and shapes ice, but he or she does not cause it to change into another substance.

Changes in Shape or Form

When you combine two substances, how do you know if just a physical change occurred or whether you have created an altogether new substance? There are ways to figure it out. For example, imagine that you pour a teaspoon of sugar into a glass of water and stir until the sugar dissolves. If you pour the sugar solution into a pan and boil away the water, the sugar will remain as a crust at the bottom of the pan. The crust may not look exactly like the sugar before you dissolved it, but it's still sugar. Therefore, dissolving is a physical change.

Other examples of physical changes include bending, crushing, breaking, and carving (**Figure 2**). Any change that alters only the shape or form of matter is a physical change. Methods of separating mixtures, such as filtration and distillation, also involve physical changes.

✓**READING CHECK** **Explain** How are melting and carving ice sculptures both examples of physical changes?

....

....

....

....

Model It

Types of Physical Changes

🖊 Make a paper airplane out of a piece of scrap paper. Draw a sketch of your paper airplane in the space provided.

1. Identify What kinds of physical changes did you cause to happen to the paper?

....

2. Connect to Society How can paper that has already been used be physically changed to make other paper products?

....

....

....

....

....

Chemical Changes in Matter

A change in matter that produces one or more new substances is a **chemical change**, or chemical reaction. In some chemical changes, a single substance breaks down into two or more other substances. For example, hydrogen peroxide breaks down into water and oxygen gas when it's poured on a cut on your skin. In other chemical changes, two or more substances combine to form different substances. Photosynthesis is a natural chemical change that occurs in plants and other photosynthetic organisms. Several compounds are combined using energy from the sun to produce new substances.

Some chemical changes can be initiated and observed in the kitchen. If you have ever baked bread with help from yeast, you have seen a chemical reaction at work. The yeast reacts with sugars in the mixture to produce bubbles of carbon dioxide, which make the dough rise (**Figure 3A**). Another chemical reaction takes place on the surface of the bread. As heat is added, the sugars turn into a brown crust (**Figure 3B**).

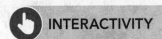 INTERACTIVITY

Investigate various properties of matter.

Chemical Change in the Kitchen

Figure 3 Adding yeast to dough causes a chemical change, which makes the dough rise.

Adding heat to the dough causes sugars to undergo a chemical change that results in a brown crust.

Tarnishing is the slow combination of a bright metal, such as silver, with sulfur or another substance, which produces a dark coating on the metal.

Oxidation is the combination of a substance with oxygen, such as when iron rusts.

Objects catch fire when a fuel combines rapidly with oxygen, producing heat, light, and new substances.

Bubbles are created by using electricity to break a compound down into elements or simpler compounds.

Types of Chemical Change

Figure 4 The images show different types of chemical changes. Next to each photo, identify the evidence that a new substance has formed.

Academic Vocabulary

Where else have you heard the term *conservation*? How does the term's meaning in that other context relate to its meaning in chemistry?

Examples of Chemical Change One common chemical change is the burning of natural gas on a gas stove. Natural gas is mostly made up of the compound methane (CH_4). When it burns, methane combines with oxygen in the air and forms new substances. The new substances include carbon dioxide gas (CO_2) and water vapor (H_2O). Both of these substances can be identified by their properties, which are different from those of methane. **Figure 4** describes some of the types of chemical changes.

Conservation of Mass When something such as a piece of paper burns, it may seem to lose mass or disappear. Scientists, however, have proved that this is false. In the 1770s, the French chemist Antoine Lavoisier measured mass both before and after a chemical change. His data showed that no mass was lost or gained during the change. The fact that matter is not created or destroyed in any chemical or physical change is called the law of **conservation** of mass. This law is also called the law of conservation of matter because mass is a measurement of matter.

....

....

....

....

HANDS-ON LAB

☑**Investigate** Explore physical and chemical changes.

Math Toolbox

Conservation of Mass

The combustion reaction that produces carbon dioxide and water from methane and oxygen does not result in any gain or loss of mass. All atoms that go into the reaction are present at the end of the reaction.

| Methane molecule | Two oxygen molecules | Carbon dioxide molecule | Two water molecules |

☐ Carbon atom(s) ☐ Hydrogen atom(s) ☐ Oxygen atom(s)   ☐ Carbon atom(s) ☐ Hydrogen atom(s) ☐ Oxygen atom(s)

1. **Interpret Diagrams** ✏️ Count the atoms of each element before and after the chemical change. Fill in the numbers in the appropriate boxes.

2. **Use Ratio Reasoning** Does the ratio of hydrogen to oxygen change during the reaction? How do you know?

....

....

3. **Ask Questions** Antoine Lavoisier was able to show that mass wasn't lost or destroyed during chemical reactions by weighing all of the matter in the system before and after reactions occurred. What questions would you ask Lavoisier about how he conducted his investigations?

....

....

....

29

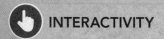
Literacy Connection

Write Explanatory Texts How can you use terms such as *thermal energy*, *particles*, *motion*, and *flow* to explain the movement of heat in our world?

....

....

....

....

....

Energy and Matter Are Related

Do you have much energy for schoolwork today? In science, energy is the ability to do work or cause change. Any kind of change to matter involves a change in energy. Bending a paper clip or chopping an onion takes energy. When ice changes to liquid water, energy is absorbed from the matter around it.

Like matter, energy is conserved in a chemical change. Energy is never created or destroyed. It is only transformed.

Temperature and Thermal Energy When you walk into a warm building on a cold winter day, you will immediately notice the difference between the cold outside and the warmth inside. We refer to the measure of how hot or cold something is as temperature. Temperature is related to the motion and energy of the particles of matter. The particles of gas in the cold outside air have less average energy of motion than the particles of air inside the warm building.

The total energy of the motion of all of the particles in an object is known as thermal energy. We usually talk about thermal energy in terms of how hot or cold something is, but thermal energy is not the same thing as temperature. Thermal energy naturally flows from warmer matter to cooler matter.

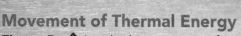

Movement of Thermal Energy

Figure 5 ✏ A polar bear swims in frigid waters of the Arctic, while people relax in a geothermal pool in Iceland. Draw arrows to indicate the direction that thermal energy moves in each image.

Thermal Energy and Changes in Matter

When matter changes, thermal energy is usually released or absorbed. For example, ice absorbs thermal energy from its surroundings when it melts, leaving the air around it feeling cold. That's why coolers for food and drinks are filled with ice. The melting of ice is an endothermic change, or a change in which energy is absorbed. An exothermic change occurs when energy is released. Combustion is an exothermic change.

Chemical energy is stored in the chemical bonds between atoms. Foods, fuels, and even the cells in your body store chemicals. Burning fuels transforms chemical energy and releases some of it as thermal energy. When you ride a bike up a hill, chemical energy from food changes into the energy of your muscles's motion, which your legs convert into mechanical energy through the bike's pedals.

Obtaining Chemical Energy
Figure 6 When this giraffe consumes food, the chemical reactions that occur during digestion are a source of energy for the giraffe.

Math Toolbox

Energy in Chemical Reactions

A student initiates two chemical reactions by adding a different substance to each of two beakers with different solutions. She observes them for 10 minutes, recording the temperature of the solution in each beaker every minute.

1. **Calculate** What was the temperature change of each solution after 10 minutes?

   ....

   ....

2. **Interpret Data** Which of the beakers had an endothermic reaction? Which had an exothermic reaction

   ....

   ....

3. **Write Explanatory Texts** Which solution could be used in a cooling pack to keep food and drinks cold in a cooler? Explain.

   ....

   ....

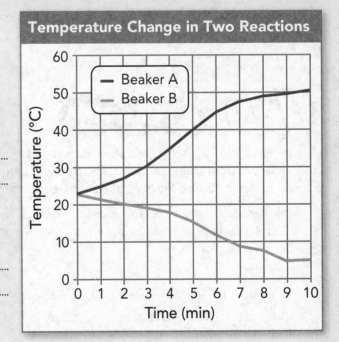

Temperature Change in Two Reactions

MS-PS1-2

1. **Classify** A large bar of solid gold is melted into liquid. The liquid is then poured into molds to make a number of gold coins. Was this a chemical or physical change? Explain.

....

....

....

2. **Infer** If you cut an apple into slices and leave them in the open air, they will slowly turn brown. What kind of chemical change is this? Explain.

....

....

....

3. **Explain** A friend notices that a nail that was left outside for a few months seems larger and heavier than it was before. He says it disproves the law of conservation of mass. Explain why he is wrong.

....

....

....

....

4. **Predict** A northern right whale migrates from warm waters off Florida to cooler waters off Nova Scotia, Canada. In which area do you think more thermal energy would move from the whale to its environment? Explain.

....

....

....

....

....

....

....

5. **Summarize** A stick of butter is melted in a saucepan. As it continues to cook, the butter turns brown. What changes have occurred?

....

....

....

....

....

Quest CHECK-INS

In this lesson, you learned the difference between a physical change and a chemical change and how changes in energy are involved. You also learned about the conservation of mass.

Evaluate Why is it important to know the difference between chemical and physical changes when designing special effects?

....

....

....

....

INTERACTIVITY

Mysterious Movie Fog

HANDS-ON LAB

Cinematic Science

Go online to learn how "dry ice" and other substances are used to make physical and chemical changes in special effects.

Gathering Speed with
SUPERCONDUCTORS

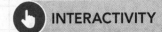

INTERACTIVITY

Find out about maglev trains and how they work.

The maglev train flashes past in a blur! If you blink, you might miss it. Maglev trains carry passengers at speeds of more than 370 miles per hour.

The Challenge: To use superconductivity to make a fast, efficient train.

Phenomenon "Maglev" is short for "magnetic levitation." A maglev train doesn't run on tracks; it floats just above them. Magnetic principles elevate the train, propel it forward, and keep it on its correct route. The magnets rely on a physical property called superconductivity.

In superconductivity, a substance loses all electrical resistance when it is cooled to a certain temperature (usually below −253°C or −423°F). At these low temperatures, certain elements and alloys become not just good conductors of electricity, but superconductors. This transition from a conductor to a superconductor is an important physical change! Once a metal is superconducting, it can generate incredibly strong magnetic fields—strong enough to elevate a train!

In the case of the maglev train, mercury is the superconductor. For the magnetic field of a maglev train to be strong enough to drive the train, the electromagnets must be cooled to a very cold −267°C!

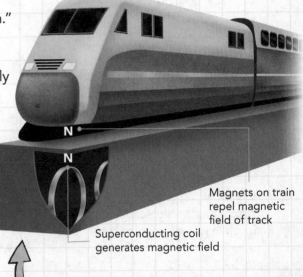

Magnets on train repel magnetic field of track

Superconducting coil generates magnetic field

Maglev trains operate on the simple principle of magnetic attraction and repulsion. The surface below a magnet is cooled enough to become superconducting, allowing the magnet to levitate.

DESIGN CHALLENGE

Can you use magnets to build a model of a maglev train? Go to the Engineering Design Notebook to find out!

MURDOCK LEARNING RESOURCE CENTER

☑TOPIC 1 Review and Assess

1 Describing and Classifying Matter

MS-PS1-1

1. Which of the following changes demonstrates a chemical property?
   - A. substance breaks in half
   - B. substance combusts
   - C. hammer bounces off substance
   - D. substance floats in water

2. Which of the following is a solution?
   - A. salt water
   - B. macaroni and cheese
   - C. cake mix
   - D. vegetable soup

3. The abilities to dissolve in water and to conduct electricity are examples of
   - A. natural properties.
   - B. chemical properties.
   - C. natural laws of matter.
   - D. physical properties.

4. **Classify** Which of the following is a substance: table salt, seawater, or sand? Explain how you know.

   ....
   ....
   ....
   ....
   ....
   ....
   ....
   ....

2 Measuring Matter

MS-PS1-2

5. Which is the correct equation for calculating density?
   - A. Density = Mass/Volume
   - B. Density = Mass/Weight
   - C. Density = Volume/Mass
   - D. Density = Volume/Weight

6. What is the density of an object whose mass is 180 grams and whose volume is 45 cm³?
   - A. 4 cm³/g
   - B. 0.25 g/cm³
   - C. 4 g/cm³
   - D. 0.25 cm³/g

7. Weight is a flawed measure of mass because it
   - A. is not used in other countries.
   - B. is affected by the force of gravity.
   - C. tends to fluctuate.
   - D. can be influenced by temperature and pressure.

8. **Summarize** Describe two ways to measure the volume of a solid object.

   ....
   ....
   ....
   ....
   ....
   ....
   ....
   ....
   ....

MURDOCK LEARNING RESOURCE CENTER

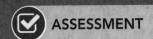

3 Changes in Matter

MS-PS1-2

9. Which of the following describes a physical change?

   A. A marshmallow burns over an open flame.

   B. Icicles melt from a rooftop.

   C. A cat eats a piece of fish.

   D. Milk turns sour.

10. Which of the following describes a chemical change?

   A. clear liquids mix, producing a cloudy liquid with yellow chunks

   B. silver coins are melted down and shaped into a solid brick

   C. salt is added to a pot of hot water, and the water's boiling point changes

   D. an apple is chopped into eight slices

11. The law of conservation of mass states that

   A. matter is neither created nor destroyed.

   B. the mass of an object remains the same even if chemical change occurs.

   C. the number of molecules before and after a chemical reaction cannot change.

   D. mass is lost when a chemical change occurs.

12. Temperature is

   A. the movement of thermal energy from a solid to a liquid.

   B. the difference in thermal energy between two objects.

   C. a measure of how hot or cold something is.

   D. a measure of how fast thermal energy is moving.

13. ....and.............................. are two types of energy that can be released when something burns.

14. Cite Evidence Look at the image of a salad with chicken on a countertop. In which direction is thermal energy moving? Cite evidence to support your answer.

....

....

....

....

....

....

....

....

....

....

MS-PS1-1

Evidence-Based Assessment

A group of students is developing models of simple molecules to help them describe and classify matter. The materials they have are pipe cleaners along with red, blue, and yellow clay.

The students are modeling four molecules. The data for these molecules is presented in the chart below.

Hydrogen	Hydrogen chloride	Ammonia	Nitrogen trichloride
2 Hydrogen atoms	1 Hydrogen atom	1 Nitrogen atom	1 Nitrogen atom
	1 Chlorine atom	3 Hydrogen atoms	3 Chlorine atoms

The students' models of the first three molecules are shown, with one of the models constructed incorrectly.

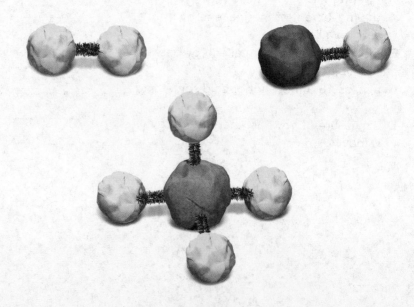

1. **Analyze Data** Based on the data and the first two models, which atom is represented by the red clay?
   A. Nitrogen   B. Hydrogen
   C. Chlorine   D. Oxygen

2. **Use Models** Which of the following can be done using the students' models? Select all that apply.
   A. Visualize the atoms bonded within the molecules
   B. Determine the thermal energy of a hydrogen chloride atom
   C. Show that some molecules are not compounds
   D. Demonstrate how elements can combine to form different types of matter

3. **Determine Differences** How does the hydrogen molecule differ from the other molecules?

   ....
   ....
   ....
   ....
   ....

4. **Make Observations** Which model has been constructed incorrectly? Explain how you would fix it.

   ....
   ....
   ....
   ....
   ....
   ....

5. **Construct Explanations** Review the chart to determine which atoms are needed to model nitrogen trichloride. Describe how you would build the model, including which colors of clay you would use.

   ....
   ....
   ....
   ....
   ....

Quest FINDINGS

Complete the Quest!

Phenomenon Determine the best way to clearly present your ideas for the movie scene and the special effects that you would propose to the film director. You may present the storyboards or run through the actual scene as though it were being filmed.

Optimize Your Solution Are there any safety considerations or other issues that you encountered when demonstrating or discussing your special effects? How would they influence a redesign of your proposal?

....
....
....
....
....
....
....
....

INTERACTIVITY

Reflect on Your Movie Scene

MS-PS1-2

Help Out the Wildlife

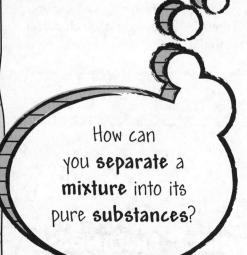

How can you **separate** a **mixture** into its pure **substances**?

Background

Phenomenon Overnight, a materials storage facility was struck by an intense hurricane. The winds destroyed the building, and the rains washed salt, sand, and iron filings into a nearby pond. You wake up to a phone call from the Department of Environmental Protection asking if you can help to clean up the contamination. Wildlife are at risk in the murky water. The owner of the storage facility also would like to recover as much salt, sand, and iron filings as possible. They should not go to waste!

Your job is to design a procedure to remove the salt, sand, and iron filings from the water.

Materials

(per group)

- 60-g mixture of salt, sand, and iron filings
- assorted materials and tools to separate the mixture

Safety

Be sure to follow all safety procedures provided by your teacher.

Murky Waters
Contaminated water can be a threat to the health of wildlife.

Sand, Salt, and
Iron Filings

Plan Your Investigation

1. Your teacher will divide the class into groups and provide each group with some water and a mixture of salt, sand, and iron filings. Your mixture will contain the same quantities as other groups so that you can compare results.

2. Design a plan to separate the mixture into its components. You may want to consider some of these questions as you design your plan:

    HANDS-ON LAB

    иDemonstrate Go online for a downloadable worksheet of this lab.

    - What materials can you use to separate each part of the mixture?

    - Are there other substances you can use to help you separate the mixture?

    - What order should your procedure follow in order to remove each part of the mixture?

    - What steps can you take to maximize the amount of each substance you recover from the mixture?

3. Identify the materials you will need to separate each substance in the mixture. Record your materials in the space provided below.

4. Develop your plan by creating a procedure. Record your procedure, paying careful attention to the order of the steps.

5. Finally, draw a data table in which you can record the mass of each substance that you recover and the material(s) that you used to do it.

Materials

Procedure

....

....

....

....

....

....

....

....

....

....

....

....

....

Observations

....

....

....

....

Data Table

Analyze and Interpret Data

1. **Compare Data** Compare your results with another group. What were the similarities and differences in your findings?

....
....
....
....
....

2. **Cause and Effect** What may be the causes of the differences in the masses recovered by each group?

....
....
....
....
....

3. **Apply Scientific Reasoning** What made you decide to do your procedural steps in the order in which you did them? Would any order have worked?

....
....
....
....
....

4. **Evaluate** Review the procedure and results of another group. If you were able to do the lab over again, what specific things would you do differently?

....
....
....
....
....
....
....

Solids, Liquids, and Gases

NGSS PERFORMANCE EXPECTATION

MS-PS1-4 Develop a model that predicts and describes changes in particle motion, temperature, and state of a pure substance when thermal energy is added or removed.

Why can you see this horse's breath in the cold?

HANDS-ON LAB

u**Connect** See if you can identify all the states of matter in three bottles.

GO ONLINE
to access your
digital course

▶ VIDEO

👆 INTERACTIVITY

🧪 VIRTUAL LAB

☑ ASSESSMENT

📖 eTEXT

📱 APP

The Essential Question

What causes matter to change from one state to another?

You can see a cloud of your breath outside on a cold day but not on a warm day. What do you think is happening to your breath in the cold air?

....

....

....

....

....

....

Quest KICKOFF

How can you use solids, liquids, and gases to lift a car?

STEM **Phenomenon** Auto mechanics often need to go under cars to repair the parts in the under-carriage, such as the shocks and exhaust system. It's much easier for them to do their job if they have more room to work, so they use lift systems to raise the cars overhead. In this problem-based Quest activity, you will design an elevator or lift system that uses a solid, liquid, or gas to raise a model car. You will explore the properties of solids, liquids, and gases to see how they can be used in a lift mechanism. You will investigate how potential changes of state affect or impose constraints on your design. By applying what you have learned through lessons, digital activities, and hands-on labs, you will design, build, test, and evaluate a model elevator or lift.

NBC LEARN ▶ VIDEO

After watching the Quest Kickoff video, which examines different ways that elevators and lifts work, write down what you already know about solids, liquids, and gases.

Solids:

....

....

Liquids:

....

....

Gases:

....

....

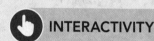

INTERACTIVITY

Getting a Lift

MS-PS1-4 Develop a model that predicts and describes changes in particle motion, temperature, and state of a pure substance when thermal energy is added or removed.

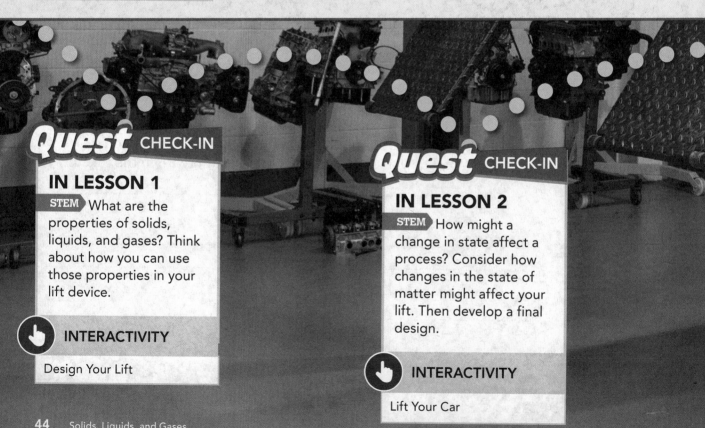

Quest CHECK-IN

IN LESSON 1

STEM What are the properties of solids, liquids, and gases? Think about how you can use those properties in your lift device.

INTERACTIVITY

Design Your Lift

Quest CHECK-IN

IN LESSON 2

STEM How might a change in state affect a process? Consider how changes in the state of matter might affect your lift. Then develop a final design.

INTERACTIVITY

Lift Your Car

Auto mechanics raise cars above their heads to repair parts such as engines and transmission systems.

Quest CHECK-IN

IN LESSON 3

STEM What criteria and constraints affect your model? Build and test your lift device. Improve and retest as needed.

HANDS-ON LAB

Phases of Matter

Quest FINDINGS

Complete the Quest!

Demonstrate your lift and evaluate its performance. Reflect on your work and consider other applications for your device.

INTERACTIVITY

Reflect on Your Lift

① States of Matter

Guiding Questions

- What are the similarities and differences between solids, liquids and gases?
- What is the relationship between particle motion and state of matter?

Connection

Literacy Write Informative Texts

MS-PS1-4

Vocabulary

solid
liquid
surface tension
viscosity
gas

Academic Vocabulary

vibrate

📱 **Vocabulary App**

Practice vocabulary on a mobile device.

Quest CONNECTION

As you learn about different states of matter, consider what types of substances would be useful for your car lift.

Connect It!

🖊 **How many solids, liquids, and gases can you find in this picture? Label the solids with an S, liquids with an L, and gases with a G.**

Infer During winter, you can sometimes ice skate outdoors on a frozen lake. Why can't you ice skate on a lake when it is not frozen?

....

....

....

Solids, Liquids, and Gases

Everything around you is made of matter. Matter exists in different forms, depending on a variety of factors, such as temperature.

Suppose you are taking a walk around a lake on a snowy day, such as in **Figure 1**. Everywhere you look, water is around you in different forms. It crunches loudly as snow beneath your feet. Liquid water on the surface of the lake flows freely when the wind blows. And invisible water particles exist in the air you breathe. The water around you is in three different phases of matter: solid, liquid, and gas.

HANDS-ON LAB

☑**Investigate** Distinguish between states of matter by understanding their properties.

Literacy Connection

Write Informative Texts Describe a solid, liquid, and gas found outdoors where you live.

....

....

....

....

....

Water Everywhere
Figure 1 Water exists in different forms on Earth.

Describing Solids

The ring box in **Figure 2** contains a ring made of pure silver. What would happen if you took the ring out of the box and placed it on your finger? Would it drip onto the floor? Of course not, because it's a solid. A **solid** has a definite shape and a definite volume. Remember that volume is the amount of space that matter fills. Volume is usually measured in cubic centimeters (cm^3), cubic meters (m^3), milliliters (mL), or liters (L).

A book is another example of a solid. If you place a book in your backpack, it will stay the same shape and size as it was before. A solid maintains its shape and volume in any position or container.

Particles of a Solid The particles that make up a solid are packed very closely together, as shown in **Figure 2**. This fixed, closely-packed arrangement of particles causes a solid to have a definite shape and volume. The particles in a solid are closely locked in position such that they cannot move around one another on their own. They can only **vibrate** in place, meaning they move back and forth slightly (see **Figure 3**).

Academic Vocabulary

Strings on a guitar vibrate to create sound waves that make music. Why does a cell phone vibrate?

....

....

....

....

A Ring of Solid Silver
Figure 2 The solid ring has a definite shape and volume.

particle arrangement in a solid

Dancing In The Crowd
Figure 3 People at a packed concert don't move very far, but if they're having fun, they're not standing still either! These people dancing in place are a lot like particles vibrating in a solid.

Apply Concepts Think about the motion of the particles in a solid and come up with your own way of describing them.

....
....
....
....
....

Physical Properties of Solids
Of course, not all solids are the same. Some are hard and brittle, while some are flexible. Some have smooth surfaces and are heavy, while others are sharp and light. Take a look at the natural quartz and the eraser in **Figure 4**. These are both solids, but they are very different!

Comparing Solids
Figure 4 Determine Differences
Write down the differences that you notice in shape, structure, and texture between the quartz and the eraser.

Eraser ....
....
....

Quartz ....
....
....

► **VIDEO**

Learn how a materials scientist uses the properties of matter to develop useful materials.

Types of Solids

The particles inside quartz are aligned in a regular, repeating pattern. This pattern creates crystals. Solids that are made up of crystals are called crystalline solids. Salt, sugar, and snow are examples of crystalline solids. When a crystalline solid is heated, it melts at a distinct temperature.

On the other hand, the material that makes up an eraser is an amorphous solid. In amorphous solids, such as the butter shown in **Figure 5**, the particles are not arranged in a regular pattern. Also, an amorphous solid does not melt at a distinct temperature. Glass is an example of an amorphous solid. It might look crystalline when it is cut into nice shapes, but it is amorphous because of its particle arrangement and the fact that it does not melt at a specific temperature. A glass blower can bend and shape glass that has been heated because it gradually becomes softer. Rubber and plastics are other examples of amorphous solids. They are very useful in manufacturing because they can be gradually heated and cooled to take specific, detailed shapes such as shoe soles and toys.

Model It !

Crystalline and Amorphous Solids

Figure 5 🖊 A pat of butter is an amorphous solid. The particles that make up the butter are not arranged in a regular pattern. The sapphire gem stones are crystalline solids. Draw what you think the particles look like in a crystalline solid.

✔ **READING CHECK** Explain In your own words, explain the main differences between crystalline solids and amorphous solids.

....
....
....
....
....
....
....

Describing Liquids

What happens when you spill a drink? It spreads into a wide, shallow puddle as shown in **Figure 6**. Without a container, your drink does not have a definite shape. Like a solid, however, it does have a constant volume. Drinks such as water, cranberry juice, and iced tea are liquids. A **liquid** has a definite volume but no shape of its own.

Spilled Liquid
Figure 6 When the water spilled, what changed: its shape or its volume?

....

150 mL

150 mL

Particles of a Liquid In general, the particles in a liquid are always in contact with one another. They are packed almost as closely together as those in a solid. However, the particles in a liquid are not fixed in place. They can move around one another. You can compare this movement to the way you might move a group of marbles around in your hand. Like the particles of a liquid, the marbles slide around one another but still touch. These freely moving particles allow a liquid to flow from place to place. For this reason, a liquid is also called a fluid, meaning a "substance that flows." Because its particles are free to move, a liquid has no definite shape. However, it does have a definite volume, as shown in **Figure 7**.

Liquids Change Shape
Figure 7 These two pools hold the same volume of water even though they have different shapes. Liquids take the shape of their containers.

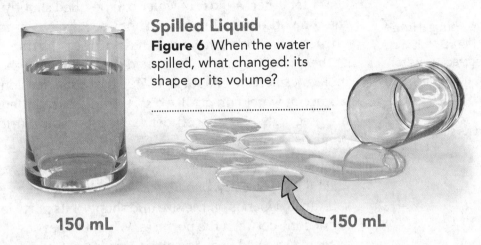

particle
arrangement
in a liquid

INTERACTIVITY

Identify the arrangement and motion of particles in solids, liquids, and gases.

Make Meaning Have you ever seen leaves sitting on top of the surface of water? In your science notebook, describe the property of the liquid water that allows the leaves to sit on its surface.

Physical Properties of Liquids

Substances can be classified by their characteristic properties—physical or chemical properties that remain the same no matter how large or small the sample. Two major characteristic properties of liquids are surface tension and viscosity.

Surface tension is an inward force, or pull, among the molecules in a liquid that brings the molecules on the surface closer together. A glass of water can be filled slightly above the rim without spilling over. That's because water molecules attract one another strongly. These attractions cause molecules at the water's surface to be pulled slightly toward the water molecules beneath its surface. Due to surface tension, the surface of water can act like a sort of skin. Surface tension lets an insect called a water strider walk on the calm surface of a pond, as in **Figure 8**.

Another characteristic property of matter that can be observed in liquids is **viscosity**, or a resistance to flowing. The viscosity of a substance depends on the size and shape of its particles and the attractions between the particles. When the particles are larger or more attracted to one another, they do not flow as freely. Liquids with high viscosities flow slowly. Honey is an example of a liquid with a very high viscosity (**Figure 9**). Liquids with low viscosity flow quickly. Water and vinegar have relatively low viscosities. Substances in other states of matter have viscosity as well. For example, solids have higher viscosity than liquids.

✓ **READING CHECK** **Write Informative Texts** Would honey be considered more viscous or less viscous than cranberry juice? Why?

....

....

....

Surface Tension

Figure 8 Does this water strider have magic powers? Not quite. Because of surface tension, the water strider is able to do the impossible: walk on water.

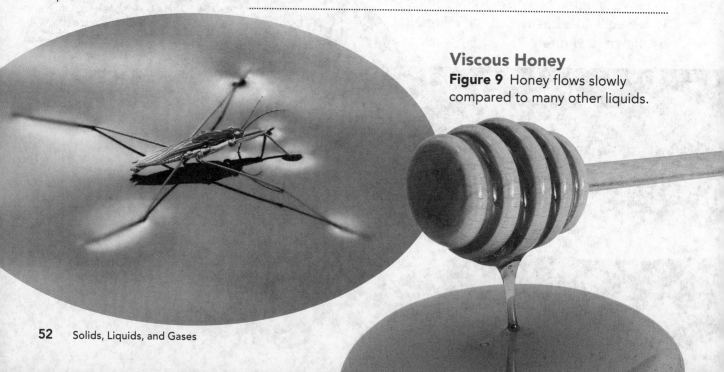

Viscous Honey

Figure 9 Honey flows slowly compared to many other liquids.

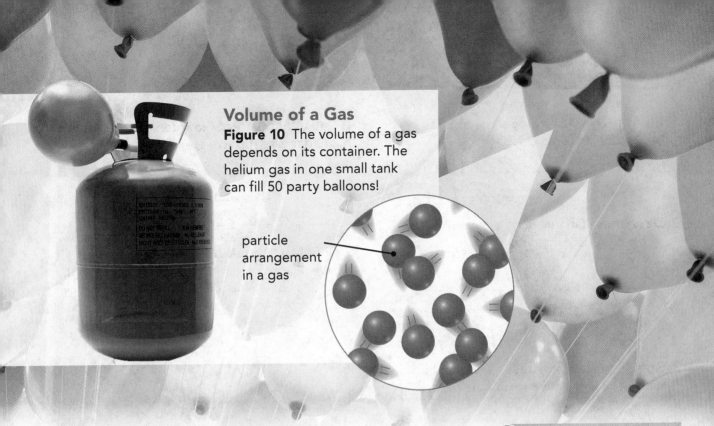

Volume of a Gas
Figure 10 The volume of a gas depends on its container. The helium gas in one small tank can fill 50 party balloons!

particle arrangement in a gas

Describing Gases

Like a liquid, a gas is a fluid. It has particles that can move around one another. However, unlike a liquid, a **gas** has neither a definite shape nor a definite volume. That's because the particles in a gas do not remain in contact with one another.

Particles of a Gas If you could see the particles that make up a gas, you would see them moving in all directions. They are widely spaced and collide with one another as they fly about. When a gas is in a closed container, the gas particles move and spread apart to fill the container.

Physical Properties of Gases Because gas particles move and fill all of the space available, the volume of a gas is the same as the volume of its container. For example, a large amount of helium gas can be compressed—or pressed together tightly—to fit into a metal tank. When you use the helium to fill balloons, it expands to fill many balloons that have a total volume much greater than the volume of the tank, as in **Figure 10**. In general, the particles of a gas flow more easily than the particles of a liquid, so gases have lower viscosity than liquids.

☑ **READING CHECK** **Determine Central Ideas** What are the main differences between gases and liquids?

....

....

....

▶ **VIDEO**

Discover the fourth state of matter: plasma!

👆 **INTERACTIVITY**

Use what you have learned to identify states of matter and describe their particles.

☑ LESSON 1 Check

1. **Identify** What two properties of a gas depend on its container?

....

....

2. **Determine Differences** How do liquids with a high viscosity differ from liquids with a low viscosity?

....

....

....

3. **Compare and Contrast** What are the similarities and differences of the particle motion in solids and liquids?

....

....

....

....

....

....

4. **Cause and Effect** How do the particles in a liquid create surface tension?

....

....

....

5. **Develop Models** 🖊 Based on what you have learned, draw models of the particles in a solid, a liquid, and a gas. Use dots for particles and arrows to show motion.

Solid   **Liquid**

Gas

Quest CHECK-IN

You have learned about the characteristics of solids, liquids, and gases. You discovered the differences in particle motion for these states of matter as well.

Predict How can you use the different states of matter to your advantage when designing a device that lifts a car? What different solids, liquids, and/or gases might you use in your design?

....

....

....

....

👆 INTERACTIVITY

Design Your Lift

Go online to review properties of solids, liquids, and gases. Then brainstorm ideas and begin your plans for a device that could lift a car.

MS-PS1-4

From "Ink" to Objects:
3D PRINTING

INTERACTIVITY

Find out about the technology and uses of 3D printing.

When you hear the word *printing*, you probably think of words and images on paper. But 3D printing has little to do with books!

The Challenge: To utilize the properties of solids and liquids to make 3D objects.

Phenomenon Have you heard of 3D printing? Unlike traditional printing, which simply binds ink onto paper or other media, 3D printing makes physical shapes that have mass and volume. How do these printers work?

Remember what you have learned about solids and liquids. In liquids, particles can move and slide past one another, while in solids, particles are fixed in place and only vibrate. This gives liquids and solids their unique properties. However, these properties can be changed by applying energy, such as heat.

Think of what happens when you melt butter. You take the butter, which is a solid, and apply heat, melting the butter into a new form—a liquid. 3D printers work in the same way. They take a solid material, usually a plastic or a metal, and apply heat until the material melts into a liquid. Then, the liquid is sprayed or squeezed onto a platform, according to a design that has been programmed into the printer. The liquid material hardens again into a solid. After many layers build up, a 3D object is completed.

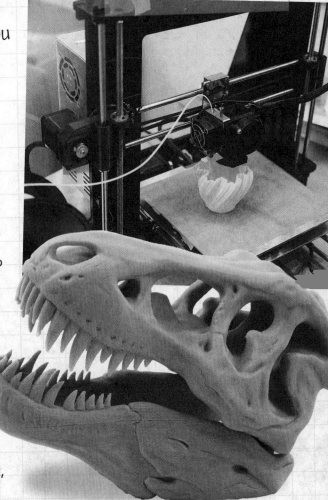

3D printers can make complex 3D objects quickly and easily. They are useful to a wide variety of production industries!

DESIGN CHALLENGE What could you design with a 3D printer? Go to the Engineering Design Notebook to find out!

② Changes of State

Guiding Questions

- How does thermal energy play a role in particle motion and changes of state?
- What happens to particles during changes of state between solids, liquids, and gases?
- How does pressure affect the change of state from liquid to gas?

Connections

Literacy Use Information

Math Draw Comparative Inferences

MS-PS1-4

Vocabulary

thermal energy
temperature
melting point
freezing point
vaporization
boiling point
evaporation
condensation
sublimation

Academic Vocabulary

suspend

 VOCABULARY APP

Practice vocabulary on a mobile device.

Quest CONNECTION

Consider the pros and cons of using substances that will change state in your car lift.

Connect It!

🖊 If you've ever watched a burning candle, you've seen how the solid wax melts into a liquid. Circle an area in the picture where you see this happening.

Determine Similarities When the liquid wax cools, it hardens. How is wax hardening similar to liquid water turning to ice?

....

....

....

Thermal Energy and Temperature

You have seen substances change state. For example, snow melts into liquid water, puddles of rain freeze in the cold, and boiling water becomes steam. What do all of these changes have in common? They involve a change in the thermal energy and temperature of the substance. Thermal energy and temperature are related, but they are not the same thing. You can understand them in terms of particles.

Thermal Energy Particles have both kinetic energy and potential energy. Kinetic energy is energy of motion, and potential energy is energy that is stored. **Thermal energy** is the total kinetic and potential energy of all the particles in an object or substance.

You can increase the thermal energy of a substance by heating it. When you apply heat, you are transferring energy from the heat source to the substance. If you add enough energy to the substance, it can become hot enough to change its state of matter, like the candle wax in **Figure 1**.

Temperature Recall that all particles of matter are constantly moving. **Temperature** is a measure of the average kinetic energy of the particles in an object or substance. The faster the particles are moving, the greater their kinetic energy and the higher the temperature of the substance.

A thermometer measures temperature in degrees, such as degrees Celsius (°C) or degrees Fahrenheit (°F). The thermometer registers a higher temperature when particles are moving faster. How do you make particles speed up? Heat a substance, such as the cider in **Figure 2**, so that its thermal energy increases and its particles move faster. As a result, the temperature of the substance will increase. On the other hand, when a substance is cooled and its thermal energy decreases, its particles slow down. The temperature of the substance decreases.

Hot Apple Cider
Figure 2 Apple cider is best served hot!

☑ READING CHECK
Integrate With Visuals
✏ Draw an arrow on **Figure 2** to show the direction of heat flow. Label the apple cider's thermal energy as increasing or decreasing.

Dripping Candles
Figure 1 The candle wax experiences a change of state as it melts.

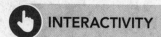

INTERACTIVITY

Examine how particles move and how temperature changes when thermal energy increases or decreases.

Changes of State Between Solid and Liquid

Have you ever let a bar of chocolate sit in a car too long on a hot day? If so, you know what it looks like when the chocolate melts. Some of the solid bar changes to liquid.

Melting When the temperature of most solids increase enough, they change to liquid. The change in state from a solid to a liquid is called melting. This change of state involves an increase in thermal energy. In general, particles of a liquid have more thermal energy than particles of the same substance in solid form.

In pure, crystalline solids, melting occurs at a specific temperature, called the **melting point**. **Figure 3** shows what happens to the temperature of an ice cube after it is taken from the freezer and left out at room temperature. At first, the energy flowing from the environment into the ice makes the water molecules vibrate faster, raising the temperature of the ice cube. At a solid's melting point, its particles vibrate so fast that they break free from their fixed positions. When the ice cube reaches the melting point of water, 0°C, its temperature stops increasing. At this point, added energy continues to change the arrangement of the water molecules from ice crystals into liquid water as the ice melts.

Write About It Have you ever eaten an ice cream cone on a hot summer day? What happened to the ice cream? Think about cause and effect, and write about what happened in your science notebook.

Changing Ice Into Water

Figure 3 The graph shows how the temperature of solid ice changes as it melts into liquid water.

Interpret Data How long did it take for the ice to completely melt once it reached the melting point?

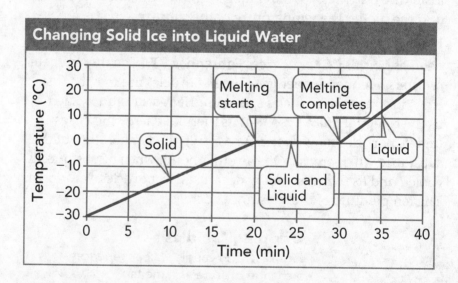

Changing Solid Ice into Liquid Water

Because the melting point is a characteristic property of a substance, chemists often compare melting points when trying to identify an unknown material. For example, silver and iron are both shiny metals with a similar color. The melting point of silver is 961.8°C, while the melting point of iron is 1,538°C. No matter how much of a substance there is, it will always melt at the same temperature.

Freezing You have probably seen many substances freeze. When you put liquid water into a freezer, for example, it turns to solid ice. The thermal energy of the liquid water decreases and the water molecules move more slowly. At 0°C, the water molecules begin to become fixed in place, and the liquid water turns to solid ice.

Freezing is the change of state from a liquid to a solid. It is the reverse of melting. Unlike water, some substances do not have to be cold to the touch in order to freeze. For example, some types of wax freeze at 63°C, which is greater than the record high surface temperature of Earth ever recorded. A substance's **freezing point** is simply the temperature at which it changes from a liquid to a solid. So, water's freezing point is 0°C, and the special wax's freezing point is 63°C. At a liquid's freezing point, its particles are moving so slowly that they begin to take on fixed positions. It doesn't matter how much of a substance there is—it will always have the same freezing point.

☑ READING CHECK **Determine Central Ideas** What is the difference between melting and freezing?

....

....

....

Math Toolbox

The Freezing Point

The graph shows a substance changing from liquid to solid.

1. **Integrate With Visuals** Based on the graph, what is the value of the freezing point for this substance?

....

2. **Draw Comparative Inferences** Think about what would happen if this substance were in the solid phase first, then melted into a liquid. What can you say about the solid's melting point compared to the liquid's freezing point?

....

....

....

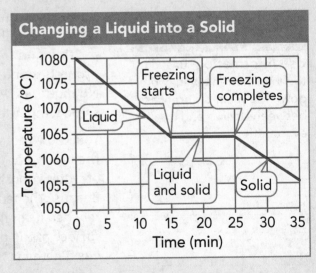

3. **Identify** 🖉 The following are four substances and their melting points. Which substance does the graph represent? Circle your answer.

Platinum: 1768.3°C   Gold: 1064.18°C   Silver: 961.78°C   Mercury: −38.83°C

Figure 4 Examples of vaporization are all around us.

Identify Label each picture as boiling, evaporation, or both.

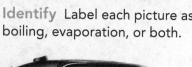

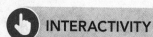

Changes of State Between Liquid and Gas

Why does a pot of hot soup create steam? How does fog form? To answer these questions, you need to look at what happens when changes occur between the liquid and gas states.

Evaporation and Boiling The change in state from a liquid to a gas is called **vaporization** (vay puhr ih ZAY shun). Vaporization occurs when the particles in a liquid gain enough energy to move independently and away from each other. There are two main types of vaporization—boiling and evaporation.

Vaporization that takes place both below and at the surface of a liquid is called boiling. When soup boils, vaporized soup molecules form bubbles below the surface. The bubbles rise and eventually break the surface of the liquid, as shown in **Figure 4**. The temperature at which a liquid boils is called its **boiling point**. The boiling point of water is 100°C at sea level. As with melting and freezing points, boiling points are characteristic properties and can be used to identify unknown substances. No matter how much of a substance you have, it will boil at the same temperature.

You know that a rain puddle eventually disappears from the ground as it changes from a liquid to a gas. The puddle of water vaporizes, but why don't we see the water boiling? Because the temperature of the water in the puddle has not reached its boiling point, only the water particles on the surface of the puddle have enough energy to turn into a gas. Energy is transferred to these particles from the sun's radiation and the surrounding air. Vaporization that takes place only on the surface of a liquid is called **evaporation**. The process continues until all of the particles evaporate and the puddle is gone. While boiling occurs only at one temperature, evaporation can occur at all temperatures.

INTERACTIVITY

Observe and describe the motion of particles in substances at different temperatures.

Literacy Connection

Use Information Based on the information given, write down the main differences between boiling and evaporation.

....

....

....

....

....

....

....

The Effect of Pressure

When you push on an object, you apply pressure to the object. The pressure depends on the force you apply and the area over which you apply the force.

Pressure = Force / Area

Gas particles constantly collide with one another and with any nearby surfaces. As a result, a gas pushes on these surfaces. The pressure a gas applies is greater if its particles collide with a surface more often, as shown in **Figure 5**.

The air that surrounds you is constantly applying pressure to you. This pressure, called atmospheric pressure, can affect how easily a liquid changes to a gas. Think about boiling water to make pasta. Atmospheric pressure is acting on the surface of the liquid water. As the water is heated on the stove, the pressure inside of the liquid increases. When the pressure inside of the liquid equals the atmospheric pressure, the liquid boils.

In locations high above sea level—such as Denver, Colorado—the atmospheric pressure is less because the air is less dense. This means that it takes less thermal energy to get a liquid to boil in these locations. In Denver, water boils at 95°C.

VIDEO

Discover how planes form vapor trails in the sky.

Pressure and Vaporization

Figure 5 🖊 Circle the image in which the liquid would require more thermal energy to change to a gas. How did you determine your answer?

....

....

....

....

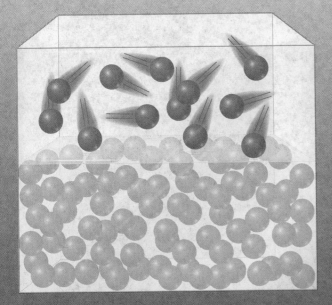
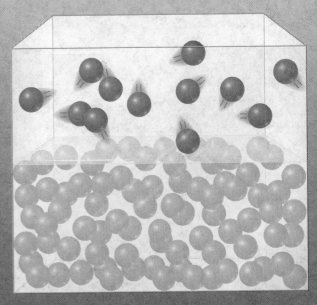

HANDS-ON LAB

☑**Investigate** Understand why fog can sometimes form on a mirror.

Academic Vocabulary

In orange juice, bits of pulp are suspended in liquid. Explain what you think *suspended* means.

....

....

....

....

....

Condensation

The reverse of vaporization is condensation. **Condensation** is the change in state from a gas to a liquid. It occurs when particles in a gas lose enough thermal energy to change state.

You can observe condensation by breathing onto a window, as shown in **Figure 6**. When warm water vapor in your breath reaches the cooler surface of the window, the water vapor condenses into liquid droplets.

Have you ever wondered how fog forms? Much like clouds in the atmosphere, fog forms (**Figure 7**) when water vapor in the air condenses into tiny liquid droplets. Water vapor is a colorless gas that you cannot see. The steam you see above a kettle of boiling water is not water vapor, and neither are clouds or fog. What you see in those cases are tiny droplets of liquid water **suspended** in air.

Condensation on a Window

Figure 6 Warm breath condenses on the cool surface of a window.

Foggy Mountains

Figure 7 Fog forms in the cool air.

☑**READING CHECK** **Draw Evidence** What is happening to the water vapor in the air in this photograph?

....

....

....

Changing State from Solid to Gas

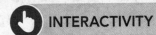

In places where the winters are very cold, the snow may disappear even when the temperature stays well below freezing. This change is the result of sublimation. **Sublimation** occurs when the surface particles of a solid gain enough energy that they form a gas. During sublimation, particles of a solid do not pass through the liquid state as they form a gas.

One example of sublimation occurs with dry ice, which is solid carbon dioxide. At ordinary atmospheric pressures, carbon dioxide cannot exist as a liquid. So instead of melting, solid carbon dioxide changes directly into a gas as shown in **Figure 8**. As it sublimes, the carbon dioxide absorbs thermal energy from its surroundings. For this reason, dry ice can be used to keep materials cold. Some fog machines use dry ice to create fog in movies. When dry ice becomes a gas, it cools water vapor in the nearby air. The water vapor then condenses into a liquid, forming fog near the dry ice.

Model It

Dry Ice

Figure 8 Dry ice sublimes, changing directly from a solid to a gas.

Developing Models 🖊 Think about what is happening to the particles of carbon dioxide as the dry ice changes from solid to gas. Draw models of the particles in the two phases of matter. Use an arrow to show the flow of thermal energy into the solid carbon dioxide.

1. **Cause and Effect** What is the main cause of any change of state?

....

....

....

2. **Explain** If there is high gas pressure above a liquid, what can you say about the amount of thermal energy required for the liquid to change to gas?

....

....

....

3. **Compare and Contrast** In terms of changes in particle motion and thermal energy, how does condensation differ from evaporation?

....

....

....

....

....

....

4. **Predict** If you left a block of dry ice in a bowl at room temperature all day, what would happen to it?

....

....

....

....

....

5. **Apply Concepts** Solid substance A has a melting point of 100°C. Liquid substance B has a freezing point of 110°C. For each substance, identify its state of matter and describe the motion of its particles when the substance is at 115°C.

....

....

....

....

....

....

....

Quest CHECK-IN

In this lesson, you learned what happens to the particles of substances during melting, freezing, evaporation, boiling, condensation, and sublimation. You also thought about how thermal energy plays a role in these changes of state.

Predict Why do you need to take the temperature of the surroundings into consideration when designing a system with materials that can change state?

....

....

....

....

👆 INTERACTIVITY

Lift Your Car

Go online to use your knowledge of changes of state to identify the benefits and drawbacks of different ideas for your design.

MS-PS1-4

FREEZE that Scalpel!

How do refrigerators and freezers keep food from spoiling? They circulate chilled air. The cold temperatures prevent bacteria from forming.

Cryosurgery works in a similar way. It uses extremely cold temperatures to treat cancers, pre-cancerous growths, warts, moles, and skin infections.

While refrigerators and freezers use freon to keep food cold, cryosurgery generally uses liquid nitrogen to freeze unwanted, harmful cells. At room temperature, nitrogen is a colorless, odorless gas. However, when it undergoes extreme cold, it condenses into a liquid. To achieve this state, the nitrogen has to be cooled to around −200°C! At this temperature, liquid nitrogen instantly freezes anything it touches, and with human tissue, it can destroy cells upon contact. After treatment, the dead cells and tumors thaw and are absorbed harmlessly into the system. If the tumor is on the skin's surface, a scab forms and eventually drops away.

Cryosurgery is very new in the field of medicine, and new techniques are being developed every day. For example, some doctors have started using liquefied argon gas, rather than liquid nitrogen, because it allows for even faster freezing of cells. Doctors and scientists are also exploring ways to use cryosurgery safely to target cells from the inside out, instead of from the outside in.

MY DISCOVERY

Type "cryosurgery" into an online search engine to learn more about this technology and the conditions it can treat.

Liquid nitrogen freeze technique treats a skin cancer.

Cryosurgery is used to kill tumors that could not be reached and cut out.

Skin lesion

Liquid nitrogen

③ Gas Behavior

Guiding Questions

- How do changes in particle motion of a gas affect physical properties?
- How are the temperature, pressure, and volume of a gas related?

Connections

Literacy Read and Comprehend

Math Graph Proportional Relationships

MS-PS1-4

Vocabulary

pressure
Charles's Law
Boyle's Law

Academic Vocabulary

proportional

 VOCABULARY APP

Practice vocabulary on a mobile device.

Quest CONNECTION

As you learn about gas behavior, think about how the pressure, volume, and temperature of a gas could factor into your car lift's design.

Connect It !

When a volleyball sits out in the sun, it becomes warmer and feels more firm.

Apply Concepts What do you think happens to the particles of air inside the ball as it warms in the sun?

....

....

Apply Scientific Reasoning What do you think happens to a volleyball outside on a cold night?

....

....

....

Pressure and Temperature of a Gas

Have you ever shaken a snow globe? If so, you've seen how the fake snowflakes fly around. They collide with each other and with the walls of the snow globe. If you shake it more slowly, the snowflakes collide less frequently.

Gas particles in a container are a lot like the snowflakes in a snow globe. The gas particles constantly collide with one another and with any walls that may contain them. As a result, a gas pushes against the walls of its container. The **pressure** of a gas is the force of its outward push (in Newtons) over an area (in square meters) of the walls of the container. Pressure is measured in units of pascals (Pa) or kilopascals (kPa) (1 kPa = 1,000 Pa).

The pressure of a gas can affect the physical properties of an object. For example, the volleyball in **Figure 1** feels firm when the pressure of the air inside of the ball is greater than the pressure of the air outside of the ball. Because the air particles inside of the ball are tightly packed, there are more frequent collisions with its inner surface. This results in a higher pressure.

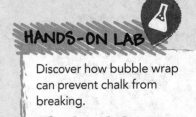

HANDS-ON LAB

Discover how bubble wrap can prevent chalk from breaking.

Volleyball in the Sun
Figure 1 The air pressure inside a volleyball increases as it warms in the sun.

Pressure in a Basketball

Figure 2 When a basketball leaks air, the pressure inside decreases. It loses its bounciness and becomes "flat."

Infer ✏ On each image, write a physical property that changes due to low gas pressure in the object.

Literacy Connection

Read and Comprehend As you read, underline the sentences that explain the motion of particles as a gas is heated.

If you get a tiny hole in a pumped-up ball, air will slowly leak out, as shown in **Figure 2**. Because the pressure inside the ball is greater than the outside air, the interior gas particles hit the inside of the ball more often. Gas particles inside the ball exit more often than gas particles outside of the ball enter. As a result, the pressure inside the ball drops until it is equal to the pressure outside.

Temperature also affects the pressure of a gas. When you heat a gas, its particles move faster, so the temperature increases. The particles will collide with the walls of their container with greater force and more frequency. A greater force over the same area results in greater pressure.

In general, when the temperature of a gas at constant volume is increased, the pressure of the gas increases. When the temperature is decreased while volume is constant, the pressure of the gas decreases.

☑ **READING CHECK** **Summarize** How does particle motion affect pressure?

....

....

Temperature and Volume

French scientist Jacques Charles examined the relationship between the temperature and volume of a gas. He measured the volume of a gas at various temperatures in a container that could change volume. Because the volume was able to change, the pressure remained fairly constant.

HANDS-ON LAB

☑**Investigate** Test Charles's and Boyle's Laws.

Charles's Law Charles discovered that when the temperature of a gas at constant pressure is increased, its volume increases. He also discovered that when the temperature of a gas at constant pressure is decreased, its volume decreases. This principle is called **Charles's law**.

Figure 3 shows Charles's Law in action. A balloon is slowly lowered into liquid nitrogen at nearly –200°C and then removed. In the process, the pressure remains more or less constant.

Cooling and Warming a Balloon

Figure 3 🖊 The volume of a gas-filled balloon changes as the temperature changes. Below each image, shade the arrows to indicate whether temperature and volume increase or decrease at each step.

A gas-filled balloon is at room temperature, 20°C.

The balloon is submerged in the liquid nitrogen at –196°C.

The balloon is removed from the liquid nitrogen.

The balloon is again at room temperature.

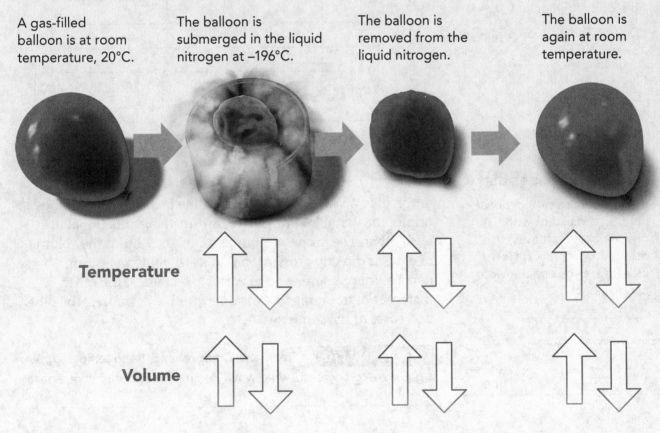

Temperature

Volume

69

Math Toolbox

Graphing Charles's Law

Suppose that you do an experiment to test Charles's law. The experiment begins with 50 mL of gas in a container that can expand. The gas is slowly heated. Each time the temperature increases by 20°C, the gas volume is recorded. The data are recorded in the data table. Note that the temperatures in the data table have been converted to kelvins, the SI unit of temperature. To convert from degrees Celsius to kelvins (K), you simply add 273.

Temperature		Volume
(°C)	(K)	(mL)
0	273	50
20	293	54
40	313	58
60	333	62
80	353	66

Graph Proportional Relationships 🖊 Plot the data from the table on the graph.

As you can see from your graph, the data points form a straight line. If you extended the line, it would pass through the origin (the point 0,0).

Draw this extension of the line on your graph.

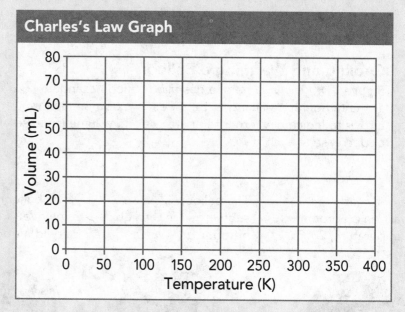

Charles's Law Graph

Academic Vocabulary

In this context, *proportional* means "consistent with." As one variable increases, the other also increases. How else might you use the word *proportional*?

....

....

....

Directly Proportional Relationships When a graph of two variables is a straight line passing through the origin, the variables are said to be directly **proportional** to each other. The graph of Charles's Law shows that the volume of a gas is directly proportional to its kelvin temperature at constant pressure. As one variable increases, the other increases at the same rate. As one variable decreases, the other decreases at the same rate.

✅ READING CHECK **Read and Comprehend** If the temperature of a gas were to decrease, what would happen to the volume of a gas?

....

Pressure and Volume

Suppose that you use a bicycle pump to inflate a tire, as shown in **Figure 4**. By pressing down on the plunger, you force the gas inside the pump through the rubber tube and out of the nozzle into the tire. What happens to the volume of air inside the pump cylinder as you push down on the plunger? What happens to the pressure?

Boyle's Law In the 1600s, the scientist Robert Boyle carried out experiments to try to improve air pumps. He measured the volumes of gases at different pressures. Boyle's experiments showed that gas volume and pressure were related.

When the pressure of a gas at constant temperature is increased, the volume of the gas decreases. When the pressure is decreased, the volume increases. This relationship between the pressure and the volume of a gas is called **Boyle's Law**. Boyle's Law describes situations in which the volume of a gas is changed. The pressure changes in the opposite way. For example, as the handle of a bike pump is pressed, it pushes the particles downward in the cylinder. The volume in the cylinder becomes smaller, and particles leave through the tube.

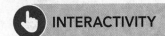

INTERACTIVITY

Watch an animation to understand Charles's Law and Boyle's Law.

Filling a Bike Tire
Figure 4 Pumping a bike pump causes an increase in gas pressure and a decrease in gas volume within the pump.

Model It

Developing Models ✏ Draw two diagrams to show the air particles in a bike pump before and after the handle is pushed down.

Air in pump before handle is pushed

Air in pump after handle is pushed

Math Toolbox

Graphing Boyle's Law

In an experiment, the volume of a gas was varied at a constant temperature. The pressure of the gas was recorded after each 50-mL change in volume. The data are shown in the table.

1. **Graph Proportional Relationships** ✏ Use the data from the table to plot points, and connect them to make a line graph.

2. **Make Generalizations** What happens to the pressure of a gas when the volume is decreased at a constant temperature?

....

3. **Calculate** Choose two points on the graph. For each point, multiply the pressure and the volume. How do these two products compare?

....

4. **Interpret Data** Is the relationship between pressure and volume directly proportional, as in Charles's Law? Explain.

....

....

....

Volume (mL)	Pressure (kPa)
300	20
250	24
200	30
150	40
100	60
50	120

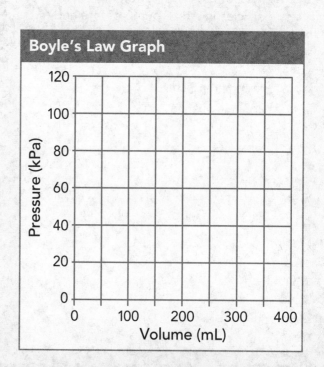

Boyle's Law Graph

Inversely Proportional Relationships

Look at the graph that you made when graphing Boyle's Law in the Math Toolbox. Notice that the points lie on a curve and not a straight line. This curved line is called a hyperbola. When volume is low, pressure is high. When pressure is high, volume is low. As the volume of a gas increases at constant temperature, the pressure of the gas decreases at a different rate. If you multiply the two variables—pressure and volume—at any point on the curve, you will find that the product does not change. This means that the two variables are inversely proportional to each other. The graph for Boyle's Law shows that gas pressure is inversely proportional to volume at constant temperature.

Real-World Gas Behavior

Pistons are often used in machines in which gas is involved. Pistons move in response to the motion of the particles of gas. For example, pistons in a car engine respond to pressure changes that occur when a mixture of fuel and air ignites. The moving pistons help to turn the crankshaft, which connects to the wheels of the car. So the pistons drive the turning of the wheels, which allows the car to move.

VIDEO

Go online to see how a car engine works.

INTERACTIVITY

Explore how a hot-air balloon uses relationships between pressure, volume, and temperature.

Pistons in an Engine

Figure 5 Pistons in car engines move up and down. This drives the turning of the wheels of the car.

How Pistons Work

Figure 6 Use what you have learned about gas behavior to understand how temperature, pressure, and volume affect pistons.

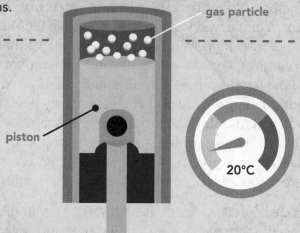

Temperature and Pressure

The image shows gas particles above a piston in a rigid container. The piston is held fixed.

Relate Change 🖊 Finish this sentence by circling the correct answer: If the temperature of the gas increases, the pressure on the piston will

(increase / decrease).

Temperature and Volume

Now, the piston is free to move up or down. Heat is applied to the gas in the cylinder.

Apply Scientific Reasoning
🖊 Finish this sentence by circling the correct answer: As temperature increases, the volume of the gas will

(increase / decrease).

Develop Models 🖊 In each cylinder, draw the piston and the gas particles based on the temperature shown.

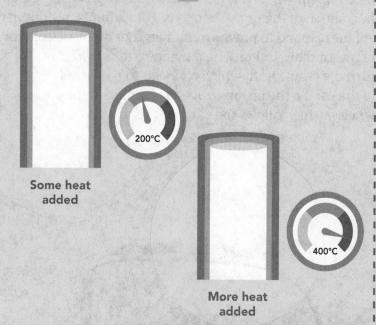

Some heat added

More heat added

Pressure and Volume

This time, the gas is kept at a fixed temperature. The piston is pushed by an outside force, so the pressure on the gas increases.

Identify What happens to the volume of the gas as the pressure increases?

....

....

Classify 🖊 Under the cylinders, rank the pressure from lowest to highest with 1 being lowest and 3 being highest. Rank the volume from lowest to highest as well.

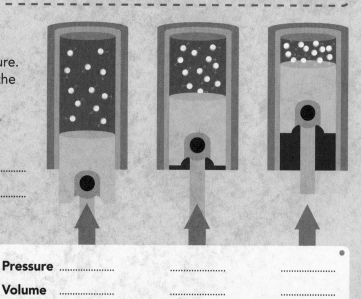

Pressure ....

Volume ....

MS-PS1-4

1. **Explain** What relationship does Charles's Law explain?

....

....

....

2. **Identify** If the gas pressure in a ball is low, how will it affect the physical properties of the ball?

....

....

....

3. **Cause and Effect** When the temperature of a gas increases, and volume is fixed, what happens to the gas pressure? Why?

....

....

....

....

....

....

4. **Synthesize Information** How do particles of gas move when there is high temperature and high pressure?

....

....

....

5. **Apply Concepts** Environmental scientists collect air samples so they can test the quality of the air. They start with rigid metal containers that are completely empty—the air has been pumped out of them. What happens to the pressure inside the container and the volume of the container as air enters it?

....

....

....

....

....

....

....

Quest CHECK-IN

You learned about the relationships between the temperature, pressure, and volume of a gas. You also modeled how the gas particles behave in different situations.

Synthesize Information Using the relationships you have learned about between temperature, pressure, and volume, what are two ways you could increase the gas pressure of a system?

....

....

....

....

....

HANDS-ON LAB

Phases of Matter

Go online to download the worksheet of this lab. Build and test your device. Redesign and retest the device as needed.

MS-PS1-4

RISING to the OCCASION:
Charles's Law in the Oven!

Have you ever baked bread or rolls? If so, you probably observed that during baking, the bread rises, increasing in volume. What causes this to happen? The answer lies in chemistry.

Chemistry in Baking

Chemistry and baking go together naturally. In fact, chemistry affects every aspect of preparing food. The ingredients in a recipe may react with one another during the mixing process. Then, when you add heat—whether from a stove, a conventional oven, or a microwave oven—another whole set of reactions may occur. Charles's Law rules the effect of heat on food.

As you have read, Charles's Law states that temperature affects the volume of a gas. Assuming constant pressure, gas expands as temperature rises.

When a chef mixes ingredients, the dry ingredients absorb the wet ingredients. In baking, the dry ingredients usually include either baking powder or baking soda. And when baking bread, the most important dry ingredient is yeast. All three of these dry ingredients react with wet ingredients, such as milk or water, by creating tiny bubbles of carbon dioxide gas. Therefore, the dough that goes into the oven is filled with gas bubbles. The oven's heat makes these bubbles expand, forcing the dough to rise. The texture within the dough then becomes more sponge-like, with tiny holes and cavities created by the expanding bubbles of carbon dioxide gas.

In the heat of an oven, gas bubbles in bread dough expand, causing the bread to rise.

Getting dough to rise properly can be a tricky task! When yeast is used, temperature affects the state of the dough before it even goes into the oven. Yeast is very active around 30°C. Putting the dough in a refrigerator, and thereby lowering the temperature around it, slows down the reaction that produces gas bubbles. Bakers need to have a good understanding of how temperature will affect their ingredients at every stage of the baking process to make sure their baked goods come out just right. In some recipes and under some conditions, bread may rise—increase in volume— by as much as 33 percent in the oven!

1. **Identify Patterns** What pattern does Charles's Law suggest about recipes with ingredients that might produce gas during cooking?

2. **Construct Explanations** Study the 3D image of a bread dough sample on the right. Explain what you see in the image, and describe the process that happens to dough in a hot oven. Use evidence to support your explanation.

3. **Predict** What would probably happen if you tried to bake bread without using yeast? Why?

4. **Refine Your Plan** Suppose you are mixing ingredients for bread, and the recipe says to bake the dough as soon as it's mixed. But, you have another task to do and are unable to bake the dough right away. What should you do to make sure your bread still turns out well?

5. **Calculate** If a baker gets the most rise out of his bread, what will be the volume of a loaf of bread that started out as a 30-cm^3 lump of dough?

1 States of Matter

MS-PS1-4

1. A substance that has neither a definite shape nor a definite volume is a
A. fluid.
B. solid.
C. liquid.
D. gas.

2. In a solid, particles do not move around each other, but they do
A. change shape.
B. vibrate.
C. flow.
D. sit completely still.

3. Sugar is considered a crystalline solid because its particles are
A. arranged in a regular pattern.
B. arranged randomly.
C. completely motionless.
D. able to move around one another.

4. Compare and Contrast How is a gas different from a liquid?

....

....

....

....

5. Compare and Contrast ✏ Use the Venn diagram to compare and contrast the characteristics of solids and liquids.

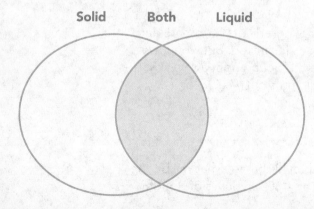

Solid   Both   Liquid

2 Changes of State

MS-PS1-4

6. Vaporization that takes place both above and below the surface is called
A. evaporation.
B. boiling.
C. condensation.
D. precipitation.

7. When a liquid freezes into a solid, the particles of the substance
A. lose energy.
B. gain energy.
C. move faster.
D. disappear.

8. Label each image as evaporation, boiling, condensation, or sublimation. Write more than one answer for an image if you notice more than one change of state.

....

....

....

....

....

....

9. When the gas pressure above a liquid increases, the amount of thermal energy required for the liquid to vaporize

....

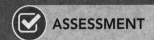
10. The melting point of aluminum is 660°C.
At what temperature will aluminum melt if
you have 5 grams? 10 grams? Explain your
answer.

....

....

....

....

....

11. Integrate With Visuals ✎ Make a
diagram with two drawings showing the
particle motion of a substance in two states
as it condenses. Use arrows on the first
drawing to show the direction thermal
energy is moving.

State of Matter: ....

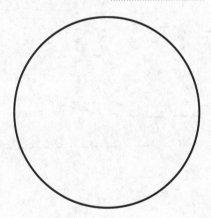

State of Matter: ....

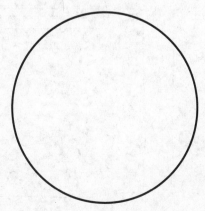

3 Gas Behavior

MS-PS1-4

12. When the temperature of a gas decreases,
and volume is held constant, the pressure of
the gas
A. stays the same.   B. increases.
C. becomes zero.   D. decreases.

13. Adding thermal energy to a gas at constant
pressure will cause
A. the volume of the gas to decrease.
B. the volume of the gas to increase.
C. the temperature of the gas to decrease.
D. the pressure of the gas to decrease.

14. Use Graphs Does this graph represent
a directly or inversely proportional
relationship? Explain what this means for the
relationship between pressure and volume.

....

....

....

....

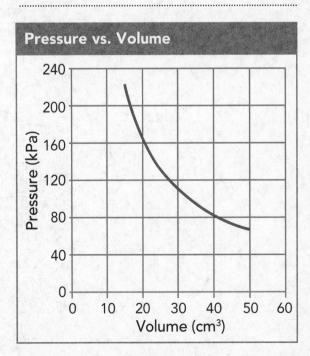

MS-PS1-4

Evidence-Based Assessment

On a sunny morning, Skyler's father fills his new swimming pool with water from a garden hose. The following day, he notices that the water level has dropped—there is less water in the pool than there was the day before. He checks the pool for any leaks, but he finds nothing.

Skyler has a hunch as to why the water level has dropped. He draws some models to help explain what has happened.

Model 1:

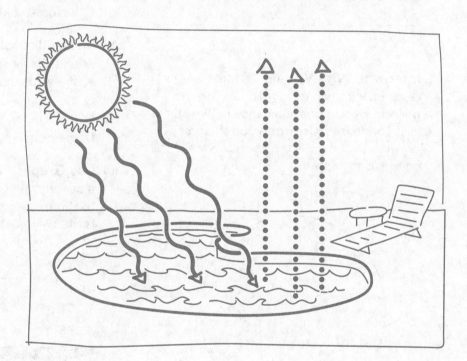

Model 2:

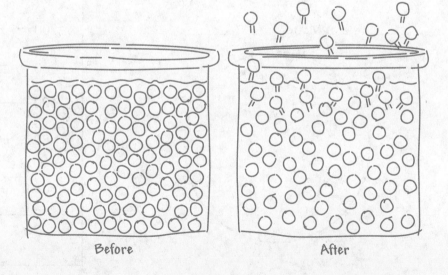

Before   After

1. **Identify** What change of state is Skyler representing with his models?
   A. condensation   B. evaporation
   C. sublimation   D. melting

2. **Use Models** Look at Model 1. What do the lines from the sun to the water represent? What do the dotted lines coming from the surface of the water represent?

....

....

....

....

....

....

3. **Develop Models** What labels and/or drawings would you add to Model 1 to improve it?

....

....

....

....

....

....

4. **Cite Evidence** Describe what is happening to the thermal energy of the water in the pool during the day. Use evidence from the models to explain your answer.

....

....

....

....

....

....

....

....

5. **Draw Comparative Inferences** Look at Model 2. What two states of matter are shown in the "After" picture? Support your answer with evidence from the model. What is happening to the kinetic energy of the water molecules at the surface? What does this imply about the temperature of the water?

....

....

....

....

....

....

....

....

Quest FINDINGS

Complete the Quest!

Phenomenon Determine the best way to present your device to your class. Think about the ways you could improve upon your device.

Apply Concepts Think of a situation in which you might need to lift a real car. Describe the situation below. If your device could be made on a larger scale, how might it work in the situation?

....

....

....

INTERACTIVITY

Reflect on Your Lift

Melting ICE

Can you develop a **model** to predict and describe how **temperature** affects the particles of a raft made of ice?

Background

Phenomenon Off the coast of Alaska, your ship has sunk, but you manage to survive by climbing on an iceberg. You need a raft to float to the mainland. The only things available are floes, which are sheets of ice. The liquid water temperature is warmer than the ice, so your raft is going to melt as you travel!

In this investigation, you will use two ice cubes to explore how the temperature of liquid water affects how quickly ice melts. Gather evidence to conclude how long an ice raft will last in two cases: where the liquid water temperature is 40–45°C, and where the liquid water temperature is 20–25°C.

Materials

(per pair)

- stopwatch or timer
- thermometer
- 2 plastic cups
- 2 plastic spoons
- 2 ice cubes, about 2 cm on each side
- warm water, 40–45°C
- room-temperature water, 20–25°C

Safety

Follow all safety guidelines provided by your teacher.

Design an Investigation

1. Begin by making a prediction about the results of the experiment using your background knowledge of ice. Include how long you think it will take each ice cube to melt completely into a liquid. Apply your prediction to your ice raft situation: assuming the mainland is far enough away that it would take 5 minutes for you to float there, would your raft stay solid long enough in 40–45°C water? How about in 20–25°C water?

....
....
....
....

2. Next, design, develop, and conduct an experiment to test your prediction. Use the space below to sketch, and the next page to write, your procedure. Think about these questions when designing your experiment.

HANDS-ON LAB

иDemonstrate Go online for a downloadable worksheet of this lab.

- How might the size of the ice cubes affect your results?

- Will the amount of water in each cup affect your results?

- Would the motion of the ice cube affect your results?

- How might you move the ice cube to model the raft's motion?

- What factors will be controls in your experiment?

3. In addition to writing your procedure, design a data table to record your observations and measurements. Be sure to use the correct metric units in your data table.

4. Tell your teacher your hypothesis and describe your procedure. Once your procedure is approved, run your experiment and record your results in the data table.

Procedure

Data Table

Analyze and Interpret Data

1. **Predict** Were your predictions about the ice cubes supported by the results of the experiment? Explain why or why not.

....

....

....

2. **Interpret Data** In which cup did the liquid water temperature change the most? Discuss your results.

....

....

....

....

3. **Apply Scientific Reasoning** When the ice melted, its particles gained enough energy to overcome the forces holding them together as solid ice. What was the source of that energy?

....

....

4. In what ways did the experiment accurately reflect icebergs melting in ocean water? In what ways did the experiment simplify the real-word scenario?

....

....

....

5. **Develop Models** In the space provided, draw two models or diagrams to show the arrangement of particles in the ice before and after thermal energy was added. For each model, identify the temperature and the state of matter.

NGSS PERFORMANCE EXPECTATIONS

MS-PS3-1 Construct and interpret graphical displays of data to describe the relationships of kinetic energy to the mass of an object and to the speed of an object.

MS-PS3-2 Develop a model to describe that when the arrangement of objects interacting at a distance changes, different amounts of potential energy are stored in the system.

MS-PS3-5 Construct, use, and present arguments to support the claim that when the kinetic energy of an object changes, energy is transferred to or from the object.

HANDS-ON LAB

uConnect Explore how changes in energy can make a playing card jump.

How do these sailors use energy and machines to move the boats faster in a race?

GO ONLINE
to access your digital course

▶ VIDEO

👆 INTERACTIVITY

📲 VIRTUAL LAB

☑ ASSESSMENT

📖 eTEXT

📱 APP

The Essential Question

How does energy cause change?

A sailboat moves due to the energy in wind. Sailors use pulleys, cranks, and other machines to adjust the sails. Sails are heavy, and machines such as pulleys help to reduce the amount of force used to move them. These machines allow the sailors to do work more easily. How does wind energy combined with machines cause a sailboat to move?

....

....

....

....

....

Quest KICKOFF

How can you build a complicated machine to do something simple?

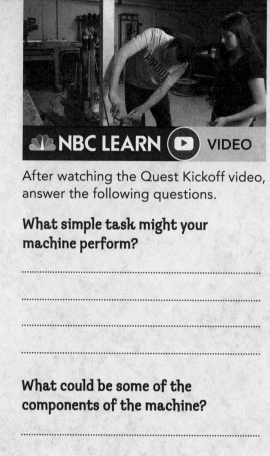

STEM **Phenomenon** Rube Goldberg was a cartoonist and inventor. Goldberg is well-known for his cartoons, which include complex and wacky machines that perform simple tasks. Today, students who study machine design and engineering can participate in contests to build the best "Rube Goldberg machine." Building these machines helps students to understand energy transformations and hone their construction skills. In this Quest, you will design and build a Rube Goldberg machine–an overly complicated machine with a simple end goal. You will use your understanding of energy transformations to construct the chain-reaction machine.

After watching the Quest Kickoff video, answer the following questions.

What simple task might your machine perform?

....

....

....

....

What could be some of the components of the machine?

....

....

....

....

 INTERACTIVITY

Outrageous Energy Contraptions

MS-PS3-2 Develop a model to describe that when the arrangement of objects interacting at a distance changes, different amounts of potential energy are stored in the system.
MS-PS3-5 Construct, use, and present arguments to support the claim that when the kinetic energy of an object changes, energy is transferred to or from the object.

Quest CHECK-IN

IN LESSON 1

STEM How do machines exert force and transfer energy? Develop a design for a chain-reaction machine that can perform a simple task.

 INTERACTIVITY

Applying Energy

Quest CHECK-IN

IN LESSON 2

STEM What are the different types of kinetic energy? Use what you have learned to finalize the design, choose materials, and build your chain-reaction machine.

HANDS-ON LAB

Build a Chain-Reaction Machine

Quest CHECK-IN

IN LESSON 3

STEM What energy transformations take place in a chain-reaction machine? Test your chain-reaction machine prototype and evaluate its performance. Revise and retest it.

HANDS-ON LAB

Test and Evaluate a Chain-Reaction Machine

Many energy transformations occur in this complicated device. In the end, it simply turns on a light bulb!

Quest CHECK-IN

IN LESSON 4

STEM How can an additional energy transformation improve your design? Modify your chain-reaction machine to include at least one additional energy transformation. Then test, evaluate, and finalize it.

HANDS-ON LAB

Redesign and Retest a Chain-Reaction Machine

Quest FINDINGS

Complete the Quest!

Determine the best way to demonstrate your machine, and show how energy is used in the working of your machine from start to finish.

INTERACTIVITY

Reflect on Your Chain-Reaction Machine

Energy, Motion, Force, and Work

Guiding Questions

- How is energy related to motion and force?
- What are the relationships among energy, motion, force, and work?

Connections

Literacy Determine Central Ideas

Math Solve Linear Equations

Vocabulary

energy
motion
force
work
power

Academic Vocabulary

maximum

 VOCABULARY APP

Practice vocabulary on a mobile device.

Quest CONNECTION

Think about how force and motion operate in machines you are familiar with. How do these factors allow machines to do work?

Connect It !

✏ **Draw curved arrows on the photograph to represent the motion of the motorcycles.**

Apply Scientific Reasoning These motorcycles need energy to move. Where does the energy come from?

....

Write Explanatory Texts Describe how the rider exerts a force on the motorcycle.

....

....

Construct Explanations In what way do you think the motorcycles perform work?

....

Energy in Motion and Force

Energy is the ability to do work or cause change. You do work when you pick up your backpack. Motorcycles do work during a race, as in **Figure 1**. The energy to do this work comes from fuel. As the fuel burns, it changes into other substances and releases energy.

Energy comes in many forms. Light, sound, and electricity are all forms of energy. Energy can also be transferred from place to place. For example, chemical energy is transferred from the food you eat to your body. Energy from the sun is transferred to Earth in the form of electromagnetic radiation. Energy is not something you can see directly. You can, however, observe its effects. When you touch something hot, you don't see the energy, but you feel the heat. You can hear the sound of a bass drum, but you can't see the sound energy itself.

Energy and Motion It takes energy for motion to occur. An object is in **motion** if its position changes relative to another object. A pitched ball would not speed toward home plate without energy supplied by the pitcher. Energy supplied by food enables a racehorse to run around a track. Energy stored in gasoline allows the motorcycles in **Figure 1** to move at high speeds. In each of these examples, the more energy that is used, the faster the object can move.

VIDEO

Watch this video to better understand energy.

Reflect Think about the different methods you used to travel from one place to another today. In your science notebook, describe two of these ways. For each, identify the energy source that caused the movement.

Racing Around the Track
Figure 1 Energy, motion, force, and work are all involved in a motorcycle race.

INTERACTIVITY

Play the role of a video game designer and test virtual machines.

Energy and Force The relationship between energy and motion also involves forces. A **force** is a push or pull. You can see many examples of this relationship on a construction site. Look at **Figure 2** and study the examples of how energy is used to apply a force that causes motion.

☑ READING CHECK **Explain** How would you describe a force?

....

....

Force

Figure 2 When energy is used to apply force, objects can move.

Apply Concepts ✎ Draw an arrow on each numbered picture to show the direction of the force being applied. Then label each arrow with "push" or "pull" to identify the type of force being applied.

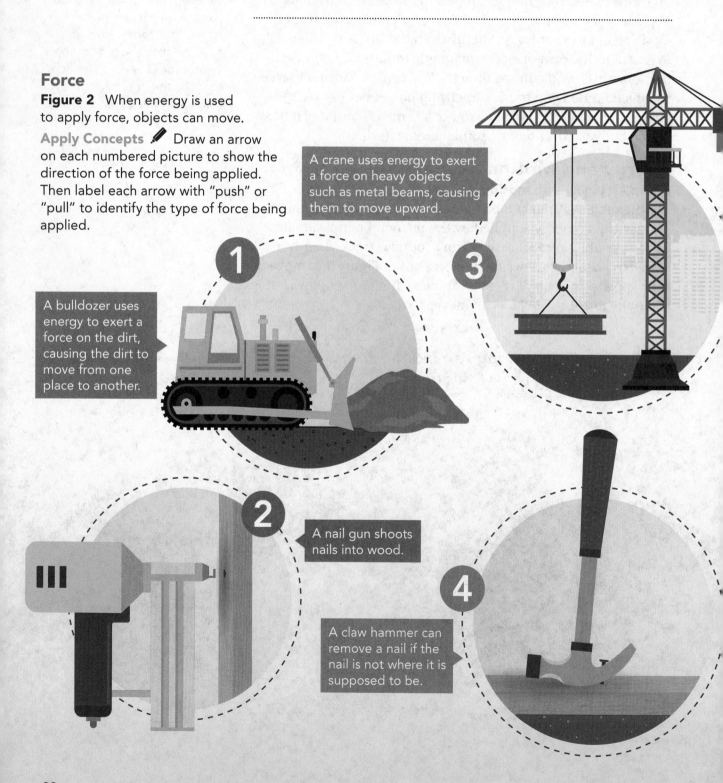

A crane uses energy to exert a force on heavy objects such as metal beams, causing them to move upward.

A bulldozer uses energy to exert a force on the dirt, causing the dirt to move from one place to another.

A nail gun shoots nails into wood.

A claw hammer can remove a nail if the nail is not where it is supposed to be.

Force and Work

You might think of "work" as a job, such as teaching, being a doctor, or bagging groceries at the local supermarket. But the scientific meaning of work is much broader than that. In scientific terms, you do **work** any time you exert a force on an object that causes the object to change its motion in the same direction in which you exert the force. All of the machines on the previous page show work being done because the forces are being applied in the same direction as the motion shown.

You probably carry your books from one class to another every school day. You know that you exert a force on the books as you carry them. However, you do very little work on them because of the direction of the force exerted. When you carry an object while walking at constant speed in a straight line, you exert an upward force on the object. Because the force is vertical and the motion is horizontal, you don't do any work on the object itself.

Figure 3 shows three different ways to move a tool bin. The weight of the bin is the same in each situation, but the amount of work varies. For a given force, the **maximum** amount of work is done when both the movement and the force are in the same direction.

INTERACTIVITY

Explore how levers work in this virtual activity.

Academic Vocabulary

Write a synonym for maximum.

....

Force, Motion, and Work

Figure 3 🖉 The amount of work that you do on something depends on the direction of the applied force and the object's motion. In the second and third pictures, label each arrow with "motion" or "force."

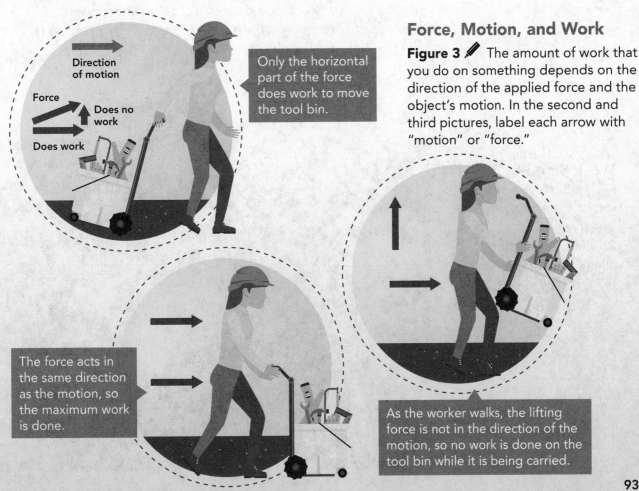

Direction of motion

Force

Does no work

Does work

Only the horizontal part of the force does work to move the tool bin.

The force acts in the same direction as the motion, so the maximum work is done.

As the worker walks, the lifting force is not in the direction of the motion, so no work is done on the tool bin while it is being carried.

Work Done, or Not?

Figure 4 This girl struggles to open a jar, but the lid does not budge.

Apply Scientific Reasoning Is the girl doing work? Explain your reasoning.

....

....

....

....

....

👆 INTERACTIVITY

Explore how energy is needed to get an object to move, and discover how work on an object affects its motion.

Work Requires Motion Imagine that you are trying to open a jar, and the lid is stuck. You exert a lot of force on the lid, but it doesn't move. Are you doing work? No. No matter how much force you exert, you don't do any work if the lid does not move.

Calculating Work Suppose you bought a new painting for your room. You have to carry the painting up three porch steps to the first floor and then up another flight of 12 steps to the second floor. (See **Figure 5**.) Is it more work to lift the painting up 12 steps than three steps? As you might guess, moving an object a greater distance requires more work than moving the same object a shorter distance. The amount of work you do depends on both the amount of force you exert and the distance the object moves.

More or Less Work Done?

Figure 5 This person carries a painting up two sets of steps.

Predict ✏️ Circle the image in which you think the person does more work.

The amount of work done on an object is calculated by multiplying force times distance. When force is measured in newtons and distance in meters, the SI unit of work is the newton-meter (N-m). This unit is also called a joule (J). One joule is the amount of work you do when you exert a force of 1 newton to move an object a distance of 1 meter.

☑ **READING CHECK** **Determine Central Ideas** What two factors affect how much work is done in any given action?

Math Toolbox

Calculating Work

A grandfather lifts a baby 1.5 m with an upward force of 80 N, as shown in the third photograph below. You can use the relationship among work, force, and distance to find out how much work is done:

Work = Force × Distance
Work = 80 N × 1.5 m
Work = 120 N-m

The amount of work done is 120 N-m, or 120 J.

Use the formula for finding work to answer questions 1–2. Show your calculations. Use joules as the unit for work.

1. **Solve Linear Equations** This woman lifts a plant 2 m with a force of 65 N. How much work does she do?

2. **Calculate** How much work is done when 300 N of force is used to lift the dog 1.5 m?

3. **Classify** Label the photos below with the words *least, medium,* and *most* to rank them from least work done to most work done.

HANDS-ON LAB

☑**Investigate** Experiment with a soda can to see how an object's energy relates to work.

Literacy Connection

Determine Central Ideas As you read, underline the main idea of each paragraph on this page.

Work Related to Energy and Power

Did you pull your shoes from the closet this morning? If so, then you did work on the shoes. As you have read, work is done when a force moves an object in the direction of the force. When an object moves, its position changes. What causes change? Recall that the ability to do work or cause change is called energy. Energy is measured in joules—the same units as work.

When you do work on an object, some of your energy is transferred to that object. Think about the plant shown in the Math Toolbox. When the gardener lifted the plant to the high shelf, she transferred energy to the plant.

If you carry a bag of groceries up a flight of stairs, the work you do is the same whether you walk or run. The time it takes to do the work does not affect the amount of work you do on an object. But something else—power—is affected. **Power** is the rate at which work is done, and it equals the amount of work done on an object in a unit of time. You can think of power in two main ways. An object that has more power than another object does more work in the same amount of time. It can also mean doing the same amount of work in less time. Look at **Figure 6** for other examples that compare power.

Work and Power

Figure 6 In each of these images, work is being done. For each image, give two examples of ways the people shown can increase the power being used.

These people load 10 items on the truck in 10 minutes. Ways power can be increased:

....

This person mows half of her backyard in one hour. Ways power can be increased:

....

Calculating Power

All you need to know to calculate power is how much and how quickly work is being done. Power is calculated by dividing the amount of work done by the amount of time it takes to do the work. This can be written as the following formula:

$$\text{Power} = \frac{\text{Work}}{\text{Time}}$$

Because work is equal to force times distance, you can rewrite the equation for power as follows:

$$\text{Power} = \frac{\text{Force} \times \text{Distance}}{\text{Time}}$$

When work is measured in joules and time in seconds, the SI unit of power is the watt (W). One watt equals one joule per second (1 W = 1 J/s). Examine **Figure 7** to learn more about calculating power.

INTERACTIVITY

Examine real-world examples of energy transformations and forces.

Power

Figure 7 Most climbers of the Himalayan Mountains would not make it to the peaks without the help of Sherpas. Sherpas are natives of Nepal, and they carry heavy loads of equipment up the mountains for the climbers. Suppose one Sherpa uses a force of 980 N to move a load of equipment to a height of 20 meters in 25 seconds. How much power is used?

Different Types of Power

Figure 8 Leaf blowers require gasoline for power, while rakes require power from your body.

Power and Energy

Recall that power is the rate at which work is done. Power is also the rate at which energy is transferred, or the amount of energy transferred in a unit of time.

$$\text{Power} = \frac{\text{Energy transferred}}{\text{Time}}$$

For example, a 60-watt lightbulb transfers 60 joules of energy per second. Different machines have different amounts of power. For instance, you can use either a rake or a leaf blower to remove leaves from your lawn (see **Figure 8**). Each tool transfers the same amount of energy to the leaves when it moves leaves the same distance. However, the leaf blower moves leaves faster than the rake. The leaf blower has more power because it transfers the same amount of energy to the leaves in less time.

☑ **READING CHECK** **Apply Concepts** What is the difference in power between a 60-watt lightbulb and a 100-watt lightbulb?

....

Model It !

Develop Models ✏ In the concept map below, label each line to show how energy, motion, force, work, and power relate to each other. One line is labeled for you as an example.

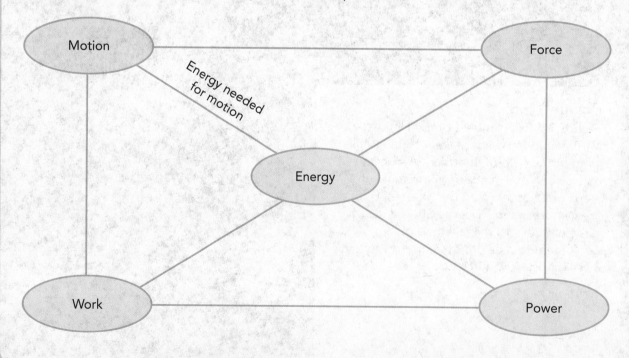

☑ LESSON 1 Check

1. **Explain** How are energy and motion related?

....

....

....

2. **Apply Concepts** Give an example in which energy produces a force that causes motion.

....

....

....

....

....

3. **Draw Conclusions** Is work done when you hold a heavy object for a long time? Why or why not?

....

....

....

....

....

4. **Calculate** What force was applied to an object if 35 J of work was done and the object moved 7 m? Show your work.

....

....

....

....

5. **Evaluate Data** A student did 24 J of work on a chair. She applied a force of 12 N and moved the chair 2 m. What else do you need to know to determine the amount of power used?

....

....

....

6. **Cause and Effect** 🖊 Use the terms *motion*, *power*, and *work* to complete the table.

Cause	Effect
Energy transferred over time	
Force applied to an object to change its position	
Force moving an object over a distance	

Quest CHECK-IN

In this lesson, you learned about the basics of energy and how force and motion relate to it. You also learned about how these concepts relate to how work is done.

Identify How do the concepts of energy, force, and motion relate to the machine you will be designing? What factors will you need to consider in your design?

....

....

....

....

....

👆 INTERACTIVITY

Applying Energy

Go online to learn about how energy, force, and motion relate to machines. Then, develop the design for your machine.

Kinetic Energy and Potential Energy

Guiding Questions

- What determines an object's kinetic energy?
- What factors affect potential energy?
- What is the relationship between potential and kinetic energy?

Connections

Literacy Integrate With Visuals

Math Evaluate Expressions

MS-PS3-1, MS-PS3-2

Vocabulary

kinetic energy
potential energy
gravitational
   potential
   energy
elastic potential
   energy

Academic Vocabulary

virtue

 VOCABULARY APP

Practice vocabulary on a mobile device.

Quest CONNECTION

Think about how your machine will use and rely on potential and kinetic energy.

Connect It!

✏️ **Draw an arrow on the image to show the direction that you think the rocks and dirt are moving.**

Construct Explanations It takes a lot of energy to move this amount of dirt and rocks. What do you think is the source of this energy?

....

....

Apply Scientific Reasoning What is another example of something that starts moving suddenly?

....

....

Kinetic Energy

Study the landslide shown in **Figure 1**. In this image, dirt and rocks are moving rapidly down the side of the hill. As you read in Lesson 1, it takes energy to cause the motion you see in this photo. When objects are in motion, they are demonstrating a certain kind of energy—kinetic energy. **Kinetic energy** is the energy that an object possesses by **virtue** of being in motion.

Examples of kinetic energy are all around us. A car moving down a road exhibits kinetic energy. So does a runner participating in a race. As you sit at your desk in school, you exhibit kinetic energy every time you turn a page in a book or type on a keyboard.

Factors Affecting Kinetic Energy The kinetic energy of an object depends on both its speed and its mass. The faster an object moves, the more kinetic energy it has. For example, if a tennis ball moves at great speed, it has more kinetic energy than if the ball had been softly lobbed over the net. Kinetic energy also increases as mass increases. A wheelbarrow full of dirt has more kinetic energy than an empty wheelbarrow has, due to its greater mass.

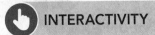
INTERACTIVITY

Interpret graphs to understand the relationships among a snowboarder's kinetic energy, mass, and speed.

Academic Vocabulary

The phrase *by virtue of* means "because of." In what other way have you heard the term virtue used?

....

....

....

Landslide!
Figure 1 A landslide is a sudden movement of rock and soil. Before the landslide, all the rocks and soil were in place and not moving.

HANDS-ON LAB

и**Investigate** Use a skateboard to model changes in kinetic energy.

Calculating Kinetic Energy Keeping in mind that the kinetic energy of an object depends on its mass and its speed, you can use the following equation to solve for the kinetic energy of an object:

$$\text{Kinetic energy} = \tfrac{1}{2} \times \text{Mass} \times \text{Speed}^2$$

The exponent "2" that follows "Speed" tells you that the speed is multiplied by itself first.

For example, suppose a girl with a mass of 50 kg is jogging at a speed of 2 meters per second (m/s). Note that $1 \text{kg·m}^2/\text{s}^2 = 1$ joule (J).

$$\begin{aligned}
\text{Kinetic energy of girl} &= \tfrac{1}{2} \times 50 \text{ kg} \times (2 \text{ m/s})^2 \\
&= \tfrac{1}{2} \times 50 \text{ kg} \times (2 \text{ m/s} \times 2 \text{ m/s}) \\
&= \tfrac{1}{2} \times 50 \text{ kg} \times 4 \text{ m}^2/\text{s}^2 \\
&= 100 \ \text{kg·m}^2/\text{s}^2 = 100 \text{ J}
\end{aligned}$$

Do changes in speed and mass both have the same effect on kinetic energy? Use the Math Toolbox to answer this question.

✓ **READING CHECK**

Apply Concepts
Underline the unit of energy you get when you calculate kinetic energy.

Math Toolbox

Mass, Speed, and Kinetic Energy

A boy and his dog are running.
The dog has a mass of 20 kg.
The boy has a mass of 45 kg.

1. **Evaluate Expressions** Suppose both the dog and the boy run at a speed of 3 m/s. Evaluate the expression for kinetic energy to find both of their kinetic energies.
Kinetic energy of dog =

....

Kinetic energy of boy =

....

2. **Calculate** Suppose the dog speeds up and is now running at a speed of 6 m/s. Calculate the dog's new kinetic energy.
New kinetic energy of dog =

....

Use your answers from questions 1 and 2 to answer these questions.

3. **Distinguish Relationships** Which variables are proportional: kinetic energy and mass, or kinetic energy and speed?

....

....

4. **Apply Mathematical Concepts** If the speed of an object is doubled, what happens to the value of the object's kinetic energy?

....

....

Potential Energy

Kinetic energy is easy to observe because there is motion involved. But an object that is not moving may still have energy. Some objects have energy simply as a result of their shapes or positions. Energy that results from the position or shape of an object is called **potential energy**. This type of energy has the potential to transform into kinetic energy, or, in other words, to do work. Recall that work involves using force to move an object over a distance.

When you raise a bottle up to your mouth to take a drink of water, or when you stretch out a rubber band, you transfer energy to the object. The energy you transfer is stored, or held in readiness by the object. It may be used later if the bottle is dropped or the rubber band is released (see **Figure 2**).

Look back again at the photo of the landslide at the beginning of the lesson. You see the dirt and rocks moving, showing kinetic energy. At some point before the photo was taken, however, the dirt and rocks were not yet moving. At that stage, they held potential energy.

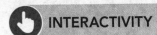

INTERACTIVITY

Investigate model racecars to see how mass affects kinetic energy.

Literacy Connection

Integrate With Visuals
In your notebook, draw an object with elastic potential energy.

Stored-Up Energy

Figure 2 This stretched rubber band is not moving, but it still contains energy—potential energy. Once the fingers that are stretching the rubber band release the band, what kind of energy will the rubber band have?

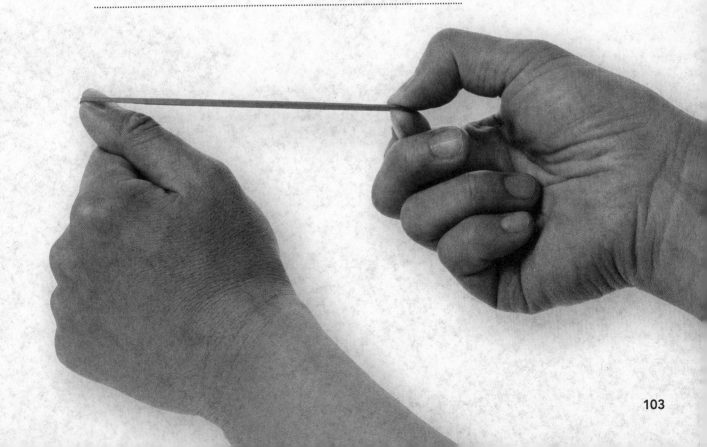

VIDEO

Explore gravitational potential energy on Earth and on the moon.

HANDS-ON LAB

Investigate Develop a model with magnets to show how the arrangement of objects affects potential energy.

Gravitational Potential Energy

Figure 3 A cyclist sitting still at the top of a hill displays gravitational potential energy. What makes it possible for the cyclist to have this type of energy?

....
....
....
....

Gravitational Potential Energy There are two types of potential energy directly related to kinetic energy. One of these types is **gravitational potential energy**. This type of potential energy is related to an object's vertical position—how high it is above the ground. The potential energy is stored as a result of the gravitational pull of Earth on the object.

Gravitational potential energy can be measured by the amount of work needed to lift an object to a certain height. Remember that work is equal to force multiplied by distance. The force you use to lift the object is equal to its weight. Weight is the force that gravity exerts on an object. The distance you move the object is its height above ground level. You can calculate an object's gravitational potential energy using this equation:

Gravitational potential energy =
Weight × Height above ground

For example, suppose a cat has a weight of 40 newtons, which is about 9 pounds. The cat is lifted 2 meters off the ground. You can calculate its potential energy:

Gravitational potential energy = 40 N × 2 m

= 80 N-m, **or** 80 J

The energy of the cyclist at the top of hill shown in **Figure 3** is another example of gravitational potential energy.

Elastic Potential Energy Sometimes, an object has a different type of potential energy due to its shape. **Elastic potential energy** is the energy associated with objects that can be compressed or stretched. This type of potential energy can be stored in such items as rubber bands, bungee cords, springs, and an arrow drawn into a bow.

Trampolines also store elastic potential energy. Take a look at **Figure 4**. When the girl presses down on the trampoline, the trampoline changes shape. The trampoline now has elastic potential energy. When the girl jumps up off the trampoline, this stored energy is transferred from the trampoline to the girl, sending the girl upward. During this energy transfer, the elastic potential energy of the trampoline is transformed into different types of energy.

☑ READING CHECK **Integrate With Visuals** Explain your rankings of the trampoline's potential energy.

....

....

....

👆 INTERACTIVITY

Explore the potential energy of roller coasters.

Elastic Potential Energy

Figure 4 The energy stored in a stretched object, such as a trampoline, is elastic potential energy. Rank the amount of elastic potential energy of the trampoline from greatest to least using the words *most*, *medium* and *least*. Write your answers in the boxes next to the images.

MS-PS3-1, MS-PS3-2

1. Explain Phenomena Explain why a running deer has kinetic energy.

....

....

....

2. Calculate Imagine the running deer has a mass of 100 kg and is running at a speed of 8 m/s. What is the deer's kinetic energy, in joules?

....

....

3. Construct Explanations Several people are using bows to shoot arrows at targets. At what point do the bows have elastic potential energy? At what point do the arrows have kinetic energy?

....

....

....

....

....

....

4. Use Equations Imagine that a bowling ball needs to be lifted 1.5 meters, and its gravitational potential energy is 90 joules. How much does the bowling ball weigh?

....

....

....

5. Determine Differences What is the main difference between gravitational potential energy and elastic potential energy?

....

....

....

....

....

....

....

....

....

Quest CHECK-IN

In this lesson, you learned about potential and kinetic energy and the different roles they play with regard to forces and motion in everyday life.

Evaluate How might the concepts of potential and kinetic energy impact the design of your machine? What factors do you need to consider?

....

....

....

HANDS-ON LAB

Build a Chain-Reaction Machine

Go online to download the lab worksheet. Finalize the design for your machine, choose construction materials, and build it! Then, analyze the moving parts of your machine and identify the different types of energy that come into play.

Prosthetics on the Move

INTERACTIVITY

Discover the properties of materials and changes in energy to guide your construction of a prosthetic limb.

How might you design a prosthetic arm that meets the needs of a modern, on-the-go person? You engineer it!

The Challenge: To design a prosthetic arm based on research into current prosthetic technology.

Phenomenon Until very recently, prosthetics, or artificial limbs, were made of wood, rubber, or plastic. These older prosthetics were solid and heavy, and they often made movement difficult.

When you walk, your foot muscles and leg muscles provide the force to push off the ground. The potential energy stored in your body becomes the kinetic energy of motion. Using an artificial leg, however, takes practice and can be uncomfortable because other muscles strain to carry the artificial limb.

Prosthetic design has advanced thanks to new technologies. In the early 2000s, engineers developed a carbon prosthetic for track athletes. This flexible leg bends and provides elastic potential energy to help the athlete run. The lighter weight of the materials allows the runner to move more efficiently with less muscle strain. Today, advanced engineers are working on limbs that are controlled by the electrical impulses in the human brain, mimicking the way our brains signal our muscles to move!

This prosthetic leg has the shape, weight, and flexibility to allow this runner to sprint again!

DESIGN CHALLENGE

How can you design and build a new kind of prosthetic limb? Go to the Engineering Design Notebook to find out!

LESSON 3 — Other Forms of Energy

Guiding Questions

- How can different forms of energy be classified, quantified, and measured?
- How are different forms of energy related to each other?

Connection

Literacy Cite Textual Evidence

MS-PS3-5

Vocabulary

mechanical energy
nuclear energy
thermal energy
chemical energy
electrical energy
electromagnetic radiation

Academic Vocabulary

medium

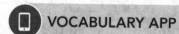 **VOCABULARY APP**

Practice vocabulary on a mobile device.

Quest CONNECTION

Think about how the machine you are designing might use different types of energy and how each type might impact the machine.

Connect It!

✏️ **Circle and label the parts of the drone that are similar to the parts of the hummingbird.**

Infer   What kinds of energy provide power to the drone and to the hummingbird?

....

....

....

Determining Mechanical Energy

👆 INTERACTIVITY

Discover several different types of energy.

The term *mechanical* may make you think of images of metal machines or a mechanic tinkering under the hood of a car. In science, *mechanical* is an adjective that refers to things that are or can be in motion, which covers just about any object we can think of, from particles all the way up to Earth itself. **Mechanical energy** is the energy an object has due to its motion, shape, position, or a combination of these factors.

An object's mechanical energy equals the total of its kinetic and potential energy. For example, a train chugging uphill has energy, and much of that energy is energy of motion—kinetic energy. But a train that is sitting idle at the top of a hill also has energy—potential energy. By adding these two energy forms together, you can determine the train's mechanical energy:

Mechanical Energy = Potential Energy + Kinetic Energy

✔️ READING CHECK **Cite Textual Evidence** What are the three factors that determine an object's mechanical energy?

Inspired by Nature

Figure 1 Engineers often look to nature for inspiration for their machines. This drone has features similar to those of the hummingbird, and they both need energy to function.

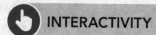

INTERACTIVITY

Investigate forms of energy involved with roller coasters and high divers.

VIDEO

Learn more about nuclear energy.

Literacy Connection

Cite Textual Evidence
As you read about different forms of energy, underline the types of evidence that can help you identify those different forms.

More Forms of Energy

Much of the energy that you observe is mechanical energy, but energy can take many other forms as well. Some other forms of energy are associated with tiny particles, such as atoms and molecules, that make up objects. These forms include nuclear energy, thermal energy, chemical energy, electric energy, and electromagnetic energy.

Nuclear Energy All matter is made of particles called atoms. The center of the atom is called the nucleus (plural: nuclei). **Nuclear energy** is a type of potential energy stored in the nucleus. It can be released through a nuclear reaction. In one type of nuclear reaction, called fission, a nucleus splits into smaller fragments. When it breaks apart, it releases energy (**Figure 2**). If fission reactions are controlled, the release of energy can be used to generate electricity. Nuclear power plants harness nuclear energy for this purpose.

Fusion is another type of nuclear reaction. In fusion, small nuclei combine to form larger nuclei. One place that fusion happens is inside the sun. Some of the energy released by this reaction makes its way to Earth as light. Fusion releases more energy than fission, but the extremely high temperatures that are required to start a fusion reaction make it more difficult to use and control.

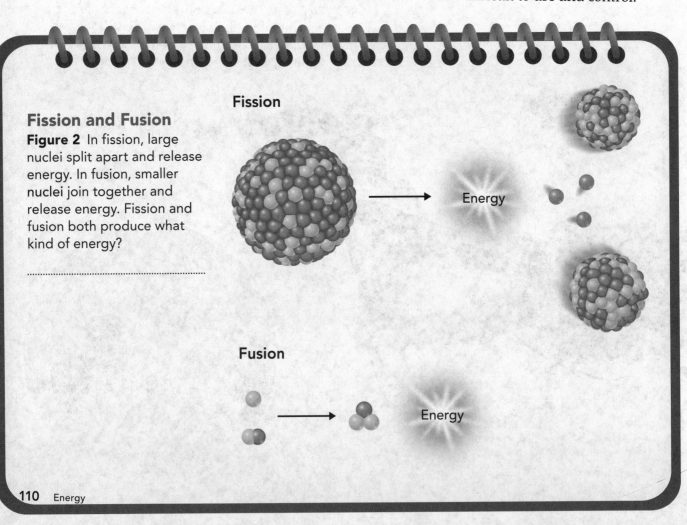

Fission and Fusion
Figure 2 In fission, large nuclei split apart and release energy. In fusion, smaller nuclei join together and release energy. Fission and fusion both produce what kind of energy?

Fission

Energy

Fusion

Energy

Use Models Read about thermal energy below. Then, in the empty circle, draw an illustration representing the particles of the warmer air inside the balloon.

Thermal Energy The total potential and kinetic energy of particles in an object is called **thermal energy**. Lots of particle movement means lots of kinetic energy, and that means a high temperature. Think of a pot of boiling water. The particles are moving very quickly, which results in a high temperature. This means the water has a lot of thermal energy. If the water is then put in the freezer, its kinetic energy will decrease. When its kinetic energy decreases, its thermal energy and temperature also decrease.

The transfer of energy into the thermal energy of an object is called heat. Heat flows from a hotter object to a cooler one through a combination of processes. These processes are called conduction, convection, and radiation. Most substances expand, or take up more space, when heated. When they lose heat, they contract and take up less space. The effect of heat allows a hot air balloon to rise. A flame heats the air inside the hot-air balloon, giving the particles more thermal energy (**Figure 3**). Since they have more thermal energy, they move faster and spread apart. The air in the balloon is then less dense than the air outside the balloon, so the balloon rises.

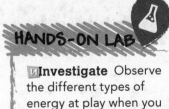

HANDS-ON LAB

Investigate Observe the different types of energy at play when you use a flashlight.

Chemical Energy What type of energy is in the food you eat, in the cells of your body, and in the substances that make a lightstick glow? It is called **chemical energy**. Chemical energy is a form of potential energy because it results from the relative positions of the particles within a material. The particles are held in those positions by chemical bonds. When these bonds are broken, energy is released.

Plants produce a form of stored chemical energy when they perform photosynthesis. In this process, plants take in energy from sunlight. They also take in water and carbon dioxide. Plant cells break the bonds of water and carbon dioxide to produce sugars. Those sugars store chemical energy. The plant later breaks the bonds of the sugar to release the chemical energy on which it lives. Similarly, your body breaks bonds of sugar from your food. Energy is released when your body breaks bonds that hold the sugar molecules together. Your body uses that energy to power your cells.

Petroleum, or oil, is another source of chemical energy. Oil is converted into gasoline and diesel fuel, which contain potential energy in the form of chemical bonds. When fuel is burned in engines, the energy in these fuels can be used to makes cars run.

Reflect What have you heard about the pros and cons of using oil for energy? In your science notebook, describe what you have heard, and write down your own conclusions about the burning of oil.

Question It !

1. **Draw Conclusions** Batteries allow us to store energy for when it's needed, such as starting a car engine or jump-starting another car whose battery has lost its charge. But batteries cannot operate without chemical reactions. What kind of energy do you think is stored in the substances within the battery?

....

2. **Apply Scientific Reasoning** When someone jump-starts a car, what do you think happens to the stored energy in the working battery?

....

....

....

....

Electrical Energy Electrical energy is the form of energy most of us use to power devices such as lights, computers, and audio systems. **Electrical energy** is the energy of electric charges. Different materials, and even particles, can have different charges. These differences in charge can result in the movement of electrical charge—a type of kinetic energy called electricity. When charges are not moving but are near one another, they have electric potential energy. This energy can be converted to electricity.

Electromagnetic Radiation Visible light is one type of electromagnetic radiation. **Electromagnetic radiation** is a form of kinetic energy that travels through space in waves. It does not need a **medium**, such as air or water, to travel through. This is why you can see the stars even though outer space does not contain a medium. Our world has a wide variety of electromagnetic energy, from X-rays that produce images of bones to microwaves that heat leftover food or transmit signals between mobile phones and towers. Other types of electromagnetic radiation include ultraviolet (UV) waves, infrared (or heat) waves, and radio waves. Like other forms of kinetic energy, all types of electromagnetic radiation can transform into thermal energy when heating something.

Academic Vocabulary

In your reading here, the word medium is used to indicate a substance through which a force acts. What are some other meanings of medium that you use or hear in everyday life?

....

....

....

....

....

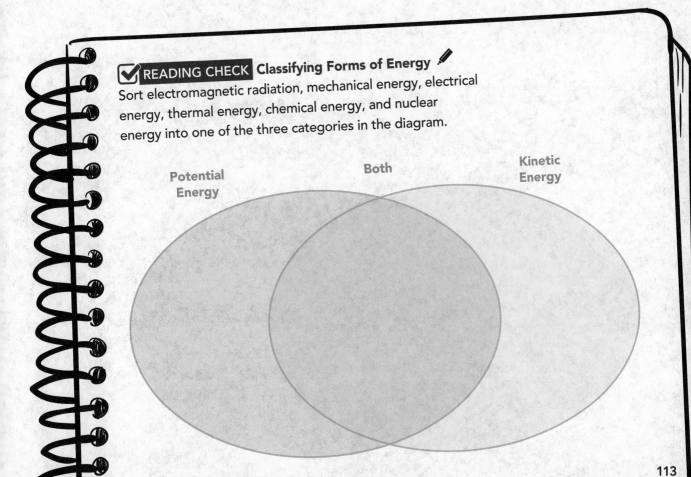

☑ READING CHECK **Classifying Forms of Energy** ✎
Sort electromagnetic radiation, mechanical energy, electrical energy, thermal energy, chemical energy, and nuclear energy into one of the three categories in the diagram.

Potential Energy

Both

Kinetic Energy

Energy at the Cookout

Figure 4 Many objects in this scene contain more than one form of energy.

1. **Integrate Information** ✏️ Label this scene with as many forms of energy as you can find.

2. **Cite Evidence** ✏️ Draw a star next to an object that contains more than one form of energy and explain your reasoning below.

....

....

3. Construct Explanations The grill converts chemical energy from propane into thermal energy that heats food. What is another example of an energy change in this image?

....

....

....

....

....

☑ LESSON 3 Check

MS-PS3-5

1. Calculate At a certain point, the kinetic energy of a falling basketball is 30.8 J and its potential energy is 16.0 J. What is its mechanical energy?

....

2. Identify Which type of nuclear energy involves splitting atoms?

....

3. Represent Relationships What are some of the relationships among thermal energy, kinetic energy, particle movement, and temperature?

....

....

....

....

....

4. Identify What type(s) of energy do you acquire when you eat a bowl of hot vegetable soup? Explain.

....

....

....

....

5. Cite Textual Evidence Why do we say the particles in a rock lying on the ground have kinetic energy and potential energy?

....

....

....

....

....

....

....

Quest CHECK-IN

In this lesson, you learned about other forms of energy, such as nuclear energy and electromagnetic radiation. You also started to think about how these forms of energy can change into other forms, and how to tell when such a change has occurred.

Evaluate Why do engineers need to keep track of potential and kinetic energy and energy transformations in prototypes of machines?

....

....

....

....

HANDS-ON LAB

Test and Evaluate a Chain-Reaction Machine

Go online to download the lab worksheet. Test your chain-reaction machine prototype and evaluate its performance. Then revise your machine's design and retest as needed. Think about energy transformations that are taking place and the roles of potential and kinetic energy.

Energy Engineer

Reinventing
ENERGY SYSTEMS

We all use energy every moment of our lives. It lights our classrooms, runs our computers, and powers our industries. For much of the twentieth century, the United States depended largely on fossil fuels for energy. This has been changing in recent decades because the supply of fossil fuels is limited, and excessive use of these fuels has caused environmental damage on a vast scale. Today, people are turning more and more to renewable sources of fuel, such as solar and wind power. This is where the energy engineers play a role.

The purpose of an energy engineer's job is simple: to make the world more energy-efficient. Energy engineers carry out a wide range of work that involves research, design, and construction.

Some energy engineers explore new methods of obtaining energy, while others develop ways to integrate renewable energy sources into the existing power grid. Energy engineers also work with architects to incorporate clean energy sources in new construction. Additionally, some of these engineers help to develop more efficient machinery, such as cars that run on alternative fuels.

This type of work involves mathematics, physics, and chemistry. It offers creative challenges and a wide variety of tasks. If you enjoy these subjects and challenges, this career might be right for you!

▶ **VIDEO**

Learn about the work an energy engineer does.

MY CAREER

Speak with an energy engineer at a local laboratory or office to learn more about this career.

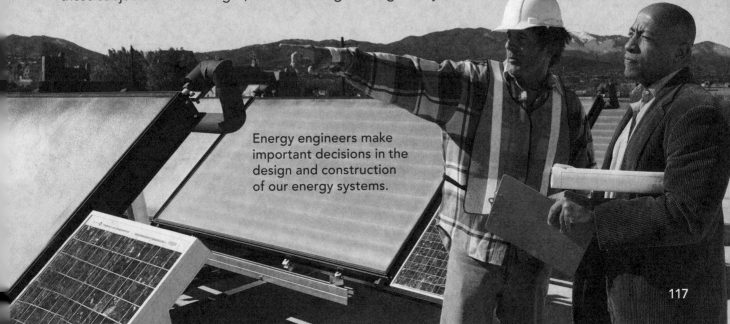

Energy engineers make important decisions in the design and construction of our energy systems.

Energy Change and Conservation

Guiding Questions

- In what ways can energy change from one form to another?
- How is energy transferred?
- How does the law of conservation of energy apply to transformations and transfers?

Connections

Literacy Cite Textual Evidence

Math Use Proportional Relationships

MS-PS3-5

Vocabulary

law of
conservation
of energy

Academic Vocabulary

pivot

 VOCABULARY APP

Practice vocabulary on a mobile device.

Quest CONNECTION

Think about how your complex machine might use transfers of energy to complete a simple task. Also consider how much energy transforms into heat as the machine works.

Connect It

✎ **Trace the movement of the snowboarder.**

Infer How is the snowboarder able to soar through the air?

....

....

....

Energy Changes Form

All forms of energy can be transformed into other forms of energy. Energy can transform once (which we call a single transformation) or multiple times. A toaster provides a good example of a single transformation. Electrical energy passes through metal wires and is transformed into thermal energy.

If you eat toast, the resulting process is an example of multiple transformations. Your body transforms chemical energy stored in cells into the kinetic energy that moves your mouth. Your digestive system uses mechanical and chemical energy to digest the bread. Some of the chemical energy in the bread is released as thermal energy that helps your body maintain its temperature. Some of the remaining chemical energy is delivered back to your body's cells. The cells then transform that chemical energy into mechanical energy that allows your body to function.

Multiple transformations also go into the making of the bread. Sunlight, which is a form of electromagnetic radiation, is harnessed by wheat plants to create chemical energy. Mechanical energy is used to grind the wheat into flour. The flour is combined with water and yeast to make dough—more chemical energy. As the dough is baked in the oven, electrical energy is used to increase the thermal energy of the oven. Heat is transferred from the oven to the dough, and the thermal energy of the dough increases as it bakes into bread. Many of the processes that we rely on daily involve multiple transformations.

Literacy Connection

Cite Textual Evidence
What evidence in the text supports the claim that energy changes form? List two examples.

....

....

....

....

....

....

Snowboard Jumping
Figure 1 The snowboarder thrusts up and forward by using her legs. But most of the energy that allows her to travel a great distance through the air is supplied by something else.

Kinetic and Potential Energy

One common energy transformation involves potential energy changing to kinetic energy. The snowboarder on the previous page had potential energy when she stood at the top of the hill. As she pushed herself off the top, gravity transformed the potential energy into kinetic energy. As she accelerated down the hill, the potential energy declined while the kinetic energy increased This is true of any falling object, such as the ball in **Figure 2**. Recall that the weight of an object and its height above the ground are proportionally related to its gravitational potential energy. And so, as the height of the ball decreases, it loses potential energy while gaining kinetic energy. The ball's kinetic energy is greatest right before it hits the ground.

A pendulum also demonstrates the relationship between kinetic and potential energy. A pendulum consists of something with mass suspended on an arm or pole that swings back and forth from a **pivot** point. A swinging boat ride at an amusement park is a kind of pendulum (**Figure 3**). At its highest point, the pendulum has no movement and therefore no kinetic energy. When it begins to swing down, potential energy declines as the kinetic energy increases. The kinetic energy and the speed of the pendulum are greatest at the bottom, or midpoint, of the swing. As the pendulum swings upward, it loses kinetic energy and gains potential energy until it is motionless again and ready to swing back to the other side.

Academic Vocabulary

The term pivot is often used in describing the action of basketball players when they keep one foot firmly in place while moving their other foot. What other things in everyday life might pivot?

....

....

....

Falling Objects

Figure 2 ✎ As an object falls, its potential energy decreases while its kinetic energy increases. Circle the location where the ball has the most kinetic energy.

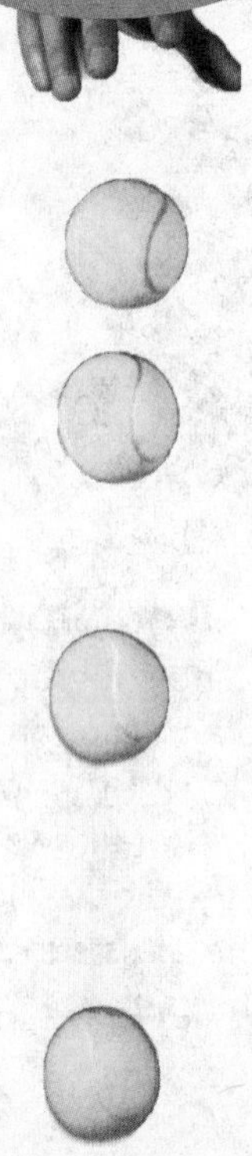

Pendulum Physics

Figure 3 This amusement park ride is basically a pendulum.

Use Models ✎ Use the abbreviation *PE* for potential energy and *KE* for kinetic energy to label the positions where the boat has maximum PE, minimum PE, maximum KE, and minimum KE.

Energy Transformation and Transfer

Energy transformation and energy transfer sometimes occur in the same process at the same time, but they are not the same thing. Energy transformation occurs when one form of energy changes into another. The potential energy of a pendulum, such as the wrecking ball in **Figure 4**, transforms into kinetic energy as it falls due to the force of gravity. Energy transfer takes place when energy moves from one object to another. When the wrecking ball hits the wall, some of the kinetic energy of the ball transfers to the wall, causing the wall to fall over. As the wrecking ball swings, energy is also transferred from the ball to the air, due to the force of friction. In this case, energy transfers, but it is also transformed. Some of the mechanical energy of the moving wrecking ball is transferred and transformed into thermal energy of the surrounding air. Whenever a moving object experiences friction, some of its mechanical energy is transformed into thermal energy.

INTERACTIVITY

Explore different examples of energy transformations.

☑ **READING CHECK** **Cite Textual Evidence** Underline the sentences that explain the difference between energy transformation and energy transfer.

Transformation and Transfer in Demolition

Figure 4 🖉 Draw pictures in the empty boxes to show what happens as the wrecking ball swings. Describe the energy transformations and transfers that are occurring.

Ball at top of swing 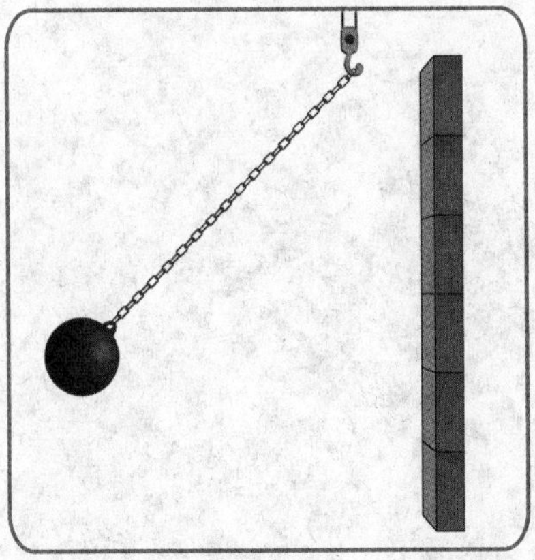	Ball at bottom of swing	Ball hitting the wall

....

VIDEO

Look into the future and learn about hydrogen fuel cell cars.

HANDS-ON LAB

☑**Investigate** Explore how the changing kinetic energy of a bouncing ball is related to conservation of energy.

Energy Is Conserved
Figure 5 After the ball is hit, it eventually slows down and falls. As it slows down, where does its kinetic energy go?

Energy Changes and the Law of Conservation

There is a certain amount of energy in the universe, and we cannot make more of it or destroy any that already exists. Another way to state this idea is to say that energy is conserved. When one object loses energy, other objects must gain it. This is known as the **law of conservation of energy**. This law is a factor in both energy transfers and energy transformations. Energy either moves from one place to another or changes forms, but no energy is created or destroyed.

When a baseball is hit by a bat, as in **Figure 5**, the ball flies through the air. The law of conservation of energy explains why it does not keep flying forever. The kinetic energy of the ball transfers to the air and transforms into thermal energy due to the force of friction. The more air particles there are, the more transfer there is. So more kinetic energy transfers to the air when the air is dense. That's why baseballs travel farther and faster at a baseball stadium in Denver, Colorado, where the air is thinner, than they do in low-altitude ballparks where the air is denser. You can learn more about this phenomenon in the Math Toolbox activity.

Conservation of Energy in Transfers Think back to the wrecking ball. Most of the kinetic energy in the moving ball is transferred directly to the wall. Any energy not transferred is transformed into thermal energy of the ball and air or the sound energy of the ball hitting the wall. Energy is conserved in this example, as it is in any example. No matter how energy is transformed or transferred, the total amount of energy in a system does not change.

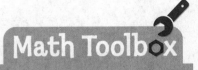

Math Toolbox

Home Runs and Air Density

For more than 20 years, major league baseball games played in Denver, Colorado, have featured a high percentage of home runs. The high altitude of Denver means the air there is less dense than in lower-altitude locations, so balls flying through the air in Denver do not transfer as much energy to the air. They keep that kinetic energy and travel farther than they do in other ballparks. This table shows how many home runs the Colorado Rockies baseball team hit at home and away over 10 seasons.

Colorado Rockies' Home Runs at Home and Away

	2007	2008	2009	2010	2011	2012	2013	2014	2015	2016
Home	103	92	98	108	94	100	88	119	102	116
Away	68	68	92	65	69	66	71	67	84	88

1. **Calculate** Over the 10-year span, how many more home runs did the Rockies score in their home ballpark in Denver than at other ballparks?

....

....

2. **Use Proportional Relationships** What is the ratio of home runs the team hit at home and home runs hit in away games over the 10-year period? Express the ratio in the smallest numbers possible.

....

....

3. **Summarize** Describe the high home-run numbers at the Rockies' home ball field in terms of kinetic energy and energy transformation.

....

....

....

....

....

....

....

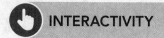

Conservation of Energy in Waves The vibrations that come from a wrecking ball smashing through a wall travel in sound waves. In a sound wave or any other type of wave, energy passes through matter without moving the matter to a new place. The matter vibrates, meaning it moves temporarily, but ends up back where it was. We can see this on the ocean surface with a floating object (**Figure 6**). An ocean wave passes under the object, lifts it, drops it, and the object ends up back where it was. That's why a surfer cannot catch a wave far out in the ocean. Once a wave breaks, matter is moved and energy is released. A surfer can ride the wave when it breaks (**Figure 7**). Energy is conserved as the breaking wave transfers its energy to the shore.

☑ READING CHECK **Connect to Engineering** Why would the energy industry be interested in developing technologies to transform the kinetic energy in ocean waves to electrical energy?

....

Waves and Matter

Figure 6 A wave's energy passes through matter. Whether the medium is air, water, or some other substance, the matter vibrates but does not end up in a new place. Similarly, a floating ball moves in a circular motion as the wave passes, and the ball ends up back where it started.

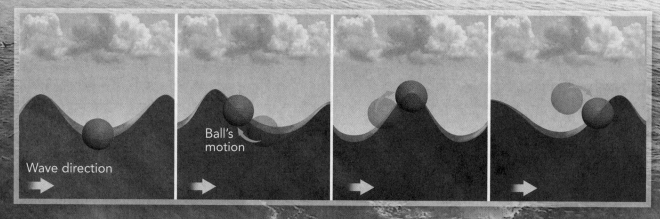

Wave direction

Ball's motion

Wave Energy

Figure 7 Ocean waves carry tremendous amounts of energy. When the wave breaks, the energy is released.

1. **Distinguish Relationships** What does it mean to say that energy is conserved in an energy transformation?

....

....

....

2. **Integrate Information** A train rumbles along the tracks at high speed. After it passes, the rail feels hot. What kind of energy transformation took place?

....

....

....

3. **Connect to Society** How are pendulums used in society? Give an example of a real-world pendulum that transfers a lot of energy.

....

....

....

4. **Construct Explanations** Explain the changes in kinetic energy (KE) and potential energy (PE) that occur when an apple falls off the table and hits the floor.

....

....

....

....

....

....

....

5. **Cite Evidence** After a tornado moves through a forest, what kinds of evidence would there be of energy transformations or transfers?

....

....

....

....

....

Quest CHECK-IN

In this lesson, you learned about energy transformations and energy transfers and how energy is conserved in both.

Evaluate Why is it important for engineers to understand and quantify how energy changes as it moves through a machine, or from one object to another?

....

....

....

....

HANDS-ON LAB

Redesign and Retest a Chain-Reaction Machine

Go online to download the lab worksheet. Modify your chain-reaction machine prototype to include at least one additional energy transformation. Then test, evaluate, and finalize the design, and present it to the class.

U.S. ENERGY CONSUMPTION

As we know from the law of conservation of energy, new energy cannot simply be created. Therefore, many people feel that it's important for countries to study how they are using their energy resources. The pie chart shows the sources of energy used in the United States.

Renewable Energy

Light and heat from the sun, energy from wind and water, and heat from wood fires were the major sources of energy until the eighteenth century, when fossil fuels began to dominate. More recently, nations of the world have begun to return to renewable energy sources. These sources exist in an unlimited supply, and they are cleaner and safer for the environment. One disadvantage to renewable energy is the high initial cost involved in switching from fossil fuel systems to renewable energy systems.

Coal

Coal comes from the Earth, and it is easily transported. However, this fossil fuel must be mined from underground. The process damages the environment, and coal miners face some of the most dangerous work there is. Burning coal also releases pollutants into the atmosphere.

Petroleum

The main advantage to petroleum, also called crude oil, is that it is a powerful fuel. However, crude oil exists only in a limited supply. Petroleum also requires drilling to access it. The process is expensive and it damages the environment. Finally, the burning and accidental spilling of petroleum results in air pollution, land pollution, and water pollution on a vast scale.

Natural Gas

Natural gas is cheap and abundant. However, it must be transported through pipelines that often leak. Like petroleum, it requires drilling, which harms the environment. And burning natural gas releases carbon dioxide, which contributes to global warming.

Nuclear Energy

Nuclear energy is the most recently discovered source of power. It is a cleaner form of energy because it does not involve the burning of fossil fuels. The United States can generate its own nuclear power, so there are economic advantages as well. The major drawbacks to nuclear power are its expensive cost, the potential for accidents, and the need to dispose of radioactive wastes that will remain dangerous for thousands of years.

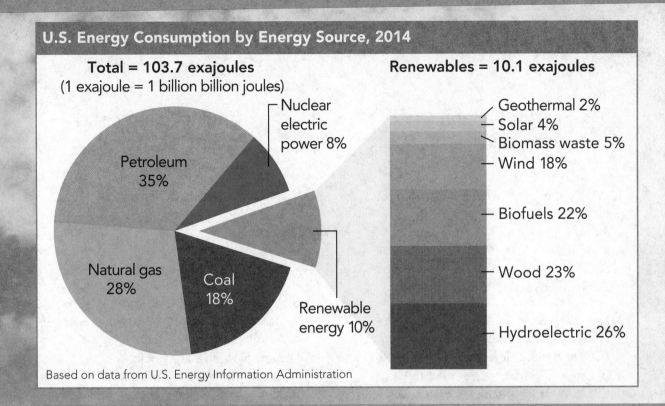

U.S. Energy Consumption by Energy Source, 2014

Total = 103.7 exajoules
(1 exajoule = 1 billion billion joules)

Renewables = 10.1 exajoules

Petroleum 35%

Nuclear electric power 8%

Natural gas 28%

Coal 18%

Renewable energy 10%

Geothermal 2%
Solar 4%
Biomass waste 5%
Wind 18%
Biofuels 22%
Wood 23%
Hydroelectric 26%

Based on data from U.S. Energy Information Administration

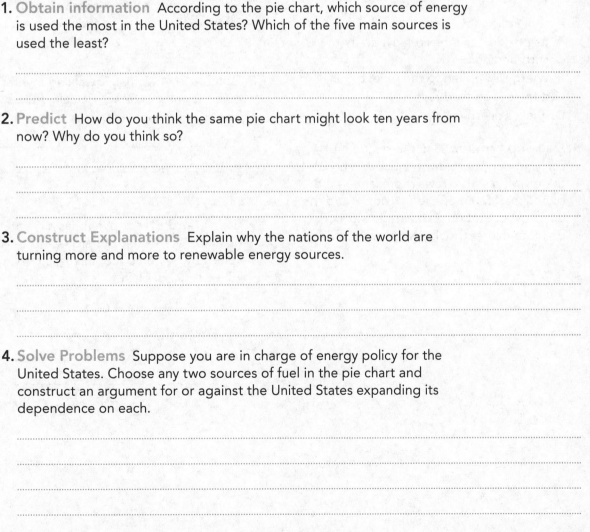

1. **Obtain information** According to the pie chart, which source of energy is used the most in the United States? Which of the five main sources is used the least?

2. **Predict** How do you think the same pie chart might look ten years from now? Why do you think so?

3. **Construct Explanations** Explain why the nations of the world are turning more and more to renewable energy sources.

4. **Solve Problems** Suppose you are in charge of energy policy for the United States. Choose any two sources of fuel in the pie chart and construct an argument for or against the United States expanding its dependence on each.

☑ TOPIC 3 Review and Assess

1 Energy, Motion, Force, and Work

1. Which of the following is not a form of energy?
   A. light
   B. sound
   C. air
   D. electricity

2. How can you increase your power when stacking shoe boxes in a closet?
   A. Spend more time stacking the boxes.
   B. Stack fewer boxes per minute.
   C. Slowly stack the boxes on a lower shelf.
   D. Stack the boxes more quickly.

3. An object is in motion if
   A. its position changes relative to its surroundings.
   B. energy is applied to the object.
   C. a force is applied to it.
   D. it loses energy.

4. **Develop Models** ✏ Draw a student carrying textbooks down a hallway. Label the drawing with arrows representing the direction of force on the textbooks and the direction of motion. Explain why no work is done on the textbooks as they are carried.

2 Kinetic Energy and Potential Energy

MS-PS3-1, MS-PS3-2

5. Kinetic energy is the energy of
   A. motion.
   B. potential.
   C. gravity.
   D. distance.

6. Which of the following is the best example of increasing an object's potential energy?
   A. rolling a bowling ball
   B. turning on a light bulb
   C. stretching a rubber band
   D. dropping a pencil

7. Gravitational potential energy is affected by the object's weight and the object's

   ....

8. **Calculate** A woman is walking at a rate of 0.5 m/s. Her mass is 62 kg. Calculate the woman's kinetic energy in joules.

   ....

   ....

   ....

9. **Cause and Effect** What has a greater effect on an object's kinetic energy—increasing its speed by 50 percent or increasing its mass by 75 percent? Explain.

   ....

   ....

   ....

   ....

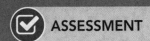
3 Other Forms of Energy

MS-PS3-5

10. In the process of fusion, nuclear energy is
A. absorbed when a nucleus splits.
B. released when a nucleus splits.
C. released when nuclei join.
D. absorbed when nuclei switch places.

11. Which of the following is a type of energy that is *not* involved in the human body's everyday processes?
A. mechanical energy
B. nuclear energy
C. thermal energy
D. chemical energy

12. An increase in the movement of particles in a substance is associated with an increase in

.... energy.

13. Chemical energy is a form of ....
.... energy.

14. Integrate Information A rubber ball that sits motionless near the edge of a tall bookshelf has no kinetic energy. However, it does have mechanical energy. Explain why this is possible.

....

....

....

....

....

4 Energy Change and Conservation

MS-PS3-5

15. Which of the following describes the law of conservation of energy?
A. Energy cannot be created or destroyed.
B. Energy can only be released through transformation.
C. When energy is conserved, it always changes form.
D. Energy increases when it is transferred from one object to another.

16. An energy ....
is the change of energy from one form to

another. An energy ....
is the movement of energy from one object to another.

17. ✏ Draw a circle where the sled rider has the most potential energy. Draw a square where the rider has the most kinetic energy.

18. Synthesize Information Explain the energy transformation that must occur for your body to participate in a physical activity, such as playing a sport.

....

....

....

MS-PS3-2, MS-PS3-5

Evidence-Based Assessment

Darnell enters a design competition at school. The challenge is to construct a doorbell that works without electricity. The bell must ring loudly enough to be heard in another room of the house.

Darnell's idea is to use the bell, a ball, and gravity. A person would insert the ball into a hole in the wall. The ball would start from rest and fall a short distance to hit a bell. The ball would continue rolling back down and out to where the person could retrieve it in order to ring the bell again. Darnell draws a model of his doorbell design, as shown below.

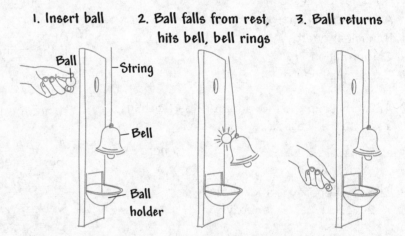

Darnell tests his design. For his first test, he uses a ping-pong ball, places the hole 1 meter above the ground, and hangs the bell 30 centimeters below the hole. He adds labels to his model to show how he set up his first test.

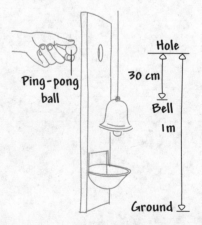

During this first test, Darnell finds that the bell does not ring loudly enough. Answer the following questions to help Darnell improve his design.

1. **Identify** Which of the following two forms of energy are at play in Darnell's design?
   A. chemical energy and nuclear energy
   B. electromagnetic radiation and kinetic energy
   C. electrical energy and gravitational potential energy
   D. gravitational potential energy and kinetic energy

2. **Define the Problem** Based on the results of his first test, Darnell needs to modify his design. What is the problem that Darnell needs to solve in his next doorbell test?

   ....
   ....
   ....

3. **Explain Phenomena** Describe the transformations and transfers of energy that are occurring in order for the bell to ring.

   ....
   ....
   ....
   ....
   ....
   ....
   ....
   ....
   ....

4. **Optimize Performance** How could Darnell change his materials or design so that the bell rings more loudly? Provide two options, and explain how they work.

   ....
   ....
   ....
   ....

....
....
....
....
....
....
....
....

Quest FINDINGS

Complete the Quest!

Phenomenon Determine the best way to demonstrate your chain-reaction machine and show how energy is transformed and transferred from start to finish.

Evaluate Change How did energy change form as it made its way through your chain-reaction machine to perform a task?

....
....
....
....
....
....
....

INTERACTIVITY

Reflect on Your Chain-Reaction Machine

131

MS-PS3-2, MS-PS3-5

3, 2, 1... Liftoff!

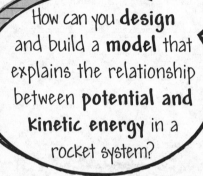

How can you **design** and build a **model** that explains the relationship between **potential and kinetic energy** in a rocket system?

Background

Phenomenon NASA is building a new website devoted to explaining the physics involved in launching rockets. They have asked you to help with a section of the website that deals with energy transfers and transformations. Your task is to design and build a model that explains the relationship between potential and kinetic energy in a rocket system.

Materials

(per group)

- scissors
- rubber bands
- meter stick
- marker
- metric ruler
- stapler
- cardboard tubes of varying diameters (from paper towels or wrapping paper)
- tape
- construction paper

Safety

Be sure to follow all safety guidelines provided by your teacher.

Design a Model

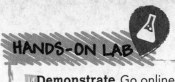

HANDS-ON LAB

🖳 **Demonstrate** Go online for a downloadable worksheet of this lab.

☐ 1. Work with your group to develop a model of a rocket and launcher using the rubber bands, cardboard tubes, stapler, and other materials listed. Keep the following criteria in mind:

    A. Your rocket must be able to launch vertically into the air. As you work with your group, think about what each of the materials in your model will represent and how the model will operate.

    B. You will need to take at least three different measurements of how far the rubber band stretches and how far your rocket travels.

Plan Your Investigation

☐ 2. As a group, design an investigation to show that the amount of elastic potential energy in the rocket launcher system affects the kinetic energy of the rocket.

As you plan your investigation, consider these questions. Write your ideas in the space below.

- How can you use the meter stick and the ruler in your investigation?
- What tests will you perform?
- How many trials of each test will you perform?
- What variables will you measure?
- What are the dependent and independent variables?

....

....

....

....

....

....

....

....

....

....

☐ 3. After getting approval from your teacher for your model design and procedure, conduct your experiment. Record the data in your table. See if you can discover a relationship between how far the rubber band stretches and how far the rocket travels.

Sketch of Rocket Launcher Model

Procedure

....

....

....

....

....

....

....

....

....

Data Table

Distance Traveled by Rocket (cm)				
Rubber band stretch (cm)	Trial 1	Trial 2	Trial 3	Average

Analyze and Interpret Data

1. **Analyze Structures** Describe how your rocket launcher works. What might you do to improve it if you could do this experiment again?

....

....

....

....

2. **Make Observations** What is the relationship between the amount of potential energy in the rocket launcher system and the kinetic energy of the rocket? Explain.

....

....

....

....

3. **Analyze Systems** What transfers of energy did you observe in the rocket launcher system? What transformation of energy did you observe? Remember to consider gravity in your answer.

....

....

....

....

4. **Construct Arguments** Use evidence from your investigation to support the argument that energy is being transferred and transformed throughout the rocket's travel. Draw a diagram that shows the rocket traveling upward, with different stages (on the ground, midway up, at its peak, and on its way down). Use labels to describe what is happening to the potential and kinetic energy at each stage. Label the position of maximum kinetic energy and the position of maximum potential energy.

TOPIC
4

Thermal Energy

NGSS PERFORMANCE EXPECTATIONS

MS-PS3-3 Apply scientific principles to design, construct, and test a device that either minimizes or maximizes thermal energy transfer.

MS-PS3-4 Plan an investigation to determine the relationships among the energy transferred, the type of matter, the mass, and the change in the average kinetic energy of the particles as measured by the temperature of the sample.

MS-PS3-5 Construct, use, and present arguments to support the claim that when the kinetic energy of an object changes, energy is transferred to or from the object.

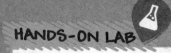

HANDS-ON LAB

uConnect See how well you can judge temperature differences.

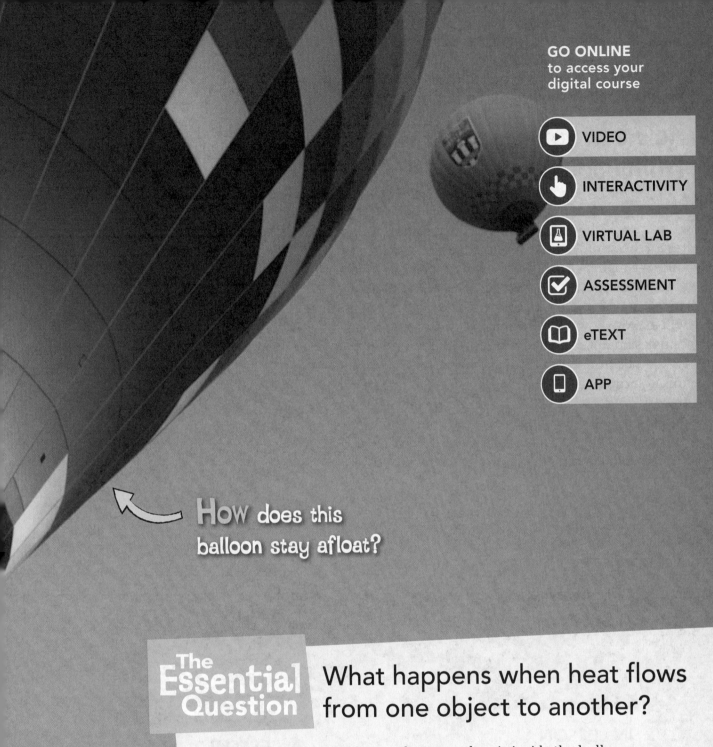

GO ONLINE
to access your
digital course

▶ VIDEO

👆 INTERACTIVITY

📱 VIRTUAL LAB

☑ ASSESSMENT

📖 eTEXT

📱 APP

How does this
balloon stay afloat?

The Essential Question

What happens when heat flows from one object to another?

An open flame from a burner heats up the air inside the balloon, allowing it to take flight. How is the pilot able to control the altitude of the balloon?

....

....

....

....

....

Quest KICKOFF

How can you keep hot water from cooling down?

STEM **Phenomenon** The Arctic is one of the harshest places on Earth. In the winter, researchers studying the Arctic climate face temperatures averaging –34°C (–30°F). In extremely cold places where it's important to stay warm, having the right gear can be a challenge. In this Quest activity, you will explore how heat is transferred between objects and design an insulating container that will keep hot liquids from cooling down quickly. As you work through the Quest, you will test and evaluate different materials. You will apply what you have learned to design and build a prototype of your container, testing and revising the design as necessary. Then you will reflect on the design process in the Findings activity.

NBC LEARN ▶ VIDEO

The Quest Kickoff video explores how humans—and even some animals—try to keep themselves warm by controlling the transfer of heat. After watching the video, write three questions you still have about how an insulating device helps limit the transfer of heat.

1
....
....

2
....
....

3
....
....

INTERACTIVITY

Keep Hot Liquids Hot

MS-PS3-3 Apply scientific principles to design, construct, and test a device that either minimizes or maximizes thermal energy transfer.

IN LESSON 1
What happens to hot liquids when exposed to cold temperatures? Think about ways your insulating container can slow the flow of heat.

Quest CHECK-IN

IN LESSON 2
STEM How does heat transfer between objects? Consider how your insulating container must function. Then evaluate different materials you can use to build your container and design a solution.

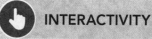

INTERACTIVITY

Contain the Heat

Researchers in the Arctic work in some of the coldest conditions on Earth.

Quest CHECK-INS

IN LESSON 3

STEM How can you apply what you know about thermal energy and heat transfer to build your container? Consider how different materials affect the flow of heat. Then build, test, and refine your design solution.

HANDS-ON LABS

- Keep the Heat In
- Keep the Cold Out

Quest FINDINGS

Complete the Quest!

Evaluate your work and reflect on the design and engineering process.

INTERACTIVITY

Reflect on Your Insulating Container

Thermal Energy, Heat, and Temperature

Guiding Questions

- What happens to a substance when it is heated?
- What is the difference between thermal energy and temperature?

Connections

Literacy Use Information

Math Convert Measurement Units

MS-PS3-4

Vocabulary

thermal energy
heat
temperature

Academic Vocabulary

transfer
absolute

 VOCABULARY APP

Practice vocabulary on a mobile device.

Quest CONNECTION

Think about how the movement of heat from one substance to another could be limited to keep liquids hot in very cold places.

Connect It!

✏️ A frozen popsicle will melt on a hot day. Circle the place on the popsicle where the particles have the most thermal energy.

Explain Phenomena Explain why you circled this place on the popsicle.

....

....

Construct Explanations With enough time, would a popsicle melt on a cool autumn day? Explain.

....

....

Thermal Energy and Heat

All objects are made up of small particles. These particles are constantly in motion. This means they have kinetic energy. Particles are arranged in specific ways in different objects, so they also have potential energy. The total kinetic and potential energy of all the particles in an object is called **thermal energy**. This total energy can also be called internal energy. Objects contain thermal, or internal, energy even if they do not feel hot. The joule is the SI unit of energy.

The thermal energy of an object changes when heat is **transferred** to or from the object. **Heat** is the energy that is transferred from a warmer object to a cooler object. As the warmer object cools down, the cooler object warms up until the two objects are the same temperature. Once this happens, heat stops transferring between the two objects.

Heating a substance can cause its particles to move more quickly. For example, when the popsicle in **Figure 1** is held in sunlight, the particles in the popsicle gain kinetic energy. As a result, the temperature of the popsicle increases.

Note that in everyday language, the term *heat* can be used to describe the thermal energy contained in an object. However, when scientists use the term *heat*, they are referring only to energy that is transferred between two objects or systems at different temperatures.

✓ READING CHECK **Compare and Contrast** What is the difference between thermal energy and heat?

....

....

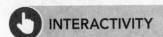

INTERACTIVITY

See how heat flows with examples from the kitchen.

Academic Vocabulary

Heat is energy transferred from one place to another. What other things can you transfer from one place to another?

....

....

....

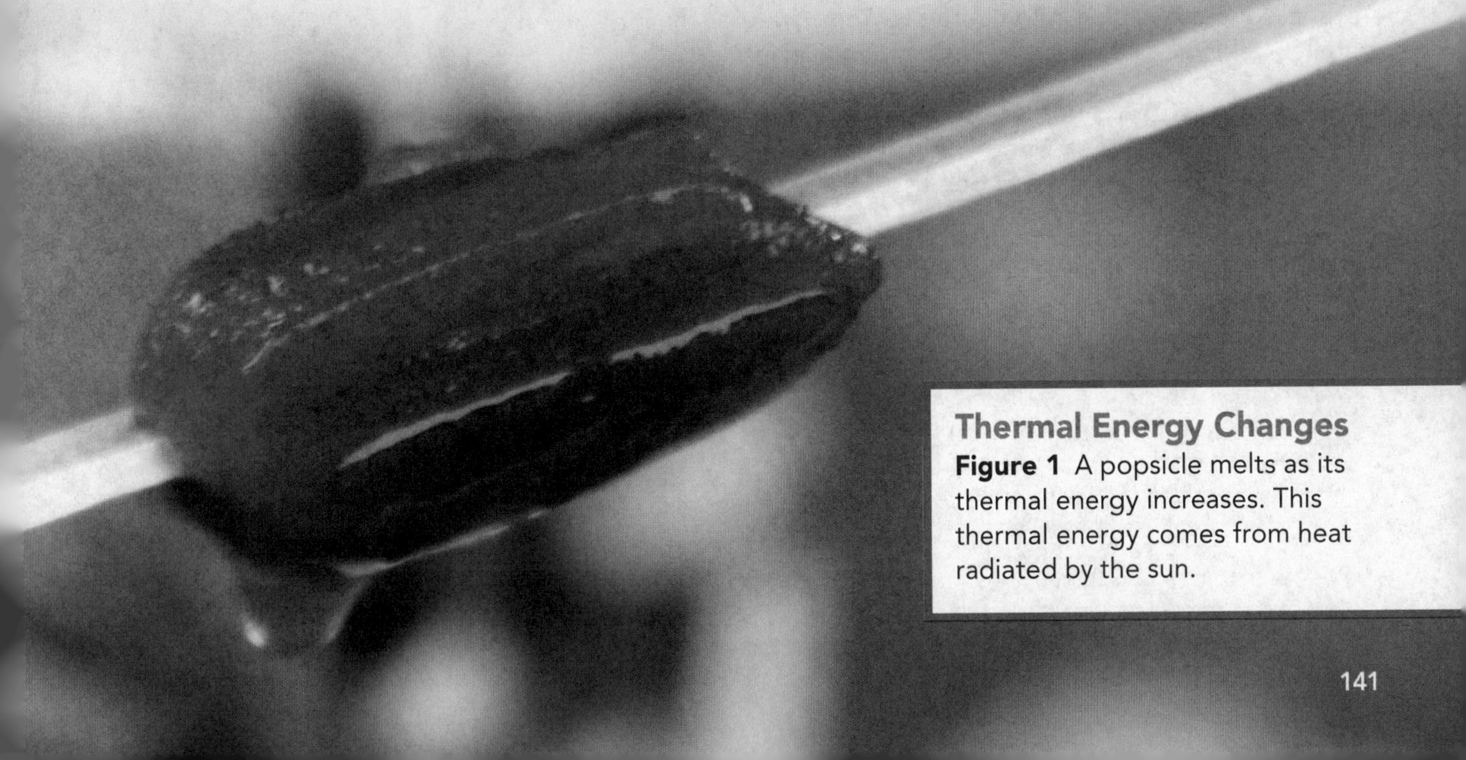

Thermal Energy Changes
Figure 1 A popsicle melts as its thermal energy increases. This thermal energy comes from heat radiated by the sun.

Temperature And Its Measurement

We use temperature as a measure of how hot or cold something is. On average, the particles in a substance move faster when the substance is hot than when it is cold. **Temperature** is a measure of the average kinetic energy of the particles in a substance. When a substance is at a higher temperature, the particles move faster and have a greater average kinetic energy than when the substance is at a lower temperature.

Temperature can be measured with a thermometer. Thermometers show how hot or cold something is compared to a reference point. The Celsius scale uses the freezing point of water at sea level as its reference point at zero degrees Celsius (0°C). The United States typically uses the Fahrenheit scale, in which the freezing point of water at sea level is 32 degrees Fahrenheit (32°F). The kelvin is the official SI unit of temperature. On the Kelvin scale, zero kelvins (0 K) refers to **absolute** zero, the lowest temperature possible. At absolute zero, particles theoretically would have no kinetic energy. They would be completely motionless! So, the Kelvin scale only goes up from zero. Units on the Kelvin scale are the same size as units on the Celsius scale. A change of 1 K is the same temperature change as 1°C. Zero K is equal to −273°C.

Academic Vocabulary

If something is absolute, it is definite or without question. How would you describe absolute silence?

....

....

....

....

Math Toolbox

Temperature Scales

If you have a thermometer with both Celsius and Fahrenheit scales, you can "eyeball" the conversion in temperature. Temperatures that line up on the parallel scales, such as 32°F and 0°C, are equivalent.

1. **Integrate with Visuals** 🖉 A comfortable room temperature is 72°F. Mark the thermometer where approximately 72°F would be. What is the approximate temperature in Celsius? ....

2. **Convert Measurement Units** 🖉 Complete the conversion table to compare the temperatures on different scales.

3. **Apply Mathematics** Write a formula for converting temperature to degrees Celsius if you are given the temperature in kelvins.

....

....

°F	°C	K
		263
	0	273
212	100	373

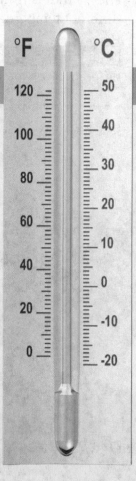

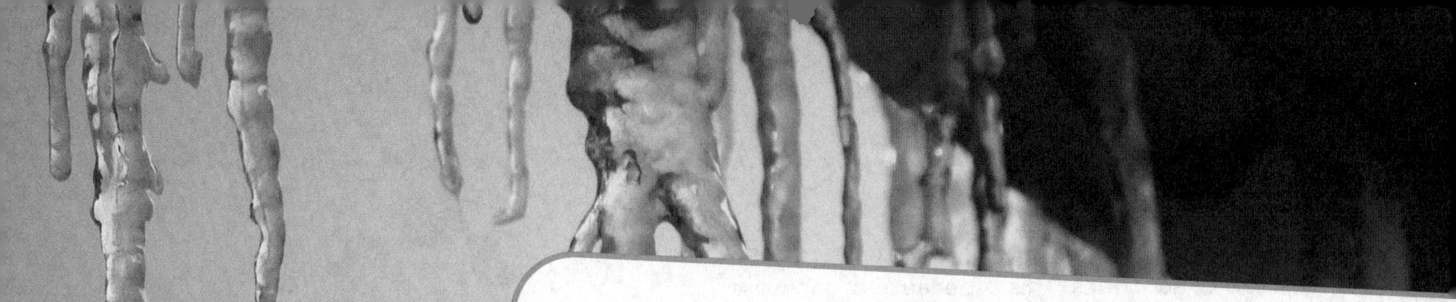

Temperature and Melting

Figure 2 Icicles melt as their thermal energy increases. However, the temperature of the melting icicles remains at 0°C during the change of state.

Predict Think about the difference between thermal energy and temperature. How might the melting icicles gain energy without changing temperature?

....

....

....

....

How Thermal Energy and Temperature Are Related

Different objects at the same temperature can have different amounts of thermal energy. This is because the thermal energy of an object is the total energy of all the particles in the object. Temperature contributes to an object's thermal energy, but it is not the only factor. Other factors include the potential energy and arrangement of the particles, as well as the states, types, and amounts of matter in the object.

Changing States When thermal energy transfers to another object in the form of heat, it can do work or cause change like all other forms of energy. If enough heat is transferred to or from a substance, the substance can change states. During a change of state, the thermal energy of a substance changes, but its temperature stays the same. For example, as heat is transferred to the melting icicles in **Figure 2**, their thermal energy continues to increase. Since these icicles have already reached their melting point (0°C), the added energy continues to break the rigid arrangement of the water molecules, rather than increase their motion. This means that the average kinetic energy of the molecules themselves does not change during a change of state. Remember, temperature is a measure of the average kinetic energy of the molecules. Therefore, as the ice melts, the thermal energy of the ice increases while the temperature remains the same.

Literacy Connection

Use Information Use the text and an internet source to help you answer the following question: How does thermal energy relate to temperature during condensation?

....

....

....

....

143

Model It!

Have you ever broken a piece of ice? You may have noticed that the break has angular edges instead of soft ones. This is because of the rigid, organized arrangement of its particles. The model shows the arrangement of water particles in a piece of solid ice just before it starts to melt.

✏️ In the empty circle, draw what the particles would look like after the ice has begun melting. Then write a caption for your drawing that describes what it shows.

1. **Identify** What is the temperature of the water in both images?

....

2. **Draw Comparative Inferences** Compare the relative amounts of thermal energy of each model.

....

....

....

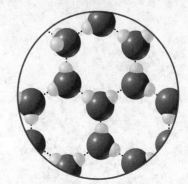

Water particles in solid form have a rigid arrangement.

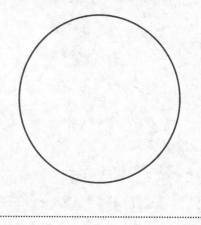

....

....

VIDEO

Watch a video to help you understand changes of state.

Comparing Thermal Energy The amount of matter in an object affects its thermal energy. This is because more matter means more particles. As you have read, the particles have stored potential energy based on their arrangement. They also have kinetic energy based on their vibration and other movement. Therefore, the more particles an object has at a given temperature, the more thermal energy it has. For example, a 1-liter pot full of tea at 85°C has more thermal energy than a 0.2-liter cup full of tea at 85°C (**Figure 3**), because the pot contains more matter.

What if the objects contain the same amount of matter? The object at the higher temperature has more thermal energy. Remember, temperature is a measure of the average kinetic energy of the particles. If the object has a higher temperature, its particles have a greater average kinetic energy. A greater kinetic energy results in a greater thermal energy. So, if two 1-liter pots of tea have two different temperatures, the pot with the higher temperature has more thermal energy.

Thermal Energy and Amount of Matter

Figure 8 Even though the pot of tea and the cup of tea are at the same temperature, the pot of tea has more thermal energy because it contains more particles.

85°C

85°C

Draw Comparative Inferences If you wanted to cool both the pot and the cup of tea to 80°C, which one would take longer to cool down?

....

....

Changes in Temperature What if we add the same amount of energy to the pot of tea and the cup of tea in **Figure 3**? Will they change to the same temperature? Not necessarily. An object's change in temperature depends on the environment and the types and amounts of matter in the object. Let's say we wanted to raise the temperature of the tea in each container by 1°C. The type of matter is the same, and the environment is the same. But the container with more tea will require more heat. It has more particles, so more energy is needed to get them all moving with the same average kinetic energy as the particles in the smaller cup of tea.

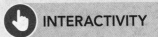 **READING CHECK** **Construct Explanations** Suppose you heat two bean burritos with the same ingredients in the microwave. One burrito weighs 0.3 pounds, while the other weighs 0.4 pounds. After microwaving each of them for one minute, which burrito will be hotter? Explain your answer.

....

....

....

INTERACTIVITY

Discover how a thermometer works.

Write About It Have you ever been served a meal that was not cooked hot enough? Write about the factors that may have contributed to your food being too cold.

145

☑ LESSON 1 Check

MS-PS3-4

1. **Define** What is the scientific definition of heat?

   ....

2. **Calculate** If the temperature outside is 297 K, what is this temperature in degrees Celsius?

   ....

   ....

   ....

   ....

3. **Describe** What is the minimum value for the Kelvin temperature scale, and what would happen at that temperature?

   ....

   ....

   ....

   ....

4. **Identify** What are the factors that determine an object's thermal energy?

   ....

   ....

   ....

5. **Apply Concepts** Suppose that you have 0.5 liters of tomato soup and 0.5 liters of split pea soup in your kitchen. Can you tell for certain which one will require more thermal energy to heat up to 60°C? Why or why not?

   ....

   ....

   ....

   ....

6. **Construct Explanations** Ice is melting at 0°C. Explain how the temperature of the melting ice stays the same while its thermal energy increases.

   ....

   ....

   ....

   ....

7. **Apply Scientific Reasoning** Object A has less thermal energy than Object B, but heat flows from Object A to Object B. What conditions would make this possible?

   ....

   ....

   ....

8. **Cause and Effect** 🖊 Jamie heats a pot of water on the stove. When the water boils, she turns the stove off and the water begins to cool. Draw a diagram with before and after pictures—before the stove is turned off, and after the stove is turned off. Add arrows to show the direction that heat flows in each picture.

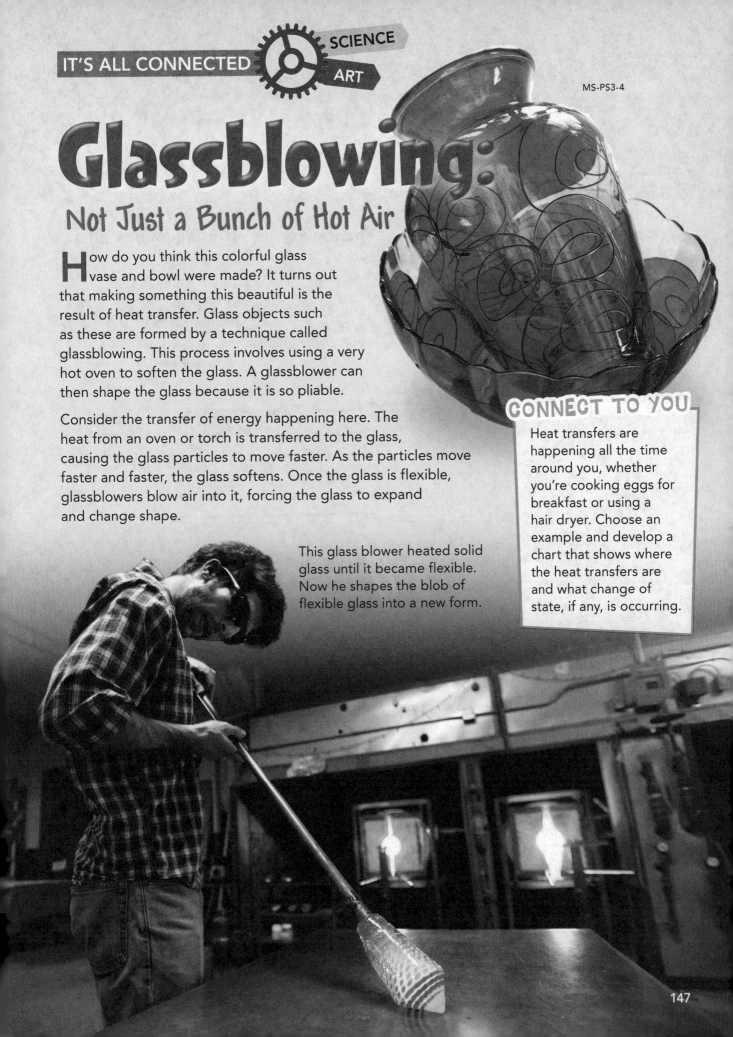

Glassblowing

Not Just a Bunch of Hot Air

How do you think this colorful glass vase and bowl were made? It turns out that making something this beautiful is the result of heat transfer. Glass objects such as these are formed by a technique called glassblowing. This process involves using a very hot oven to soften the glass. A glassblower can then shape the glass because it is so pliable.

Consider the transfer of energy happening here. The heat from an oven or torch is transferred to the glass, causing the glass particles to move faster. As the particles move faster and faster, the glass softens. Once the glass is flexible, glassblowers blow air into it, forcing the glass to expand and change shape.

This glass blower heated solid glass until it became flexible. Now he shapes the blob of flexible glass into a new form.

CONNECT TO YOU

Heat transfers are happening all the time around you, whether you're cooking eggs for breakfast or using a hair dryer. Choose an example and develop a chart that shows where the heat transfers are and what change of state, if any, is occurring.

② Heat Transfer

Guiding Questions

- How is heat transferred?
- How is energy conserved during transformations?

Connections

Literacy Conduct Research Projects

Math Reason Quantitatively

MS-PS3-4, MS-PS3-5

Vocabulary

conduction
convection
convection current
radiation

Academic Vocabulary

transform

 VOCABULARY APP

Practice vocabulary on a mobile device.

Quest CONNECTION

Think about how heat flows between different types of materials, both liquids and solids. What materials prevent the transfer of heat?

Connect It!

🖊 **When you're outside on a cold day, it's nice to stay warm near a fire. Draw an arrow on Figure 1 to show the direction of heat flow between the fire and the person's hands.**

Predict What happens in terms of heat transfer the longer you sit near the fire?

....

....

Infer Why would you rather have hot cocoa than lemonade on a cold day?

....

....

Types of Heat Transfer

Heat is transferring around you all the time. Heat doesn't transfer in random directions, though. It is transferred from warmer areas to cooler areas by conduction, convection, and radiation.

Conduction is the transfer of energy from one particle of matter to another within an object or between two objects that are in direct contact. Conduction occurs when you place your head on a cool pillow. The fast-moving particles in your skin collide with the slow-moving particles in the pillow. This causes the particles in the pillow to move faster. The pillow becomes warmer, while your skin becomes cooler.

Convection is a type of heat transfer that occurs through the movement of fluids, which can be solid, liquid, or gas. Fluids are materials that flow. When air is heated, its particles speed up and move farther apart. This makes the heated air less dense. The heated air rises to float on top of the denser, cooler air. Cooler air flows into its place, heats up, and rises. Previously heated air cools down, sinks, and the cycle repeats. This flow creates a circular motion known as a **convection current**. Convection currents in air cause wind and changes in the weather.

Radiation is the transfer of energy by electromagnetic waves. Radiation is the only form of heat transfer that does not require matter. You can feel the radiation from a fire without touching the flames, as in **Figure 1**. The sun's transfer of energy to Earth is another example of radiation. Sunlight travels 150 million kilometers through empty space before it warms Earth.

INTERACTIVITY

Watch this visual summary of conduction, convection, and radiation.

Warming Up

Figure 1 A fire feels especially warm to your hands on a cold day, when heat from your body quickly transfers to the frigid air.

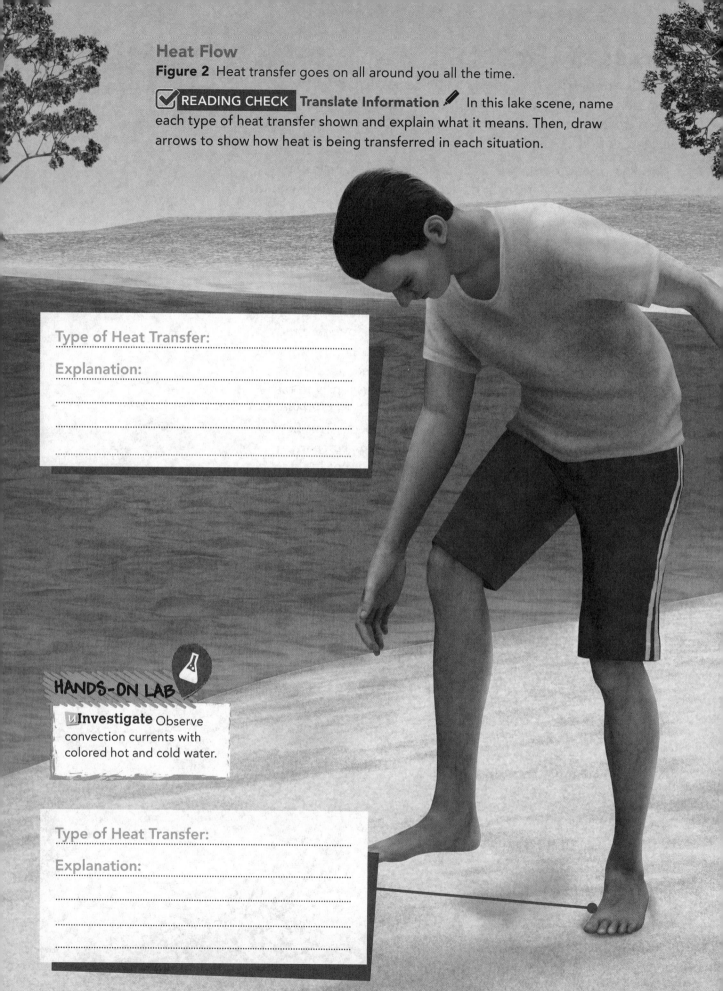

Heat Flow

Figure 2 Heat transfer goes on all around you all the time.

☑ READING CHECK **Translate Information** 🖊 In this lake scene, name each type of heat transfer shown and explain what it means. Then, draw arrows to show how heat is being transferred in each situation.

Type of Heat Transfer:

Explanation:

HANDS-ON LAB

✋Investigate Observe convection currents with colored hot and cold water.

Type of Heat Transfer:

Explanation:

Type of Heat Transfer: ....

Explanation: ....

....

....

Math Toolbox

Graphing Changes in Temperature

It's a hot day at the lake, with an air temperature of 30°C (86°F). Jeremy has two cups of water—one at 10°C and the other at 50°C. He places them on a picnic table where they receive the same amount of sunlight and no wind for a half an hour. The air temperature does not change during this time.

1. **Reason Quantitatively** ✏ Sketch two trend lines on the graph showing how the temperature of the water in the two cups would change over the 30 minutes. Create a legend to distinguish which line represents which cup (for example, the warmer cup = dotted line).

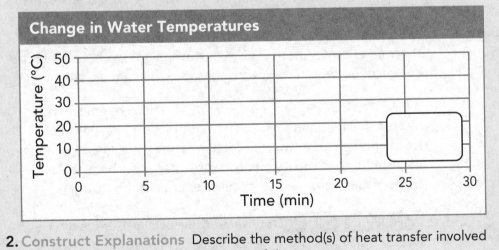

Change in Water Temperatures

Cup 1

10°C

Cup 2

50°C

2. **Construct Explanations** Describe the method(s) of heat transfer involved in causing the change in temperature of the two cups.

....

....

....

151

Figure 3 A wood-fired pizza oven demonstrates all three types of heat transfer: conduction, convection, and radiation.

Apply Scientific Reasoning ✎
Draw arrows to show the direction of heat transfer. How is energy conserved in the system of the pizza and the wood-fired oven?

....

....

....

....

....

▶ **VIDEO**

See what it's like to become a firefighter.

Academic Vocabulary

What is another way of saying that energy can transform?

....

....

....

👆 **INTERACTIVITY**

Figure out the best method for reheating a pizza.

Energy Conservation

In conduction, convection, and radiation, energy is transferred from one place to another. Even though the energy moves, it is always conserved within a system. For instance, in the pizza oven shown in **Figure 3**, the oven loses energy, but the pizza gains that energy. So the total energy of the oven-pizza system is conserved. By the law of conservation of energy, energy cannot be created or destroyed.

Energy Transformations The law of conservation of energy applies to everything—even when energy **transforms**. Many energy transformations involve thermal energy. For example, an electric stove transforms electrical energy into thermal energy. Another kind of stove, a gas oven, converts the chemical energy from natural gas into thermal energy.

Thermal Energy and Work Thermal energy can be transformed to do work. For example, some types of train engines heat water to create steam. This causes pistons in the engine to move. The thermal energy of the water is transformed into the mechanical energy of the train.

☑ **READING CHECK** **Determine Conclusions** Is there a type of energy transformation in which the system destroys or creates energy? What conclusion can you draw?

....

....

Question It !

Alicia performed an experiment on squash soup. She wanted to see whether stirring the soup would really help it cool down faster. She heated two 10-ounce bowls of soup in a microwave for 120 seconds. Then, she stirred one bowl of soup with a spoon for 60 seconds and let the other sit for 60 seconds. She used two thermometers to make measurements, and she recorded her data in the chart below.

Temp of soup after heating (°F)	Stir or let sit for 60 seconds?	Temp after 60 seconds (°F)
150	Stir	137
150	Let sit	145

1. **Apply Scientific Reasoning** Describe the energy transformations involved in heating the soup in the microwave. Which method of heat transfer is involved in heating the soup?

....

....

....

....

....

....

....

....

2. **Analyze Quantitative Relationships** Based on the data, summarize Alicia's results. Describe how stirring the soup affects heat transfer.

....

....

....

....

....

....

....

....

....

....

....

....

Literacy Connection

Conduct Research Projects Perform the experiment, and think about what you've learned about heat transfer in this lesson. Then, write a new question that would explore these concepts further. Discuss the possible answers to your question with a partner or teacher.

....

....

....

Write About It Think about how your breakfast or lunch was prepared. How did thermal energy come into play?

MS-PS3-4, MS-PS3-5

1. **Classify** What type of heat transfer occurs when eggs fry in a hot pan?

....

2. **Identify** What type of heat transfer occurs when you roast a marshmallow by holding it over a campfire?

....

3. **Describe** Name a type of food in which convection helps the cooking process. Explain your answer.

....

....

....

4. **Explain Phenomena** When you touch a warm picnic table, your hand becomes warmer. Explain how energy conservation applies to this situation.

....

....

....

5. **Develop Models** 🖊 Draw a picture that shows a convection current in a real-life situation. Use arrows to represent the convection current.

6. **Apply Scientific Reasoning** Give a real-world example of how energy is transformed from electrical energy to thermal energy. Describe how the heat can be transferred to other objects through conduction, convection, or radiation.

....

....

....

....

....

Quest CHECK-IN

So far, you have learned how energy can be transferred by means of conduction, convection, and radiation.

Evaluate Why is it important to consider the types of materials that are available and how those materials interact with cold exterior temperatures and warm interior temperatures of a food container?

....

....

....

👆 INTERACTIVITY

Contain the Heat

Go online to apply what you've learned about thermal energy and heat transfer. How can you use this knowledge to design your insulating container? Brainstorm possible solutions with a group, and record your work in a graphic organizer. Then select the best method and materials to use in your design.

SHOCKWAVE TO THE FUTURE

 VIDEO

See how engineers use energy transformations to develop a real-world solution.

How do you make car engines more efficient? You engineer them! The new shockwave engine offers a better way to get where you are going.

The Challenge: To build a more efficient engine.

Phenomenon Most cars on the road today still contain combustion engines. These engines use pistons to run. The pistons make the car heavier, and they also cause friction that wastes energy.

The shockwave engine does not contain pistons. It is more like a fan, circular in shape and ringed with blades. The shockwave engine converts the chemical energy of fuel into heat, and pressure increases within the engine. The thermal energy is converted to mechanical energy when the blades begin to spin. These spinning blades cause a crankshaft to turn, which causes the wheels of the car to spin.

The shockwave engine has fewer moving parts, and it is lighter than combustion engines. It can improve fuel economy by about 60 percent!

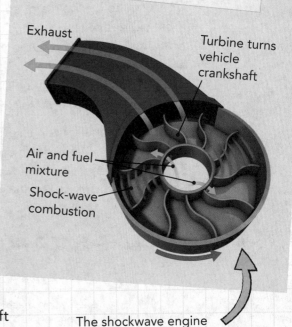

Exhaust

Turbine turns vehicle crankshaft

Air and fuel mixture

Shock-wave combustion

The shockwave engine works with thermal energy and pressure, causing a simple spinning motion. No pistons required!

DESIGN CHALLENGE

How can you build a simple heat engine? Go to the Engineering Design Notebook to find out!

MS-PS3-4, MS-PS3-5

Earth Power

Electricity is the largest form of energy used in the United States. Power plants generate this energy using a variety of sources. These sources include fossil fuels (such as natural gas and coal), nuclear power, hydroelectric, wind, and solar.

Coal used to be the major source of electricity, but it is one of the most expensive sources. It is also harmful to human health and the environment. Many coal plants, which produce soot and toxic gases, are now changing to natural gas, which is cheaper and cleaner. The burning of all fossil fuels releases carbon dioxide, which is a greenhouse gas that affects the climate.

Geothermal energy can also be used to generate electricity. In this process, warm water deep underground is pumped to the surface. The thermal energy of the water is transformed into electricity within a power plant. Review the steps in the diagram.

How a Geothermal POWER PLANT Works

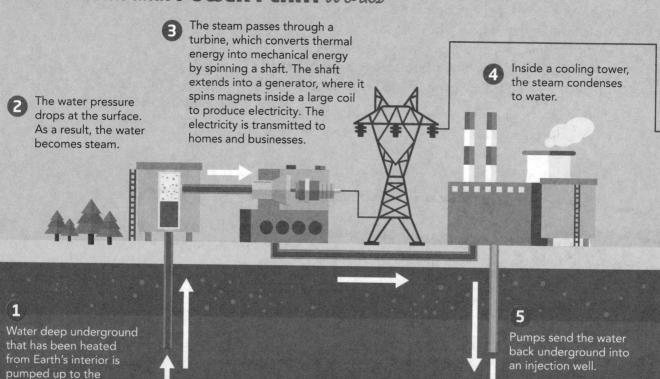

3 The steam passes through a turbine, which converts thermal energy into mechanical energy by spinning a shaft. The shaft extends into a generator, where it spins magnets inside a large coil to produce electricity. The electricity is transmitted to homes and businesses.

4 Inside a cooling tower, the steam condenses to water.

2 The water pressure drops at the surface. As a result, the water becomes steam.

1 Water deep underground that has been heated from Earth's interior is pumped up to the surface.

5 Pumps send the water back underground into an injection well.

Geothermal on the Rise

Over the past 10 years, the demand for geothermal energy has increased greatly. While it is still one of the less common ways to generate electricity, it is a much cleaner method than burning coal, and it has garnered public support. A disadvantage to using geothermal energy is that it is very expensive to generate and transmit, and the number of sites where geothermal energy is accessible from Earth's surface is not as high as the number of sites where natural gas, oil, and coal can be found. Still, there are significant efforts to increase demand for renewable energy resources, such as geothermal, solar, and wind, to reduce our impact on the environment.

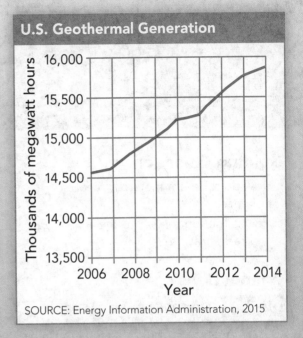

U.S. Geothermal Generation

SOURCE: Energy Information Administration, 2015

Use the graph to answer the following questions.

1. **Patterns** Describe any patterns you see in the graph.

   ....

   ....

2. **Predict** What do you think the data will look like for the generation of geothermal energy through the year 2040 in the United States? Why?

   ....

   ....

   ....

3. **Construct Explanations** The country of Iceland resides in a very volcanically active location. Geothermal plants provide 25 percent of Iceland's electricity. What factors do you think contribute to the high percentage of energy supplied by geothermal sources in Iceland?

   ....

   ....

4. **Communicate** What do you think could be done to encourage more people to use geothermal energy?

   ....

   ....

Heat and Materials

Guiding Questions

• How do different materials respond to heat?

• How is friction related to thermal energy and temperature?

Connections

Literacy Integrate with Visuals

Math Analyze Proportional Relationships

MS-PS3-4, MS-PS3-5

Vocabulary

conductor
insulator
specific heat
thermal
 expansion

Academic Vocabulary

contract

 VOCABULARY APP

Practice vocabulary on a mobile device.

Quest CONNECTION

Think about how different objects and materials transfer heat. Do they retain thermal energy or does heat transfer quickly to nearby objects?

Connect It!

🖊 **When divers explore deep ocean waters, the temperatures they encounter are very cold. In the space provided, describe how you think the wetsuit keeps the diver warm in cold water.**

Communicate You also use special clothing to stay warm and perform different functions. What items of clothing do you use for specific activities?

....

....

Relate Structure and Function What materials are those items made of?

....

Thermal Properties of Materials

When you bake something in the oven, you use dishes made of glass, ceramic, or metal instead of plastic. Some materials can stand up to the heat of an oven better than others. Materials respond to heat in different ways. The thermal properties of an object determine how it will respond to heat.

Conductors and Insulators

If you walk barefoot from your living room rug to the tile floor of your kitchen, you will notice that the tile feels colder than the rug. But the temperature of the rug and the tile are the same—room temperature! The difference has to do with how materials conduct heat, which is another way of saying how well they absorb or transmit heat.

A material that conducts heat well is called a **conductor**. Metals such as silver are good conductors. Some materials are good conductors because of the particles they contain and how those particles are arranged. A good conductor, such as the tile floor, feels cold to the touch because heat easily transfers out of your skin and into the tile. However, heat also transfers out of conductors easily. A metal flagpole feels much hotter on a summer day than a wooden pole would in the same place because heat easily conducts out of the metal pole and into your hand.

A wooden pole and your living room rug are good insulators. **Insulators** are materials that do not conduct heat well. Other good insulators include air and wool. For example, wool blankets slow the transfer of heat out of your body.

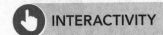

INTERACTIVITY

Determine what kind of container to use when taking lunch to the beach.

Reflect Conductors and insulators are all around you. In your science notebook, write one conductor and one insulator that you see. Describe their materials and why you believe they are conductors or insulators.

Surviving the Cold Water
Figure 1 A diver stays warm in a special wetsuit.

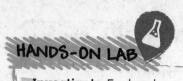
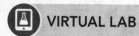

VIRTUAL LAB

Explore energy changes with a calorimeter and investigate the amount of calories in different foods.

Specific Heat

Specific Heat Imagine running across hot sand toward the ocean. You run to the water's edge, but you don't go any farther— the water is too cold. How can the sand be so hot and the water so cold? After all, the sun heats both of them. The answer is that water requires more heat to raise its temperature than sand does.

When a substance or material is heated, its temperature rises. But the temperature does not rise at the same rate for all materials. The amount of heat required to raise the temperature of a material depends on the material's chemical makeup. Different materials require different amounts of energy to have the same temperature increase.

The amount of energy required to raise the temperature of 1 kilogram of a material by 1 kelvin is called its **specific heat**. It is measured in joules per kilogram-kelvin, or J/(kg·K), where kelvin is a measure of temperature. A material with a high specific heat can absorb a great deal of energy without a great change in temperature.

If a material's temperature changes, you can calculate how its energy changes with a formula.

Energy Change = Mass × Specific Heat × Temperature Change

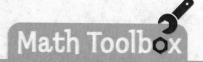

Math Toolbox

Energy Change, Specific Heat, and Mass

A chef is preparing vegetables in two pans. The pans are the same mass, but one is made of aluminum and the other is made of iron. She heats both pans to the same temperature before adding the vegetables.

1. **Analyze Proportional Relationships** The ratio of the specific heat of aluminum to the specific heat of iron is 2:1. How much energy must be transferred to the aluminum pan, compared with the amount of energy transferred to the iron pan?

....

....

2. **Apply Scientific Reasoning** If the chef used an aluminum pan and a silver pan of equal mass, which would undergo a greater energy change?

....

....

Material	Specific Heat (J/(kg·K))
Aluminum	900
Water	4,180
Silver	235
Iron	450

3. **Predict** Suppose the chef used two silver pans instead, but one was three times the mass of the other. How would the energy change of the two pans compare?

....

....

....

Pop!

Figure 2 When you make popcorn, heat flows to a tiny droplet of water inside the kernel. This causes the liquid water to change into vapor. The expanding water vapor builds up pressure inside the kernel. Finally, the kernel explodes, turning into a piece of popcorn!

Thermal Expansion Have you ever tried to open a jar, but the lid was firmly stuck? Thermal expansion could help you in this situation. To loosen a jar lid, you can hold it under a stream of hot water. This works because the metal lid expands more than the glass does as it gets hotter.

As the thermal energy of matter increases, its particles usually spread out, causing the substance to expand. This is true for almost all types of matter. The expansion of matter when it is heated is known as **thermal expansion**. When matter is cooled, the opposite happens. Thermal energy is released. This causes the particles to slow down and move closer together. As matter cools, it usually decreases in volume, or **contracts**. Different materials expand and contract at different rates and to different volumes.

Academic Vocabulary

In this context, the verb *contract* means to decrease in size. Write a sentence using the word *contract*.

....

....

Expansion Joints

Figure 3 Bridge joints allow room for the bridge to expand in the heat.

✔ READING CHECK Write Informative Texts

What might happen if thermal expansion had not been considered in the building of this bridge?

....

....

....

....

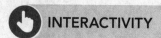
Temperature, Energy, and Friction

The kinetic energy of particles can change, as in thermal expansion, but an entire object's kinetic energy can change as well. A change in an object's kinetic energy indicates that a transfer of energy to or from the object is happening. If the kinetic energy of the object increases, then some form of energy is being transferred to the object. If the kinetic energy decreases, then the object is transferring kinetic energy to something else. This is true because energy is always conserved. The kinetic energy is not created or destroyed—it is transferred and sometimes transformed to other forms of energy in the process.

Friction and Energy Transformation

Some objects lose kinetic energy because of friction. The law of conservation of energy accounts for this change in energy. For example, when a bike skids to a stop, as in **Figure 4**, the tires experience friction with the ground. When this happens, the kinetic energy of the entire bike changes—the bike slows down. Where does that kinetic energy go? If you could feel the bike tire or the ground, you would observe the answer. They both become hot. As friction slows the bike, the kinetic energy transforms into thermal energy of the tire and the ground. As the tire and the ground cool down, that thermal energy transfers to the surrounding air.

From Fast to Warm
Figure 4 As this bike skids to a stop, the tires and the ground become warmer.

Literacy Connection

Integrate With Visuals
How does friction between the bike tires and the ground relate to thermal energy and temperature?

....

....

....

....

Model It

Friction and Energy Transformation
In the space provided, draw an example in which friction causes kinetic energy to transfer and transform. Describe the transfers or transformations that are occurring.

....

....

....

Space Shuttle Entering Atmosphere
Figure 5 This NASA illustration shows how a space shuttle burns through the atmosphere as it returns to Earth.

Materials for Space Shuttles When space shuttles were used for various missions, friction occurred between the space shuttles and the air in Earth's atmosphere. When a shuttle returned from space and re-entered the atmosphere, as in **Figure 5**, it experienced compression and friction from the atmospheric gas. Even though the upper atmosphere is cold, the space shuttle experienced high temperatures due to friction. Some of the kinetic energy of the moving space shuttle transformed into thermal energy.

Space shuttles were built with materials that can withstand both the high temperatures when moving through the atmosphere and the cold temperatures of outer space. Scientists developed Ultra High Temperature Ceramics for the front end of space shuttles. These materials withstood extremely high temperatures. A space shuttle also had a layer of insulating material below its outer layer. The insulation layer prevented the heat from transferring into the interior of the shuttle. It also prevented heat from transferring out of the shuttle's interior once the shuttle entered the cold of outer space.

INTERACTIVITY

Evaluate and recommend materials in the design of a playhouse for a park.

☑ READING CHECK **Infer** Which type of material, an insulator or a conductor, should be used to keep an airplane warm inside? Why?

....

....

Plan It!

Materials for Airplanes

Figure 6 Various materials including titanium, graphite-epoxy, and wood have have been used to construct airplanes. Use the information in the table to help you answer the questions.

Material	Advantages	Disadvantages
Wood	Lightweight, strong	Splinters, requires maintenance
Aluminum	Lightweight, strong	Cannot withstand temperatures at high speeds
Steel	Stronger than aluminum, stiff	heavy
Graphite-epoxy	Lighter than aluminum, strong, thin sheets can be stacked	Not as strong as steel
Titanium	As strong as steel, lightweight	expensive

1. **Construct an Argument** Which material do you think would be best for the outside of a high-speed airplane? Use the information in the table to construct an argument for your choice.

....
....
....
....

2. **Identify Criteria** What additional information would you like to know to ensure that it is suitable for the outside of the aircraft?

....
....
....
....

MS-PS3-4, MS-PS3-5

1. Construct an Explanation Why do some materials feel hotter than others, even if the two materials are at the same temperature?

....

....

....

....

....

2. Classify Foam picnic coolers keep food cool on a hot day. Is foam a conductor or an insulator? Explain.

....

....

....

3. Calculate Suppose you have two slices of cheese. They have the same specific heat, but one is twice the mass of the other. How much energy is needed to melt the larger slice compared to the amount of energy needed to melt the smaller slice?

....

....

....

4. Explain Why do objects tend to expand when they are heated?

....

....

....

....

....

....

....

5. Cause and Effect The driver of a car slams on the brakes so that his car does not crash into a deer in the road. What happens to the thermal energy of the tires as the car skids to a stop? What causes this change in thermal energy?

....

....

....

....

....

Quest CHECK-INS

In this lesson, you learned how the specific heat of different substances affects how they transfer heat and whether they're likely to be classified as insulators or conductors.

Evaluate How could the specific heat of the substance your container will hold affect the performance of the container?

....

....

....

HANDS-ON LABS

- Keep the Heat In
- Keep the Cold Out

Go online to download the lab worksheets. You will finalize the design of your container, and then build, test, and evaluate the finished product.

☑ TOPIC 4 Review and Assess

1 Thermal Energy, Heat, and Temperature

MS-PS3-4

1. What is the total energy of all of the particles in an object called?
A. chemical energy
B. thermal energy
C. potential energy
D. nuclear energy

2. Energy that is transferred from a warmer object to a cooler object is called
A. temperature.
B. substance.
C. heat.
D. mechanical energy.

3. When the kinetic energy of the particles in an object increases, the temperature of the object
A. increases.
B. decreases.
C. remains the same.
D. becomes fixed at 100°C.

4. A/an .... is an instrument that can be used to measure temperature.

5. Predict What happens to the state of liquid water if enough heat is added?

....
....

6. Draw Comparative Inferences A 2-ounce apple and a 4-ounce apple are at the same temperature. Which requires more thermal energy to raise its temperature by 1°F? Why?

....
....
....
....

Use the illustration to answer questions 7 and 8.

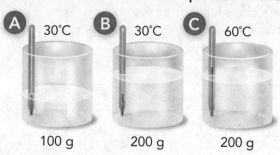

A 30°C B 30°C C 60°C

100 g   200 g   200 g

7. Interpret Diagrams Compare the average motion of the particles in the three containers of water. Explain your answer. (Note: The same substance is in each container.)

....
....
....
....

8. Draw Conclusions Compare the amount of thermal energy in containers A and B. Explain your answer.

....
....
....

2 Heat Transfer

MS-PS3-4, MS-PS3-5

9. What is the process by which heat transfers from one particle of matter to another when the particles collide?
A. conduction   B. convection
C. expansion   D. radiation

10. When energy transforms from one form to another, the total amount of energy in the system
A. decreases.   B. increases.
C. is conserved.   D. drops to zero.

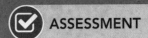
11. Air currents transfer energy by the method of heat transfer called ....

12. Identify each example of heat transfer as conduction, convection, or radiation.

A.

B.

C.

13. Explain How can heat be transferred across empty space? Explain your answer.

....

....

14. Make Judgments Suppose you try to heat up your home using a fireplace in one of the rooms. Would a fan be helpful? Explain.

....

....

....

3 Heat and Materials

MS-PS3-4, MS-PS3-5

15. Which kinds of materials do not conduct heat well?
A. insulators
B. conductors
C. metals
D. radiators

16. The amount of energy per kilogram needed to increase the temperature of a material by 1 K is called the
A. specific heat.
B. heat sensitivity.
C. heat resistance.
D. thermal heat.

17. The speeds of two bumper cars decrease as their bumpers rub against each other. What happens to the temperatures of the bumpers due to the force of friction?
A. Both bumpers cool down.
B. Both bumpers warm up.
C. One bumper cools down while the other warms up.
D. Both bumpers remain the same temperature.

18. Develop Models ✏ Draw before and after diagrams of the particles in a log that is heated. Does the log expand or contract?

MS-PS3-4, MS-PS3-5

Evidence-Based Assessment

Out in space, sand-sized particles of rock approach Earth every single day. However, they do not reach Earth's surface because they burn up in the atmosphere. Sometimes, larger space rocks called meteoroids also travel through the atmosphere. Once the meteoroid enters the atmosphere, it appears as a bright light moving through the sky, called a meteor. A meteoroid typically enters the atmosphere with an average speed in the range of 10–70 km/s. The rock burns as it travels, losing mass and speed in the process. The burning is due to friction between the meteoroid and the air particles in the atmosphere. The density of the air particles in the atmosphere is greater closer to Earth's surface. Some meteoroids do not burn up completely, and they reach Earth's surface as meteorites.

The following data provides information about three meteoroids traveling towards Earth's surface. The meteoroids are all roughly spherical and of the same density.

Meteoroid	Initial Mass (kg)	Surface temperature of meteoroid in space, before entering atmosphere (°C)	Surface temperature of meteoroid in atmosphere, 150 km above Earth's surface (°C)
1	0.52	90	1730
2	3.24	92	1727
3	1.05	91	1735

1. **Identify** Which statement describes what happens to the kinetic energy of the particles in the atmosphere as they come into contact with the meteoroid?

   A. The kinetic energy of the surrounding air particles is converted to electrical energy.

   B. The average kinetic energy of the surrounding air particles increases.

   C. The kinetic energy of the surrounding air particles is converted to potential energy.

   D. The average kinetic energy of the surrounding air particles decreases.

2. **Cite Evidence** What happens to the kinetic energy of a meteoroid as it travels farther through the atmosphere towards Earth's surface? Support your claim with evidence from the information provided.

   ....

   ....

   ....

   ....

   ....

   ....

   ....

   ....

3. **Infer** Explain how two methods of heat transfer are involved as the meteoroid burns.

   ....

   ....

   ....

   ....

   ....

   ....

   ....

   ....

   ....

4. **Apply Scientific Reasoning** Which meteoroid is most likely to reach Earth's surface? Explain why this is so, in terms of heat transfer. Use data from the table to support your response.

   ....

   ....

   ....

   ....

   ....

   ....

   ....

   ....

Quest FINDINGS

Complete the Quest!

Phenomenon After applying what you learned to the design and construction of an insulating container, reflect on the use of models and scientific principles in the design of your containers.

Evaluate How did concepts related to thermal energy and heat transfer guide your design process?

....

....

....

....

....

👆 **INTERACTIVITY**

Reflect on Your Insulating Container

Testing Thermal Conductivity

How can you **design** an experiment to determine the best **metal** to use for a **heat sink**?

Background

Phenomenon Electronics manufacturers use heat sinks to draw heat away from components that can overheat. Engineers for a new tablet company have designed a super-fast processor. The problem is, the processor gets very hot, causing the tablet to shut down. The company has asked you to design an experiment to provide evidence for the best metal to use for a heat sink in their new tablet.

Materials

(per group)

- 3 metal conducting strips (10 cm x 2 cm each): copper, aluminum, and brass
- 6 insulating foam cups (5 cm tall)
- aluminum foil
- 2 plastic-backed thermometers
- boiling water (75 mL)
- room-temperature water (40 mL)
- graduated cylinder
- scissors
- stopwatch

Safety

Be sure to follow all safety procedures provided by your teacher. Appendix B of your textbook provides additional details about the safety icons.

heat sink

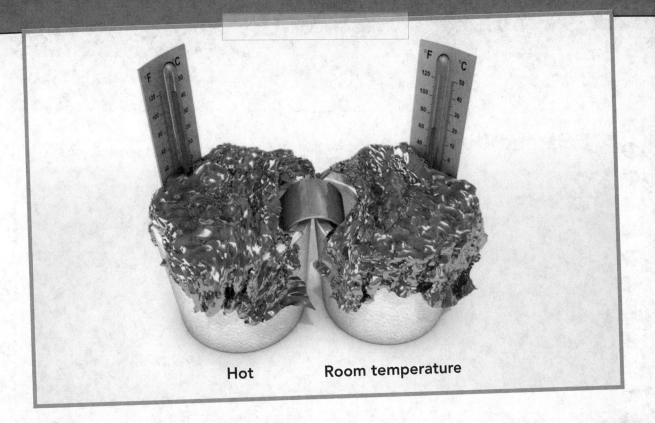

Hot   Room temperature

Develop Possible Solutions

⚠️ You will conduct an experiment to investigate how each of the three metals conducts heat from a cup of hot water to a cup of room-temperature water. Design an experiment using the materials provided. Write out a procedure below, and then conduct the experiment. Construct a data table to record the results of your experiment, and note any important observations you make.

HANDS-ON LAB

и**Demonstrate** Go online for a downloadable worksheet of this lab.

....

....

....

....

....

....

....

....

....

....

....

....

....

....

....

....

....

Data and Observations

Analyze and Interpret Data

1. **Apply Scientific Reasoning** What is the direction of heat flow between the cups? How does this transfer take place? Explain your answer.

   ....

   ....

   ....

   ....

2. **Calculate** Determine the temperature change of the room temperature water after 10 minutes for each metal used.

   Copper: ....

   Aluminum: ....

   Brass: ....

3. **Calculate** Determine the average rate of temperature change of the room temperature water for each metal used.

   Copper: ....

   Aluminum: ....

   Brass: ....

4. **Engage In Argument From Evidence** Brass costs about $0.90 per pound, copper costs $2.15 per pound, and aluminum costs $0.75 per pound. Which metal would you recommend be used for for use as a heat sink in the tablet? Explain your choice.

   ....

   ....

   ....

5. **Provide Critique** Examine the setup and procedure for another group's experiment. Make recommendations to the group for improving the design of its experiment.

   ....

   ....

   ....

   ....

NGSS PERFORMANCE EXPECTATIONS

MS-ESS2-1 Develop a model to describe the
cycling of Earth's materials and the flow of energy
that drives this process.

MS-ESS2-4 Develop a model to describe the
cycling of water through Earth's systems driven by
energy from the sun and the force of gravity.

HANDS-ON LAB

uConnect Develop a model to
describe interactions among
Earth's spheres.

HOW do all the things in this photo interact with each other?

▶ VIDEO

👆 INTERACTIVITY

🧪 VIRTUAL LAB

☑ ASSESSMENT

📖 eTEXT

📱 APP

The Essential Question

How do matter and energy cycle through Earth's systems?

How do water, rock, air, and organisms interact to make Earth's surface features and systems?

....

....

....

....

....

....

....

Quest KICKOFF

NBC LEARN ▶ VIDEO

How can you predict the effects of a forest fire?

Phenomenon You just watched a news report about a wildfire that is burning just north of your town. The fire is not under control, and you wonder what will happen to the forest. In this problem-based Quest activity, you will take on the role of a scientist whose task is to educate and inform local residents about the harmful effects of a forest fire. You will consider how all the spheres of the Earth system interact, then use that information to make predictions about the outcome of the fire's damage. Your presentation will take the form of a poster, photo essay, or a multimedia report.

After watching the Quest Kickoff video, which explores the effects of a forest fire, record ways in which a fire will impact Earth's spheres.

Organisms:

....

....

Ground/Earth:

....

....

Air:

....

....

Water:

....

....

 INTERACTIVITY

Forest Fires

MS-ESS2-1 Develop a model to describe the cycling of Earth's materials and the flow of energy that drives this process.
MS-ESS2-4 Develop a model to describe the cycling of water through Earth's systems driven by energy from the sun and the force of gravity.

Quest CHECK-IN

IN LESSON 1

How can an event in one sphere, such as the atmosphere, have an impact on another sphere? Think about the flow of energy as the fire started, then spread.

 INTERACTIVITY

Fire and Earth's Spheres

Quest CHECK-IN

IN LESSON 2

How do all of Earth's spheres interact? Consider these interactions as you learn how fire affects the geosphere.

 INTERACTIVITY

Disrupting the Geosphere

Fires are part of the natural life cycle of a forest. However, when they happen at the wrong time or burn for too long, forest fires have a devastating effect on plant and animal populations. Fires also affect the surrounding air, water, and land.

Quest CHECK-IN

IN LESSON 3

How does the hydrosphere interact with the other spheres, and vice versa? Examine the effects of fire on the hydrosphere. Then review all data and finalize your predictions.

👆 **INTERACTIVITY**

Impact on the Hydrosphere

Quest FINDINGS

Complete the Quest!

Create an engaging presentation to summarize your findings. Reflect on how the spheres influence each other—and your town.

👆 **INTERACTIVITY**

Reflect on Forest Fires

1 Matter and Energy in Earth's System

Guiding Questions

- What are the different components of the Earth system?
- What are the sources of energy for the processes that affect Earth?
- How can you model the cycling of matter in the Earth system?

Connections

Literacy Cite Textual Evidence

Math Interpret a Line Graph

MS-ESS2-1

Vocabulary

atmosphere
geosphere
hydrosphere
cryosphere
biosphere
energy

Academic Vocabulary

system
feedback

 VOCABULARY APP

Practice vocabulary on a mobile device.

Quest CONNECTION

Think about how an event, such as a fire, in one sphere can have an impact on another sphere.

Connect It !

✎ **Draw a line on the photo to indicate where the surface of the lake was in the past.**

Cause and Effect What happened to the water in this lake? Why do you think this happened?

....

....

The Earth System

Lake Mead, shown in **Figure 1**, is part of a large system consisting of the Colorado River, Hoover Dam, and Las Vegas, Nevada. A **system** is a group of parts that work together as a whole. If we zoom way out, the universe is the biggest system of all, and it contains all other systems. Earth is a system, too.

Water and Rock Cycles

The Earth system involves flows of matter and energy through different components. In the water cycle, water evaporates from the ocean and other bodies of water. Then it rises into the atmosphere and eventually falls back to Earth's surface as precipitation. Rain and meltwater then flow to rivers, lakes, and the ocean. Eventually the water cycles back into the atmosphere. At each step of a cycle of matter, some change in energy occurs to keep the cycle going. Evaporation of water requires heat energy. The heat energy may come from the sun or from within Earth, as in a hot spring.

Rock also cycles through the Earth system. Hot molten material inside Earth, called magma, flows up through cracks in Earth's crust. This new material cools—loses heat energy—to form solid rock. Over time, the rock can be eroded into small pieces. If enough small pieces collect, they may get packed together to form new rock.

☑ **READING CHECK** **Compare and Contrast** How are the rock and water cycles similar? How are they different?

....

....

....

INTERACTIVITY

Explore different types of systems.

Academic Vocabulary

Much of science involves identifying components of different systems. List two systems you hear about in everyday life. What are their components?

....

....

....

....

....

....

....

The Cycling of Water
Figure 1 Drought has had a serious impact on Lake Mead, a reservoir in Nevada.

VIDEO

Learn about the main spheres of Earth's system and how they interact.

Literacy Connection

Cite Textual Evidence
Reread the sections about the atmosphere. Underline the evidence that supports the idea that the atmosphere affects Earth's climate.

Earth's Spheres The Earth system is made up of four main spheres, or subsystems, shown in **Figure 2**. Earth's **atmosphere** (AT muh sfeer) is the relatively thin envelope of gases that forms Earth's outermost layer. It is made of air— a mixture of gases including nitrogen, oxygen, water vapor, and carbon dioxide—and dust particles. It contains Earth's weather, and it is the foundation for the different climates around the world. Most of Earth's mass is in the form of rock and metal of the **geosphere** (GEE uh sfeer). The geosphere includes the solid metal inner core, the liquid metal outer core, and the rocky mantle and crust. All of Earth's water, including water that cycles through the atmosphere, is called the **hydrosphere** (HI druh sfeer). The **cryosphere** (CRY uh sfeer) is the frozen component of the hydrosphere. It is made up of all the ice and snow on land, plus sea and lake ice. The parts of Earth that contain all living organisms are collectively known as the **biosphere** (BI uh sfeer).

Earth's outermost layer receives energy in the form of sunlight that passes through it and from heat that rises from Earth's surface, including the ocean. Heat rising from Earth's surface creates wind, which distributes heat as well as water through the atmosphere.

Earth's rock and metal contain an enormous amount of energy. Exposed rock absorbs sunlight and radiates heat into the atmosphere. In some locations, energy and new material make up the rocky outer layer of the geosphere in the form of lava. Major eruptions can affect the atmosphere, which in turn affects the hydrosphere and biosphere.

Energy Flow The constant flow, or cycling, of matter through the Earth system requires energy. **Energy** is the ability to do work. The Earth system has two main sources of energy: heat from the sun and heat from Earth's interior. These energy sources drive cycles of matter in the four spheres.

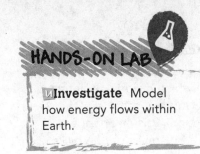

HANDS-ON LAB

☑**Investigate** Model how energy flows within Earth.

☑ **READING CHECK** **Use Information** Which part of each sphere do you interact with in your daily life? Give one example for each of the main spheres.

....

....

....

Earth's Spheres

Figure 2 Earth has four major spheres that cycle matter and energy and shape Earth's surface. Label each box with the correct sphere name. Then, list at least two spheres that show an interaction within the photo.

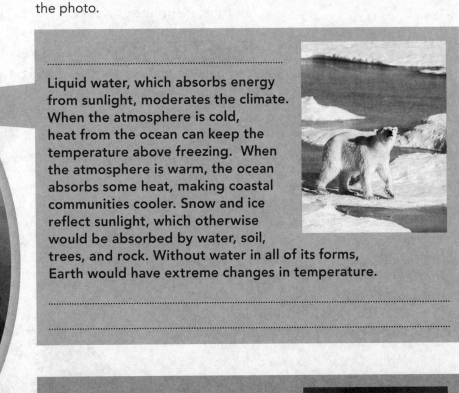

....

Liquid water, which absorbs energy from sunlight, moderates the climate. When the atmosphere is cold, heat from the ocean can keep the temperature above freezing. When the atmosphere is warm, the ocean absorbs some heat, making coastal communities cooler. Snow and ice reflect sunlight, which otherwise would be absorbed by water, soil, trees, and rock. Without water in all of its forms, Earth would have extreme changes in temperature.

....

....

Life has been found in virtually every part of Earth, from deep below the continental ice shelf of Antarctica to high up in the Himalayan Mountains.

....

....

Academic Vocabulary

Feedback involves a loop in which a signal or action triggers another signal or action. This can happen when a microphone picks up sound from a speaker that is amplifying the microphone's signal. The equipment passes the signal back and forth, and it becomes louder and harsher. What is one form of feedback that you encounter in your life?

....

....

....

System Feedback

Glaciers, part of the cryosphere, are large blocks of ancient ice, usually found near mountains and in polar regions. Like a freezer pack in a cooler, a glacier keeps the surrounding air and land cool. But many glaciers are melting around the world. As glaciers melt, they lose mass and volume and turn into liquid water that drains away or evaporates. This allows the land underneath to absorb more sunlight, which causes the surrounding air and land to get warmer. The warmer air makes glaciers melt even faster. This is an example of **feedback**. The system returns, or feeds back, information about itself, and that information results in change.

Positive and Negative Feedback
Sometimes feedback is negative: it causes a process to slow down, or go in reverse. But some types of feedback are positive: they reinforce, speed up, or enhance the process that's already underway. Feedback may result in stability or it may cause more change. The melting glaciers are an example of positive feedback and change. A similar process is causing change in the Arctic.

☑ READING CHECK **Cite Textual Evidence** Name a reason why melting glaciers are considered positive feedback.

....

....

Model It !

Sea Ice and Climate

Figure 3 Liquid and solid water are important factors in controlling climate. A large body of water can absorb energy from the sun, while snow or ice reflects solar energy back into space. In recent years, the amount of sea ice—frozen water—in the Arctic Circle has been dwindling because the air and water have been warmer than usual. As more of the Arctic Ocean is exposed due to loss of ice, it absorbs more sunlight and gets warmer. This makes it less likely for sea ice to form even when the air is well below freezing.

Develop Models 🖎 On the image provided, draw and label a cycle diagram for the feedback that is occurring in the Arctic among ice, liquid seawater, atmosphere, and solar energy.

Sea Ice

Arctic Sea Ice

Historically in the Arctic, winter brought virtually endless nights and frigid air that could freeze seawater. In summer, much of the sea ice melted as the days grew longer and temperatures rose. Today, more ice is melting than ever before. The total area of Arctic sea ice has changed in recent years as the globe has warmed. The graph shows the amount of sea ice found in the Arctic Ocean for the following years: 1986, 1996, 2006, and 2016.

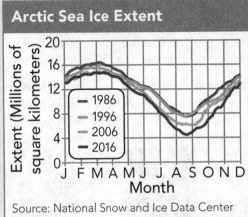

Arctic Sea Ice Extent

Source: National Snow and Ice Data Center

1. **Interpret a Line Graph** What is the trend in the data?

   ....

2. **Interpret a Line Graph** What was the lowest extent of sea ice in the data, and when did it occur?

   ....

3. **Predict** What will happen to the extent of sea ice in the Arctic if temperatures continue to rise? Incorporate what you know about "feedback" into your prediction.

   ....

   ....

   ....

Interacting Spheres
An event in one sphere can affect another, which in turn can affect another. For example, Greenland is losing about 250 billion tons of ice each year. As the massive ice sheet thins, the weight of the ice decreases. As a result, in some parts of Greenland, the land is rising about 1.0 cm per year. How can this happen? Earth's rocky outer layer is floating on a denser layer of rock below the crust.

A landmass that gets heavier by gaining more water or other material will "sink," while a landmass that gets lighter by losing material will rise. It's like a boat in the water with its cargo off-loaded, as shown in **Figure 4**. As containers are removed, there's less mass on the boat. This causes the boat to sit higher in the water because it is more buoyant.

INTERACTIVITY

Examine thermal energy and the cycling of matter in Earth's spheres.

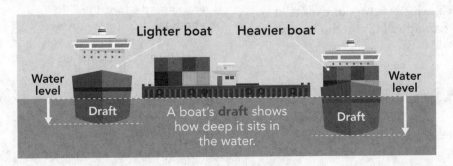

Lighter boat   Heavier boat

Water level   Water level

Draft   Draft

A boat's **draft** shows how deep it sits in the water.

Buoyancy of Landmasses
Figure 4 A landmass can rise and sit higher on Earth's surface if it sheds a lot of mass, just like a boat floating on water.

☑ LESSON 1 Check

MS-ESS2-1

1. **Identify** What is the term for the part of the hydrosphere that is frozen?

....

2. **Use Models** Use the rock cycle diagram below to describe how energy is involved in the cycling of matter in the geosphere.

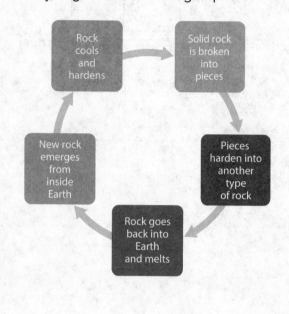

....
....
....
....

3. **Cause and Effect** During the water cycle, water evaporates, rises into the atmosphere, and eventually falls back to Earth's surface as precipitation. What is the original source of energy that produces these changes?

....
....
....
....

4. **Describe** Give an example of the hydrosphere interacting with the geosphere.

....
....
....
....
....

5. **Connect to the Environment** Give an example of how changes in the cryosphere affect the biosphere.

....
....
....
....

Quest CHECK-IN

In this lesson, you learned about the different spheres that make up Earth. You also learned how these spheres affect and shape each other, and how feedback within or between spheres produces stability or change.

Evaluate What are three ways in which factors or events in the atmosphere could increase the damage of fire in the biosphere?

....
....
....
....

 INTERACTIVITY

Fire and Earth's Spheres

Go online to trace how the forest fire started and discover factors that can start and spread a forest fire. Think about the flow of energy as the fire spreads and how you might use this information in your presentation.

MS-ESS2-1, MS-ESS2-4

When the ICE MELTS

Florida, a semi-tropical paradise far from the northern latitudes, might seem to have nothing to do with Greenland, the island of ice between the Atlantic and Arctic Oceans. But Florida is a coastal state with one of the largest populations in the United States.

And if you live near the coast, then you'll definitely want to pay attention to what's happening in Greenland. About 82 percent of Greenland is covered by an ice sheet. But in recent years, this ice sheet has been melting at an advanced rate due to warming global temperatures. When ice on land melts and runs into the ocean, it has the potential to raise sea levels around the world.

Sea levels have risen at an average rate of 1.5 cm every year for the last century. But during the last 25 years, that rate has doubled, mostly as a result of ice melting in Greenland and Antarctica.

Higher sea levels threaten infrastructure, such as roadways or utility lines, as well as lives and property. The higher the sea level, the more vulnerable Florida is to deadly storms and coastal flooding. Government officials and scientists from a variety of fields are working together to create and implement protection measures to deal with potential problems in the future.

MY COMMUNITY

How would you deal with the problem of rising sea levels? Go online to research what Florida or another coastal state is doing to protect its coastline from the encroaching ocean.

If the entire ice sheet on Greenland melted, sea levels would rise about 7 meters.

LESSON 2
Surface Features in the Geosphere

Guiding Questions

- What are the different landforms found on Earth?
- What forces and energy make the different landforms?
- What are the various ways to model landforms?

Connections

Literacy Write Explanatory Texts

Math Analyze Quantitative Relationships

MS-ESS2-1

Vocabulary

topography
landform
mountain
coastline
dune
river
delta
surveying

Academic Vocabulary

model

 VOCABULARY APP

Practice vocabulary on a mobile device.

 **CONNECTION**

Think about how the geosphere interacts with the atmosphere and biosphere.

Connect It

🖊 **Circle the places of high elevation in the Western and Eastern United States. What other features do you notice on the map?**

Make Observations What observations can you make about the elevations of the coasts and center of the United States?

....

....

Apply Scientific Reasoning Do you think other countries around the world also have a variety of land elevations? Explain.

....

....

Topography of the Geosphere

If you drove across the United States, you would observe many changes in topography, as shown in **Figure 1**. **Topography** (tuh PAWG ruh fee) is the shape of the land. Land can be described using elevation, relief, and landforms.

The height of a point above sea level on Earth's surface is its elevation. California has the lowest and highest points of elevation in the contiguous United States. The lowest point, found at Badwater Basin in Death Valley, is 86 meters below sea level. The highest elevation is Mount Whitney at 4,418 meters. The difference in elevation between the highest and lowest points of an area is its relief. An area's relief is the result of the different landforms found there. **Landforms** are features such as coastlines, dunes, and mountains. Different landforms have different combinations of elevation and relief.

☑ **READING CHECK** **Determine Central Ideas** Explain the three ways that land can be described.

....

....

....

....

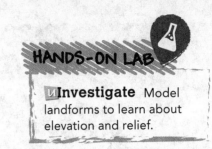

HANDS-ON LAB

ᵁ**Investigate** Model landforms to learn about elevation and relief.

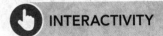

INTERACTIVITY

Think about landforms that can be found in Florida.

Relief Map

Figure 1 The United States has many different land features such as mountains, rivers, and plains.

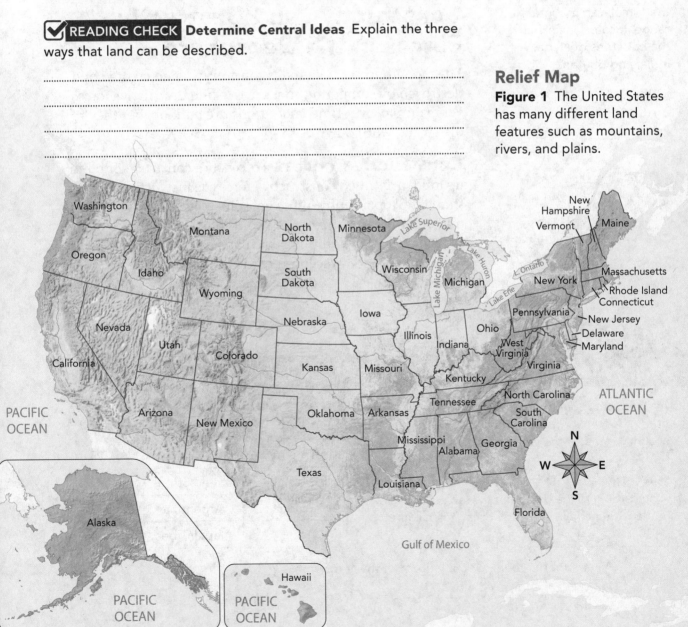

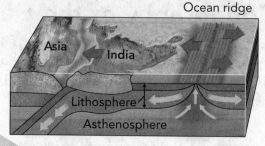

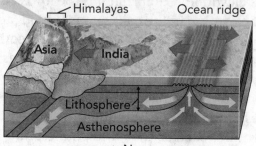

Ocean ridge

Asia India

Lithosphere
Asthenosphere

Himalayas   Ocean ridge

Asia   India

Lithosphere
Asthenosphere

←N

Plates Collide

Figure 2 India was pushed against Asia, which caused the formation of the Himalayan mountain range, located mainly in the countries of Nepal, India, and Bhutan.

Constructive and Destructive Forces in the Geosphere

The topography of the land is constantly being created and destroyed by competing constructive and destructive forces. For example, over time, mountains are built up, but they're also being worn down.

Constructive Forces Forces that construct, or build up land, are called constructive forces. Constructive forces shape the topography in the geosphere by creating mountains and other huge landmasses. The Himalayan mountain range in Asia formed over millions of years, as India collided with Asia and pushed up sections of the ocean floor, as shown in **Figure 2**.

Math Toolbox

Tallest Mountains

As the plates continue to push against each other, the Himalayas are still rising to new heights. Mount Everest is the world's tallest mountain.

Mountain	Location	Height (meters)
Kilimanjaro	Tanzania	5,895
Denali	United States	6,190
Aconcagua	Argentina	6,962
Everest	Nepal/Tibet	8,850

1. **Analyze Quantitative Relationships** According to the data from the table, about how many times taller is Everest than Kilimanjaro?

....

2. **Infer** What might account for the heights of these mountains?

....

A volcano erupts.

....

The eruption sends ash and gases into the air.

....

Lava and ash flow down into the surrounding habitats.

....

Mudflows form when ash and other volcanic material mix with water.

....

Destructive Forces The Himalayas were formed because land was built up, but there are destructive forces that also change Earth's topography. For example, rain, wind, ice, and fire destroy and wear away landmasses and affect the geosphere.

The geosphere, atmosphere, hydrosphere, and biosphere interact with each other to affect Earth. For example, an event that occurs in the geosphere, such as the volcano in **Figure 3**, will change the other spheres. A volcano releases ash and gases into the atmosphere and volcanic material into the hydrosphere. Initially, the volcanic material and gases may kill organisms in the biosphere. However, ash can enrich the soil and give new plants more nutrients. Hardened lava may cut off old river channels but form a new lake.

✓ READING CHECK **Integrate With Visuals** Refer to the art in **Figure 2** that shows the collision of India with Asia. How did changes in the geosphere cause the Himalayas to form?

....

....

A Volcano Changes Everything

Figure 3 ✏ A volcano causes changes in four spheres. Record which sphere is affected during each step in an eruption.

Literacy Connection

Write Explanatory Texts As you read, number the steps in which an erupting volcano starts the cycle of change. Then, think about a forest fire. Explain how a fire would affect the geosphere, atmosphere, hydrosphere, and biosphere.

189

Exploring Earth's Surface

There are a variety of landforms on Earth because Earth's surface differs from place to place. In addition, landforms change over time due to constructive and destructive forces. Some landforms are snow-capped mountains, some are giant glaciers, and others are ever-changing sand dunes. **Figure 4** shows some of the landforms found on Earth.

Mountains A **mountain** is a landform with both high elevation and high relief. Mountains that are closely related in shape, structure, location, and age are called a mountain range. Different mountain ranges in one region make up a mountain system. The Rocky Mountains are a famous mountain system. Mountain ranges and mountain systems in a long, connected chain form a larger unit called a mountain belt.

Plateaus and Plains Landforms that have high elevation and low relief are called plateaus. Streams and rivers may cut into the plateau's surface. Landforms that have low elevation and low relief are called plains. A plain that lies along a seacoast is called a coastal plain. In North America, the Atlantic coastal plain extends from Florida all the way up to Cape Cod in Massachusetts.

Many Landforms

Figure 4 ✏ There are so many different landforms, but they are all connected. Choose two landforms. Draw a line from one landform to another and tell how they are connected to each other.

....

....

....

....

....

Plateau

Lake

Plain

Dune

Coastlines The boundary between the land and the ocean or a lake is the **coastline**. Among the 50 states, the mainland of Alaska has the longest coastline at 10,686 kilometers. The mainland of Florida has the second longest coastline, measuring 2,170 kilometers.

Dunes The land that extends from a coastline may be rocky cliffs, sandy beaches, or dunes. A **dune** is a hill of sand piled up by the wind. Dunes in the coastal regions are parallel to the coastline and protect the land from ocean waves.

Rivers and Deltas A **river** is a natural stream of water that flows into another body of water such as an ocean, lake, or another river. When a river reaches an ocean, the water slows and sand, clay, and sediment in the water sink. When the sediment builds up, it makes a landform called a **delta**. In Florida, the Apalachicola River supplies sand to St. Vincent's Island, a barrier island and wildlife refuge.

☑ READING CHECK **Compare and Contrast** How are dunes and deltas similar and different?

....

....

Mountain

Glacier

River

Plain

Delta

Coastline

191

Academic Vocabulary

Making a model of something helps you understand how things work. You can make a model using many different materials. Describe a model you have made and the materials you used.

....

....

....

Modeling Landforms

Before modern technology, scientists and mapmakers studied the land and drew maps by hand. They spent hundreds of hours walking over landforms or sailing along coastlines to **model** what they saw. Then people used a process called surveying. In **surveying**, mapmakers determine distances and elevations using instruments and the principles of geometry. Today, people use computers to create topographic and other maps from aerial photography and satellite imagery.

Topographic Maps Imagine that you are in a plane flying high above the United States. How does it look? A topographic map portrays the surface features of an area as if being viewed from above. Topographic maps provide accurate information on the elevation, relief, and slope of the ground, as shown in **Figure 5**.

Contour Lines Topographic maps have contour lines to show elevation, relief, and slope. A contour line connects points of equal elevation. Contour lines also show how steep or gradual a slope is. Contour lines that are far apart represent flat areas or areas with gradual slopes. Lines that are close together represent areas with steep slopes.

The change in elevation from one contour line to the next is called a contour interval. On a given map, the contour interval is always consistent. Every fifth contour line is known as an index contour. These lines are darker and heavier than the other lines.

Topographic Map of Mt. Grinnell

Figure 5 The contour lines on the map can be used to determine a feature's elevation. Use the contour lines to determine the elevation of Mt. Grinnell.

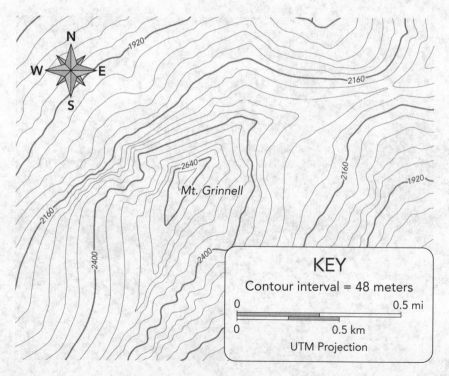

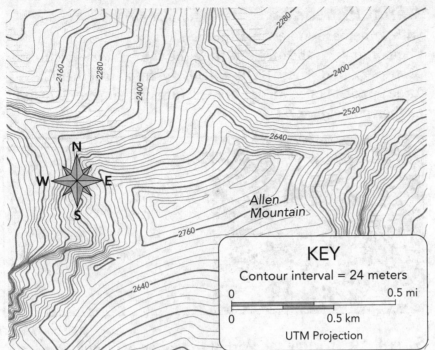

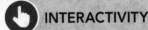

KEY

Contour interval = 24 meters

0   0.5 mi

0   0.5 km

UTM Projection

Shape of Contour Lines

Figure 6 🖉 The area around Allen Mountain has many features. Circle the hilltops. Mark the steepest slopes with an *X*.

INTERACTIVITY

Investigate how constructive and destructive forces affect Earth's landforms.

Reading a Topographic Map In the United States, the scale of many topographic maps is 1 centimeter on the map for every 0.24 kilometers on the ground. This scale allows mapmakers to show land features such as rivers and coastlines. Large human-made structures, such as airports and highways, appear as outlines, while small structures, such as houses, are represented with symbols.

To find the elevation of a feature on the map in **Figure 6**, begin at an index contour line and count the number of lines up or down the feature. The shape of contour lines also provides information. V-shaped contour lines pointing away from a summit indicate a ridge line. V-shaped contour lines pointing toward a summit indicate a valley. A contour line that forms a closed loop indicates a hilltop. A closed loop with dashes inside indicates a depression, or hollow in the ground.

Model It 🖉

A map is a way to model Earth. What features are modeled by the topographic map in **Figure 6**?

Develop Models 🖉 Use the topographic map to create a drawing of the features it represents. Use the contour lines to help determine whether the area has a steep or gradual elevation. Be sure to label your illustration with the elevation of each feature.

193

Aerial Photography

When photographs are taken with cameras mounted in airplanes, it is called aerial photography. As the airplane flies, the camera takes pictures of strips of land. These picture strips are fitted together like a large puzzle to form an accurate picture of a large area of land, as shown in **Figure 7**.

Aerial Photograph

Figure 7 🖊 Mapmakers use aerial photographs such as this one to create a map. Use the photo to make a street map of the neighborhood in the photograph. Be sure to add your own street names.

Satellite Imagery

With the creation of computers, mapping has become easier and more accurate. Mapmakers can make maps of Earth using computers that interpret satellite data. Mapping satellites use electronic devices to collect data about the land surface. Pictures of the surface based on these data are called satellite images. These images are made up of pixels, and each pixel has information about the color and brightness of a part of Earth's surface, as shown in **Figure 8**.

Satellites orbit Earth collecting and storing data. Then, computers use the data to create images. Satellite images show details including plants, soil, rock, water, snow, and ice that cover Earth's surface.

Satellite Image of North America

Figure 8 🖊 Scientists and mapmakers identify special features on an image by their color and shape. For example, forests appear green, water may be blue or black, and snow is white. Draw an *X* to show where your state is.

Interpret Photos Write about the features you see in the satellite image.

....

....

....

....

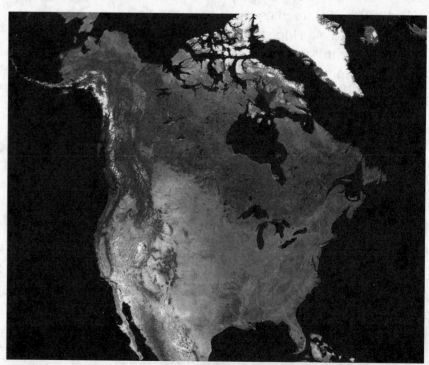

GPS The Global Positioning System, or GPS, is a navigational system that uses satellite signals to fix the location of a radio receiver on Earth. GPS helps anyone with a receiver locate his or her position anywhere on or above Earth.

You may have used GPS on a phone or in a car to navigate, but do you know how it works? Twenty-four orbiting satellites continuously send their current location and time to a GPS receiver on Earth. A user's receiver, such as a phone, needs information from at least three satellites to determine its location.

GIS A Geographic Information System, or GIS, is a system of computer hardware and software used to produce interactive maps. GIS uses GPS, satellite images, statistics about an area, and other maps to display and analyze geographic data.

The different types of information stored in a GIS are called data layers. The data layers help scientists and city planners to solve problems by understanding patterns, relationships, and trends. **Figure 9** shows how GIS could be used to determine a neighborhood's flood risk by analyzing data layers about the location of a river, its floodplain boundary, and the streets in a neighborhood.

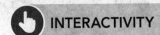

INTERACTIVITY

Explore how maps can help solve problems.

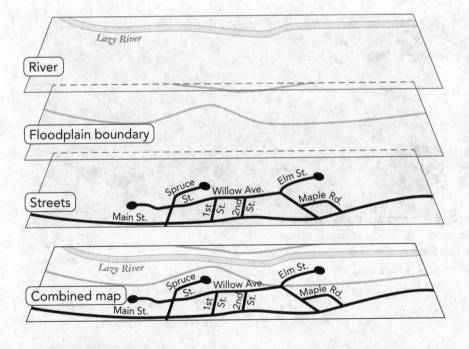

GIS Map

Figure 9 ✏️ A GIS map has many data layers that can be used to analyze how different systems interact. Shade in the floodplain on the combined map. Where should a city planner avoid building houses? Why?

....

....

☑️ **READING CHECK** **Write Explanatory Texts** Explain ways in which GPS and GIS are more useful than a topographic map.

....

....

....

MS-ESS2-1

1. Define What is topography?

....

....

....

....

2. Identify A mountain is a landform with both

high .... and high ....

3. Interpret a Diagram ✏ Match each set of contour lines to the correct drawing.

4. Compare and Contrast Compare and contrast constructive and destructive forces.

....

....

....

....

....

5. Infer The owner of a car wash wants to open a new location in a different neighborhood. How could the owner use GIS to figure out where to put the new car wash? Explain what information should be included in the data layers.

....

....

....

....

6. Apply Concepts Explain how water can be both a destructive and constructive force.

....

....

....

....

Quest CHECK-IN

In this lesson, you learned about the topography of the geosphere and the various landforms. You learned how different forces shape these landforms. You also discovered how scientists model landforms to better understand the topography.

Evaluate How might a fire have a destructive effect on the geosphere?

....

....

....

🖑 INTERACTIVITY

Disrupting the Geosphere

Go online to determine how the interactions among the geosphere, atmosphere, and biosphere affect the course of the forest fire and the damage it causes.

A DARING BRIDGE

Do you know how to build a bridge with some tough budget and environmental constraints? You engineer it! Plans for the Bixby Bridge in California show us how.

The Challenge: To design a cost-effective bridge across a canyon that withstands the elements.

Phenomenon Every winter, people in Big Sur, California, were trapped. Bad weather made the Old Coast Road impossible to travel. That changed in the 1930s when the state built a bridge across the canyon cut by Bixby Creek.

In designing the bridge, engineers weighed its impact on the environment. Then they considered costs and appearance. The country had entered the Great Depression. Funds were scarce, and a steel bridge would be costly. Also, a steel bridge so close to the Pacific Ocean would rust.

Finally, the engineers decided on an uncovered arch bridge 713 feet long and more than 260 feet above the canyon floor. They used concrete—45,000 sacks of it. Its appearance fit better alongside the area's stone cliffs. This design was also much less expensive. The Bixby Bridge reached completion on time and under budget—a success for any building project!

INTERACTIVITY

Learn how engineers considered each sphere when building the Bixby Bridge.

During the 1930s and 1940s, the lack of good roads and bridges could sometimes make traveling by car impossible.

DESIGN CHALLENGE Can you design a bridge? Go to the Engineering Design Notebook to find out!

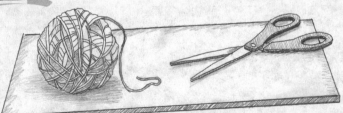

3 The Hydrosphere

Guiding Questions

- Where and in what features is water found on Earth?
- How does water cycle through Earth's systems?

Connection

Literacy Determine Central Ideas

MS-ESS2-4

Vocabulary

water cycle
evaporation
transpiration
condensation
precipitation
watershed
aquifer
well

Academic Vocabulary

process

 VOCABULARY APP

Practice vocabulary on a mobile device.

Quest CONNECTION

Think about how the hydrosphere interacts with the other spheres and how fire affects them all.

Connect It!

✎ **Circle the different areas of water in this photo.**

Infer Why is water important to human beings?

....

....

Apply Scientific Reasoning Why is water important to our planet?

....

....

....

The Water Cycle

Without water, life as we know it would not exist. As shown in **Figure 1**, water is an important characteristic of Earth. All living things require water to live. Fortunately, Earth has its own built-in water recycling system: the water cycle.

The **water cycle** is the continuous process by which water moves from Earth's surface to the atmosphere and back again. This movement is driven by energy from the sun and by gravity. In the water cycle, water moves through the geosphere, the biosphere, the hydrosphere, and the atmosphere.

Evaporation The sun heats up the surface of bodies of water and causes water molecules to undergo a change. The process by which molecules at the surface of a liquid absorb enough energy to change to a gas is called **evaporation**. Water constantly evaporates from the surfaces of bodies of water.

Elements of the geosphere and biosphere can also add water vapor to the atmosphere. Water evaporates from soil in the geosphere. Animals in the biosphere release water vapor as they breathe. Water even evaporates from your skin.

Plants also play a role in this step of the water cycle. Plants draw in water from the soil through their roots. Eventually the water vapor is given off through the leaves in a process called **transpiration**.

INTERACTIVITY

Discuss ways you depend on the hydrosphere.

Importance of Water
Figure 1 Water makes life on Earth possible.

The Water Cycle

Figure 2 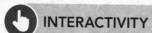 This diagram shows some of the major processes that make up the water cycle. Draw arrows to show the way that water moves through the cycle. Then, in the blank spaces, write the process that is at work.

👆 **INTERACTIVITY**

Review all of the processes of the water cycle.

Literacy Connection

Determine Central Ideas As you read, underline the central idea of each paragraph. Note how this idea is developed through examples and details.

Condensation After a water molecule evaporates into the atmosphere, warm air carries the water molecule upward. **Condensation** is the process by which water vapor becomes liquid water. As water vapor rises into the colder air, some water vapor cools and condenses into liquid or solid water. Droplets of liquid water and ice crystals collect around solid particles in the air, forming clouds. Eventually, this results in precipitation.

Precipitation As more water vapor condenses, the water droplets and ice crystals grow larger. Eventually, they become so heavy that gravity causes them to fall back to Earth in the form of precipitation. Water that forms in clouds and falls to Earth as rain, snow, hail, or sleet is called **precipitation**. Once it falls, it collects in rivers, lakes, and streams. It is also absorbed by the soil in the geosphere. Precipitation is the source of almost all fresh water on and below Earth's surface.

For millions of years, the total amount of water cycling through the Earth's system has remained fairly constant—the rates of evaporation and precipitation are balanced. That means that the water you use today is the same water that your ancestors used.

☑ **READING CHECK** **Draw Evidence** The biosphere interacts with the hydrosphere within the water cycle. Cite one example of that interaction.

....

....

....

Distribution of Earth's Water

Most of the water in the hydrosphere—roughly 97 percent—is salt water found mostly in the ocean. Only 3 percent is fresh water, as shown in **Figure 3**.

Fresh Water Of the 3 percent that is fresh water, about two-thirds is frozen in huge masses of ice near the North and South poles. Much of Earth's fresh water is frozen into thickened ice masses called glaciers. Massive glacial ice sheets cover most of Greenland and Antarctica.

About a third of Earth's fresh water is underground. A tiny fraction of fresh water occurs in lakes and rivers. An even tinier fraction is found in the atmosphere, most of it in the form of invisible water vapor, the gaseous form of water.

Most precipitation falls directly into the ocean. Of the precipitation that falls on land, most evaporates. A small amount of the remaining water runs off the surface into streams and lakes in a **process** called runoff, but most of it seeps into the ground. After a long time, this groundwater eventually comes to the surface and evaporates again.

Salt Water Atlantic, Indian, Pacific, and Arctic are the names for the different parts of the ocean. The Pacific Ocean is the largest, covering an area greater than all the land on Earth. Smaller saltwater bodies are called seas. Seas are generally inland and landlocked. A small percentage of Earth's salt water is found in some saline lakes.

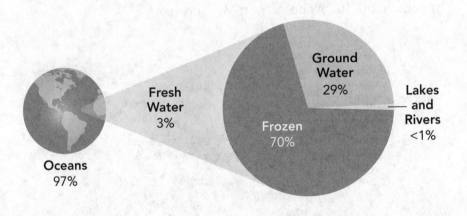

Oceans 97%

Fresh Water 3%

Frozen 70%

Ground Water 29%

Lakes and Rivers <1%

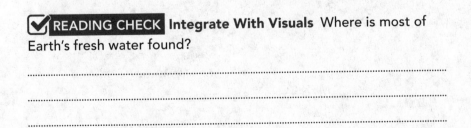

READING CHECK **Integrate With Visuals** Where is most of Earth's fresh water found?

....

....

HANDS-ON LAB

Investigate Model the distribution of water on Earth.

Academic Vocabulary

A process is a series of actions or operations leading toward a particular result. List some processes you are familiar with in your daily life.

....

....

....

....

Water Resources

Figure 3 Most of the water on Earth is salt water in the ocean.

Reflect NASA satellite data show that the ice sheets are melting at a rate of about 350 billion tons of ice each year, which is far above historic averages. What do you think is causing this to happen? What effect would this increased amount of ice melt have on the ocean?

The Mississippi River

Figure 4 Many tributaries contribute to the Mississippi River.

▶ **VIDEO**

Discover how an aquaculture manager helps meet the needs of people while protecting the habitats of living things.

Watersheds

Figure 5 ✏ This map shows the watersheds of some large rivers in the United States. Draw a line on the map to represent the Great Divide. Use arrows to show the direction in which the water flows on each side of the divide.

Surface Water

Surface water includes all the water found on the surface of Earth. The ocean, rivers, lakes, and ponds are all part of the surface water in the hydrosphere.

Rivers Even large rivers, such as the Mississippi River or St. Johns River, start as a trickle of water that originates from a source—an underground stream, runoff from rain, or melting snow or ice. Gravity causes these tiny streams to flow downhill. These small streams join others to form a larger stream. Larger streams join others to form a river that flows into the ocean. The streams and smaller rivers that feed into a main river are called tributaries. A river and all the tributaries that flow into it make up a river system, as shown in **Figure 4**.

Watersheds The land area that supplies water to a river system is called a **watershed**. When rivers join another river system, the areas they drain become part of the largest river's watershed. **Figure 5** shows the major watersheds that cover the United States.

Divides Watersheds stay separated from each other by a ridge of land called a divide. Streams on each side of the divide flow in different directions. The Great Divide, the longest divide in North America, follows the Rocky Mountains. West of this divide, water flows toward the Pacific Ocean. Some water stays in the Great Basin between the Rocky and Sierra Nevada Mountains. East of the divide, water flows toward the Mississippi River and into the Gulf of Mexico, joining rivers flowing from the Appalachian Mountains.

Ponds and Lakes

Ponds and lakes form when water collects in hollows and low-lying areas of land. Unlike streams and rivers, ponds and lakes contain mostly still water. Ponds are smaller and shallower than lakes. Like other bodies of water, lakes and ponds are supplied by rainfall, melting snow and ice, and runoff. Some are fed by rivers or groundwater.

Lakes, such as the ones in **Figure 6**, form through several natural processes. When a river bends, a new channel may form, cutting off a loop to form an oxbow lake. Some lakes, such as the Great Lakes, formed in depressions created by ice sheets that melted at the end of the Ice Age. Other lakes were created by movements of Earth's crust that formed long, deep valleys called rift valleys. Lakes can also form in the empty craters of volcanoes.

> ☑ **READING CHECK** **Summarize** How do river systems, watersheds, and divides interact?
>
> ....
> ....
> ....
> ....
> ....
> ....

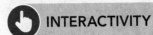
INTERACTIVITY

Discover the best site on which to locate a fish farm.

Lakes in Mountains
Figure 6 Lakes are important because they hold some of Earth's fresh water.

Plan It !

Building a Reservoir

Research 🖉 A reservoir is a storage space for water. Consider why people build reservoirs. Do some research to help you plan how to build a reservoir in your region of the country. Use the space provided to draw a diagram showing the features of your reservoir. Write out the steps of your plan below.

....
....
....
....

Groundwater

Figure 7 ✏ This diagram shows how water travels underground. Add arrows to identify the paths that water takes.

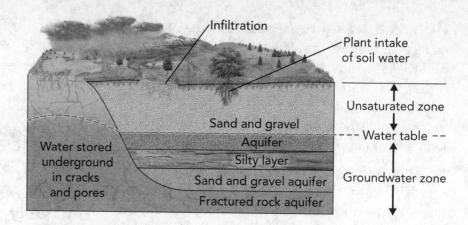

Infiltration

Plant intake of soil water

Unsaturated zone

Water table

Groundwater zone

Sand and gravel
Aquifer
Silty layer
Sand and gravel aquifer
Fractured rock aquifer

Water stored underground in cracks and pores

INTERACTIVITY

Explore how the Floridan aquifer formed and describe its importance today.

VIDEO

Learn more about the role of groundwater in the water cycle.

Groundwater

A large portion of fresh water in the hydrosphere is underground, as shown in **Figure 7**. Water that fills the cracks and spaces in soil and rock layers is called groundwater. Far more fresh water is located underground than in all of Earth's rivers and lakes.

Aquifers As precipitation falls to Earth, it moves through the soil and the small spaces within underground rock layers. These layers contain air as well as water, so they are not saturated, or filled, with water. This top layer is called the unsaturated zone.

Eventually, the water reaches a level where the openings in the layers are filled with water, or saturated. The upper level of the saturated zone is called the water table. Below the saturated zone there are layers of rock that hold water called **aquifers**.

Aquifers range in size from a small patch to an area the size of several states. Aquifers and other groundwater sources provide 55 percent of the drinking water for the United States. In rural areas, aquifers provide as much as 99 percent of the water used.

Wells People can get groundwater from an aquifer by digging a well that reaches below the water table. A **well** is a hole sunk into the earth to reach a supply of water. Long ago, people dug wells by hand and used buckets to bring up the water. Today, most wells are created with drilling equipment and the water is retrieved using mechanical pumps that run on electricity.

✓ READING CHECK **Determine Central Ideas** What is an aquifer?

....

....

....

....

Exploring the Ocean

There are several ways that the ocean is unique in the hydrosphere. The water in Earth's ocean varies in salinity, temperature, and depth.

Salinity The total amount of dissolved salts in a sample of water is the salinity. Near the ocean's surface, rain, snow, and melting ice add fresh water, lowering the salinity. Evaporation, on the other hand, increases salinity. Salinity is also higher near the poles because the forming of sea ice leaves some salt behind in the seawater.

Salinity affects ocean water in different ways. For instance, fresh water freezes at 0°C but ocean water freezes at about –1.9°C because the salt interferes with the formation of ice. Salt water also has a higher density than fresh water. Therefore, seawater lifts, or buoys up, less dense objects floating in it.

Temperature The broad surface of the ocean absorbs energy from the sun. Temperatures at the surface of the ocean vary with location and the seasons. Near the equator, surface ocean temperatures often reach 25°C, about room temperature. The temperatures drop as you travel away from the equator.

Depth The ocean is very deep—3.8 kilometers deep on average. That's more than twice as deep as the Grand Canyon. As you descend through the ocean, the water temperature decreases. Water pressure, the force exerted by the weight of water, increases by 1 bar, the air pressure at sea level, with each 10 meters of depth. Use **Figure 8** to explore temperature, pressure, and depth.

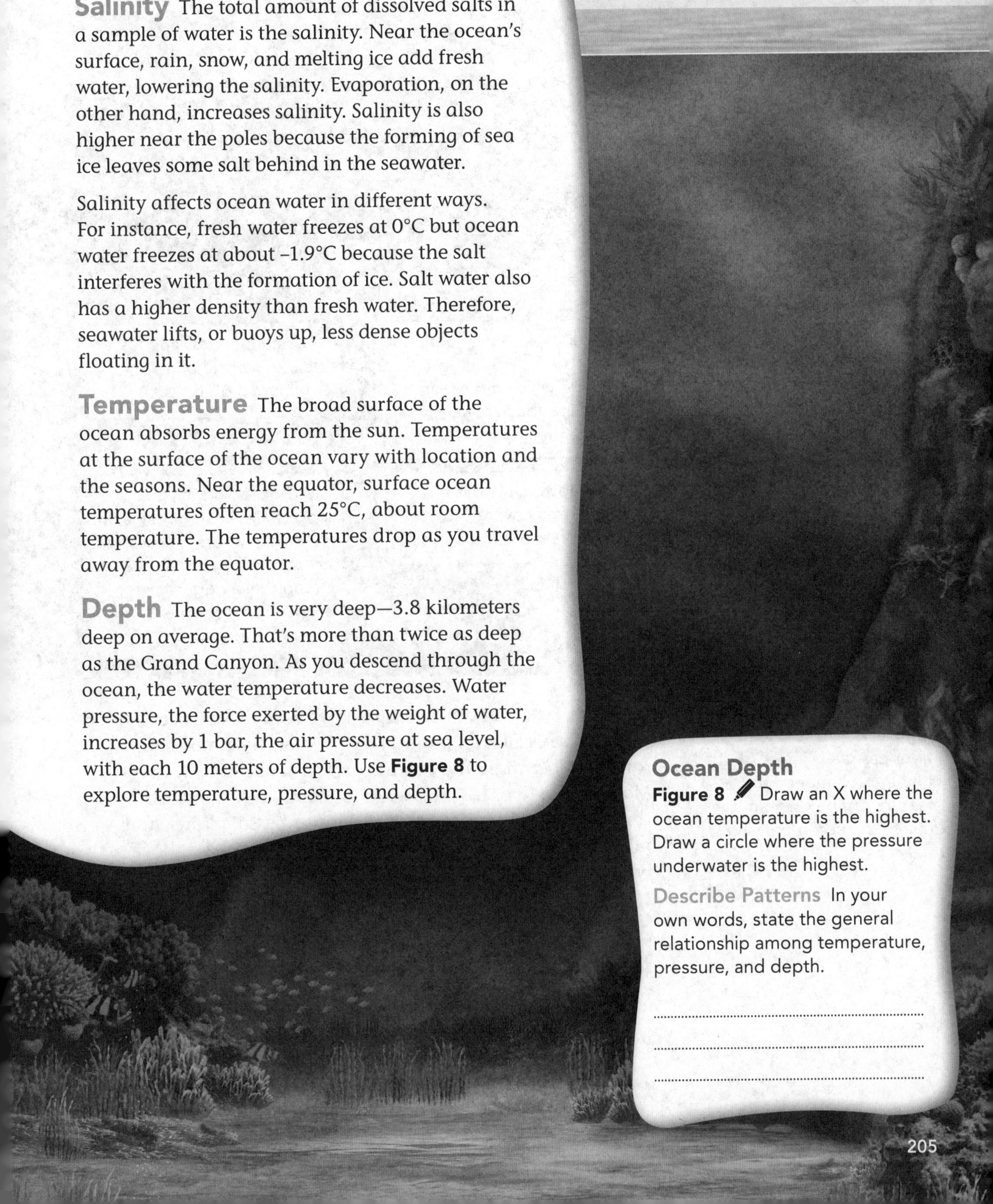

Ocean Depth

Figure 8 ✎ Draw an X where the ocean temperature is the highest. Draw a circle where the pressure underwater is the highest.

Describe Patterns In your own words, state the general relationship among temperature, pressure, and depth.

....

....

....

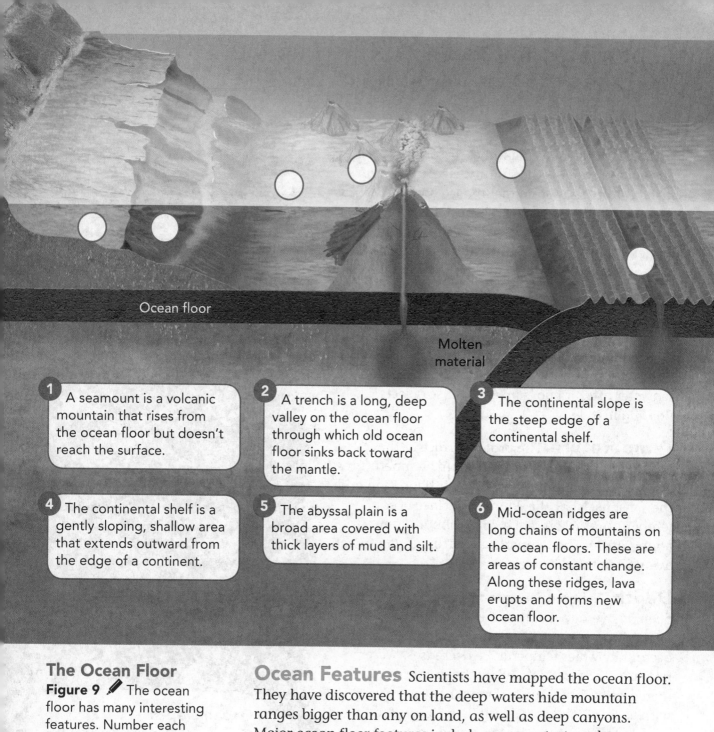

Ocean floor

Molten
material

1 A seamount is a volcanic mountain that rises from the ocean floor but doesn't reach the surface.

2 A trench is a long, deep valley on the ocean floor through which old ocean floor sinks back toward the mantle.

3 The continental slope is the steep edge of a continental shelf.

4 The continental shelf is a gently sloping, shallow area that extends outward from the edge of a continent.

5 The abyssal plain is a broad area covered with thick layers of mud and silt.

6 Mid-ocean ridges are long chains of mountains on the ocean floors. These are areas of constant change. Along these ridges, lava erupts and forms new ocean floor.

The Ocean Floor

Figure 9 ✏ The ocean floor has many interesting features. Number each feature on the diagram to match the accompanying descriptions.

Ocean Features Scientists have mapped the ocean floor. They have discovered that the deep waters hide mountain ranges bigger than any on land, as well as deep canyons. Major ocean floor features include seamounts, trenches, continental shelves, continental slopes, abyssal plains, and mid-ocean ridges. These features, shown in **Figure 9**, have all been formed by the interaction of Earth's plates.

☑ **READING CHECK** **Draw Conclusions** How do the temperature and pressure most likely differ at the top of a seamount and the bottom of a trench?

....

....

....

....

1. **Identify** What are the important processes in the water cycle?

....

....

....

2. **Describe** What are the components of a river system?

....

....

....

....

3. **Summarize** What are the main features of the ocean floor?

....

....

....

....

....

....

4. **Infer** How does the interaction between the hydrosphere and the geosphere affect the supply of drinking water?

....

....

....

....

....

....

5. **Compare and Contrast** ✏ Create a Venn diagram comparing fresh water and salt water.

Quest CHECK-IN

In this lesson, you learned how the water of the hydrosphere is cycled and how it interacts with the other spheres. You also learned about the characteristics of each portion of the hydrosphere, including surface water, ocean water, and groundwater.

Evaluate How might a natural disaster, such as a forest fire, affect the elements of the hydrosphere?

....

....

....

....

☞ INTERACTIVITY

Impact on the Hydrosphere

Go online to examine how the hydrosphere interacts with other spheres and the effect of a forest fire on those interactions. Then review the data and finalize your predictions about the fire's damage.

1989

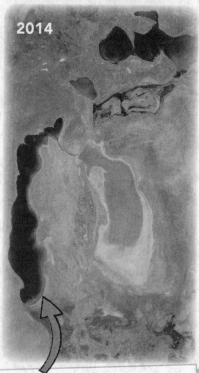

2014

The remaining areas of water now cover only 10 to 25 percent of the former surface area. The volume of water has been reduced by 90 percent.

The CASE of the
Shrinking Sea

The Aral Sea in Central Asia was once the fourth largest lake in the world, and it supported many fisheries and shipping lines. Bordered by the countries of Uzbekistan and Kazakhstan, the lake is fed by water from melting glaciers and the rivers of the Aral Sea Basin, which flow from five countries in the region.

But the Aral Sea has been rapidly disappearing since the 1960s. As the population in the area grew to more than 60 million, people diverted major rivers flowing into the lake for agricultural and industrial use. However, up to one quarter of this diverted water was wasted due to poor management and planning. This wasted water was either absorbed by dry desert soil surrounding the lake or flowed into unused run-off ditches. Additionally, the rate of evaporation from the Aral Sea has increased, contributing to its disappearance.

In the past 50 years, the water levels have dropped so rapidly that the lake has fragmented into several smaller bodies of water separated by barren desert in between.

Effects of a Disappearing Sea

As the lake evaporates and shrinks, its salinity increases. Between the 1960s and the 1980s, the salt concentration of the Aral Sea increased dramatically, killing wildlife and destroying the fishing trade. The concentration of salt is so high in some areas that efforts to reintroduce fish have failed. Concentrated salt, minerals, and pollutants from the now-exposed sea floor are whipped into sandstorms that also threaten the health of the human population in the area.

To improve the conditions in the area, some water management efforts started in the 1990s. Then, in 2005, the Kok-Aral Dam was built to keep water from the northern fragment from flowing to the southern fragment. The dam was a success and the North Aral Sea rose more than 3 meters in the first year. Surveyors hope that in the future the water levels in the north will rise to the point that they can begin to let water flow to the South Aral Sea as well.

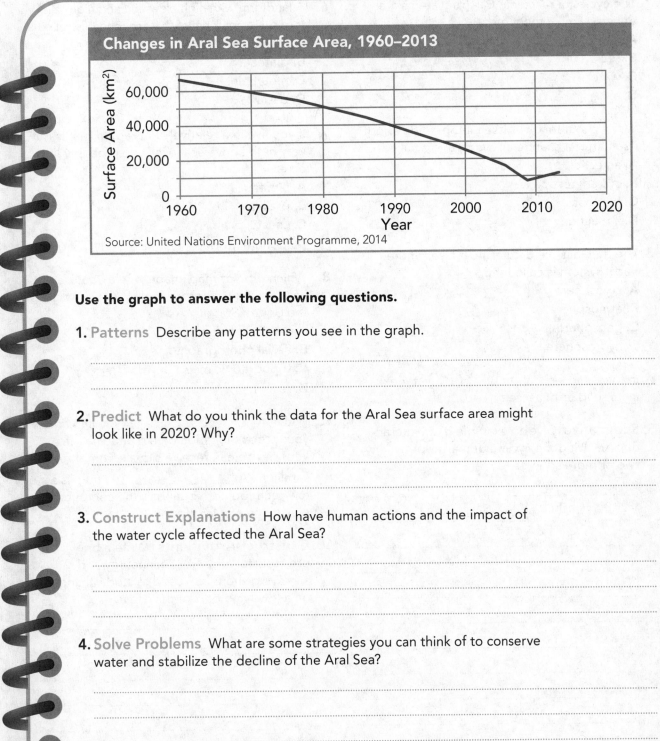

Changes in Aral Sea Surface Area, 1960–2013

Source: United Nations Environment Programme, 2014

Use the graph to answer the following questions.

1. Patterns Describe any patterns you see in the graph.

2. Predict What do you think the data for the Aral Sea surface area might look like in 2020? Why?

3. Construct Explanations How have human actions and the impact of the water cycle affected the Aral Sea?

4. Solve Problems What are some strategies you can think of to conserve water and stabilize the decline of the Aral Sea?

☑TOPIC 5 Review and Assess

① Matter and Energy in Earth's System

MS-ESS2-1

1. The cycles of matter in Earth's systems are driven by movement of
A. heat.
B. rock.
C. water.
D. air.

2. When a system gives itself information about itself after a change or event, this is called
A. an echo.
B. system response.
C. feedback.
D. a reaction.

3. The thin, gas-filled outermost layer of the Earth system is called the
A. cryosphere.
B. atmosphere.
C. geosphere.
D. hydrosphere.

4. In the ...., water exists in its solid form as ice.

5. Summarize Give an example of an interaction involving the cycling of matter between two or more spheres.

....
....
....
....
....
....
....
....
....

② Surface Features in the Geosphere

MS-ESS2-1

6. A landform with high elevation and high relief formed by material of the geosphere is called a
A. plain.
B. plateau.
C. mountain.
D. basin.

7. If you live in a relatively flat region that is not very high above sea level, you probably live on a
A. plateau.
B. prairie.
C. coastal plain.
D. mountaintop.

8. Which type of map image would you use if you wanted to represent plant density across the United States?
A. satellite imagery
B. aerial photography
C. topographic map
D. relief map

9. With ...., you can find your precise location on a digital map if your device can receive signals from three satellites. A .... map is a low-tech tool for visualizing the contours and elevations of a landform.

10. Construct Arguments Write a brief proposal for why GPS technology and surveying should be used to study changes on a low-lying part of the coast.

....
....
....
....
....

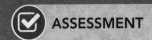

3 The Hydrosphere

MS-ESS2-4

11. Which is not a part of the hydrosphere?
A. sediment
B. pond
C. rain
D. ice

12. When ocean water reaches the poles, some of it turns to ice. Some salt is trapped between ice crystals, but most is left behind in the unfrozen seawater. This causes an increase in
A. evaporation.   B. salinity.
C. pressure.   D. temperature.

13. About 97 percent of the hydrosphere is
A. salt water in lakes, seas, and the ocean.
B. water vapor in the atmosphere.
C. fresh water in ice and snow.
D. also part of the cryosphere.

14. .... from plants and

.... from bodies
of water both add water vapor to the

....

15. In this photo, the .... is

interacting with the ....
by wearing down the rocks as the water flows.

16. Summarize Describe how groundwater is replenished.

....

....

....

....

....

17. Develop Models ✏ How might water from a lake move through the water cycle and eventually fall as rain? Draw a diagram to model the cycle.

MS-ESS2-4

Evidence-Based Assessment

Scientists have been monitoring the enormous volumes of ice at Earth's poles with curiosity and concern. In western Antarctica, the ice shelves are deteriorating. An ice shelf acts as a dam between land-based glaciers and the ocean. As a shelf crumbles into the ocean, glacial ice behind the ice shelf can flow more freely from higher elevations. The collapsing ice shelf, which floats on the ocean, does not directly contribute to sea level rise. However, scientists predict that the increased flow of glacial ice and meltwater from land will contribute to a global sea level rise of two meters by 2100.

The graph provides data about the volume of ice lost at four different glacier systems.

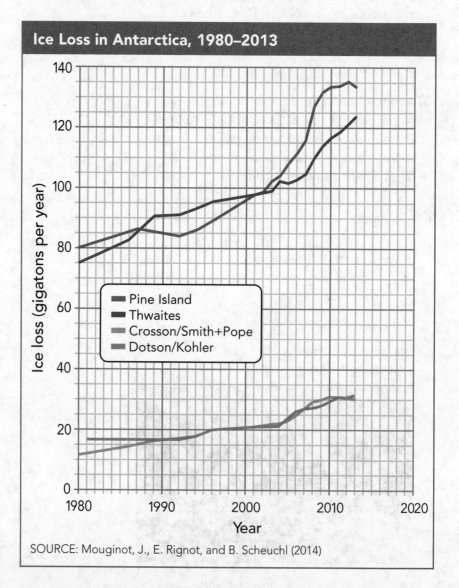

Ice Loss in Antarctica, 1980–2013

Legend:
- Pine Island
- Thwaites
- Crosson/Smith+Pope
- Dotson/Kohler

y-axis: Ice loss (gigatons per year)
x-axis: Year

SOURCE: Mouginot, J., E. Rignot, and B. Scheuchl (2014)

1. **Analyze Data** What is the overall trend in ice loss at the four locations?

A. Ice loss has been increasing at all four locations, but the rate has been getting higher since about 2000.

B. Ice loss has remained at a steady rate at all four locations.

C. Ice loss was decreasing at all four locations until 2005, when it began to increase.

D. Ice loss has been decreasing at a steady rate at all four locations.

2. **Examine Change** Which location lost the most ice in 2013? Approximately how much ice was lost from the four locations in 2013? Show your work.

....

....

....

....

....

....

....

....

....

....

3. **Apply Concepts** What role does the sun play in driving the water cycle in Antarctica?

....

....

....

....

....

....

....

....

....

4. **Construct Arguments** Average temperatures on the Antarctic Peninsula have risen 3°C over the last 50 years. If this trend continues, what effect would it have on the water cycle in Antarctica? In your answer, explain the impact on ice flows.

....

....

....

....

....

....

Quest FINDINGS

Complete the Quest!

Phenomenon Determine the best medium for presenting your findings, such as a map or a multimedia presentation.

Summarize How does a forest fire demonstrate how the different spheres of Earth interact with each other?

....

....

....

....

....

....

....

....

INTERACTIVITY

Reflect on Forest Fires

Modeling a Watershed

How can you **model** the effects of **pollution** on a watershed?

Background

Phenomenon A factory has released pollutants into a nearby river. You discovered dead fish far downstream from the factory. But the factory claims that it can't be responsible because the fish were found so far away. You have been asked to help biologists demonstrate that when contaminated water enters one part of a watershed, it can affect the entire watershed.

In this investigation, you will model the effects of pollution on surface water in a watershed and demonstrate the importance of protecting watershed areas.

(per group)

- small wooden or plastic blocks
- paper or plastic drinking cups
- newspaper
- markers
- craft sticks
- plastic CD cases
- light paper
- aluminum foil
- plastic wrap
- large pan
- water
- red food coloring
- metric ruler
- tape
- digital camera (optional)
- goggles
- apron
- gloves

Procedure

1. Use the materials provided by your teacher to design and build a model watershed for your demonstration. Use a camera or drawings to record and analyze information to show how pollution affects an entire watershed.

2. Consider the following questions before you begin planning your model:

   • How can the materials help you to model a watershed?

   • How will you form highlands in your model?

   • How can you include streams and rivers in your model?

   • How can you use food coloring to represent the effects of pollution on surface water in the watershed?

   • What are some ways that a watershed can be polluted?

3. Once you have worked out a design, draw a sketch of your model. Label the objects in your model and identify the materials you are using.

4. Write a short procedure that details the steps you will follow to model how pollution can affect surface water in a watershed.

5. Once your teacher has approved your design and procedure, carry out the investigation. If possible, use a camera to photograph your model during the investigation. Record observations about how your model represents the effects of pollution in a watershed.

HANDS-ON LAB

Demonstrate Go online for a downloadable worksheet of this lab.

Sketch Design and sketch your model here.

Observations

Analyze and Interpret Data

1. **Use Models** Describe the path that the food coloring took through your model. What does the pattern of the food coloring's path tell you about the effect of pollution on surface water in a watershed? Based on your observations and evidence, could the factory's pollution have caused the fish to die?

....

....

....

....

2. **Cause and Effect** What other human activity takes place in the watersheds that might lead to pollution?

....

....

....

3. **Identify Limitations** Compare your model to other models. How can you improve your model based on other examples? What parts of a watershed, if any, are missing from your model?

....

....

....

4. **Construct Explanations** Explain the importance of laws that restrict and punish individuals or businesses that pollute healthy watersheds. Include a description of any cause-and-effect relationships that you think scientists might observe when pollutants are introduced into a watershed area. Use your model and your observations in this lab as evidence for your answer.

....

....

....

....

....

TOPIC
6

Weather in the Atmosphere

NGSS PERFORMANCE EXPECTATIONS

MS-ESS2-4 Develop a model to describe the cycling of water through Earth's systems driven by energy from the sun and the force of gravity.

MS-ESS2-5 Collect data to provide evidence for how the motions and complex interactions of air masses results in changes in weather conditions.

MS-ESS2-6 Develop and use a model to describe how unequal heating and rotation of the Earth cause patterns of atmospheric and oceanic circulation that determine regional climates.

MS-ESS3-2 Analyze and interpret data on natural hazards to forecast future catastrophic events and inform the development of technologies to mitigate their effects.

MS-PS1-4 Develop a model that predicts and describes changes in particle motion, temperature, and state of a pure substance when thermal energy is added or removed.

HANDS-ON LAB

uConnect Explore the role of plants in the water cycle.

What happened to this house?

GO ONLINE
to access your
digital course

▶ VIDEO

👆 INTERACTIVITY

🌡 VIRTUAL LAB

☑ ASSESSMENT

📖 eTEXT

📱 APP

The Essential Question

What determines weather on Earth?

One of the first things you might have done this morning was to look out the window to see what the weather was like. It might be warm and sunny, or you might be expecting a severe storm. Is your weather today typical for the climate in which you live? List some ways in which your life depends on weather.

....

....

....

....

....

....

Quest KICKOFF

How can you prepare for severe weather?

Phenomenon Severe weather can put people's lives and property at risk. Part of the job of a meteorologist, or a scientist who studies the weather, is to help keep the public safe by informing them about severe weather events. In this Quest activity, you will explore the factors that cause severe weather and the ways people can protect themselves and reduce damage during these weather events. Applying what you learn in each lesson, you will develop a public service announcement (PSA) to teach people about severe weather and what they can do to prepare for it and stay safe. In the Findings activity, you will present your PSA and reflect on your work.

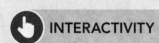 **INTERACTIVITY**

Preparing a Plan

MS-ESS2-5 Collect data to provide evidence for how the motions and complex interactions of air masses results in changes in weather conditions.
MS-ESS3-2 Analyze and interpret data on natural hazards to forecast future catastrophic events and inform the development of technologies to mitigate their effects.

NBC LEARN ▶ VIDEO

After watching the video, which explores the tools that meteorologists use to study and predict the weather, complete the 3-2-1 activity.

3 tools that a meteorologist uses

....

....

....

2 types of severe weather that a meteorologist might predict

....

....

....

1 question I have for the meteorologist

....

....

IN LESSON 1
How does the atmosphere affect the weather? Think about conditions in the atmosphere and how they are related to severe weather.

Quest CHECK-IN

IN LESSON 2
How is the water cycle involved in severe weather? Consider the information you should include in your PSA.

 INTERACTIVITY

Weather and Severe Weather

Quest CHECK-IN

IN LESSON 3
What happens when different air masses interact? Explore how tornadoes form and decide what information about air masses you will include in your PSA.

 INTERACTIVITY

All About Air Masses

A tornado is one of the most destructive types of severe weather that occurs in the United States.

Quest CHECK-IN

IN LESSON 4

How can forecasts help people to prepare for severe weather? Record ideas about weather predictions that your PSA should address.

 INTERACTIVITY

Predicting Severe Weather

Quest CHECK-IN

IN LESSON 5

How does examining past data help prepare people for future weather hazards? Analyze historical data about tornadoes in the United States.

HANDS-ON LAB

The History of Hazardous Weather

Quest FINDINGS

Complete the Quest!

Create your PSA to help people to understand, predict, prepare for, and avoid the dangers of severe weather.

 INTERACTIVITY

Reflect on Your PSA

The Atmosphere Around You

Guiding Questions

- What is the composition and structure of Earth's atmosphere?
- How does energy from the sun affect Earth's atmosphere?

Connections

Literacy Support Author's Claim

Math Represent Quantitative Relationships

MS-ESS2-5, MS-ESS2-6, MS-ESS3-2, MS-PS1-4

Vocabulary

atmosphere
air pressure
altitude
wind

Academic Vocabulary

stable

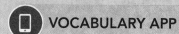 **VOCABULARY APP**

Practice vocabulary on a mobile device.

Quest CONNECTION

Consider how knowing more about the atmosphere might help people prepare for severe weather.

Connect It !

✏️ **Draw a line on the image showing how far from Earth's surface you think the atmosphere extends. What do you notice about the structure of the atmosphere?**

Make Observations Where is most of the gas in the atmosphere found?

....

....

Apply Scientific Reasoning How does the atmosphere protect life on Earth?

....

....

....

Earth's Insulator

The thin envelope of gases that surrounds the planet, shown in **Figure 1**, is called the **atmosphere**. This envelope acts like a coat for Earth. Just as you wear a coat to protect you from the elements and keep warm, the atmosphere protects the planet from harmful solar radiation and keeps the planet's temperature within a range that allows life to exist.

The protection our atmosphere provides is "just right." Too heavy a coat, and you would be too warm. Too light a coat, and you would be too cold. Venus and Mars, our planetary neighbors, are good examples of this. Venus's thick atmosphere traps heat and smothers the planet, while Mars's thin atmosphere retains little heat and results in huge temperature swings on the planet.

Earth's atmosphere includes air, water, and energy all connected within a system. All parts of the system interact with each other to produce the weather and climate around our planet. The atmosphere also interacts with Earth's other systems, such as the biosphere and the ocean, and its motions are driven by energy from the sun.

Reflect Many parts of the system that make up the atmosphere cannot be seen, such as the movement of air. In your science notebook, describe how you think evidence of these parts could be observed and measured.

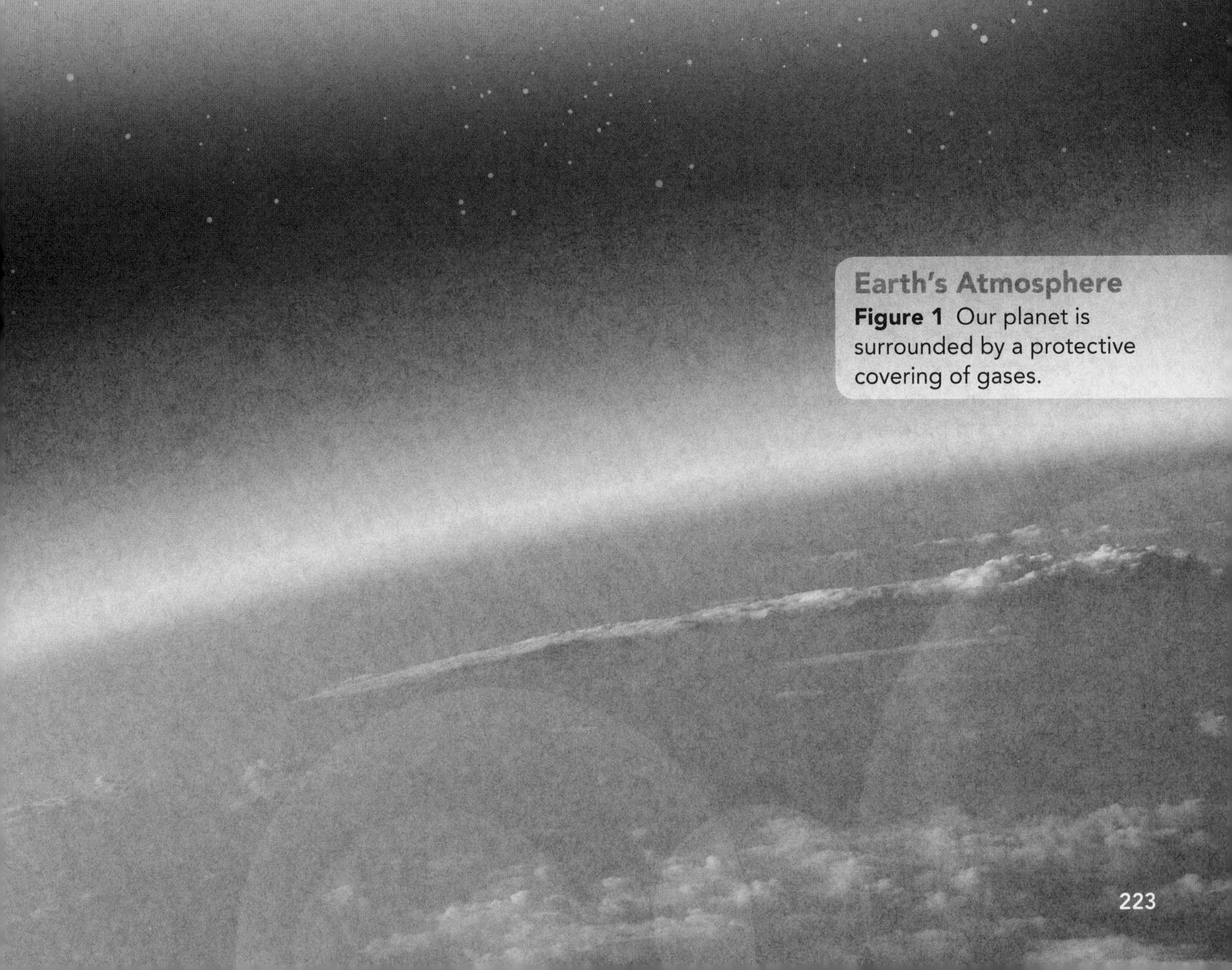

Earth's Atmosphere
Figure 1 Our planet is surrounded by a protective covering of gases.

Composition of the Atmosphere

Composition of the Atmosphere The air that makes up the atmosphere is a mixture of various gases, including water vapor, and other fine particles. The most abundant gases found in the atmosphere are nitrogen and oxygen. These two gases account for 99 percent of the atmosphere.

Nitrogen makes up about 78 percent of the air we breathe. Oxygen is essential for animal life, and makes up about 21 percent of the atmosphere's gases. The remaining one percent of the gases in our atmosphere consists of trace, or very small, amounts of gases such as argon, carbon dioxide, methane, and ozone. Though these gases are far less abundant, they help insulate Earth by trapping solar energy before it escapes into space. Burning fuels can increase the amount of carbon dioxide in the air.

The atmosphere also contains water vapor, which is the gaseous form of water. The amount of water vapor in the atmosphere varies from nearly zero percent in the driest deserts to as high as four percent in the extremely humid tropics. Water vapor cannot be seen, but when it condenses into tiny droplets of liquid water or frozen ice, it forms the clouds we see in the sky. In addition, fine particles of dust, ash, and other chemicals can be suspended in air. These particles can be seen as smog or smoke when they occur in large enough amounts, as shown in **Figure 2**.

Suspended Particles

Figure 2 During a volcanic eruption, fine particles of ash spew into the atmosphere. How might suspended particles in the atmosphere affect life on Earth?

....

....

....

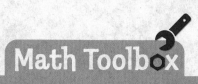

Math Toolbox

Temperature Scales

1. **Construct Graphs** ✏ Create a circle graph of the gases that make up air. Fill in the circle using percentages from the text. Use a different color for each gas and provide a key.

2. **Hypothesize** If gases like carbon dioxide and methane make up less than 1% of the total atmosphere, why is it important for scientists to monitor changes in percentages of these gases?

....

....

....

....

Composition of Air

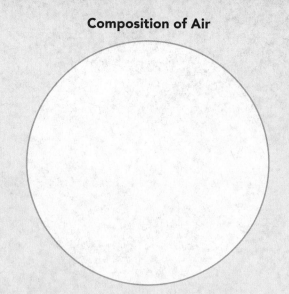

Model It!

Altitude and Air Density

Figure 3 The density of air decreases at higher altitudes because there is less pressure forcing the air molecules together.

Develop Models ✏️

Consider the molecules of air at different altitudes. The bottom magnification shows the air molecules near sea level. The center magnification shows the air molecules halfway up the mountain. Draw how you think the air molecules would be arranged at the top of the mountain.

Air Pressure The atmosphere is composed of tiny molecules of gases, water vapor, and particles. Each molecule exerts a small amount of force when it collides with other particles or a surface. Imagine the column of air above you that extends all the way into space. This column of air exerts a force on you called **air pressure**.

Earth's gravity pulls the molecules in the atmosphere toward the surface. The weight of the molecules presses down on the molecules below them. As a result, the molecules closest to the surface of Earth are pressed the most closely together. As you move up through the atmosphere, the density, or amount of air particles found within a certain volume, decreases. The molecules are more and more spread out. The distance above sea level is called **altitude**. The higher the altitude, the lower the air pressure because there is less air pushing down on you. Air pressure is measured using a barometer (**Figure 4**).

Gravity is not the only force that affects air pressure. Air pressure is also affected by temperature. When air is warm, heat energy causes the particles to move more rapidly, forcing the particles around them to spread out. Warm air is less dense than cold air, so it exerts less pressure.

☑ **READING CHECK** **Summarize** How does altitude affect air pressure?

....

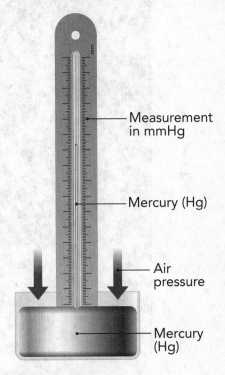

— Measurement in mmHg

— Mercury (Hg)

— Air pressure

— Mercury (Hg)

Measuring Air Pressure

Figure 4 As the column of air pushes on the mercury in the barometer, it causes the mercury to rise in a tube. The measurements are read as millimeters of mercury, or mmHg.

225

Identifying the Atmosphere's Layers

Figure 5 The atmosphere is divided into different layers by how the temperature (the yellow line in the graph) changes with altitude.

1. **Synthesize Information** ✎ Read each caption. Draw dotted lines to represent the boundary between each layer of the atmosphere.

2. **Cite Data** ✎ Beneath each caption, write the range of altitude (km) for that layer of the atmosphere and the position of each layer relative to the other three.

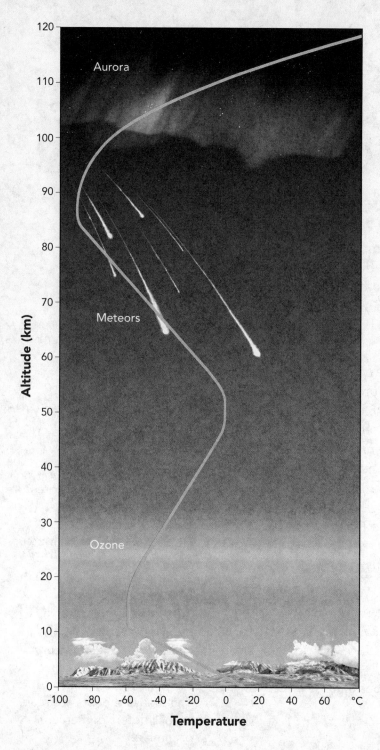

Thermosphere: This is the uppermost layer of the atmosphere, with the lowest density of air. The thermosphere is Earth's boundary with space. Radiation from the sun is absorbed by molecules in this layer, causing the temperatures to reach up to 1,800°C. But the molecules are so far apart that it would feel extremely cold.

Altitude Range:

Mesosphere: This layer of the atmosphere is directly above the stratosphere. It protects Earth from most meteoroids, which burn up due to friction as they strike the gases in this layer. The temperature in this layer decreases as the altitude increases.

Altitude Range:

Stratosphere: This layer of Earth's atmosphere contains the most ozone. As ozone in this layer absorbs ultraviolet radiation from the sun, it heats up the molecules of air. The temperature increases as altitude increases.

Altitude Range:

Troposphere: This is the layer where Earth's weather occurs. The troposphere is the closest to Earth's surface and experiences changeable conditions. This layer also contains 80 percent of the atmosphere by weight. The temperature decreases quickly as the altitude increases.

Altitude Range:

Layers of the Atmosphere As you have learned, the density of air in the atmosphere decreases the farther up you travel from the surface. In fact, those changes create distinct layers around Earth, which scientists identify based on the temperature characteristics of each layer. There are four main layers of the atmosphere: the troposphere, the stratosphere, the mesosphere, and the thermosphere (see **Figure 5**).

Energy in the Atmosphere

The sun provides most of the energy that drives Earth's systems, including the atmosphere. Solar energy in the form of light travels through space and reaches Earth. Some is reflected back into space, but most passes through the atmosphere to be trapped by the air or absorbed as heat at the surface. This energy drives the processes in the atmosphere, such as the water cycle and the movement of air.

The solar energy absorbed and stored by the atmosphere causes Earth's surface temperatures to remain relatively **stable**, or constant. Recall that the thin atmosphere of Mars causes huge temperatures changes on the planet, and the thick atmosphere of Venus traps so much heat that the planet is smothered and extremely hot. Earth's atmosphere is unique because it holds just the right amount of solar energy to protect life.

Heating of Earth The atmosphere plays an important role in transferring heat to and from Earth's surface. Heat is transferred in three ways: convection, conduction, and radiation.

Energy from the sun warms Earth's atmosphere as it reaches its surface by radiation. Some of the energy that hits Earth's surface is absorbed by land or water, some is reflected back into space, and some warms the air that touches Earth's surface through conduction.

Convection currents are also always moving Earth's air and water to redistribute heat to and from cool and warm places. This constant transfer of energy in the atmosphere and hydrosphere is responsible for the movement and cycling of air and water around Earth.

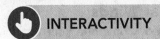

INTERACTIVITY

Explore the structure of the atmosphere.

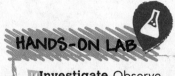

HANDS-ON LAB

Investigate Observe how changes in altitude affect the atmosphere.

Academic Vocabulary

How is the term *stable* used in the text?

....

....

Literacy Connection

Support Author's Claim As you read, underline evidence in the text that you think supports the idea that our atmosphere provides stable conditions that support life on Earth.

Global Winds

Figure 6 Convection currents caused by the uneven heating of Earth's surface and Earth's rotation interact to create the global wind patterns shown in the diagram.

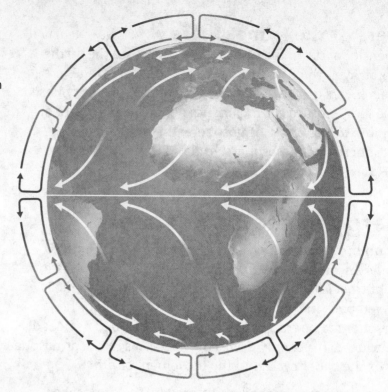

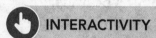 **INTERACTIVITY**

Learn about patterns in the wind.

Winds As the air in the atmosphere is heated by solar energy and Earth's surface, the unequal heating causes changes in air pressure. Warm air expands and becomes less dense. Cool, dense air nearby pushes in underneath, causing the warmer air to rise. This movement of air parallel to Earth's surface is called **wind**. Air moves as wind from areas of higher pressure to areas of lower pressure.

Unequal heating over small areas results in local winds, which are winds that blow over short distances. Two examples of local winds seen along shorelines are sea breezes and land breezes. Unequal heating causes sea breezes to occur during the day, when the land heats up faster than the water. Through conduction, the land heats up the air above it, causing the air to expand and rise. The cooler air over the water moves into the low-pressure area over the land. At night, the reverse happens and land breezes occur. The land cools off faster than the water and the cool, dense air blows from the land to the water, where the air pressure is lower.

Global winds, shown in **Figure 6**, are also caused by unequal heating, but they occur over much larger areas. As solar energy warms the areas near the equator, cold air near the poles moves in global winds to areas of low pressure. Convection currents caused by cool and warm air produce global winds.

✓ **READING CHECK Determine Central Ideas** Why is the atmosphere heated unequally by the sun?

....

....

MS-ESS2-5, MS-ESS2-6, MS-ESS3-2, MS-PS1-4

1. **Identify** What is the relative abundance of oxygen in the atmosphere?

....

....

....

2. **Compare and Contrast** How are the troposphere and the stratosphere different?

....

....

....

....

....

3. **Apply Concepts** Suppose a plane is flying at an altitude of 11,000 meters. Describe how the air pressure and temperature will change as the airplane comes down to land.

....

....

....

....

....

4. **Cause and Effect** How does the atmosphere affect life on Earth? Include both positive and negative effects in your response.

....

....

....

....

....

....

....

5. **Explain Phenomena** Explain how temperature and air pressure play a role in creating wind.

....

....

....

....

6. **Develop Models** 🖍 Draw a model of the atmosphere showing the transfer of solar energy through radiation, conduction, and convection.

Water in the Atmosphere

Guiding Questions

- What processes make up the water cycle?
- How does energy drive the processes of the water cycle?
- How does the water cycle affect weather?

Connections

Literacy Summarize Text

Math Convert Measurements

MS-ESS2-4

Vocabulary

water cycle
evaporation
condensation
dew point
humidity
relative humidity
precipitation

Academic Vocabulary

cycle

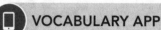 **VOCABULARY APP**

Practice vocabulary on a mobile device.

Quest CONNECTION

Think about how the water cycle can affect severe weather.

 **Connect It!**

✏️ **Circle the organisms in the photo. Do the organisms have any effect on the water in the stream?**

Construct Explanations How does the grass in the photo affect the movement of water?

....

....

....

Apply Scientific Reasoning How might the cattle affect the movement of water?

....

....

Water Enters the Atmosphere

During a humid day, the air around you may feel moist and thick. On a clear, cloudless day, the air may feel dry. The difference between these feelings is caused by the amount of water in the air. Water is always moving between the surface of Earth and the atmosphere. This process is known as the **water cycle**. A **cycle** is any series of events that repeat in the same order over and over again.

In one phase of the water cycle, water vapor enters the atmosphere through a number of processes. One of these processes is **evaporation**. During evaporation, molecules of liquid water in oceans, lakes, and other bodies of water are heated by the sun. The energy of the sun causes the water molecules to speed up and collide more often. As the molecules collide, some of them "escape" and enter the surrounding air.

The stream in **Figure 1** is not the only source of water for the atmosphere. Plants and animals also release water vapor into the air. In plants, water enters through the roots, rises to the leaves, and is released into the air as water vapor. This is known as transpiration. Animals (and people!) release water vapor into the air every time they breathe out, or exhale. This is known as respiration.

HANDS-ON LAB

Explore the conditions under which water vapor becomes liquid water.

Academic Vocabulary

How do the four seasons also represent a cycle?

....

....

....

Water Enters the Atmosphere

Figure 1 Water is released into the atmosphere as water vapor from bodies of water such as this stream and living things, such as grass and cattle.

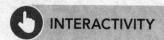

INTERACTIVITY

Investigate the stages of the water cycle.

HANDS-ON LAB

Investigate Investigate how clouds and fog form.

Forming a Cloud

Figure 2 ✏️ Complete the diagram to show how clouds form when warm, moist air rises and cools. Use the following terms: *evaporation, cooling air, condensation,* and *particles.*

Condensation Recall that water vapor is a gas mixed in with the rest of the air. **Condensation** occurs when water vapor changes into liquid water.

For condensation to occur, tiny particles must be present in the atmosphere so that the water has a surface on which to condense. Most of these particles are salt crystals, dust from soil, bacteria, or particles contained in smoke. During condensation, molecules of water vapor mix with these particles.

Temperature is also a major factor in condensation. Warm air can hold more water vapor than cold air can. Therefore, as warm air cools, the amount of water vapor it can hold decreases, and the water vapor starts to condense. Liquid water that condenses from the air onto a cooler surface is called dew. The temperature at which condensation begins is called the **dew point**. If the dew point is above freezing, the water vapor forms droplets. If the dew point is below freezing, the water vapor may change directly into ice crystals called frost.

One result of condensation of water vapor in the atmosphere is cloud formation. Clouds form when water vapor in the air condenses to form liquid water or ice crystals. When you look at a cloud, such as the one in **Figure 2,** you are seeing millions of these tiny water droplets or ice crystals. When water vapor condenses near ground level, it can take the form of fog. Water can condense as dew on any solid surface, such as a blade of grass or a window pane.

Relative Humidity

Relative Humidity Meteorologists often warn of high or low humidity during their weather forecasts. **Humidity** is a measure of the amount of water vapor in the air.

The ability of air to hold water vapor depends on temperature. Warm air can hold more water than cool air. So, in their weather reports, meteorologists usually refer to the amount of water vapor in the air as relative humidity.

Relative humidity is the percent of water vapor in the air compared to the maximum amount of water vapor the air can hold at a particular temperature. For example, 1 cubic meter of air can hold no more than 8 grams of water vapor at 10°C. If there are 8 grams of water vapor in the air, then the relative humidity is 100 percent and the air would be said to be saturated. Similarly, the relative humidity is 50 percent if the air has only 4 grams of water vapor per cubic meter.

Relative humidity is a better reflection of how the air feels than humidity. For example, air that holds 4 grams of water vapor per cubic meter can feel moist on a cold day or dry on a hot day. Relative humidity reflects this feeling. It would be near 100 percent on a cold day, and much lower on a hot day.

Relative humidity can be measured using a psychrometer It is a device made up of two thermometers, a wet-bulb thermometer and a dry-bulb thermometer. This device is called a psychrometer. As shown in **Figure 3**, a moist cloth covers the wet bulb. When the psychrometer is "slung," or spun around, air flows over both thermometers. The wet-bulb thermometer is cooled by evaporation, causing its temperature reading to fall. If the relative humidity is high, evaporation occurs slowly and the wet-bulb temperature does not change much. If the relative humidity is low, evaporation occurs rapidly and the wet-bulb temperature drops by a large amount. Relative humidity is measured by comparing the temperatures of the two bulbs.

☑ READING CHECK **Determine Conclusions** Suppose the two thermometers on a sling psychrometer show almost identical readings. Was the psychrometer more likely used on a Florida beach or in an Arizona desert? Explain your answer.

....

....

....

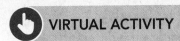
VIRTUAL ACTIVITY

Observe how water moves in the water cycle.

Literacy Connection

Summarize Text As you read, underline sentences that contain information you consider important to remember.

Tools for Measuring Humidity

Figure 3 Digital hygrometers and sling psychrometers like the ones shown are used to find relative humidity.

Write About It
What are the different types of precipitation you encounter in your daily life? In your science notebook, describe how precipitation impacts your life.

Water Leaves the Atmosphere

Water is continually evaporating and condensing in the atmosphere, and this process forms clouds. When enough condensation occurs within a cloud, water droplets form. At first, the droplets are very small, but they grow larger as condensation continues. Depending on temperature and other conditions in the atmosphere, the droplets may grow heavy enough that gravity pulls them down toward Earth's surface. When this happens, precipitation occurs. **Precipitation** is any form of water that falls from clouds and reaches Earth's surface.

Types of Precipitation The most common kind of precipitation is rain. Rain comes in various forms depending on the size of the water droplets that form, as seen in **Figure 4**. Rain starts out as cloud droplets. When cloud droplets grow a bit bigger, they become mist. When droplets reach a size of 0.05 to 0.5 millimeters in diameter, they are known as drizzle. Drops of water are called rain when they are larger than 0.5 millimeters in diameter.

Water Droplets

Figure 4 ✎ On the diagram, label the drops as *mist, rain, drizzle,* or *droplet.*

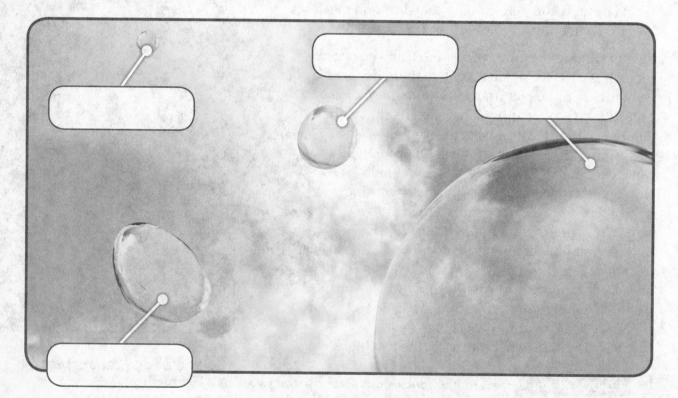

Temperature is a very important factor in determining the type of precipitation an area may get at any given time. In warm climates, precipitation is almost always rain. However, there are many other types of precipitation. In colder regions, precipitation often falls as snow or ice. Besides rain, common types of precipitation include sleet, freezing rain, snow, and hail, as shown in **Figure 5**.

Freezing Precipitation

Figure 5 Draw a check mark on the photos showing the precipitation that occurs when the air temperature is above 0°C and the ground temperature is below 0°C. Draw an X on the photos showing the precipitation that occurs when the air temperature is below 0°C and the ground temperature is above 0°C. Draw a triangle on the photos showing the precipitation that occurs when both air and ground temperature are below 0°C.

Freezing Rain Raindrops sometimes freeze when they hit a cold surface. This kind of precipitation is called freezing rain.

Hail A hailstone is a round pellet of ice at least 5 millimeters in diameter. Hail starts as an ice pellet inside a cold region of a cloud. Strong updrafts of wind carry the hailstone up through the cold region many times, adding ice in layers to the outside of the hailstone. Eventually the hailstone becomes heavy enough for gravity to pull it to the ground.

Sleet Raindrops that fall through a layer of air below 0°C freeze into solid particles of ice before they hit the ground. Ice particles smaller than hailstones are called sleet.

Snow Snow forms when water vapor in a cloud is converted directly into ice crystals that clump together. The clumps fall in the form of ice crystals called snowflakes.

235

VIDEO

Watch a single drop of water as it moves through the water cycle.

Measuring Precipitation If a town receives a large snowfall, meteorologists need to track how much snow fell to determine how safe it is to travel. Similarly, if a big storm delivers a lot of rain, people would need to know how much rain fell to determine whether flooding might occur.

Rain can be measured by using a rain gauge, which is an open-ended tube that collects rain. The amount of rain is measured either by dipping a ruler into the water in the tube or by reading a scale printed on the tube. Snowfall is usually measured in two ways: by using a simple measuring stick or by melting collected snow and measuring the depth of water it produces. On average, 10 centimeters of snow contain about the same amount of water as 1 centimeter of rain. However, light, fluffy snow contains far less water than heavy, wet snow does.

☑ READING CHECK **Determine Central Ideas** How are snow and rain formation similar? How are they different?

....

....

....

....

Math Toolbox

Measuring Precipitation

In late September and early October of 2016, Hurricane Matthew brought a huge amount of rain to the Caribbean and then the southeastern United States, causing major flooding and damage. The table shows approximate rainfall during the hurricane. Use the table to answer the questions about this powerful storm.

1. **Convert Measurements** ✏ Complete the table. Use the fact that 1 inch is equal to 25.4 millimeters.

2. **Draw Conclusions** Does the data in the table support the conclusion that the hurricane weakened before reaching the United States? Explain.

Rainfall During Hurricane Matthew		
Location	Rain in mm	Rain in inches
Hewanorra, Saint Lucia		12.6
Santo Domingo, Dominican Republic		9.21
Fayetteville, NC, United States	355	

....

....

The Water Cycle

The water cycle describes the way that water moves through Earth's systems and affects our lives in many ways. As the sun heats the land, ocean, lakes, and other bodies of water, its energy changes the amount of water in the atmosphere. Through evaporation, transpiration, and respiration, water rises up and forms clouds. Rain, snow, and other forms of precipitation fall from the clouds toward Earth's surface. The water then runs off the surface or moves through the ground, back into lakes, streams, and eventually the ocean. As seen in **Figure 6**, gravity and energy from the sun together drive water molecules through this never-ending cycle.

INTERACTIVITY

Examine your own role in the water cycle.

☑ READING CHECK **Summarize Text** What role does energy play in the water cycle?

....

....

....

Model It!

Figure 6 Identify Patterns ✏ Study this diagram of the water cycle in action. Label the various processes you see in the diagram.

☑LESSON 2 Check

1. **Generalize** Besides energy from the sun, what force helps move water molecules through the water cycle?

....

2. **Explain** What conditions must change for rain to become snow?

....
....
....
....
....

3. **Identify** Suppose you use a sling psychrometer in two different locations. How will you know which location has lower relative humidity?

....
....
....
....
....
....

4. **Analyze Systems** Explain how animals affect the water cycle as they breathe.

....
....
....

5. **Use Models** ✎ Create a diagram that shows how water cycles through the environment around your neighborhood.

Quest CHECK-IN

In this lesson, you learned how water cycles through Earth's systems. You also discovered that the water cycle can influence the weather.

Evaluate How does each part of the water cycle contribute to the weather?

....
....
....
....
....
....

👆 INTERACTIVITY

Weather and Severe Weather

Go online to analyze how the water cycle is involved in weather, especially severe weather. Then consider possible causes and effects of various weather events, and suggest how people can prepare for those events.

MS-ESS2-4

CATCHING WATER
With a Net

INTERACTIVITY

Explore the factors affecting the amount of water that a dew catcher can collect.

How can you provide safe drinking water for small villages far from any clean water source? By extracting it from the air!

The Challenge: To reclaim clean drinking water from humidity in the air.

Phenomenon You can get a fresh drink of water almost anywhere in the United States simply by turning on a faucet. However, in many villages and cities around the world, people have to go a long way to find clean water that is safe to drink.

Scientists have taken up the challenge of bringing water to these people through the ancient method of collecting dew. Recall that dew is the moisture that condenses on surfaces as a result of cooling temperatures and the available humidity in the air.

In rural villages across the world, people are putting up nets. Cooler night temperatures cause moisture in the air from higher humidity or fog to condense and cover the nets with water. The water drains into a container, providing a lifeline to thirsty communities. The water is safe for drinking, cooking, bathing, and tending crops.

Members of the Swakopmund People of the Topnaar tribe work on a fog collection system in the Namib Desert in Namibia.

DESIGN CHALLENGE Can you build a device to catch dew from the air? Go to the Engineering Design Notebook to find out!

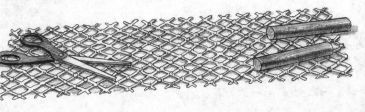

239

③ Air Masses

Guiding Questions

- How do global patterns, such as the jet stream, affect air masses?
- How do air masses interact to form fronts?
- How do the interactions of air masses result in changes in weather?

Connections

Literacy Read and Comprehend

MS-ESS2-5

Vocabulary

air mass
jet stream
front
cyclone
anticyclone

Academic Vocabulary

prevailing
stationary

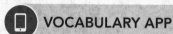 **VOCABULARY APP**

Practice vocabulary on a mobile device.

Quest CONNECTION

Think about how interacting air masses can cause severe weather.

Connect It !

✎ **Make a checkmark on something in the picture that indicates whether the air is warm or cool. Make an X on something that indicates the relative humidity.**

Construct Explanations Do you think the air at this beach is humid or dry? Why do you think so? Explain.

....

Apply Scientific Reasoning What factors affect the temperature at this beach?

....

....

Major Air Masses

Look outside your window. What is the weather like where you are today? The weather you see is happening due to the influence of air masses. An **air mass** is a huge body of air that has similar temperature, humidity, and air pressure at any given height. Scientists classify air masses based on temperature and humidity.

The characteristics of an air mass depend on the temperature and moisture content of the region over which the air mass forms. Whether an air mass is humid or dry depends on whether it forms over water or dry land. For example, an air mass that forms above the ocean in **Figure 1** would have different characteristics than an air mass that forms over a desert.

How Air Masses Move Air masses are always on the move. In the continental United States, air masses are commonly moved by the **prevailing** westerlies and jet streams.

In general, the major wind belts over the continental United States, known as the prevailing westerlies, push air masses from west to east. For example, cool, moist air masses from the Pacific Ocean may be blown onto the West Coast, bringing low clouds and showers. Embedded within the prevailing westerlies are jet streams. A **jet stream** is a band of high-speed winds about 6 to 14 km above Earth's surface. As jet streams blow from west to east, the surface air masses beneath them are carried along. The movement of these air masses, and their interactions have a great impact on weather.

INTERACTIVITY

Explore the characteristics of air masses.

Academic Vocabulary

Think about the meaning of *prevailing* in terms of wind. Keeping this in mind, what might be the prevailing noise at a concert?

....

....

....

Air Masses

Figure 1 Air masses near this beach have specific temperature and humidity profiles based on conditions where the air masses formed.

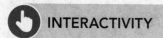

INTERACTIVITY

Describe the properties and characteristics of the different kinds of air masses.

Types of Air Masses

Figure 2 These four major types of air masses affect North American weather.

Integrate with Visuals ✏
Label each type of air mass with two words that describe its temperature and humidity such as *warm* and *dry*.

Types of Air Masses

Is it often windy or rainy where you live? Your local weather, and all the weather in North America, is influenced by one of four major types of air masses: maritime tropical, continental tropical, maritime polar, and continental polar. These air masses are shown in **Figure 2**.

Tropical, or warm, air masses form in the tropics and have low air pressure. Polar, or cold, air masses form in the high latitudes and have high air pressure. Maritime air masses form over the ocean and are very humid. Continental air masses have less exposure to large amounts of moisture, and are drier than maritime air masses. The high and low temperatures in continental air masses can be more extreme than the temperatures in maritime air masses. This is because large bodies of water moderate air temperatures.

✔ **READING CHECK** **Read and Comprehend** What types of air masses affect the weather in North America?

....

....

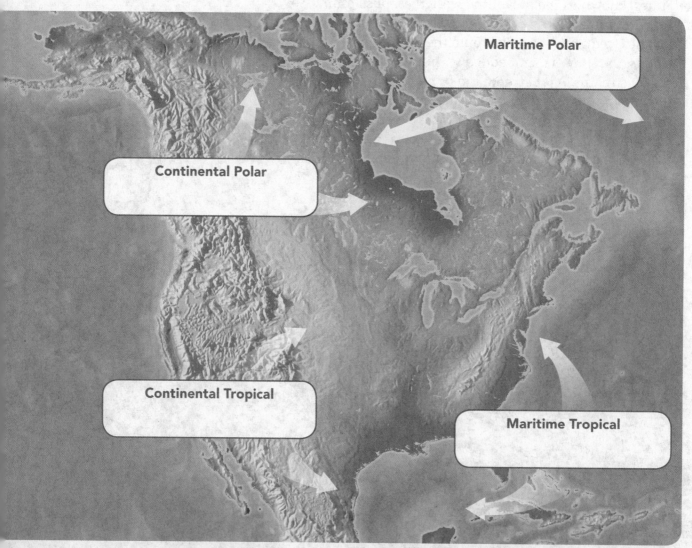

Types of Fronts

Think about a bottle of oil and water. What happens when you shake the bottle? If you try this, you will see that the two substances do not mix—the less-dense oil winds up floating on top of the water. Air masses of different temperatures and humidity act the same way. Although they move across the land and frequently collide with each other, they do not mix easily. Instead, the boundary where the air masses meet becomes a **front**. Storms and changeable weather often develop along fronts like the one in **Figure 3**.

The weather may be different when you leave school this afternoon than it was when you arrived in the morning. The change might be due to a front passing through your area. Colliding air masses can form four types of fronts: cold fronts, warm fronts, stationary fronts, and occluded fronts, as shown on the next two pages in **Figure 4**. The kind of front that develops depends on the characteristics of the air masses and the direction in which they move.

How a Front Forms
Figure 3 A front may be 15 to 600 km wide and extend high into the troposphere.

Predict What kind of weather would develop along the front shown in the photo?

....

....

HANDS-ON LAB

Investigate Model the behavior of cold and warm fronts.

243

Cold Front

Warm Front

Literacy Connection

Read and Comprehend
As you read about each type of front, underline any effects caused by its formation. Think about how the interactions of these fronts affect the weather.

Academic Vocabulary

A *stationary* front occurs when two air masses meet but neither one can move the other. Knowing that, in what way would a population be said to be stationary?

....

....

....

....

....

Cold Fronts A cold front forms when a cold air mass runs into a warm air mass. Because cold air is denser than warm air, the warm air is pushed up rapidly as the colder air slides beneath it. Cold fronts can result in abrupt and hazardous weather such as heavy rains and winds, thunderstorms, and even tornadoes. After the front passes, the weather usually cools and the skies become clear.

Warm Fronts A warm front forms when a fast-moving warm air mass overtakes a slower-moving cold air mass. Because the warm air mass is less dense, it rises above the cold air mass. Along the front, light rain or snow can fall if the warm air is humid. Scattered clouds can form if the warm air mass is dry. These fronts often move slowly, so there may be rain and clouds for a few days. The weather usually cools is warmer and more humid after a warm front moves by.

Occluded Fronts Sometimes, a warm air mass gets caught between two cold air masses, forming an occluded front. Because the cooler air is denser, it moves under the warm air, causing the warm air to rise. When the two cold air masses meet, they mix together. Air temperature drops as the warm air mass becomes occluded, or prevented from reaching the ground. As the warm air mass rises and cools, clouds gather, and rain or snow may fall.

Stationary Fronts Sometimes cold and warm air masses meet, but neither one can move the other. This non-moving front is called a **stationary** front. Where the warm and cool air meet, water vapor in the warm air condenses into rain, snow, fog, or clouds. A stationary front may bring many days of clouds and precipitation.

✓ READING CHECK **Determine Central Ideas** What do all of these different types of fronts have in common?

....

....

Occluded Front

Stationary Front

Model It!

Develop Models ✎ Draw a diagram to model what would happen when a cold air mass moving from the south collides with a warm air mass moving from the north.

Types of Fronts

Figure 4 Different types of fronts occur, depending on how the different air masses interact.

Synthesize Information How are cold and warm fronts different?

....

....

....

....

▶ **VIDEO**

Watch how the different fronts could affect the weather.

Cyclone

Figure 5 🖊 This image shows a specific type of Northern Hemisphere cyclone known as a hurricane. On the image, draw arrows to show the direction the cyclone is swirling. How do you know this picture is of a cyclone and not an anticyclone?

....

....

....

....

INTERACTIVITY

Identify the types of weather that take place in different locations.

Write About It Watch water swirl down a drain. In your science notebook, describe how this swirling water is related to a cyclone.

Cyclones and Anticyclones

When air masses collide, they form fronts that can sometimes become distorted by surface features, such as mountains, or by strong winds, such as a jet stream. When this happens, the air begins to swirl, causing a low-pressure center to form.

Cyclones When you read a weather map, you may often notice a circled L that indicates a "low," or an area of relatively low air pressure. As shown in **Figure 5**, a swirling center of low air pressure can form a **cyclone**. As warm air at the center of a cyclone rises, the air pressure decreases. Cooler air blows inward from nearby areas of higher air pressure. Winds spiral inward toward the center. In the Northern Hemisphere, the Coriolis effect deflects these winds towards the right, so the cyclone winds spin counterclockwise when viewed from above. As air rises in a cyclone, the air cools, forming clouds and precipitation.

Anticyclones An **anticyclone** is the opposite of a cyclone. It is a high-pressure center of dry air, shown by an H on a weather map. In an anticyclone, winds spiral outward from the center, moving toward areas of lower pressure. The Coriolis effect, which is the deflection of the winds towards the right, causes the winds in an anticyclone to spin clockwise in the Northern Hemisphere. As air moves out from the center, cool air moves downward from higher in the atmosphere. As the cool air warms up, its relative humidity drops, so no clouds form and the weather is clear and dry.

✓ READING CHECK **Read and Comprehend** How do cyclones and anticyclones differ?

....

....

....

1. Compare and Contrast What is the difference between an air mass and a front?

....

....

....

....

....

....

....

2. Cause and Effect A state often has cold, snowy winters and cool, rainy summers. Is this state more likely to be New York or Nebraska? Explain your answer.

....

....

....

....

....

....

....

....

....

....

3. Use Tables 🖉 For each description in the table, write the name of the type of front it describes.

Type	Description
	A cold air mass pushes under a warm air mass.
	A warm air mass is trapped by two cold air masses.
	A warm air mass rises over a cold air mass.
	The front does not move.

4. Develop Models 🖉 Use the two models to show the air pattern in a cyclone and in an anticyclone. On each sketch, draw arrows that trace the direction of the air and label the cyclone and anticyclone.

Quest CHECK-IN

In this lesson, you learned that air masses interact at fronts. You also discovered that interacting air masses can cause severe weather.

Infer Why is it important for people to understand how interacting air masses can affect the weather?

....

....

....

....

✋ INTERACTIVITY

All About Air Masses

Go online to explore what happens when different air masses interact. Then find out how and where tornadoes form.

LESSON 4

Predicting Weather Changes

Guiding Questions

- How do meteorologists use the interactions of air masses to forecast changes in weather?
- How does technology aid in collecting and analyzing weather data?
- How do weather maps help to model current weather and predict future weather?

Connections

Literacy Determine Central Ideas

Math Analyze Quantitative Relationships

MS-ESS2-5, MS-ESS2-6

Vocabulary

meteorologist

Academic Vocabulary

synthesize

 VOCABULARY APP

Practice vocabulary on a mobile device.

Quest CONNECTION

Think about how weather forecasts help people to prepare for severe weather.

Connect It !

🖉 **On two different places in the photo, draw a symbol to indicate the type of weather occurring in that location.**

Make Observations What details in the photo support your predictions?

....

....

....

How To Predict Weather

Whether you're planning on going on a hike, driving to an amusement park, or having a picnic in the park, you'll need to know the day's weather to make your plans. Before you're able to predict the weather, you'll first need to collect data, either through direct observations or by using special instruments, such as a barometer. A barometer measures air pressure. If the reading is falling, meaning the air pressure in the area is decreasing, then you can expect stormy weather.

Making observations is a simple way of predicting how the weather might change. Looking at the sky shown in **Figure 1** might make you wonder how you can use your observations to forecast weather. You might read signs of changing weather in the clouds. On a warm day, you may see clouds that slowly grow larger and taller, which could indicate that a thunderstorm is on the way. If you can see thin, high clouds in the sky, a warm front may be approaching.

Usually, your observations won't tell you everything you need to know. Even careful observers often turn to meteorologists for weather information. A **meteorologist** (mee tee uh RAHL uh jist) is a scientist who studies and predicts weather.

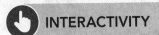

INTERACTIVITY

Explore some of the factors that make it difficult to predict the weather.

Predicting Weather Changes
Figure 1 Meteorologists forecast the weather using direct observations about the conditions.

HANDS-ON LAB

Investigate Consider how barometric pressure is related to weather conditions.

Weather Technology

Figure 2 Technological improvements in gathering weather data have improved the accuracy of weather forecasts.

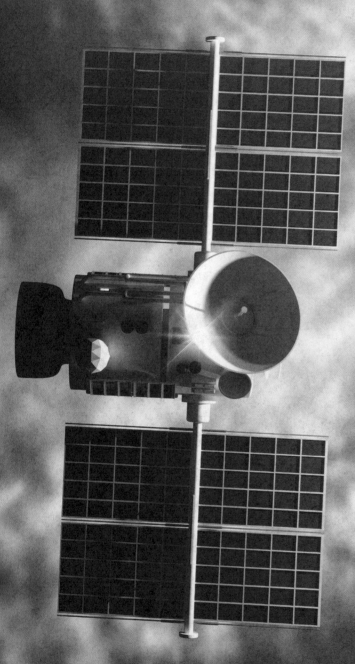

Weather Satellites Satellites orbit high above Earth collecting data as well as images of Earth's surface and atmosphere.

Weather Balloons Weather balloons carry instruments for collecting weather data high into the atmosphere where human observation is not feasible.

Automated Weather Stations Weather stations in many locations can gather real-time weather data.

Computer Forecasts Computers process weather data quickly, which enables forecasters to make timely predictions.

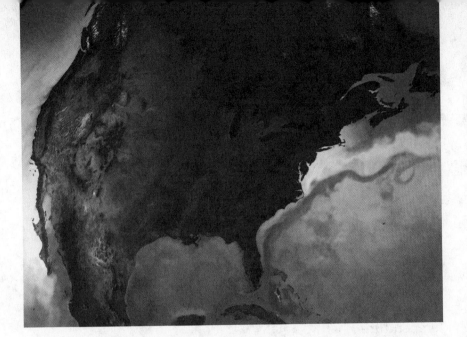

Weather Technology

In recent years, new technologies have been developed to help meteorologists predict the weather, as shown in **Figure 2**. Short-range forecasts—forecasts for up to five days—are now fairly reliable. Meteorologists can also make somewhat accurate long-range predictions.

Global Patterns and Local Weather

Recognizing patterns is another component of weather forecasting. A large part of the job of a meteorologist is to determine how global patterns affect the local weather. Meteorologists look at many different factors, including temperature, wind, air pressure, humidity, and precipitation. They closely observe and track the movements of jet streams and ocean currents to help predict future weather changes.

Jet streams help to move air masses and weather systems around the globe. While the weather may be warm and sunny one day, a jet stream can push a cold, moist air mass into the area and change the forecast to cooler, stormy days.

Ocean currents, which move warm and cold water around the world, also affect local weather. Warm ocean currents cause the air masses above them to become warmer, while cold currents lower the temperature of air masses above them. These currents affect local air temperatures and precipitation, and they also cause changes in wind speed and direction. Observe **Figure 3** to see how one ocean current, the Gulf Stream, influences the temperatures on the east coast of North America.

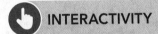

INTERACTIVITY

Discover how air masses can be used to predict weather.

VIDEO

Learn how weather satellites are used in meteorology.

☑ READING CHECK **Determine Conclusions** Based on the image in **Figure 3**, how does the Gulf Stream most likely affect temperatures on the East Coast?

....

....

Learning from Weather Maps

Do you ever check the weather on your phone or a tablet? In addition to telling you the temperature and atmospheric conditions, many apps will show you a weather map. A weather map is a model that shows the weather conditions at a particular time over a large area. There are many types of weather maps.

Academic Vocabulary

What do you think it means to synthesize a chemical?

....

....

Reading Weather Maps Data from many local weather stations all over the country are **synthesized** into weather maps at the National Weather Service. Some weather maps show curved lines. These lines connect places with similar conditions of temperature or air pressure. Isobars are lines joining places on the map that have the same air pressure. Isotherms are lines joining places that have the same temperature.

Figure 4 shows a typical newspaper weather map. Standard symbols on weather maps show many features, including fronts, areas of high and low pressure (measured in millibars), types of precipitation, and temperatures.

Math Toolbox

Isobars

The black lines on this map of the United States are isobars, which connect points of equal air pressure, measured in millibars.

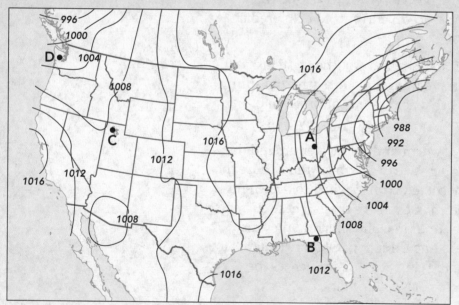

Analyze Quantitative Relationships Use the locations A, B, C, and D from the map to answer the questions about air pressure.

1. Which two locations have approximately the same air pressure? _____

2. Which two locations have the greatest difference in air pressure? _____

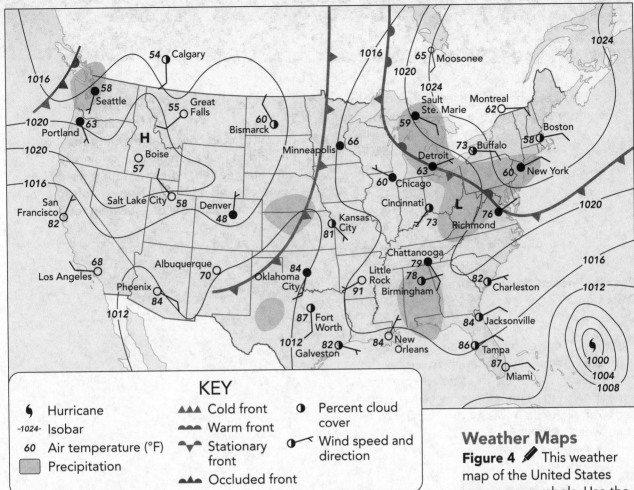

KEY

⚓ Hurricane
-1024- Isobar
60 Air temperature (°F)
▨ Precipitation

▲▲▲ Cold front
⌒⌒⌒ Warm front
⌄⌄⌄ Stationary front
▲▲▲ Occluded front

◑ Percent cloud cover
◑⌐ Wind speed and direction

The Future of Meteorology

As computers, satellites, and radar technologies become more sophisticated, scientists can make better forecasts. But even with these advanced tools, no forecaster will ever be one hundred percent accurate. This is because the atmosphere works in such a way that a small change in the weather today can mean a larger change in the weather a week later! A tiny event might cause a larger disturbance that could—eventually—grow into a large storm.

☑ **READING CHECK Determine Central Ideas** How are isobars and isotherms alike? How are they different?

....

....

....

Weather Maps

Figure 4 🖉 This weather map of the United States uses many symbols. Use the key to interpret the symbols. Underline the cities with the highest and lowest temperatures. (Note that the temperatures are given in degrees Fahrenheit.) Then circle the area showing the highest levels of atmospheric pressure.

Literacy Connection

Determine Central Ideas
Compare the information you read about weather forecasts in the text with the information you gained about forecasts from looking at the weather map. Use the central idea from the reading and map reading to compare the information.

MS-ESS2-5, MS-ESS2-6

1. **Summarize** What does a meteorologist do? Use information from the lesson to summarize.

....

....

....

....

....

Use the information in Figure 4 to answer Question 2.

2. **Patterns** From the temperatures shown on the weather map and the knowledge that air masses are usually pushed eastward by the prevailing westerlies, what do you predict will happen to the temperature in Kansas City the day after the map was made? Explain your answer.

....

....

....

....

....

3. **Develop Models** ✏ Describe a weather station that will be used to collect weather data. It should collect all the data that are needed to make forecasts. Explain what data are needed, how the station would be powered, and any other relevant information. Then sketch a model of your weather station.

....

....

....

....

Quest CHECK-IN

In this lesson, you learned how meteorologists use observations, patterns, and tools to predict the weather.

Infer How might accurate weather forecasting help people who work as farmers or fishers? How does it help everyone?

....

....

....

....

....

....

INTERACTIVITY

Predicting Severe Weather

Go online to determine how weather forecasts help people to prepare for severe weather. Then identify which weather conditions you should address in your PSA.

CAREERS

Meteorologist

Watching the CLOUDS GO BY

People have been trying to predict the weather for thousands of years. In ancient times, people observed the clouds, the wind, and the temperature changes. They recognized patterns that helped them to forecast the weather with some accuracy.

Today, forecasting the weather combines data collection with the old skill of pattern recognition. Scientists called meteorologists collect weather data using computers and other tools. They analyze and interpret the data and compare it to their knowledge and experience. This process allows meteorologists to make predictions about the weather days and even weeks in advance.

There are many different types of meteorologists. Broadcast meteorologists report the weather on television. Research meteorologists work at government agencies and study particular issues related to weather and climate. Forensic meteorologists are called upon to research past weather events for court cases or insurance claims.

Meteorologists often have a good background in subjects such as physics, astronomy, and math. It also helps if you like different kinds of weather and if you are observant and curious!

▶ VIDEO

Find out how a meteorologist predicts the weather in an area.

Meteorologists check instruments at an automated weather station in a remote desert location at the Jornada Biosphere Reserve in southern New Mexico.

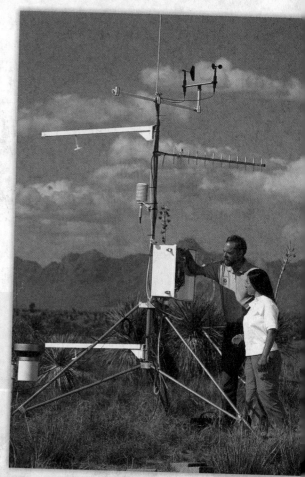

MY CAREER

Type "meteorologist" into an online search engine to learn more about this career.

Severe Weather and Floods

Guiding Questions

- How does severe weather affect human life?
- How do humans protect themselves from severe weather?

Connections

Literacy Cite Textual Evidence

MS-ESS3-2

Vocabulary

storm
thunderstorm
hurricane
tornado
storm surge
flood
drought

Academic Vocabulary

approximate

 VOCABULARY APP

Practice vocabulary on a mobile device.

Quest CONNECTION

Think about how data from past events might help to prepare people for future weather hazards.

Connect It!

✏ **Label the center, or eye, of this North Atlantic hurricane.**

Explain Phenomena In what direction are the winds swirling around the location you identified?

....

Predict How might this storm affect people living near its path?

....

....

Types of Severe Storms

In October 2016, Hurricane Matthew struck the Caribbean and the southeastern United States with torrential rains and winds that reached **approximate** speeds of 250 km/h. Shown in the satellite image in **Figure 1**, it was one of the most intense storms ever to hit that part of the United States.

The death toll due to Hurricane Matthew surpassed 1000, with most of those deaths occurring in Haiti. In the United States, approximately 40 people died, more than half of these in North Carolina. Florida did not receive the extremely strong winds that some areas did, but the hurricane dropped between 7 and 10 inches of rain in the eastern half of the state.

In addition to casualties, property damage from the hurricane was extreme. Many areas were battered by winds or flooded for days. Many buildings were blown down and roads washed away.

A hurricane is one example of a storm. A **storm** is a violent disturbance in the atmosphere. Storms involve sudden changes in air pressure, which cause rapid air movements and often precipitation. There are several types of severe storms: winter storms, thunderstorms, hurricanes, and tornadoes.

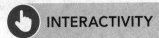

INTERACTIVITY

Write about your experiences with severe weather.

Academic Vocabulary

What is the difference between an approximate and an exact number?

....

....

....

Hurricane Matthew

Figure 1 This satellite image shows Hurricane Matthew swirling north of Cuba and beginning to engulf the Florida peninsula.

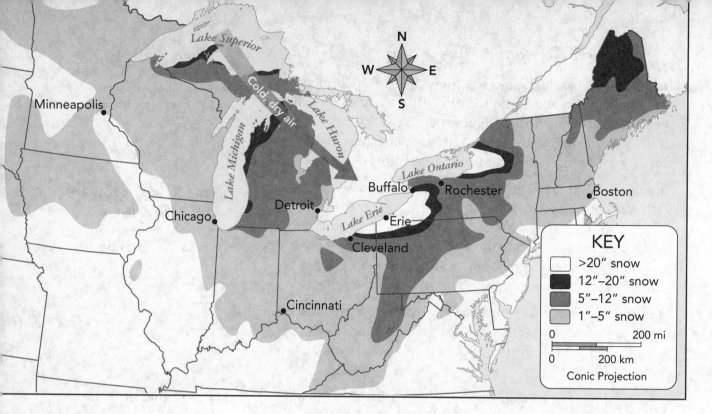

Map labels: Lake Superior, Cold, dry air, Lake Huron, Lake Michigan, Minneapolis, Chicago, Detroit, Lake Erie, Lake Ontario, Buffalo, Rochester, Erie, Cleveland, Cincinnati, Boston

KEY

- >20" snow
- 12"–20" snow
- 5"–12" snow
- 1"–5" snow

0   200 mi

0   200 km

Conic Projection

Lake-Effect Snow

Figure 2 This map shows the snow totals after a certain winter storm. The higher totals are a result of lake-effect snow. Draw arrows on the map to represent the wind blowing across the lakes.

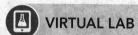 **Write About It** Identify the actions you can take to remain safe during a severe storm of any kind.

VIRTUAL LAB

Investigate conditions that favor snowfall.

Winter Storms

In the winter in the northern United States, most of the precipitation that occurs is in the form of snow. If the air is colder than 0°C all the way to the ground, the precipitation falls as snow. Heavy snow can block roads, trap people in their homes, and delay emergency vehicles. Extreme cold can cause water pipes to burst.

Some places, including Buffalo, New York, and Erie, Pennsylvania, get more snow than other places relatively close by. In an average winter, nearly 118 inches of snow fall on these cities due to lake-effect snow, as shown in **Figure 2.**

In the fall and winter, the land near the Great Lakes cools much more rapidly than the water in the lakes. When a cold, dry air mass moves southeast across the lakes, it picks up water vapor and heat. As soon as the air mass reaches the other side of the lake, the air rises and cools again. The water vapor condenses and falls as snow.

Some winter storms are more intense than others. In February 1978, a huge blizzard hit the northeastern United States. During this storm, weather stations recorded hurricane-force winds and record-breaking amounts of snow. The storm hovered over New England, and heavy snow fell for almost 33 hours without letting up.

People driving on highways abandoned their cars when the snow became too deep. Rescuers traveled on cross-country skis and snowmobiles to help stranded drivers. It was almost a week until the roads opened again.

Thunderstorms Spring and summer are often associated with clear, warm weather, but they are also the times when hazardous thunderstorms can form.

A **thunderstorm** is a localized storm often accompanied by heavy precipitation, frequent thunder, and dangerous lightning. It forms when warm air carrying lots of moisture is forced upward along a cold front. The warm, humid air rises rapidly, forming dense thunderheads. Thunderstorms can bring heavy rain and hail.

During a thunderstorm, positive and negative electrical charges build up and discharge in the thunderheads. Lightning occurs as these charges jump between parts of a cloud, between nearby clouds, or between a cloud and the ground, all of which are shown in **Figure 3**.

The terrifying booms of thunder that can keep us up at night are produced when lightning heats the air near it to as much as 30,000°C. That's hotter than the sun's surface! The rapidly heated air expands explosively, creating the shockwave we call thunder in the surrounding air as it is compressed.

Thunderstorms cause severe damage. Their heavy rains may flood low-lying areas. Large hailstones ruin crops, damage property such as cars and windows, and may even cause fatalities to people and animals out in the open. Lightning strikes start fires and damage structures or sometimes just the electrical equipment within a structure. If lightning strikes a person, it can cause unconsciousness, serious burns, and even death.

Thunder and Lightning
Figure 3 Lightning strikes can cause severe damage during thunderstorms.

Model It

How Thunderstorms Form

Develop Models ✏ Draw a labeled diagram to show the formation of a thunderstorm.

Hurricanes

Hurricanes When a cyclone's winds exceed 119 km/h, we call it a hurricane. A **hurricane** can stretch more than 600 kilometers across and it may have winds as strong as 320 km/h. In the western Pacific Ocean, these storms are called typhoons. When they occur in the Indian Ocean, they are known simply as cyclones.

A typical hurricane that strikes the United States forms in the Atlantic Ocean north of the equator during the late summer. It begins as a low-pressure area, or tropical disturbance, over ocean water warmed by solar radiation.

A hurricane draws its energy from the warm, humid air near the warm ocean's surface. This air rises, forming clouds and drawing surrounding air into the area, as shown in **Figure 4**. Bands of heavy rains and high winds spiral inward toward the area of lowest pressure at the center. The lower the air pressure at the center of the storm, the faster the winds blow toward it.

Hurricane winds are strongest in a narrow band or ring of clouds at the storm's center called the eyewall, which encloses the storm's "eye." When the eye arrives, the weather changes suddenly, growing calm and clear. After the eye passes, the storm resumes, but the winds blow from the opposite direction.

Hurricanes often result in severe flooding, which in turn contaminates drinking water supplies. Wind damage and severe flooding often mean that travel after the storm will be difficult. Residents of hurricane-prone areas are encouraged to stock a three-day supply of drinking water, ready-to-eat food, and any other necessary items, such as medications or diapers, to help them through the aftermath of a hurricane.

Literacy Connection

Cite Textual Evidence
Textual evidence is information or clues that reinforce or support an idea. Reread the third and fourth paragraphs on this page. Underline the evidence that supports the statement that hurricane winds are strongest around the storm's center.

Formation of a Hurricane

Figure 4 ✏ Draw arrows to show how warm, humid air rises to form clouds and how winds spiral toward the area of low pressure.

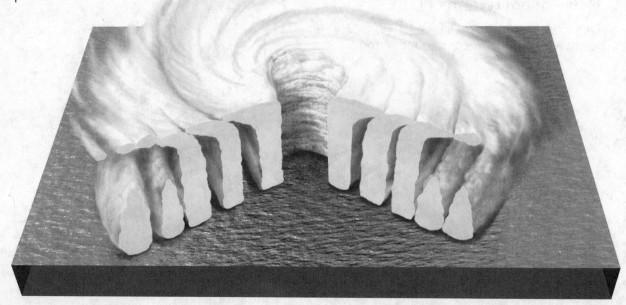

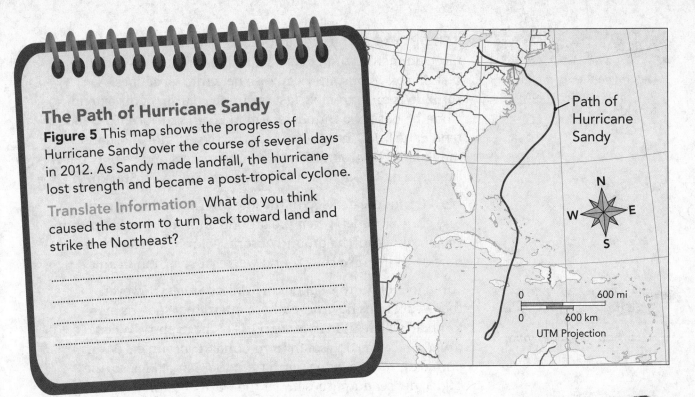

The Path of Hurricane Sandy

Figure 5 This map shows the progress of Hurricane Sandy over the course of several days in 2012. As Sandy made landfall, the hurricane lost strength and became a post-tropical cyclone.

Translate Information What do you think caused the storm to turn back toward land and strike the Northeast?

....

....

....

....

Path of Hurricane Sandy

| 0 | | 600 mi |
| 0 | 600 km | |

UTM Projection

How Hurricanes Move Hurricanes are long-lasting storms, existing for a week or more. They can travel thousands of kilometers from where they originally formed. Hurricanes that form in the Atlantic Ocean are usually steered by easterly trade winds toward the Caribbean islands and then up toward the southeastern and eastern United States, as was Hurricane Sandy in 2012 (**Figure 5**). Once a hurricane passes over land, it loses its energy source: warm, moist air. If the hurricane doesn't travel over another source of warm, moist air to fuel it, it will gradually weaken.

When a hurricane makes landfall, high waves, severe flooding, and wind damage often accompany it. A hurricane's low pressure and high winds can raise the level of the water in the ocean below it by as much as 6 meters above normal sea level. The result is a **storm surge**, a "dome" of water that sweeps across the coast where the hurricane is traveling. Storm surges can cause great damage, destroying human-made structures as well as coastal ecosystems.

✓ READING CHECK **Determine Conclusions** Why don't hurricanes form in oceans in northern latitudes of the world?

....

....

....

HANDS-ON LAB

Investigate Record and analyze historical hurricane data to predict future events.

 INTERACTIVITY

Determine the conditions that favor the formation of tornadoes.

 VIDEO

Watch how tornadoes form.

Tornadoes Thunderstorms can lead to something even more dangerous than heavy rains, flooding, or hail. Under certain conditions, they can also generate tornadoes. A **tornado** is an extremely fast spinning column of air extending from the base of a thunderstorm to Earth's surface. Tornadoes tend to be brief, intense, and destructive. While a tornado may touch the ground for 15 minutes or less and be only a few hundred meters across, its wind speed can reach 500 km/h.

Most tornadoes develop in the late afternoon during spring and early summer, when the ground tends to be warmer than the air above it. The ground absorbs solar radiation more quickly than air so the ground warms faster than the air.

Tornadoes occur throughout the United States. However, the Great Plains have a weather pattern that spawns more tornadoes there than in other parts of the country. When a cold, dry air mass moving south from Canada encounters a warm, humid air mass moving north from the Gulf of Mexico, the colder, denser air pushes under the warmer air mass, forcing it to rise. Warm ground can "turbo-charge" this process by releasing some of the heat it absorbed from the sun. This extra heat forces the air above to rise even faster. An area of low pressure develops and rapidly draws surrounding air inward and up. This fast-moving air rotates as it rises and forms a funnel. If the funnel touches Earth's surface, it becomes a tornado.

Tornado damage comes from both strong winds and the flying debris those winds carry. Tornadoes can move large objects and scatter debris many miles away. The Fujita Scale, shown in **Figure 6**, allows meteorologists to categorize tornadoes based on the amount and type of damage they cause. Only about one percent of tornadoes is ranked as F4 or F5. In 2007, the original Fujita Scale was replaced by the Enhanced Fujita Scale to more closely align high wind speeds with the types of damage they typically cause to structures.

Tornado Damage
Figure 6 Use the image to rate the damage shown by circling a rating on the Fujita Scale.

Fujita Scale	Types of Damage
F0	Branches broken off trees
F1	Mobile homes overturned
F2	Trees uprooted
F3	Roofs torn off
F4	Houses leveled
F5	Houses carried away

Floods and Drought

Storms are not the only type of hazardous severe weather. Floods, droughts, and excessive heat can occur in many different areas in the United States.

Floods Flooding is a major danger during severe storms, such as the one shown in **Figure 7**. A **flood** is an overflowing of water in a normally dry area. Some floods occur when excess water from rain or melting snow overflows a stream or river. In urban areas, floods occur when the ground can't absorb any water because it is already saturated.

Dams and levees are used to control flooding near rivers. A dam is a barrier across a river that may redirect the flow of the river or store floodwaters so that they can be released slowly. An embankment built along a river to prevent flooding of the surrounding land is a levee.

Droughts and Excessive Heat Having too little water can also cause problems. A long period with little or no rainfall is known as a **drought**. Drought is caused by hot, dry weather systems that stay in one place for weeks or months at a time. Long-term droughts can lead to crop failures and wild-fires. Streams, reservoirs, and wells dry up, causing shortages of water for homes, businesses, plants, and animals. People can help lessen the impacts of drought by conserving water.

The excessive heat caused by heat waves can also be harmful to people. Prolonged exposure to heat and the sun can cause skin damage, heat stroke, and dehydration. To prevent over-exposure to the sun, wear protective clothing, sunglasses, and sunscreen, and avoid direct sunlight between the hours of 10 am and 2 pm.

☑ **READING CHECK** Cite Textual Evidence What are two ways to help prevent floods?

Flood Damage
Figure 7 In 2012, as Sandy made landfall, the hurricane lost strength and became a post-tropical cyclone, causing heavy damage from flooding.

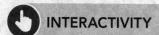

INTERACTIVITY

Examine the technologies used to predict and mitigate the effects of severe weather.

Storm Safety

When potentially dangerous storms are likely, weather announcements indicate where there is a storm "watch" and where there is a storm "warning." A watch means that conditions are right for producing severe weather, but the severe weather has not yet developed. A warning signifies that severe weather is approaching and people should take shelter. **Figure 8** shows the precautions people should take for each type of severe storm.

Severe Storm Safety

Figure 8 Different severe storms require different safety measures.

Tornado If you hear a tornado warning, go to a safe area quickly. Move to the middle of the ground floor. Stay away from windows and doors.

Winter Storm Winter storms can limit your vision and make it easy to get lost. Strong winds cool bodies rapidly. Stay or get indoors and keep a supply of water and food on hand in case of a power outage.

Thunderstorm Get and stay indoors. If in a car, it's safe to stay there. But if you are outside, find a low area away from trees, fences, and poles. If you are swimming or in a boat, get to shore and find shelter.

Hurricane Today, weather satellites can track and warn people well in advance of an approaching hurricane. You should be prepared to evacuate, or move away temporarily. If you hear a hurricane warning and are told to evacuate, leave the area immediately.

☑ READING CHECK Determine Central Ideas What safety precautions are common to all types of severe weather?

....

....

1. Identify What are four types of severe storms?

....

....

2. Patterns A certain severe storm causes much property damage from heavy rain and winds that travel in a straight line. What type of severe storm has these characteristics? Why don't the other types of storms apply to this description?

....

....

....

....

3. Draw Conclusions When hurricanes or thunderstorms strike, damage from the floods they may produce can last much longer than the storms themselves. Why do floods cause damage for longer periods of time?

....

....

....

....

....

4. Develop Models 🖊 Assume a tornado warning has been issued for where you live. Draw a diagram of your home and show where in it you would go to be safe during a tornado. Then, beneath your diagram, explain why that location would be safe.

....

....

....

....

Quest CHECK-IN

In this lesson, you studied how storms like thunderstorms, hurricanes, and tornadoes form. You also learned about the damage these storms can cause and how people can protect themselves from severe storms.

Summarize Choose a severe storm. What information about this storm would you include in a public service announcement about storm safety?

....

....

....

....

....

HANDS-ON LAB

The History of Hazardous Weather

Do the Hands-On lab to determine how examining past data help to prepare people for future weather hazards. Then analyze data about tornadoes in the United States.

MS-ESS2-5, MS-ESS3-2

THE CASE OF THE

Runaway Hurricane

Have you ever lived through a hurricane? If so, you know how dangerous they can be. Hurricane winds range from 74 to nearly 200 miles per hour. Storm surges can be greater than 8 feet. These major storms can submerge whole neighborhoods and destroy houses.

During a hurricane, downed power lines result in widespread power outages, flooding can reach as high as the second floor of houses, and downed trees and telephone poles make roads dangerous or impassable. Roofs can be torn off buildings and hurled violently through the air, along with other movable property such as lawn chairs. The powerful storm can even cause some buildings to collapse.

Hurricanes generate far out at sea. They may pick up strength and speed over warm water as they move toward the coast, or weaken in cold water before they reach land. Florida's exceptionally long coastline and tropical location make it a prime target for hurricanes. These two factors explain why Florida is hit by more major hurricanes than any other U.S. state.

In 2016, Hurricane Matthew did not hit Florida directly, but it dumped flooding rains on the state. Insurance claims for damage have thus far added up to more than $218 million.

There's no changing the fact that many states lie in the path of many hurricanes. Officials high-risk areas are working hard to find ways to lower the risks, including issuing new rules for storm-resistant structures and spending more money on disaster planning, so that communities will be better prepared for future storms.

Hurricane Matthew caused severe flooding and major property damage in Florida in 2016.

Use the map to answer questions 1–2.

1. Make Observations
What general observations can you make about hurricane risk in the U.S.?

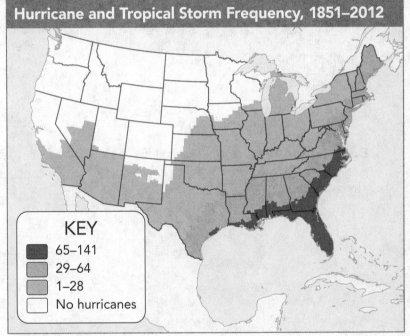

Hurricane and Tropical Storm Frequency, 1851–2012

KEY
- 65–141
- 29–64
- 1–28
- No hurricanes

Source: FEMA

2. Construct Explanations
How would you characterize the risk of a hurricane strike where you live? Use evidence from the map to support your explanation.

3. Solve Problems Besides the solutions mentioned in the text, what do you think people living in areas where hurricanes are common might do to address the continual threat of major hurricanes?

☑ TOPIC 6 Review and Assess

1 The Atmosphere Around You

MS-ESS2-5, MS-ESS2-6, MS-ESS3-2, MS-PS1-4

1. The atmosphere is mostly made up of the gases .... and ....

2. **Explain Phenomena** In what sense does Earth's atmosphere help to keep Earth "just right"?

....
....
....
....
....
....

3. **Develop Models** In the space below, draw a simple diagram of the layers of Earth's atmosphere.

2 Water in the Atmosphere

MS-ESS2-4

4. What is the measure of the amount of water vapor in the air?
   A. dew point   B. evaporation
   C. precipitation   D. humidity

5. What process in the water cycle is driven directly by the sun's energy?
   A. precipitation   B. condensation
   C. evaporation   D. transpiration

6. In the water cycle, water vapor becomes liquid water during

....

7. **Construct Explanations** Describe how clouds form during the water cycle.

....
....
....
....
....
....
....
....
....
....
....
....
....
....
....

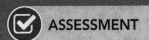
3 Air Masses

MS-ESS2-5

8. Which type of front does not move?
   A. cold
   B. occluded
   C. stationary
   D. warm

9. Which term describes the boundary where two air masses meet?
   A. anticyclone
   B. cyclone
   C. front
   D. jet stream

10. What type of air mass is most likely to form over the Atlantic Ocean near the equator?

....

4 Predicting Weather Changes

MS-ESS2-5, MS-ESS2-6

11. What does an isobar show on a weather map?
    A. areas of low humidity
    B. areas of high wind speeds
    C. areas of equal air pressure
    D. areas of equal temperature

12. A person who collects and analyzes weather data and uses the results to make weather forecasts is a(n)

....

13. **Communicate** How are cold fronts and warm fronts represented on a weather map?

....

....

....

....

5 Severe Weather and Floods

MS-ESS3-2

14. Which type of storm always forms over and pulls energy from a large body of warm water?
    A. hurricane
    B. thunderstorm
    C. tornado
    D. winter storm

15. Which of the following are <u>not</u> used to prevent flooding during storms?
    A. dams
    B. levees
    C. boats
    D. sandbags

16. What type of storm is associated with the term "lake effect"?
    A. hurricane
    B. thunderstorm
    C. tornado
    D. winter storm

17. **Develop Models** ✏ Thunderstorms are rainstorms that include thunder and lightning. Draw a diagram that illustrates how thunder and lightning occur during a thunderstorm. Be sure to use labels to explain your diagram.

MS-ESS2-5

Evidence-Based Assessment

Kamiko is researching local weather patterns in her region. She observes the air pressure each day at noon and records it in millibars, a unit for measuring pressure in the atmosphere. She displays these data in a graph. In addition to recording the air pressure each day, Kamiko records her observations about the general weather, as well as wind direction and speed. The data she records are shown in the table.

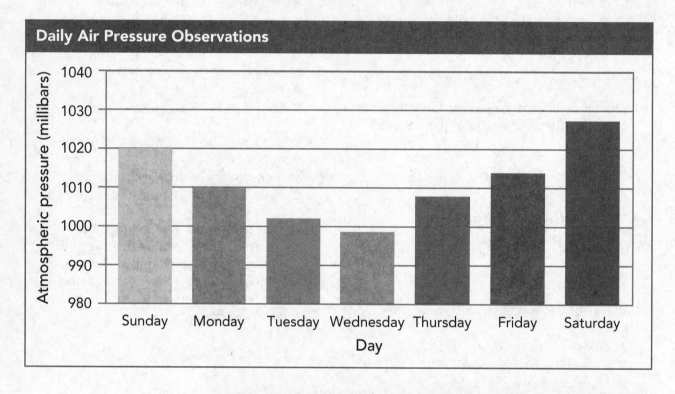

Daily Air Pressure Observations

Day	Weather	Wind (kilometers per hour)
Sunday	sunny	11 from south
Monday	cloudy	15 from south
Tuesday	rain	22 from south
Wednesday	snow	22 from northwest
Thursday	breezy	30 from northwest
Friday	sunny	19 from northwest
Saturday	sunny	9 from north

1. **Analyze Data** Between which two days did Kamiko observe the greatest change in air pressure?

    A. Sunday to Monday
    B. Tuesday to Wednesday
    C. Thursday to Friday
    D. Friday to Saturday

2. **Patterns** What pattern do you notice in the wind speed data? What is responsible for this pattern?

    ....

    ....

    ....

    ....

    ....

    ....

    ....

    ....

    ....

    ....

    ....

    ....

3. **Apply Scientific Reasoning** Which of the following statements about Kamiko's observations from Sunday to Monday are true?

    ☐ The increase in wind speed indicated that temperatures would begin to rise.

    ☐ The drop in air pressure indicated that rain was probably on its way.

    ☐ The decrease in wind speed indicated that a high pressure system was moving in.

    ☐ The increase in clouds and wind speed indicated that inclement weather was coming.

4. **Construct Arguments** Use evidence from the graph and data table to explain why Kamiko observed rain on Tuesday, but snow on Wednesday.

    ....

    ....

    ....

    ....

    ....

    ....

    ....

    ....

    ....

    ....

Quest FINDINGS

Complete the Quest!

Phenomenon Create your PSA to help people understand, predict, prepare for, and avoid the dangers of severe weather.

Apply Concepts Severe storms can harm people and damage property. What climate and weather factors do meteorologists track to help people stay informed about severe weather events? Explain.

....

....

....

....

....

INTERACTIVITY

Reflect on Your PSA

MS-ESS2-4

Water From Trees

How can you **gather evidence** that **plants** are part of the **water cycle**?

Background

Phenomenon A local horticultural society that opposes the construction of a new mall in the community has enlisted your help.

The group members believe that cutting down thousands of trees will have a negative impact on the environment. In this lab, you will design an investigation to collect evidence that trees play an important role in the water cycle.

Materials

(per group)

- balance scale
- 3 plastic sandwich bags
- 3 small pebbles
- 3 twist ties

Plan Your Investigation

HANDS-ON LAB

☑ **Demonstrate** Go online for a downloadable worksheet of this lab.

☐ 1. You will use the materials provided by your teacher to design and conduct an investigation to identify the mass of water released by several plant leaves outside over a 7-day period.

☐ 2. Consider the following questions before you begin planning your investigation:

   • How can you use the bag, pebble, and twist tie to collect water from several leaves of a tree?

   • How many trials will you conduct?

   • What data will you collect?

   • How can you determine the mass of water released by the plant leaf after 7 days?

☐ 3. In the space provided, write out a procedure that identifies the steps you will follow to conduct your investigation. Include a sketch of your setup.

☐ 4. Create a data table in the space provided to record the data you collect.

☐ 5. After receiving your teacher's approval for your plan, conduct your investigation.

uDemonstrate Lab

Procedure and Sketch

Data Table

Analyze and Interpret Data

1. **Make Observations** What did you observe in the plastic bags after 7 days? Where did the water you observed come from?

   ....

   ....

   ....

2. **Calculate** A large, mature tree can contain as many as 200,000 leaves. Using the data you collected, calculate the mass of water that might transpire from a mature tree in one day.

   ....

   ....

3. **Evaluate Your Plan** Review the data table from another group's investigation. How might your group modify your data table?

   ....

   ....

   ....

4. **Construct Arguments** In the space provided, sketch a diagram of Earth's water cycle. Use arrows and labels to indicate water's movement through the cycle. Based on your evidence, include a tree in your diagram to show the role that trees and other plants play in the water cycle.

NGSS PERFORMANCE EXPECTATION

MS-ESS2-1 Develop a model to describe the cycling of Earth's materials and the flow of energy that drives this process.

What caused
this rock to look
like this?

GO ONLINE
to access your
digital course

 VIDEO

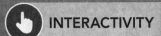 INTERACTIVITY

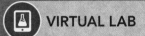 VIRTUAL LAB

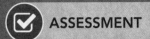 ASSESSMENT

 eTEXT

 APP

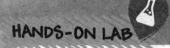

HANDS-ON LAB

µConnect Explore and model Earth's structure.

The Essential Question

What events form Earth's rocks?

Shiprock is a rock formation in New Mexico that stands about 480 meters (about 1,600 feet) tall. How do you think this rock formed?

....

....

....

....

....

Quest KICKOFF

How can you depict Earth processes in a movie script?

Phenomenon A movie producer is working on an exciting new adventure film. Much of the action takes place not in space, not on Earth, but *under* the surface of Earth. The producer wants to present a realistic view of this world, so she hires a science consultant to help get the facts right. In this problem-based Quest activity, you will help evaluate and revise movie scripts whose plots involve action that takes place within Earth. Based on your research and understanding of Earth's structure, you will suggest changes that reflect accurate science. In the Findings activity, you will reflect on how accurately movies depict scientific facts.

 INTERACTIVITY

Science in the Movies

MS-ESS2-1 Develop a model to describe the cycling of Earth's materials and the flow of energy that drives this process.

NBC LEARN ▶ VIDEO

After watching the Quest Kickoff video and reacting to some movie scenes, think about a scientific falsehood that you have seen in a movie. How do you suggest changing the script to reflect the science accurately?

The scene and its false science

....

....

....

....

How the scene should be changed

....

....

....

....

....

Quest CHECK-IN

IN LESSON 1

What is the structure of Earth's mantle and core? How could a movie accurately depict these regions inside Earth?

 INTERACTIVITY

The Deep Drill

Quest CHECK-INS

IN LESSON 2

How do stalactites and stalagmites form? Model the formation of these structures.

HANDS-ON LAB

Make Your Own Stalactites and Stalagmites

Quest CHECK-IN

IN LESSON 3

What are the three types of rocks and how do they form? Consider how different types of rock form and represent that information accurately in a movie script.

 INTERACTIVITY

Rocky Business

The 1959 movie *Journey to the Center of the Earth* was based on Jules Verne's novel, published in 1864. In the story, a professor and several other characters travel through the center of Earth, entering through a volcano in Iceland and exiting through a volcano in Italy.

Quest CHECK-IN

IN LESSON 4

What processes affect rock formation? Understand different rock cycle processes and appropriately depict those processes in a script.

👆 **INTERACTIVITY**

The Rock Cyclers

Quest FINDINGS

Complete the Quest!

Now that you have revised movie scripts to be more scientifically accurate, consider how you will view the science in other movies differently.

👆 **INTERACTIVITY**

Reflect on Science in Movies

① Earth's Interior

Guiding Questions

- How do geologists study Earth's layered interior?
- What roles do heat and pressure in Earth's interior play in the cycling of matter?
- What are the patterns and effects of convection in Earth's mantle?

Connections

Literacy Translate Information

Math Construct Graphs

MS-ESS2-1

Vocabulary

seismic wave
crust
mantle
outer core
inner core

Academic Vocabulary

evidence
elements

 VOCABULARY APP

Practice vocabulary on a mobile device.

Quest CONNECTION

Think about how understanding the structure of Earth's interior can help you to evaluate Earth processes depicted in a movie script.

Connect It !

What do you observe about the rock shown in Figure 1?

Determine Differences How do the xenoliths compare to the surrounding rock?

....

....

Apply Scientific Reasoning How might xenoliths help geologists understand Earth's interior?

....

....

Learning About Earth's Interior

How do we study Earth's interior and connect those interior processes to things we see or experience on Earth's surface? This question is difficult to answer because geologists are unable to see deep inside Earth. However, geologists have found other ways to study the unseen interior of Earth. Their methods focus on two main types of **evidence**: direct evidence from rock samples and indirect evidence from seismic waves.

Academic Vocabulary

Suppose you think the air temperature is getting colder. Give two examples of evidence you could use to support your idea.

....

....

....

....

....

....

Rock Hitchhikers

Figure 1 These yellowish-green pieces of rock are *xenoliths*, from ancient Greek words *xeno*, meaning "foreign," and *lith*, meaning "rock." These xenoliths are fragments of peridotite, a rock that forms at least 50 to 60 kilometers deep inside Earth. They were picked up and carried to the surface by melted rock that later hardened and formed the grayish surrounding rock.

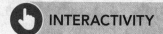

INTERACTIVITY

Explore how to investigate something you cannot directly observe.

Evidence From Rock Samples Geologists have drilled holes as deep as 12.3 kilometers into Earth. Drilling brings up many samples of rock and gives geologists many clues. They learn about Earth's structure and conditions deep inside Earth where the rocks are formed. In addition, volcanoes sometimes carry rocks to the surface from depths of more than 100 kilometers. These rocks provide more information about Earth's interior, including clues about how matter and energy flow there. Some rocks from mountain ranges show evidence that they formed deep within Earth's crust and later were elevated as mountains formed. Also, in laboratories, geologists have used models to recreate conditions similar to those inside Earth to see how those conditions affect rock.

Evidence From Seismic Waves To study Earth's interior, geologists also use an indirect method. When earthquakes occur, they produce **seismic waves** (SIZE mik). Geologists record the seismic waves and study how they travel through Earth. The paths of seismic waves reveal where the makeup or form of the rocks change, as shown in **Figure 2**.

Waves

Figure 2 Earthquakes produce different types of seismic waves that travel through Earth. The speed of these waves and the paths they take give geologists clues about the structure of the planet's interior.

Make Observations Compare and contrast the paths that P-waves and S-waves take through Earth. How do you think this information helps geologists understand Earth's interior?

....

....

....

....

....

....

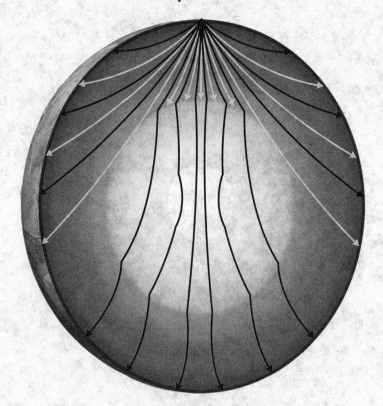

Earthquake epicenter

→ P-waves travel through solids and liquids.

→ S-waves only travel through solids.

Earth's Layers

After many years of research, scientists today know that Earth's interior is made up of three main layers: crust, mantle, and core. These layers vary greatly in thickness, composition, temperature, and pressure.

Pressure results from a force pressing on an area. Within Earth's interior, the mass of rock that is pressing down from above causes an increase of pressure on the rocks below. The deeper inside Earth's interior, the greater the pressure becomes. Pressure inside Earth increases much like water pressure in the swimming pool increases as you dive down deeper, as in **Figure 3**.

The temperature inside Earth increases as depth increases. Just beneath Earth's surface, the surrounding rock is cool. At about 20 meters down, the rock starts to get warmer. For every 40 meters of depth from that point, the temperature typically rises 1 degree Celsius. The rapid rise in temperature continues for several tens of kilometers. Eventually, the temperature increases more slowly, but steadily. The high temperatures inside Earth are mostly the result of the release of energy from radioactive substances and heat left over from the formation of Earth 4.6 billion years ago.

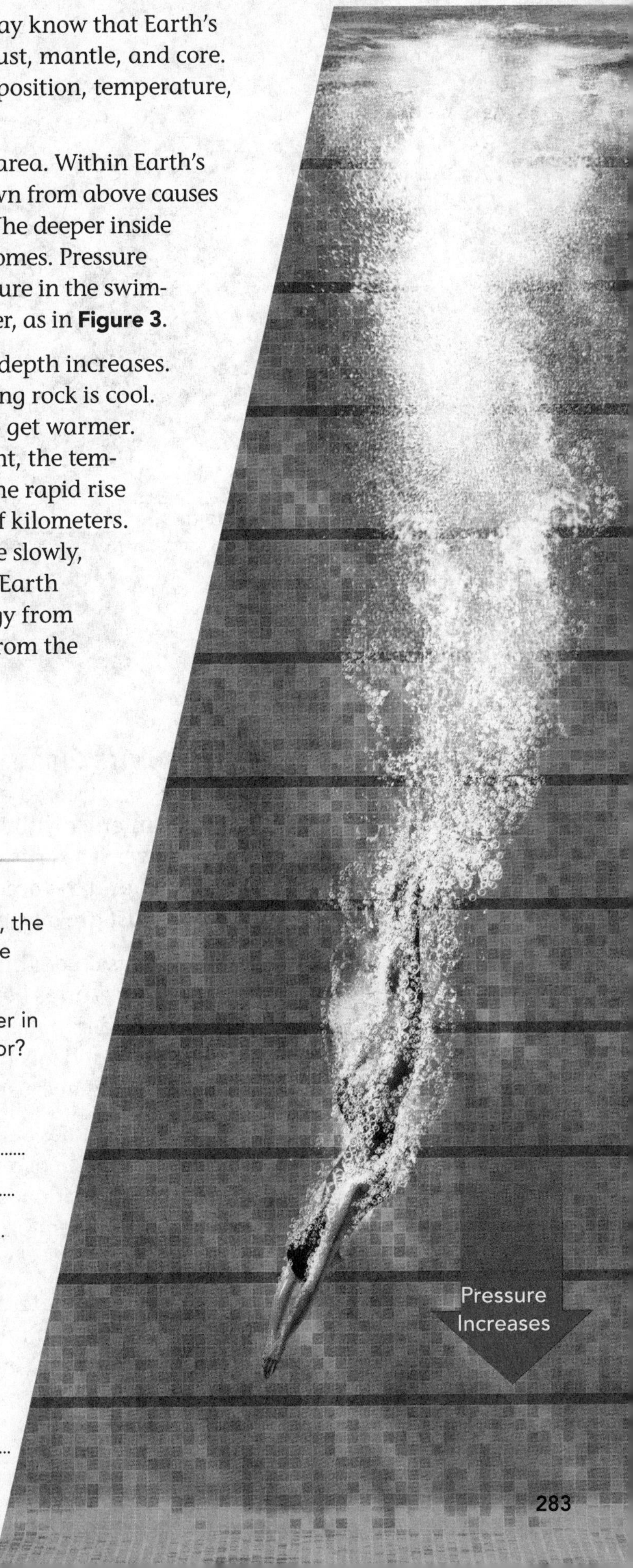

Pressure and Depth

Figure 3 The deeper that the swimmer goes, the greater the pressure on the swimmer from the surrounding water.

1. Compare and Contrast How is the water in the swimming pool similar to Earth's interior? How is it different? (*Hint:* Consider both temperature and pressure in your answer.)

   ....

   ....

   ....

   ....

   ....

2. Use Proportional Relationships At what location in the pool would the water pressure be greatest?

   ....

Pressure Increases

Earth's Layers

Figure 4 The crust and uppermost mantle make up the rigid lithosphere. The lithosphere rests on the softer material of the asthenosphere.

Translate Information Use the diagram to identify the layers and contrast how rigid they are.

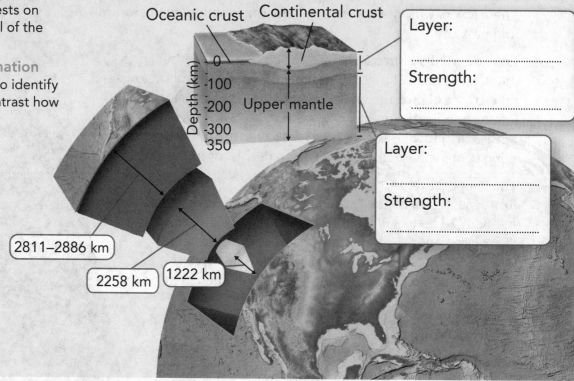

Oceanic crust   Continental crust

Layer:

....

Strength:

....

Depth (km)

0
-100
-200 Upper mantle
-300
350

Layer:

....

Strength:

....

2811–2886 km

2258 km   1222 km

Academic Vocabulary

Oxygen and silicon are two of the chemical elements that make up the crust. *Elements* can also refer to the smallest or most basic parts of something, such as machine. Describe the elements of something, such as parts of a machine, that you used today.

....

....

....

The Crust

Have you ever hiked up a mountain, toured a mine, or explored a cave? During each of these activities people interact with Earth's **crust**, the rock that forms Earth's outer layer. The crust is a layer of solid rock that includes both dry land and the ocean floor. The main **elements** of the rocks in the crust are oxygen and silicon.

The crust is much thinner than the layers beneath it. In most places, the crust is between 5 and 40 kilometers thick. It is thickest under high mountains, where it can be as thick as 80 kilometers, and it is thinnest beneath the ocean floor. There are two types of crust: oceanic crust and continental crust.

The crust that lies beneath the ocean is called oceanic crust. The composition of all oceanic crust is nearly the same. Its overall composition is much like basalt, with small amounts of ocean sediment on top. Basalt (buh SAWLT) is a dark, fine-grained rock.

Continental crust forms the continents. It contains many types of rocks. But overall the composition of continental crust is much like granite. Granite is a rock that usually is a light color and has coarse grains.

The Mantle Directly below the crust, the rock in Earth's interior changes. Rock here contains more magnesium and iron than does the rock above it. The rock below the crust is the solid material of the **mantle**, a layer of hot rock. Overall, the mantle is nearly 3,000 kilometers thick.

The uppermost part of the mantle is brittle rock, like the rock of the crust. Both the crust and the uppermost part of the mantle are strong, hard, and rigid. Geologists often group the crust and uppermost mantle into a single layer called the lithosphere. As shown in **Figure 4**, Earth's lithosphere is about 100 kilometers thick.

Below the lithosphere, the material is increasingly hotter. As a result, the part of the mantle just beneath the lithosphere is less rigid than the lithosphere itself. Over thousands of years, this part of the mantle may bend like a metal spoon, but it is still solid. This solid yet bendable layer is called the asthenosphere.

Beneath the asthenosphere is the lower mantle, which is hot, rigid, and under intense pressure. The lower mantle extends down to Earth's core.

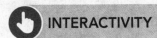

INTERACTIVITY

Examine the different layers of Earth.

Math Toolbox

Temperature in Earth's Layers

1. **Construct Graphs** ✏ Use the data in the table to complete the line graph.

2. **Interpret Graphs** How does temperature change with depth in Earth's mantle?

....

....

....

....

Depth (km)	Temperature (°C)
500	1,600°C
1,000	1,800°C
1,500	2,200°C
2,000	2,500°C
2,500	2,900°C

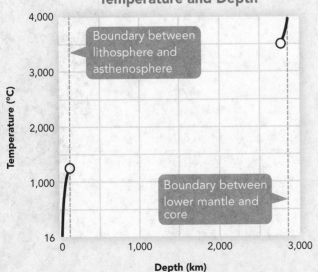

Temperature and Depth

Boundary between lithosphere and asthenosphere

Boundary between lower mantle and core

Temperature (°C)

Depth (km)

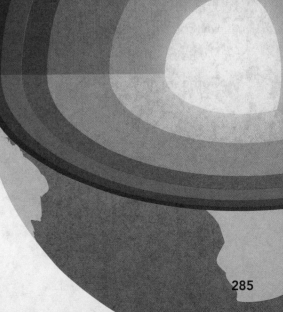

285

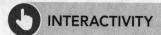
The Core Below the mantle is Earth's dense core. Earth's core occupies the center of the planet. It consists of two parts, a liquid outer core and a solid inner core. The outer core is 2,260 kilometers thick. The inner core is a solid ball with a radius of about 1,220 kilometers. Therefore, total radius of the entire core is approximately 3,480 kilometers.

The **outer core** is a layer of molten metal surrounding the inner core. Despite enormous pressure, the outer core is liquid. The **inner core** is a dense ball of solid metal. In the inner core, extreme pressure squeezes the atoms of iron and nickel so much that they cannot spread out to become liquid despite the extremely high temperatures.

Currently, most evidence suggests that both parts of the core are mostly made of iron and nickel. Scientists have found data suggesting that the core also contains smaller amounts oxygen, sulfur, and silicon.

Model It

1. **Develop Models** Label Earth's layers and use the text on the page to fill in the table with details about the layers.

	Thickness	Composition	Solid/Liquid
Crust:			
Mantle:			
Outer core:			
Inner core:			
Total:	6,370 km		

2. **Compare and Contrast** Pick any two points inside Earth and label them A and B. Record their locations.

My Point A is in the ....

My Point B is in the ....

Compare and contrast Earth at those two points.

....

....

....

The Core and Earth's Magnetic Field
Scientists think that movements in the liquid outer core produce Earth's magnetic field. Earth's magnetic field affects the whole planet.

To understand how a magnetic field affects an object, think about a bar magnet. If you place the magnet on a piece of paper and sprinkle iron filings on the paper, the iron filings automatically line up in a pattern matching the bar's magnetic field. If you could surround Earth with iron filings, they would form a similar pattern. This is also what happens when you use a compass. The compass needle aligns with Earth's magnetic field.

☑ READING CHECK **Identify Evidence** How can iron filings provide evidence that a bar magnet has a magnetic field?

....

....

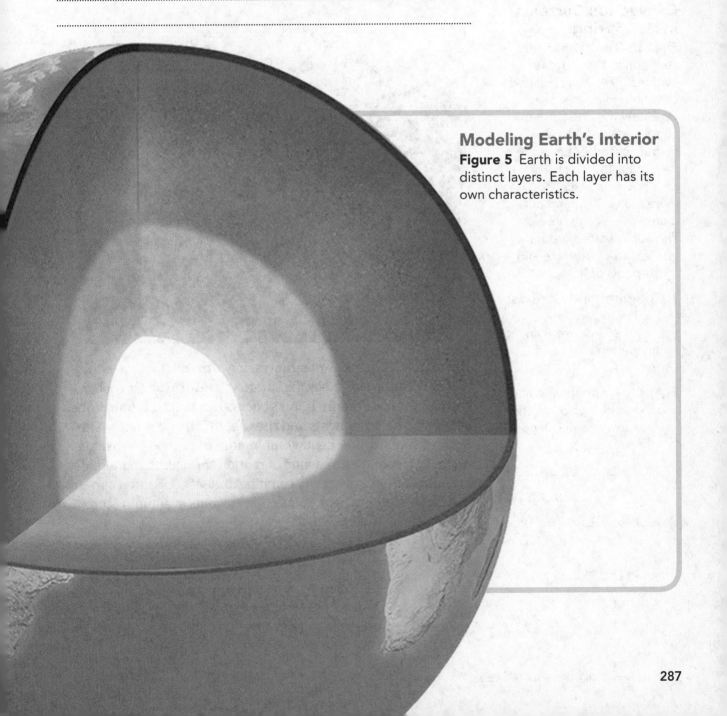

Modeling Earth's Interior
Figure 5 Earth is divided into distinct layers. Each layer has its own characteristics.

Movement in Earth's Mantle

Recall that Earth's mantle and core are extremely hot. Heat is a form of energy that flows. It transfers from matter at a higher temperature to matter at a lower temperature. The transfer of heat in the mantle drives a process called convection. This process is how matter and energy cycle through Earth's interior as well as its surface.

Convection Currents When you heat water on a stove, the water at the bottom of the pot gets hot and expands. As the heated water expands, its density decreases. Less-dense fluids flow up through denser fluids.

Convection Currents in Hot Springs

Figure 6 Hot springs are common in Yellowstone National Park. Here, melted snow and rainwater seep far below the crust into the mantle, where a shallow magma chamber heats the rock of Earth's crust. The rock heats the water to more than 200°C and puts it under very high pressure. This superheated groundwater rises to the surface and forms pools of hot water.

1. **Compare and Contrast** The heated water is (more/less) dense than the melted snow and rainwater.

2. **Apply Concepts** What process causes convection currents to form in a hot spring?

....

....

....

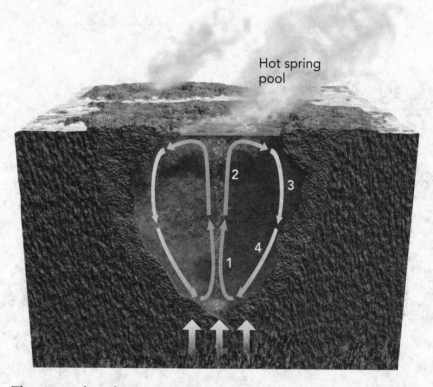

Hot spring pool

The warm, less dense water moves upward and floats over the cooler, denser water. Near the surface, the warm water cools, becoming denser again. It sinks back down to the bottom of the pot. Here, the water heats and rises again. The flows shown in **Figure 6** that transfer heat within matter are called convection currents. Heating and cooling of matter, changes in matter's density, and the force of gravity combine and set convection currents in motion. Without heat, convection currents eventually stop.

✓ **READING CHECK** **Cause and Effect** What three processes or forces combine to set convection currents in motion?

....

....

....

Convection Currents in Earth Heat from the core and from the mantle itself drives convection currents. These currents carry hot, solid rock of the mantle outward and cooled, solid rock inward in a never-ending cycle.

As the oceanic lithosphere cools and sinks, it drives a pattern of mantle convection. The cold lithosphere moves down into the mantle, where it is heated. An upward return flow of hot rock completes the cycle, as shown in **Figure 7**. Over and over, the cycle of sinking and rising takes place. One full cycle takes millions of years. Convection currents are involved in the production of new rock at Earth's surface. There are also convection currents in the outer core.

Literacy Connection

Translate Information As you look at the visuals depicting convection, come up with an explanation for how the directions of two side-by-side convection currents determine whether material in the mantle rises or descends.

....

....

....

....

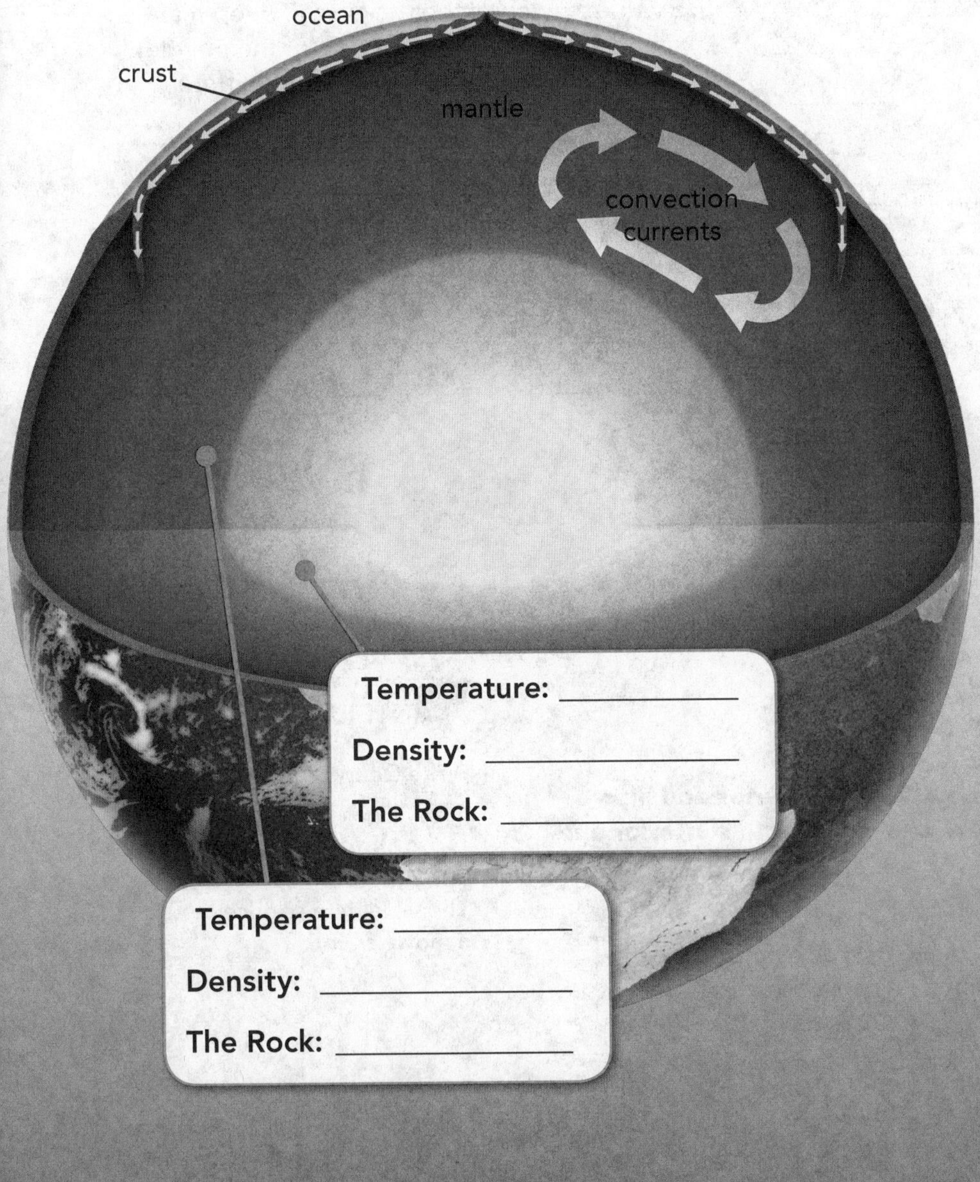

ocean
crust
mantle
convection currents

Temperature: _____

Density: _____

The Rock: _____

Temperature: _____

Density: _____

The Rock: _____

Mantle Convection

Figure 7 Complete the model by drawing the missing convection currents.

Use Models Then complete the figure labels by using the terms in the box.

hotter

colder

less dense

more dense

sinks

rises

Make Meaning How can a solid such as mantle rock flow? Think about candle wax. In your science notebook, describe how you can make candle wax flow. What other solids have you observed that can flow?

MS-ESS2-1

1. Identify Name each layer of Earth, starting from Earth's center.

....

....

....

....

2. Apply Concepts Give examples of direct evidence and indirect evidence that geologists use to learn about Earth's interior.

....

....

....

....

....

....

3. Predict What would happen to the convection currents in the mantle if Earth's interior cooled down? Why?

....

....

....

4. Explain How does convection cause movement of material and energy in Earth's interior?

....

....

....

....

....

....

5. Evaluate How is the rock in the deep mantle similar to the rock in the parts of the mantle nearest the surface? How are they different?

....

....

....

....

....

....

Quest CHECK-IN

In this lesson, you learned about Earth's interior and also how energy and material move between Earth's interior and its surface.

Engage in Argument Explain why you think it is or isn't important for science fiction films to depict natural processes and geological events as accurately as possible.

....

....

....

....

👆 INTERACTIVITY

The Deep Drill

Go online to find out more about Earth's interior structure. Then evaluate science facts in a movie script.

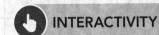 INTERACTIVITY

Design a satellite that can collect electromagnetic field data.

Examining **Earth's Interior** from **Space**

How can you study Earth's interior? You engineer it! Geologist use satellites to help them visualize what they cannot see.

The Challenge: To understand how scientists study what they can't observe directly.

Phenomenon As Earth rotates, its liquid outer core spins. The flow and movement of Earth's oceans also create electric currents that generate secondary magnetic fields. Scientists call this process "motional induction." The European Space Agency (ESA) has launched three satellites into Earth's orbit that are sensitive to these electric currents.

The satellites also tell us many details about the electrical conductivity inside Earth's core—both the liquid of the outer core and the solid metallic sphere found at the center of the planet. A rock's ability to conduct electricity is related to its temperature, mineral composition, and water content. A satellite cannot directly measure these things. However, scientists can now draw reasonable conclusions about them by studying satellite data about the electric currents that flow through and just below Earth's surface.

Swarm Satellites launched in November 2013. The ESA's three-satellite Swarm mission is helping to improve our understanding of Earth's interior by taking measurements of its magnetic fields.

DESIGN CHALLENGE Can you design your own satellite? Go to the Engineering Design Notebook to find out!

LESSON 2 Minerals

Guiding Questions

- What are the characteristics and properties of minerals?
- What processes result in the formation of minerals?
- What processes explain the distribution of mineral resources on Earth?

Connections

Literacy Integrate With Visuals

Math Calculate

MS-ESS2-1, MS-ESS3-1

Vocabulary

mineral
crystal
crystallization

Academic Vocabulary

organic

 VOCABULARY APP

Practice vocabulary on a mobile device.

Quest CONNECTION

Consider how understanding the ways in which minerals form helps you accurately evaluate Earth processes depicted in a movie script.

Connect It !

✎ **Circle two crystals in the photo.**

Relate Change Do you think these crystals formed in conditions that were stable or that changed often? Explain.

....

....

....

....

Defining Minerals

Look at the objects in **Figure 1**. They are solid matter that formed deep beneath Earth's surface. They are beautiful, gigantic crystals of the mineral selenite, which is a form of gypsum. But what is a mineral?

Characteristics

A **mineral** is a naturally occurring solid that can form by inorganic processes and has a crystal structure and definite chemical composition. For a substance to be a mineral, it must have the following five characteristics.

Naturally Occurring All minerals are substances that form by natural processes. Gypsum forms naturally from chemical elements that precipitate from water.

Solid A mineral is always a solid, which means it has a definite volume and shape. The particles in a solid are packed tightly together. Gypsum is a solid.

Forms by Inorganic Processes All minerals must form by inorganic processes. That is, they can form from materials that were not a part of living things. Gypsum forms naturally as sulfate-rich solutions evaporate. Some minerals, such as calcite, form from both inorganic and organic processes.

Crystal Structure The particles of a mineral line up in a pattern that repeats over and over again. The repeating pattern of a mineral's particles forms a solid called a **crystal**. The gypsum in the image has a crystal structure.

Definite Chemical Composition A mineral has a definite chemical composition. This means it always contains the same elements in certain proportions. Gypsum always contains calcium, oxygen, sulfur, and hydrogen, in set proportions.

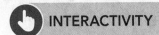

INTERACTIVITY

Explain what the term *mineral* means to you.

Reflect Write down where you have heard of minerals before, and the names of any minerals that play a role in your everyday life.

Mineral Giants

Figure 1 Dwarfed by megacrystals of the mineral selenite, miners explore Mexico's Cave of Crystals. Located about 300 meters below Earth's surface, the cave contains some of the largest crystals ever discovered in nature—up to 12 meters long!

INTERACTIVITY

Compare and contrast the different properties of minerals.

Mineral Properties Geologists have identified and named more than 5,000 minerals, though only about 20 make up most of the rocks of Earth's crust. Because there are so many minerals, telling them apart can be challenging. Each mineral has characteristic properties that are used to identify and describe it. **Figure 2** shows some of the properties of the mineral pyrite.

Luster Luster is the term that describes how light reflects from a mineral's surface. Terms used to describe luster include *metallic, glassy, earthy, silky, waxy,* and *pearly.*

Streak The streak of a mineral is the color of its powder. Although the color of a mineral can vary, its streak does not.

Color Minerals come in many colors. Only a few minerals have their own characteristic color.

Identifying Minerals

Figure 2 🖉 You can identify a mineral such as pyrite by its properties. Describe the color and luster of pyrite.

Properties of Pyrite	
Color	
Streak	Greenish black
Luster	
Hardness	6–6.5
Density	5 g/cm³
Crystal structure	Isometric (cubes or octahedrons)
Cleavage or fracture	None; uneven
Special	Becomes magnetic when heated

Density Each mineral has a characteristic density, or mass in a given volume. To calculate a mineral's density, use this formula:
Density = Mass/Volume

Cleavage and Fracture A mineral that splits easily along flat surfaces has the property called cleavage. Whether a mineral has cleavage depends on how the atoms in its crystals are arranged. Most minerals do not split apart evenly. Instead, they have a characteristic type of fracture. Fracture describes how a mineral looks when it breaks apart in an irregular way.

Special Properties Some minerals can be identified by special physical properties. For example, calcite bends light to produce double images. Other minerals conduct electricity, glow when placed under ultraviolet light, or are magnetic.

Crystal Structure All the crystals of a mineral have the same crystal structure. Different minerals have crystals that are shaped differently. Geologists classify crystals by the number of faces, or sides, on the crystal and the angles at which the faces meet.

Math Toolbox

Calculate Density

A sample of the mineral cinnabar has a mass of 251.1 g and a volume of 31.0 cm³.

Calculate What is the density of cinnabar?

....

....

....

....

Hardness The Mohs hardness scale is used to rank the hardness of minerals from 1 being the softest to 10 being the hardest. A mineral can scratch any mineral softer than itself but can be scratched by any mineral that is harder.

Where Minerals Form

Figure 3 ✎ Minerals can form by crystallization of magma and lava or precipitation of materials dissolved in water. Circle the area where you might find a cave with crystals similar to the large crystals shown in **Figure 1**.

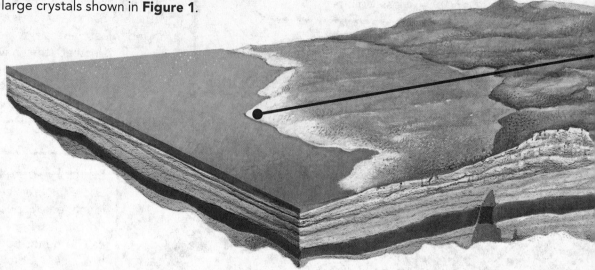

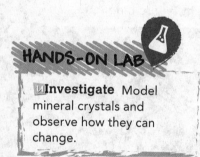

HANDS-ON LAB

Investigate Model mineral crystals and observe how they can change.

Academic Vocabulary

You might be familiar with term *organic food*. How does this meaning of *organic* differ from the scientific meaning?

....

....

....

....

Mineral Formation

In general, minerals can form in a few different ways and at different locations at or below Earth's surface. Some minerals form from organic processes. Other minerals form from the materials dissolved in evaporating solutions of water. Many minerals form when magma and lava originally heated by the energy of Earth's interior cool and solidify. Finally, some minerals form when other minerals are heated or compressed, which causes the material to deform.

Organic Minerals All minerals can form by inorganic processes. However, many **organic** processes can also form minerals. For instance, animals such as cows and humans produce skeletons made of the mineral calcium phosphate. Ultimately, the energy used to drive the processes of mineral formation in most living things can be traced all the way back to the sun and the plants that use its energy.

Minerals From Solutions Sometimes the elements and compounds that form minerals dissolve in water and form solutions. On Earth's surface, energy from the sun can cause water to evaporate, leaving behind minerals. Water below Earth's surface, which is under intense pressure and at high temperatures, can pick up elements and compounds from surrounding rock. When these elements and compounds leave the water solution through precipitation, crystallization can occur.

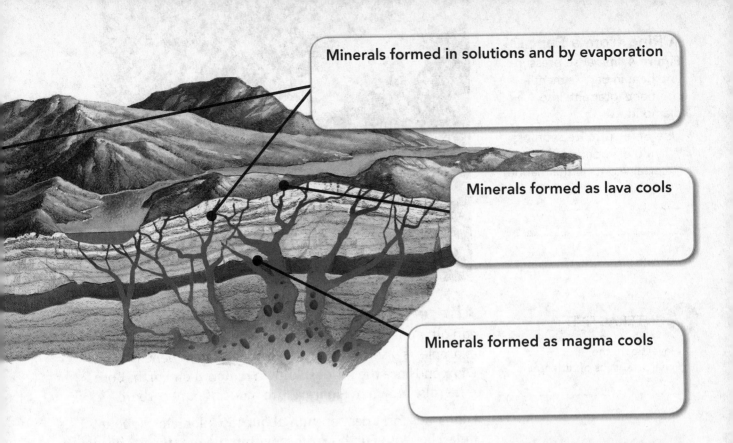

Minerals formed in solutions and by evaporation

Minerals formed as lava cools

Minerals formed as magma cools

Crystallization is the process by which atoms are arranged to form a material that has a crystal structure. Minerals such as halite, calcite, and gypsum form through crystallization when bodies of water on Earth's surface evaporate.

In another example, the huge crystals in **Figure 1** formed from a solution of water heated by energy from Earth's interior that eventually cooled underground. But the process was an extremely long one, taking place over millions of years.

Minerals From Magma and Lava

Many minerals form when hot magma from Earth's interior cools higher up in the crust, or as lava cools and hardens on the surface. When these liquids cool to a solid state, they form crystals.

The size of the crystals depends on several factors, including the rate at which the melted rock cools. Slow cooling leads to the formation of large crystals, such as coarse quartz and feldspar crystals found in granite that slowly cools underground. Fast cooling leaves very little time for crystals to grow. Lava cools quickly on the surface or under water and forms small crystals, such as pyroxene and fine-grained olivine in basalt rock of the oceanic crust.

☑ **READING CHECK** **Summarize Text** What type of minerals might a geologist expect to find near the site of an ancient lava flow? Explain.

....

....

Literacy Connection

Integrate With Visuals
Underline the name of each mineral mentioned on this page. Then, record each mineral in its correct place in **Figure 3**.

A Ring from a Pencil?

Figure 4 Immense pressure and heat in Earth's mantle compacts graphite into diamond.

Use Scientific Reasoning
Why do diamonds only form in certain spots in the mantle?

....

....

....

graphite

cut diamond

 INTERACTIVITY

Investigate the characteristics of different rocks.

Altered Minerals A change of temperature or pressure can alter one mineral into a new mineral. Graphite, for example, is a soft mineral commonly used in pencils. Diamonds are the hardest known material on Earth. Both minerals, shown in **Figure 4**, are made of pure carbon.

Diamonds form deeper than about 150 kilometers (about 90 miles) beneath Earth's surface within the mantle. At this depth below continental crust, temperatures reach between 900°C to 1,300°C, and the pressure is about 50,000 times greater than at Earth's surface. The intense pressure and high temperature alter the structure of the carbon atoms in graphite, forming diamond.

These diamond zones may also contain magma. Long ago, the pressure that formed diamonds also caused magma to squeeze toward Earth's surface, where it might erupt. Sometimes, diamonds were carried along for the ride. When the magma cooled in pipe-like formations, the diamonds were embedded in this rock.

Model It

Diamond Formation

Develop Models 🖊 Use the information in the text and **Figure 3** to draw a diagram that shows how diamonds form. Your model should show and label the following parts of the process:

1. Graphite in the mantle that is under intense pressure becomes diamonds.

2. In the past, magma from the mantle moved quickly toward Earth's surface, forming pipes.

3. The magma cooled with the diamonds trapped within it.

Mineral Distribution The common minerals that make up the rocks of Earth's crust are found abundantly throughout Earth's surface. Other minerals are much less common because their formation depends on certain materials and conditions that may be limited. Other minerals may form as the result of processes that take a very long time, which will limit where and how much of the mineral can form. The process by which diamonds are formed is one example.

Geological processes often tied to plate tectonics, such as volcanic eruptions or evaporations in ocean basins, can cause certain minerals to collect in concentrated deposits. These deposits, or ores, are mined for the valuable materials they contain. **Figure 5** shows the distribution of some of Earth's mineral resources.

INTERACTIVITY

Identify a mineral based on its characteristic properties.

☑ READING CHECK **Integrate With Visuals** What ideas from the text are illustrated in the map in **Figure 5**?

....

....

Mineral Resources

Figure 5 The map shows the location of some important mineral resources. Many of the minerals represented on the map are not evenly distributed across the planet.

Patterns What patterns do you notice in the distributions of different minerals on Earth?

....
....
....
....
....

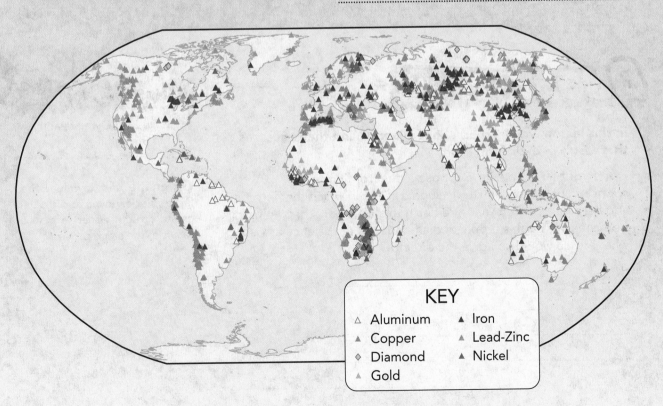

KEY
△ Aluminum   ▲ Iron
▲ Copper   ▲ Lead-Zinc
◇ Diamond   ▲ Nickel
▲ Gold

1. **Analyze Properties** What are some of the properties that geologists use to identify and describe minerals?

....

....

....

2. **Cause and Effect** Why aren't diamonds found evenly distributed on Earth?

....

....

....

....

....

3. **Apply Concepts** Amber is a solid material used in jewelry. It forms in nature only by the process of pine tree resin hardening. Explain why you think amber is or is not a mineral.

....

....

....

....

4. **Apply Concepts** What role does the sun's energy play in the formation of minerals from solutions?

....

....

....

....

....

5. **Develop Models** ✏ Draw a flow chart or cycle diagram to show one way a mineral gets recycled in nature and forms a new mineral.

Quest CHECK-INS

In this lesson, you learned about minerals and the processes that result in their formation.

Construct Arguments Suppose a director filming a science fiction film wants to include a scene in which the hero and heroine travel down inside Earth to stop a band of criminals from stealing Earth's supply of diamonds. As the science advisor, what advice would you give the director?

....

....

....

....

HANDS-ON LAB

Make Your Own Stalactites and Stalagmites

Go online and download the lab to model how two different crystal structures can form as a result of the same process.

MS-ESS2-1

The Cost of TECHNOLOGY

Coltan ore before processing to extract tantalum.

Yyou may never have heard of the element tantalum, but you probably use it every day. The electrical properties of tantalum make it a good material to use in capacitors in electronic devices. And it's found in all the smartphones, laptops, and other electronics that billions of people use to stay organized, get work done, and communicate with each other.

Tantalum must be extracted from an ore called coltan. The ore must be mined and refined before the tantalum can be used. By the turn of the 21st century, worldwide demand for electronics reached a peak, which increased demand for tantalum. Prior to 2000, most of the world's tantalum was extracted from coltan mined in Australia and Brazil. These countries have stricter mining regulations, which increases the cost of mining tantalum.

When demand for tantalum exploded, coltan mining increased in the Democratic Republic of Congo (DRC) and neighboring countries in Africa. But the DRC has been torn apart by civil war, which has lured armed coltan miners looking for a fast profit. The government does little to regulate how the coltan is mined. The unregulated, often illegal, mining provides inexpensive tantalum but destroys vital wildlife habitats and helps to fund continued conflict in this war-ravaged country.

MY COMMUNITY

How would you solve the problem of the need for coltan versus the need to source the coltan responsibly? Work in a small group to identify possible solutions. Conduct internet research to find facts and evidence that support your arguments.

These miners search for coltan, iron ore, and manganese at the Mudere mine in eastern Democratic Republic of Congo.

LESSON
3 Rocks

Guiding Questions

- What are the three major types of rocks and how do they form?
- How is the formation of rocks the result of the flow of energy and cycling of matter within Earth?

Connections

Literacy Summarize Text

Math Analyze Relationships

MS-ESS2-1

Vocabulary

igneous rock
sedimentary rock
sediment
metamorphic
   rock

Academic Vocabulary

apply

 VOCABULARY APP

Practice vocabulary on a mobile device.

Quest CONNECTION

Consider how understanding the ways in which rocks form can help you determine whether scenes in a movie are scientifically accurate.

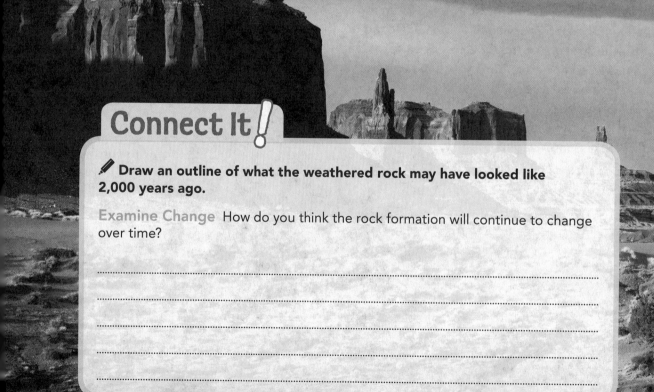

Connect It !

✏️ **Draw an outline of what the weathered rock may have looked like 2,000 years ago.**

Examine Change How do you think the rock formation will continue to change over time?

....

....

....

....

....

Describing Rocks

In southern Utah, spires and buttes of red sandstone rise up into the sky in Monument Valley (**Figure 1**). To a tourist or other casual observer, these rock formations seem to stand motionless and unchanging. But every moment of every day, forces are at work on these rocks, slowly changing their shapes and sizes. Weathering, erosion, transportation, and deposition all work to wear away and alter the appearance of the rock formations.

Rocks, like the sandstone in Monument Valley, are made of mixtures of minerals and other materials. To describe rocks, geologists observe mineral composition, color, and texture.

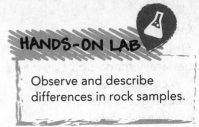

HANDS-ON LAB

Observe and describe differences in rock samples.

Towers of Rock

Figure 1 The striking red color of Monument Valley is the result of iron oxide minerals exposed within the rock.

Granite

Figure 2 Granite is generally made up of only a few common minerals. This coarse granite formed when magma cooled slowly.

Classify ✏ Circle the best word to complete each sentence.

Granite is generally (dark/light) in color.

Granite has a (high/low) silica content.

The grains in granite are (fine/coarse).

Mica

Quartz

Granite

Feldspar

Hornblende

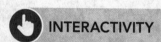

INTERACTIVITY

Identify and evaluate the characteristics of different rocks.

Mineral Composition and Color

Some rocks contain only a single mineral. Other rocks contain several minerals. About 20 minerals make up most of the rocks of Earth's crust. These minerals are known as rock-forming minerals.

A rock's color provides clues to the rock's mineral composition. Granite, as shown in **Figure 2**, is generally a light-colored rock that has high silica content, meaning it is rich in the elements silicon and oxygen.

Texture

Most rocks are made up of particles of minerals or other rocks, which geologists call grains. To describe the texture of a rock, geologists use terms that are based on the size, shape, and pattern of the grains. For example, rocks with grains that are large and easy to see are coarse-grained. In fine-grained rocks, grains can be seen only with a microscope.

Origin

Using mineral composition, color, and texture, geologists classify a rock's origin—how the rock formed. Geologists have classified rocks into three major groups based on origin: igneous rock, sedimentary rock, and metamorphic rock.

☑ **READING CHECK** **Determine Meaning** *Ignis* means "fire" in Latin. What is "fiery" about igneous rocks?

....

Plan It !

Rocky Observations

As part of a geological investigation you are conducting, you observe three rock samples.

Collect Data What characteristics would you examine to help you distinguish among the three rocks?

....

....

How Rocks Form

Each type of rock, whether its igneous, sedimentary, or metamorphic, forms in a different way.

Igneous Rock Rock that forms from cooled magma or lava is **igneous rock** (IG nee us). Igneous rocks can look very different from each other. The temperature and composition of the molten rock determine the kind of igneous rock that is formed.

Igneous rock may form on or beneath Earth's surface from molten material that cools and hardens. Extrusive rock is igneous rock formed from lava that erupted onto Earth's surface. Basalt is the most common extrusive rock, making up a large part of oceanic crust. Igneous rock that formed when magma hardened beneath the surface of Earth is called intrusive rock. The most abundant type of intrusive rock in the continental crust is granite. Granite forms tens of kilometers below Earth's surface and over hundreds of thousands of years or longer. When granite ends up close to the surface, it may be mined for use as road-building material, in a crushed state, or as a building material, in large polished slabs.

The texture of most igneous rock depends on the size and shape of its mineral crystals (**Figure 3**). Rapidly cooling lava found at or near Earth's surface forms fine-grained igneous rocks with small crystals or no minerals at all. Slowly cooling magma below Earth's surface forms coarse-grained rocks, such as granite and diorite, with large crystals. Intrusive rocks have larger grains than extrusive rocks. Extrusive rocks that cool too quickly to form any minerals are called glass.

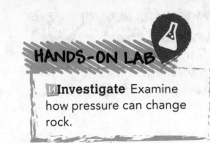

HANDS-ON LAB

⊔**Investigate** Examine how pressure can change rock.

Igneous Rock Formation

Figure 3 The texture of igneous rock varies according to how it forms.

Interpret Diagrams ✎ Did the rocks in the photographs form at A or B? Write your answers in the spaces provided.

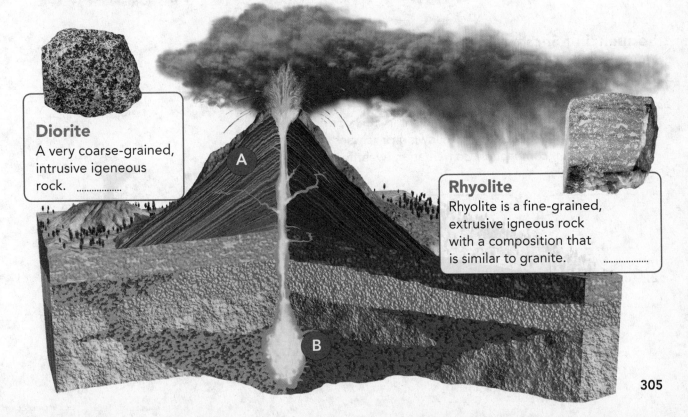

Diorite
A very coarse-grained, intrusive igeneous rock. ....

Rhyolite
Rhyolite is a fine-grained, extrusive igneous rock with a composition that is similar to granite. ....

Literacy Connection

Summarize Text Underline the sentence that best summarizes the paragraph.

Sedimentary Rock

Most **sedimentary rock** (sed uh MEN tur ee) forms when small particles of rocks or the remains of plants and animals are pressed and cemented together. The raw material is **sediment**—small, solid pieces of material that come from rocks or living things. As shown in **Figure 4**, sediment forms and becomes sedimentary rock through a sequence of processes: weathering and erosion, transportation, deposition, compaction, and cementation. Examples of sedimentary rock include sandstone, shale, and limestone.

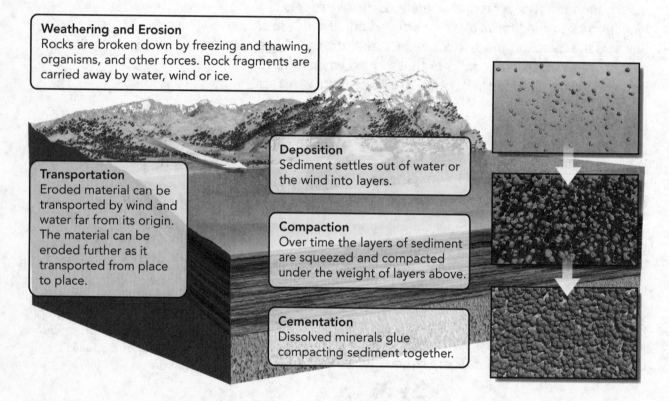

Weathering and Erosion
Rocks are broken down by freezing and thawing, organisms, and other forces. Rock fragments are carried away by water, wind or ice.

Transportation
Eroded material can be transported by wind and water far from its origin. The material can be eroded further as it transported from place to place.

Deposition
Sediment settles out of water or the wind into layers.

Compaction
Over time the layers of sediment are squeezed and compacted under the weight of layers above.

Cementation
Dissolved minerals glue compacting sediment together.

Sequencing Sedimentary Rock Formation

Figure 4 Sedimentary rock forms in layers that are then buried below the surface. Formation occurs through a series of processes over millions of years.

1. Organize 🖉 Summarize how sedimentary rock forms by using the flow chart to sequence the following processes correctly: *transportation, compaction, cementation, weathering and erosion,* and *deposition*.

2. Synthesize Information Which two processes turn layers of loose sediment into hard sedimentary rock?

....

....

Metamorphic Rock

Metamorphic rock (met uh MOR fik) forms when a rock is changed by heat or pressure or by chemical reactions. When high heat and pressure are **applied** to rock, the rock's shape, texture, or composition can change, as shown in **Figure 5**.

Most metamorphic rock forms deep inside Earth, where both heat and pressure are much greater than at Earth's surface. Collisions between Earth's plates can push rock down toward the deeper, hotter mantle, altering the rock. The heat that changes rock into metamorphic rock can also come from very hot magma that rises up into colder rock. The high heat of this magma changes surrounding rock into metamorphic rock.

Very high pressure can also change rock into metamorphic rock. When plates collide, or when rock is buried deep beneath millions of tons of rock, the pressure can be enough to chemically change the rock's minerals to other types. The physical appearance, texture, and crystal structure of the minerals changes as a result.

Metamorphic rocks whose grains are arranged in parallel layers or bands are said to be foliated. For example, the crystals in granite can be flattened to form the foliated texture of gneiss. Some metamorphic rocks, such as marble, are nonfoliated. Their mineral grains are arranged randomly.

✅ **READING CHECK** **Summarize Text** Explain the basic difference between igneous and metamorphic rock.

....

....

Academic Vocabulary

Applied is the past tense of the verb *apply*. What is applied to rock that causes the rock to change shape and composition? Underline your answer in the text.

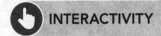

INTERACTIVITY

Explore different regions' rocks.

Granite

Heat and Pressure

Gneiss

Marble

Heat and Pressure

Limestone

Metamorphic Changes

Figure 5 🖉 Heat and pressure can change one type of rock into another. Label each rock *sedimentary*, *igneous*, or *metamorphic*. Indicate whether the metamorphic rocks are foliated. Then shade the correct arrowhead to show which rock can form from the other rock.

Eruption!

Figure 6 A volcanic eruption brings up magma that will be subject to weathering and erosion when it cools.

Evaluate Change Would you describe the processes that change the rocks making up this volcano as fast or slow? Explain.

....

....

....

....

....

The Flow of Energy No matter what type of rock is formed, it formed as a result of the energy that flows through the Earth system. The energy that drives forces affecting the formation of sedimentary rock, such as weathering, erosion, transportation, and deposition, comes in the form of heat from the sun. Heat from Earth's interior drives the processes that control the formation of igneous and metamorphic rocks.

✓ **READING CHECK** **Summarize Text** What are the sources of energy that drive volcanic processes?

....

....

....

Math Toolbox

Pressure and Depth

Pressure increases inside Earth as depth increases.

1. **Interpret Data** About how far must one travel to experience the greatest pressure inside Earth?

....

2. **Analyze Relationships** How is pressure related to depth?

....

....

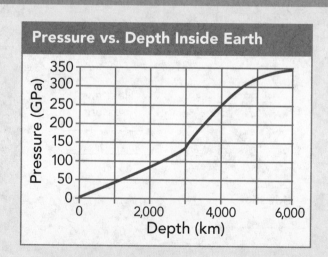

Pressure vs. Depth Inside Earth

☑ LESSON 3 Check

MS-ESS2-1

1. Identify What are the three major kinds of rocks?

....

....

2. Cause and Effect What is the source of energy that drives the weathering and erosion of sedimentary rock? Explain.

....

....

....

....

....

3. Apply Concepts High heat melts a deposit of sedimentary rock, which then hardens into new rock. What kind of rock forms? Explain your answer.

....

....

....

....

....

4. Analyze Properties You are examining a sample of igneous rock. What factors affect the kind of igneous rock found in the sample?

....

....

....

....

....

5. Quantify Change If rocks, such as the sandstone formations in **Figure 1**, are constantly changing as a result of weathering and erosion, then why do they appear to be stable and unchanging to us?

....

....

....

....

....

....

....

Quest CHECK-IN

In this lesson, you learned about rocks and how energy from the sun and Earth's interior drives their formation.

Use Models How could the formation of metamorphic rock be modeled in a science fiction film through special effects?

....

....

....

....

👆 INTERACTIVITY

Rocky Business

Go online to evaluate the science facts in a movie script and the ways they are presented, revising the script as necessary.

LESSON

(4) Cycling of Rocks

Guiding Questions

- How are Earth's materials cycled in the rock cycle?
- How does the flow of energy drive the processes of the rock cycle?

Connection

Literacy Translate Information

MS-ESS2-1

Vocabulary

rock cycle

Academic Vocabulary

process
source

 VOCABULARY APP

Practice vocabulary on a mobile device.

Quest CONNECTION

Think about how understanding the processes that change rocks from one kind to another can help you to determine the scientific accuracy of a movie script.

Connect It!

✏️ **Look closely at the desert photograph in Figure 1. Circle a change that you can observe in the image.**

Interpret Photographs What change did you observe? What agent is causing the change?

....

....

Apply Scientific Reasoning What rock-forming processes are taking place?

....

....

The Cycling of Earth's Materials

The rock in Earth's crust is always changing. Forces deep inside Earth and at the surface build, destroy, and change the rocks in the crust. The **rock cycle** is the series of processes that occur on Earth's surface and in the crust and mantle that slowly change rocks from one kind to another. For example, the **process** of weathering breaks down granite into sediment that gets carried away and dropped by the wind. Some of that sediment can later form sandstone.

INTERACTIVITY

Explore the different phases of the rock cycle.

Academic Vocabulary

Circle the name of a process in the text. Then name two processes you go through in your daily life.

....

Rock Cycle in Action

Figure 1 In Death Valley, California, and other locations on Earth's surface, processes of the rock cycle continuously move and change sediment and rocks.

HANDS-ON LAB

🖐Investigate Determine the relative ages of rocks.

Translate Information
Review the sequence of events described in the text. Then number the materials from Granite Mountain in the order in which they move through the rock cycle.

Sandstone ....

Granite ....

Quartzite ....

Sediment ....

Granite Mountain

Figure 2 Processes in the rock cycle change the granite in Granite Mountain.

Relate Change Circle the words that best complete the sentences.

The (leaves/roots) of the trees on the mountain cause (weathering/erosion) of the granite. (Erosion/Deposition) by streams transports sediment away.

Reason Quantitatively How long will it most likely take for processes in the rock cycle to change most of Granite Mountain into sediment? Check the box next to the correct answer.

☐ less than 1 million years
☐ 1 million years
☐ 10 million years or more

The Flow of Energy in the Rock Cycle

There are many pathways by which rocks move through the rock cycle. These pathways and the processes and events they include are patterns that repeat again and again. For example, **Figure 2** shows Granite Mountain in Arizona. The granite in Granite Mountain formed millions of years ago below Earth's surface as magma cooled.

After the granite formed, the forces of mountain building slowly pushed the granite up to the surface. Since then, weathering and erosion have been breaking down and carrying away the granite. Transportation by streams carries some of the pieces of granite, called sediment, to rivers and eventually to the ocean. What might happen next?

Over millions of years, layers of sediment build up on the ocean floor. Slowly, the weight of the layers would physically compact the sediment. Then calcite that is dissolved in the ocean water could cement the particles together, causing a chemical change in the material. Over time, the material that once formed the igneous rock granite of Granite Mountain could become the sedimentary rock sandstone.

Sediment could keep piling up and burying the sandstone. The motion of Earth's plates could move the sandstone even deeper below the surface. Eventually, extreme pressure could deform the rocks by compacting them and causing physical and chemical changes in the rock particles. Some of the particles might crystallize. Silica, the main ingredient in quartz, would replace the calcite cement. The rock's physical texture would change from gritty to smooth. After millions of years, the sandstone could change into the metamorphic rock quartzite. Or, the heat below Earth's surface could melt the sandstone and form magma, starting the cycle over again. **Figure 3** shows this process.

The Rock Cycle

Figure 3 Patterns of repeating events in the rock cycle, including melting, weathering, erosion, and the application of heat and pressure, constantly change rocks from one type into another type. Through these events, Earth's materials get recycled.

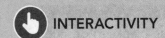

1. 🖉 Study the photographs of the Earth materials. Fill in each blank box in the rock cycle diagram with the correct material.

2. 🖉 Study the diagram. Then label each arrow with the correct term: *melting, weathering and erosion, heat and pressure, volcanic activity,* or *deposition.* (*Hint:* To fit your answers, abbreviate "weathering and erosion" as "w & e.")

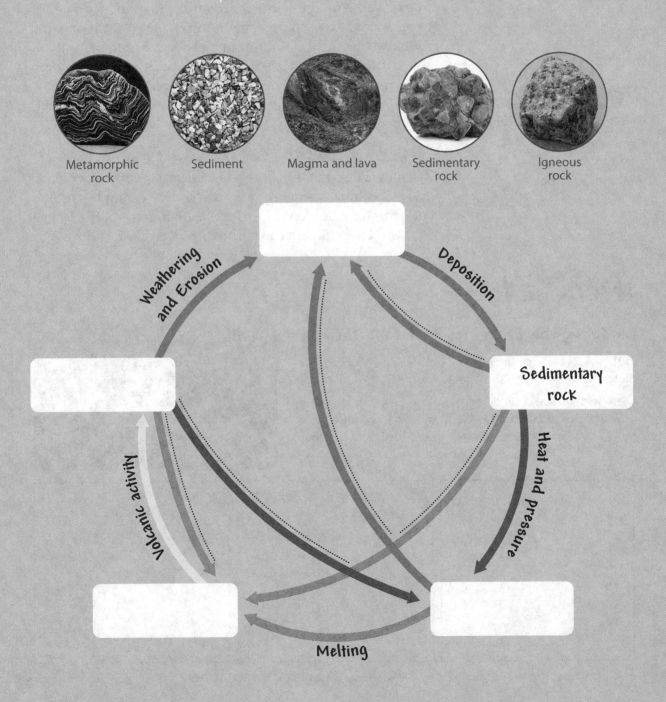

313

Fill in the blanks to describe
two sources.
.... is the source of
igneous rocks.
.... is the source of the
energy my body needs.

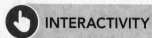

INTERACTIVITY

Track Earth materials as
they move through the
rock cycle.

READING CHECK

Cause and Effect Underline
the plate motion that can
lead to rock changing into
metamorphic rock.

Plate Tectonics and the Rock Cycle The rock cycle
is driven in part by plate tectonics. Recall that Earth's lithosphere
is made up of huge plates that slowly move over Earth's surface
due to convection currents in the mantle. As the plates move,
they carry the continents and ocean floors with them. Plate
movements help drive the rock cycle by helping to form magma,
the **source** of igneous rock.

Where oceanic plates move apart, magma moves upward and
fills the gap with new igneous rock. Where an oceanic plate
moves beneath a continental plate, magma forms and rises.
The result is a volcano where lava flows onto the overlying plate,
forming igneous rock. Sedimentary rock can also result from
plate movement. The collision of continental plates can be
strong enough to push up a mountain range. Weathering and
erosion wear away mountains and produce sediment that
may eventually become sedimentary rock. Finally, a collision
between continental plates can push rocks down deep beneath
the surface. Here, heat and pressure could change the rocks to
metamorphic rock.

Cycling of Earth's Materials As the rock in Earth's
crust moves through the rock cycle, material is not lost or gained.
Instead it changes form and gets recycled. For example, basalt
that forms from hardened lava can weather and erode to form
sediment. The sediment can eventually form new rock.

Model It

Modeling the Cycling of Rock Material

Figure 4 New rock forms from erupting lava where two
plates move apart on the ocean floor.

Develop Models ✏ Complete the diagram to model
how rock material might cycle from lava to sedimentary
rock. Draw and label three more possible events in this
pattern of change in the rock cycle.

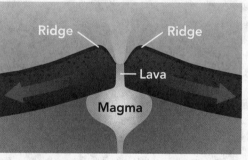

☑ LESSON 4 Check

MS-ESS2-1

1. Relate Change What processes can recycle sedimentary rock into sediment?

....

....

....

2. Patterns Describe a process that happens again and again in the rock cycle.

....

....

....

....

3. Apply Concepts Explain why the change from metamorphic rock to magma almost always occurs below Earth's surface.

....

....

....

....

....

....

4. Evaluate Do you think that plate tectonics plays a major or minor role in the rock cycle? Explain your answer.

....

....

....

....

....

....

Use the rock cycle diagram in Figure 3 to help you answer Question 5.

5. Use Models Describe two different ways that sedimentary rock can become igneous rock.

....

....

....

....

....

....

Quest CHECK-IN

In this lesson, you learned how Earth's materials move through the rock cycle. You also learned about the flow of energy that drives the processes of the rock cycle.

Ask Questions Suppose you could meet with a science consultant for movies and scripts. What questions would you have for the consultant about reviewing, evaluating, and revising scripts to make them more scientifically accurate?

....

....

....

👆 INTERACTIVITY

The Rock Cyclers

Go online to identify and evaluate scientific facts of the rock cycle in a movie script, and then revise the script to make it more accurate.

Mighty Mauna Loa

The high summit of Mauna Loa is often surrounded by tropical rain clouds. The large volcano, outlined in red on the satellite image below, makes up a majority of the area of the main island of Hawaii.

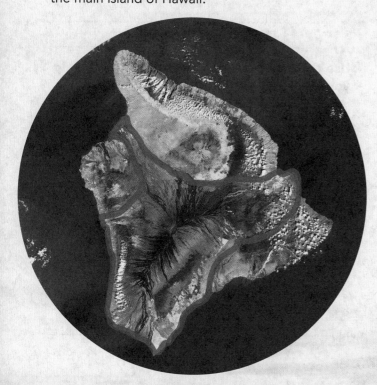

Mauna Loa is one of Hawaii's most active volcanoes, located on the largest of the islands. The volcano sits on an active hotspot. For more than 80 million years, the Hawaiian Islands and seamounts have formed as the Pacific Plate has been sliding northwest over a hotspot—a plume of magma that causes eruptions through the overlying plate.

Mauna Loa illustrates the rock cycle in action. Over time, rock will continue to be buried as more lava flows and more sediment is carried down the volcano. Under high temperatures and pressure, some of the sedimentary rock will become metamorphic rock.

When Mauna Loa erupts, magma from inside Earth pours out of the volcano as lava. The lava flows down the slopes of the volcano.

Lava cools to form igneous rock. Some lava cools on the slopes of the volcano. Other lava flows to the ocean, where the lava cools and slowly increases the size of the island.

Weathering and erosion break down some of the igneous rock. Through the process of deposition, some of this sediment is carried down the volcano. As the sediment becomes compacted, it forms sedimentary rock.

1. **Develop Models**  Complete the diagram using arrows, labels, and captions to describe the processes that drive the rock cycle on Mauna Loa.

2. **Patterns** The last few eruptions of Mauna Loa happened in 1942, 1949, 1950, 1975, and 1984. The volcano has erupted 33 times since 1843. When do you think the next eruption will occur, and why do you think so?

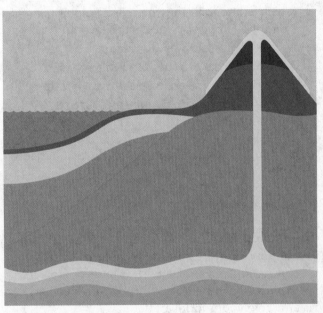

....
....
....
....
....

3. **Construct an Explanation** Why do you think Mauna Loa erupts periodically instead of steadily?

....
....
....
....
....
....

☑ TOPIC 7 Review and Assess

1 Earth's Interior

MS-ESS2-1

1. Which part(s) of Earth's interior has two distinct layers?
   - **A.** crust
   - **B.** mantle
   - **C.** core
   - **D.** crust and core

2. Which is Earth's thinnest layer?
   - **A.** crust
   - **B.** inner core
   - **C.** mantle
   - **D.** outer core

3. Which of the following is an example of indirect evidence about Earth's layers?
   - **A.** rock samples obtained by drilling
   - **B.** mantle rocks produced by volcanoes
   - **C.** changes observed in seismic wave data
   - **D.** data gathered from high–pressure lab experiments

4. Heat in the core and the .... cause ...., which help to cycle material on Earth.

5. **Develop Models** 🖊 Draw a model to show the flow of energy and rock material through convection currents in Earth's interior. Be sure to show movement, label the layers involved, and give your model a title.

2 Minerals

MS-ESS2-1

6. Which statement best identifies the substance whose characteristics are listed in the table?

Characteristic	Observation
Naturally occurring	Yes
Can form by inorganic processes	No
Solid	Yes
Crystal structure	No
Definite chemical composition	No

   - **A.** It is not a mineral because it is a solid.
   - **B.** It is a mineral because it occurs naturally.
   - **C.** It is not a mineral because it doesn't have a crystal structure.
   - **D.** It is a mineral because it forms only organically.

7. What causes the crystals in gneiss to line up in bands?
   - **A.** deposition
   - **B.** erosion
   - **C.** pressure
   - **D.** weathering

8. *Metallic, glassy, earthy,* and *pearly* are words that describe a mineral's ....

9. **Apply Concepts** Mineral A has a hardness of 5. Mineral B has a hardness of 7. Mineral C can scratch Mineral A, but it can be scratched by Mineral B. What ranking on the Mohs hardness scale should Mineral C be assigned? Explain.

....

....

....

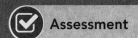
 Rocks

MS-ESS2-1

10. Which process acts on Earth's surface to break rocks into pieces?
   A. compaction   **B.** deposition
   C. erosion   **D.** weathering

11. Metamorphic rock forms as a result of

changes in .... and

....in Earth's interior.

12. Apply Concepts An igneous rock contains large crystals of quartz, feldspar, and horn-blende. How did the rock most likely form?

....

....

13. Classify A rock sample contains tiny pieces of other rocks that are cemented together. Is it an igneous, sedimentary, or metamorphic rock? Explain your answer.

....

....

....

4 **Cycling of Rocks**

MS-ESS2-1

14. Which of the following leads most directly to the production of igneous rock?
   A. formation of magma
   B. cementation of rocks
   C. weathering of rocks
   D. deposition of sediment

Use the model of the rock cycle to answer questions 15 and 16.

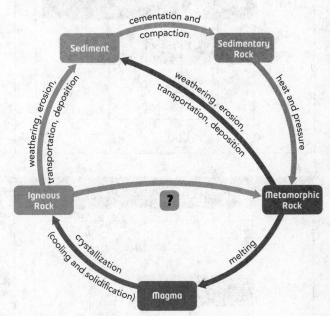

15. Which is the **best** way to complete this model of the rock cycle?
   A. crystallization
   B. solidification
   C. heat and pressure
   D. melting

16. What is a step in the process of a rock changing from sedimentary to igneous?
   A. crystallization
   B. deposition
   C. erosion
   D. melting

MS-ESS2-1

Evidence-Based Assessment

Earth's layers vary in thickness, temperature, pressure, density, state of matter, and composition. The infographic below compares some of these characteristics of Earth's layers.

Analyze the infographic to answer the questions.

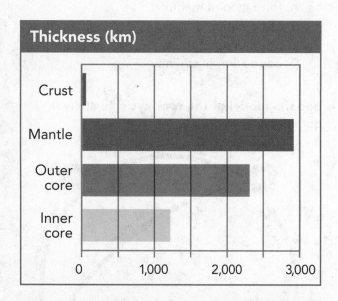

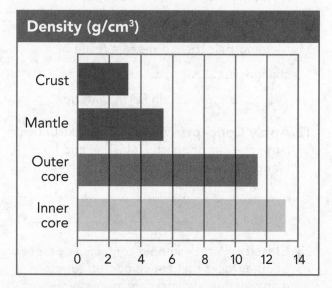

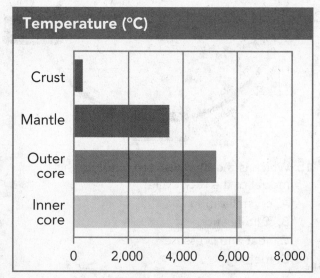

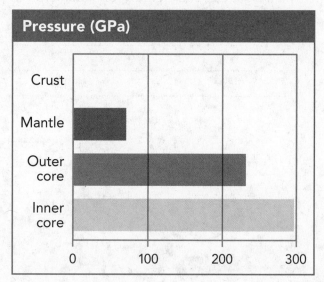

1. **Analyze Data** Which of the following correctly lists Earth's layers from thickest to thinnest?
   A. crust, mantle, outer core, inner core
   B. mantle, outer core, inner core, crust
   C. inner core, outer core, mantle, crust
   D. mantle, crust, outer core, inner core

2. **Analyze Data** About how many times denser is the liquid outer core than the solid crust?
   A. 6   B. 4
   C. 2   D. 3

3. **Cause and Effect** Suppose the mantle were thicker than it is. What effect would this have on the pressure in the outer core? Explain.

   ....
   ....
   ....
   ....
   ....

4. **Identify Patterns** What is the relationship among density, pressure, and temperature across the different layers of Earth? What explains this relationship?

   ....
   ....
   ....
   ....
   ....
   ....
   ....
   ....
   ....
   ....
   ....

5. **Synthesize Information** Both the inner and outer core are made of iron and nickel. The inner core is hotter and denser than the outer core, yet the outer core is in a liquid state and the inner core is solid. Why is this the case? Use evidence from the data tables to support your response.

   ....
   ....
   ....
   ....
   ....
   ....
   ....

Quest FINDINGS

Complete the Quest!

Phenomenon Review and revise the movie scripts. Consider how you can stage readings of the scripts.

Defend Your Claim Do you think producers of fictional films that depict scientific processes should be required to hire a science consultant? Support your opinion with facts and details.

....
....
....
....
....
....

INTERACTIVITY

Reflect on Science in the Movies

The Rock Cycle in Action

Can you make **models** that show **third-grade students** how sedimentary, igneous, and metamorphic **rocks** form?

Background

Phenomenon At first glance, rock formations—such as the Vasquez Rocks in California shown here—don't seem to do much other than sit motionless. But rocks are constantly being cycled through processes that can take just a few minutes or thousands of years.

Your task is to work with a partner to design and build models that could be used to show how the rock cycle works to someone who has never heard of it. Your teacher will assign you a specific type of rock—sedimentary, metamorphic, or igneous—and you will design a model of its formation.

Materials

(per pair)

- crayons or crayon rocks of a few different colors
- plastic knife
- paper plates
- aluminum foil
- books or other heavy objects
- hot water or hot plate
- tongs or oven mitts
- beaker

Safety

Be sure to follow all safety guidelines provided by your teacher. Appendix B of your textbook provides more details about the safety icons.

Plan Your Investigation

☐ You will create a plan and design a procedure to model the processes that form the type of rock that has been assigned to you. You must consider:

- the roles that weathering and erosion, deposition, and cementation play in forming sedimentary rock
- the role that high amounts of pressure and energy play in forming metamorphic rock
- the role that high amounts of heat and energy play in forming igneous rock

☐ As you design your model, consider these questions:

- What will the different crayons represent in your model?
- How can you use the available materials to represent specific processes such as weathering and erosion, or melting and cementation?
- How can you use the available materials to simulate the processes and flow of energy, such as heat and pressure, that result in the formation of sedimentary, metamorphic, and igneous rocks?

☐ Organize your ideas in the table. Then plan your procedure.

HANDS-ON LAB

☑**Demonstrate** Go online for a downloadable worksheet for this lab.

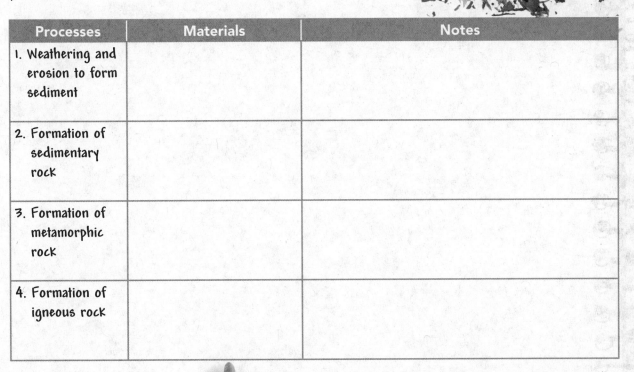

Processes	Materials	Notes
1. Weathering and erosion to form sediment		
2. Formation of sedimentary rock		
3. Formation of metamorphic rock		
4. Formation of igneous rock		

Procedure

Use the space below to describe your model(s) and list steps in a procedure to demonstrate the formation of your assigned rock type. You may wish to use sketches to show some steps.

Analyze and Interpret Data

1. **Develop Models** Work with other pairs to develop a complete model of the rock cycle. Draw your model in the space provided. Include labels to explain what each part of the model represents.

2. **Relate Change** Describe the flow of energy and cycling of matter represented by your pair's model. How does your model help you to understand processes that can last thousands of years?

....

....

....

....

3. **Identify Limitations** How does your model differ from the actual rock cycle on Earth? How could you make your model more accurate?

....

....

....

....

....

....

TOPIC

8

Plate Tectonics

NGSS PERFORMANCE EXPECTATIONS

MS-ESS2-2 Construct an explanation based on evidence for how geoscience processes have changed Earth's surface at varying time and spatial scales.

MS-ESS2-3 Analyze and interpret data on the distribution of fossils and rocks, continental shapes, and seafloor structures to provide evidence of the past plate motions.

MS-ESS3-2 Analyze and interpret data on natural hazards to forecast future catastrophic events and inform the development of technologies to mitigate their effects.

How did this island get here?

HANDS-ON LAB

u**Connect** Explore how Earth's continents can be linked together.

GO ONLINE
to access your
digital course

 VIDEO

 INTERACTIVITY

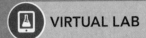 VIRTUAL LAB

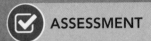 ASSESSMENT

 eTEXT

 APP

The Essential Question

How do geological processes change Earth's surface?

This island in the South Pacific formed as the result of a violent eruption of material from deep inside Earth. What role does this kind of event play in shaping Earth's surface?

....

....

....

....

....

....

Quest KICKOFF

How safe is it to hike around Mount Rainier?

Phenomenon Camping and hiking in the mountains are popular pastimes for people all over the world. But what if the mountain is actually an active volcano? It hasn't erupted for thousands of years—but it *could*. Would volcanologists say it is safe to hike? What kinds of data do they collect to predict eruptions? In this problem-based Quest activity, you will determine whether it is safe to take an extended camping and hiking trip on Mount Rainier. Through hands-on labs and digital activities, you'll gather evidence about Rainier's history and look into current research on the mountain's volcanic activity. You will use this information to create a presentation that supports your claim and synthesizes your findings.

NBC LEARN ▶ VIDEO

After watching the Quest Kickoff video, which explains volcanic processes, think about the pros and cons of hiking on Mount Rainier. Record your ideas.

PROS

....

....

....

CONS

....

....

....

👆 **INTERACTIVITY**

To Hike or Not to Hike

MS-ESS2-2 Construct an explanation based on evidence for how geoscience processes have changed Earth's surface at varying time and spatial scales.

MS-ESS3-2 Analyze and interpret data on natural hazards to forecast future catastrophic events and inform the development of technologies to mitigate their effects.

Quest CHECK-IN

IN LESSON 1

STEM What is Mount Rainier's history of eruption? Investigate the mountain range's history and draw conclusions about the likelihood of an eruption.

🧪

HANDS-ON LAB

Patterns in the Cascade Range

Quest CHECK-IN

IN LESSON 2

How is volcanic activity related to tectonic plate movements? Explore the science behind the connection.

👆 **INTERACTIVITY**

Mount Rainier's Threat

IN LESSON 3

What processes cause earthquakes and tsunamis to form? Think about the possible risks caused by movements of the ground beneath your feet.

The Cascade Range stretches from northern California all the way up through British Columbia, Canada. Mount Rainier is just one of many volcanoes that lie within the range and are considered "active."

Quest CHECK-INS

STEM IN LESSON 3

What kinds of data can be used to predict an eruption? Investigate the tools and methods that volcanologists use to study volcanoes. Then analyze some data to determine the likelihood of an eruption.

👆 INTERACTIVITY

Monitoring a Volcano

HANDS-ON LAB

Signs of Eruption?

Quest FINDINGS

Complete the Quest!

Present information on Mount Rainier's history and current geological research, along with your evidence-based argument about whether it is safe to hike and camp there.

👆 INTERACTIVITY

Reflect on Mount Rainier's Safety

1 Evidence of Plate Motions

Guiding Questions

- What evidence supported the hypothesis of continental drift?
- What roles do mid-ocean ridges and ocean trenches play in the movement of plates?

Connection

Literacy Cite Textual Evidence

MS-ESS2-3

Vocabulary

mid-ocean ridge
sea-floor
  spreading
subduction
ocean trench

Academic Vocabulary

hypothesis

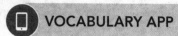 **VOCABULARY APP**

Practice vocabulary on a mobile device.

Quest CONNECTION

Learn about processes that affect Earth's surface, including structures such as Mount Rainier.

Connect It!

✏️ **Draw lines between South America and Africa to show how the contours of the two continents could fit together.**

Patterns What might you infer about South America and Africa if you thought the continents were movable objects?

....

Hypothesis of Continental Drift

For many centuries, scientists and map-makers had been curious about why some continents look as though they could fit together like the pieces of a jigsaw puzzle. The continents on the east and west sides of the South Atlantic Ocean, for example, looked like they would fit together perfectly (**Figure 1**). In the mid 1800s, scientists began to gather clues that suggested the slow movement, or drift, of continents. In 1912, German meteorologist Alfred Wegener (VAY guh nur) further developed the **hypothesis** that all of of the continents had once been fused together, and that over time they had drifted apart. This hypothesis became known as "continental drift."

In 1915, after gathering evidence that supported the hypothesis, Wegener published *The Origin of Continents and Oceans*. The book connected clues from studies of land features, fossils, and climate to make a compelling case for the hypothesis that a supercontinent called Pangaea (pan JEE uh) had broken up into the continents we know today.

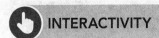

INTERACTIVITY

Try your hand at piecing together puzzles.

Academic Vocabulary

In science, a hypothesis is an idea that can be tested by experimentation or investigation. It is an evidence-based idea that serves as a starting point, whereas a scientific theory is what science produces when a hypothesis has been shown to be true through a broad range of studies. As you read this lesson, highlight or underline the key components of the hypothesis of continental drift.

Pieces of the Puzzle

Figure 1 Scientists wondered whether the continents' coastlines seemed to fit like jigsaw puzzle pieces because they had once been joined together.

Cite Textual Evidence Use your science notebook to organize the evidence that supports the hypothesis of continental drift. Identify a common theme among the different pieces of evidence.

Evidence From Land Features

There were other pieces of evidence to support the hypothesis of continental drift. Mountain ranges near those continents' coasts seemed to line up, as though they had been made in the same place and at the same time. Coal deposits, made of the remains of plants that thrived in warm locations millions of years ago, were found on multiple continents and in regions that no longer supported that kind of plant life. The separate, scattered locations of these features (**Figure 2**) suggested that they hadn't always been separate.

Evidence From Fossils

Geologists noticed that evidence from the fossil record supported continental drift. (**Figure 2**). Fossils are traces of organisms preserved in rock. Geologist Edward Suess noted that fossils of *Glossopteris* (glaw SAHP tuh ris), a fernlike plant from 250 million years ago, were found on five continents. This suggested that those landmasses had once been connected, as part of Pangaea. Fossils of animals told a similar story. *Mesosaurus* was a reptile that lived in fresh-water habitats millions of years ago, yet *Mesosaurus* fossils were found in both South America and Africa.

Evidence for Continental Drift

Figure 2 Study the map key to see how Wegener pieced together similar pieces of evidence from separate sites to support his hypothesis.

Interpret Visuals Present-day India is in South Asia, at the northern end of the Indian Ocean. What evidence found in India matches that of other locations?

....

....

....

ATLANTIC OCEAN

PACIFIC OCEAN

KEY

- Folded mountains
- Coal beds
- Glacial deposits
- *Glossopteris* fossils
- *Lystrosaurus* fossils
- *Mesosaurus* fossils

Evidence From Climate Wegener, whose own expertise was in the study of weather and climate and not geology, also gathered evidence that showed Earth's continents had experienced different climates than the ones they have today. For example, Spitsbergen, an island in the Arctic Ocean, has fossils of plants that could have survived only in a tropical climate. This doesn't mean that the Arctic Ocean once had a tropical climate. That isn't possible, because the poles do not receive enough sunlight to produce tropical weather or support tropical plants. Instead, this evidence means Spitsbergen used to be at the equator, part of a supercontinent. The supercontinent slowly broke apart, and the island now known as Spitsbergen drifted far to the north over the course of millions of years.

HANDS-ON LAB

☐**Investigate** Piece Pangaea together.

✓ READING CHECK **Summarize Text** What is the general pattern in the evidence that supports the hypothesis of continental drift?

....

....

Reflect Think of some organic item (such as a flower or type of fruit) that you've found in at least two places that are many miles apart. Do the items have a common origin? Why do you think so? What conclusions can you draw from the item's presence in widely-different locations?

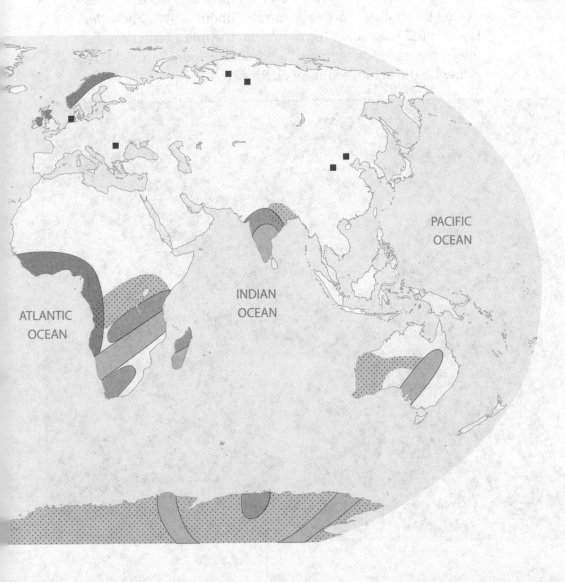

PACIFIC OCEAN

ATLANTIC OCEAN

INDIAN OCEAN

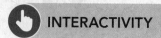
Mid-Ocean Ridges

The hypothesis of continental drift included evidence from different areas of science, but it had a major flaw. It lacked a good explanation for *how* the continents could have broken up and moved apart. Many scientists rejected the hypothesis for that reason. By the middle of the twentieth century, advances in oceanography—the study of Earth's oceans—allowed a mapping of the ocean floor that renewed interest in continental drift. Undersea exploration provided evidence that Earth's surface was composed of moving plates—large pieces of the lithosphere.

By measuring distances from the sea surface to its floor, scientists now had a clear visual of what Earth's surface looked like under the oceans. What surprised many was the presence of long, zipper-like chains of undersea mountains called **mid-ocean ridges**. One such chain, called the Mid-Atlantic Ridge, ran down the middle of the Atlantic Ocean, curving in a pattern that seemed to mirror the contours of the surrounding continental coastlines. Further modeling and mapping of the ocean floor in the 1990s showed that these mid-ocean ridges extend throughout Earth's oceans for about 70,000 kilometers. If you could hold Earth in your hand, the mid-ocean ridges might resemble the seams on a baseball (**Figure 3**). Could these ridges be the actual seams of Earth's crust?

Mid-Ocean Ridges

Figure 3 Mapping of mid-ocean ridges in the mid-twentieth century provided supporting evidence that Earth's surface was composed of moving plates.

Interpret Visuals Do any of the mid-ocean ridges appear to extend into continents? Which ones?

....

....

....

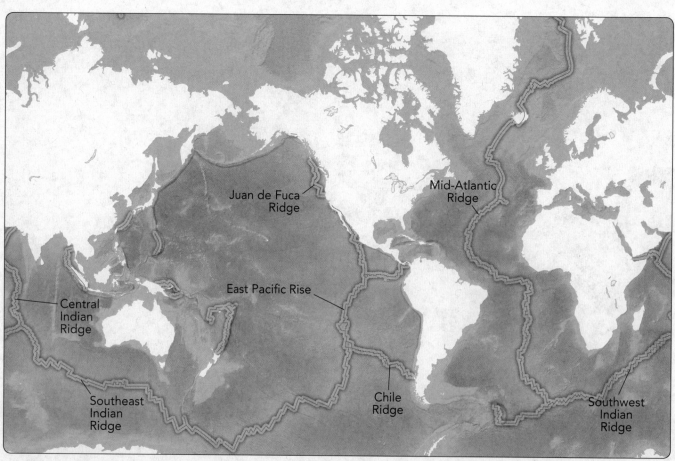

Juan de Fuca Ridge

Mid-Atlantic Ridge

East Pacific Rise

Central Indian Ridge

Chile Ridge

Southeast Indian Ridge

Southwest Indian Ridge

Aged Rock Samples The globe image shows the relative ages of the ocean floor on either side of the Mid-Atlantic Ridge, with red being young rock, yellow older rock, and green, the oldest of all.

Ocean surface

Fresh Ocean Material In the central valleys of mid-ocean ridges, scientists find rocks shaped like pillows. These pillow rocks form only when molten material hardens very quickly after erupting into cold water. This is evidence of volcanic activity in the mid-ocean ridges.

Oceanic crust

Mantle

Sea-Floor Spreading

While ocean-floor mapping was underway, geologists began to gather samples of rock from the ocean floor. They learned that mid-ocean ridges are the sources of new spans of the ocean floor. In a process called **sea-floor spreading**, molten rock flows up through a crack in Earth's crust and hardens into solid strips of new rock on both sides of the crack. The entire floor on either side of the ridge moves away when this occurs, meaning the older strips of rock move farther from the ridge over time. It's like a two-way conveyer belt with new material appearing at the ridge while older material is carried farther away. **Figure 4** shows a model and describes some specific evidence of sea-floor spreading.

✓ READING CHECK Cite Textual Evidence Why was undersea exploration important for developing the theory of plate tectonics?

Sea-Floor Spreading

Figure 4 Sea-floor spreading continually adds material to the ocean floor on both sides of the ridge.

Develop Models 🖊
Label the different features that play a role in sea-floor spreading.

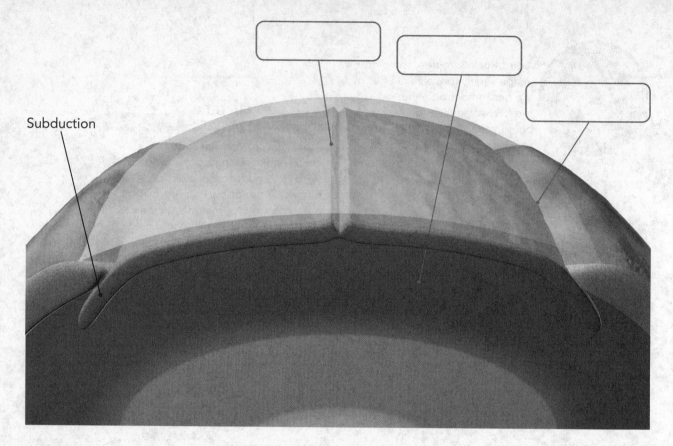

Subduction

Subduction

Figure 5 Oceanic plates, which form from sea-floor spreading, sink back into the mantle at subduction zones.

Summarize Label the mantle, mid-ocean ridge, and ocean trench.

▶ VIDEO

Watch what happens at ocean ridges and trenches.

Ocean Trenches

You may be wondering why all of the oceans aren't getting wider, or why Earth as a whole is not expanding, with all of the sea-floor spreading going on. The answer to that is **subduction** (sub DUC shun), or the sinking movement of ocean floor back into the mantle. Subduction occurs where a dense plate of oceanic crust goes under an adjacent section of Earth's crust. This occurs at **ocean trenches**, which are undersea valleys that are the deepest parts of the ocean (**Figure 5**).

The Process of Subduction New oceanic crust is relatively warm. As the rock cools and moves away from a mid-ocean ridge, it gets denser. At some point, the dense slab of oceanic crust may meet another section of ocean floor, or a continent. What happens? Because the oceanic crust is cooler than the mantle underneath, it is denser and will sink into the mantle if given the chance. At an ocean trench, it has that chance, and the oceanic crust will sink under the edge of a continent or a younger, less-dense slab of oceanic crust. The oceanic plate that sinks back into the mantle gets recycled. This process can produce volcanic eruptions at the surface. If the oceanic crust meets continental crust, then a chain of volcanoes will form. If it meets more oceanic crust, then there will likely be a chain of volcanic islands.

Subduction and the Oceans

Subduction and the Oceans An ocean basin can have a spreading ridge, subduction zones, or both, depending on its age. An ocean basin starts with just a spreading ridge. The Atlantic Ocean, for example, has the Mid-Atlantic Ridge running down its full length, but no subduction zones. This means that the Atlantic Ocean is still getting wider—by about 2 to 5 centimeters per year. At some point, part of the oceanic plate will begin to sink back into the mantle and a subduction zone will form.

The Pacific Ocean is a more mature ocean basin. While it still has a spreading ridge, the Pacific basin is surrounded by subduction zones. The oceanic crust in the Pacific is being recycled back into the mantle faster than it is being created. This means that the Pacific Ocean basin is getting smaller.

Eventually, hundreds of millions of years from now, as Africa collides into Europe and the Pacific Ocean closes up, a new supercontinent may appear.

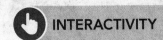

INTERACTIVITY

Learn about the slow and steady movement on Earth.

☑ READING CHECK **Cite Textual Evidence** What features are evidence of the Pacific Ocean's maturity?

Model It !

Predict North America's Movement

Figure 6 The map shows the layout of some of Earth's landmasses, the mid-ocean ridges where plates are made, and ocean trenches where plates are recycled.

Predict 🖊 Draw a line to indicate where you think the west coast of North America will eventually be located.

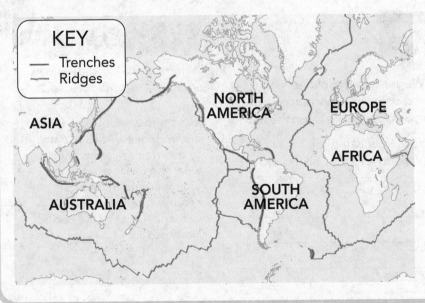

☑ LESSON 1 Check

MS-ESS2-3

1. **Summarize** Describe the hypothesis of continental drift.

....

....

....

....

2. **Evaluate Evidence** How did the study of fossils provide support for the ideas behind the existence of Pangaea?

....

....

....

....

....

....

....

....

....

....

3. **Explain** How did the discovery of mid-ocean ridges support the hypothesis of continental drift?

....

....

4. **Predict** A large oceanic crust collides with the edge of a continent. What will happen?

....

....

....

5. **Infer** A remotely-operated vehicle is sent to the deepest part of the Mariana Trench. It returns with a sample of rock from the ocean floor. Would this rock be old or young? Explain.

....

....

....

....

....

....

....

....

Quest CHECK-IN

In this lesson you learned about Wegener's hypothesis of continental drift and how he pieced together evidence from different areas of natural history to support his hypothesis.

Connect to the Nature of Science How can the history of Mount Rainier's eruptions help you decide whether hiking around Mount Rainier is safe?

....

....

....

HANDS-ON LAB

Patterns in the Cascade Range

Go online to download the lab worksheet. Analyze data to determine whether there is a pattern to Mount Rainier's eruptions and those of other nearby volcanoes in the Cascade Range of the Pacific Northwest.

The Slow Acceptance of
Continental Drift

"Utter rot," a "fairy tale," and "delirious ravings." These statements are how some scientists in the early 1900s responded to Alfred Wegener's book describing the hypothesis continental drift.

PANGAEA   EQUATOR

CONNECT TO YOU

Do you think skepticism is an important quality for a scientist to have? Why or why not? Discuss your ideas with a partner.

This case demonstrates that scientific thought doesn't always advance neatly or without controversy. Long-held scientific attitudes can be slow to change when new evidence or interpretations are encountered.

The hypothesis of continental drift faced a number of challenges. Though there was evidence to support it, there was not a convincing explanation of how continental drift actually occurred. Scientists who were already skeptical of the idea only heaped additional ridicule on Wegener.

In addition, Wegener was a trained meteorologist, but the hypothesis crossed multiple scientific disciplines. Many experts in their respective fields felt threatened because Wegener—viewed as an outsider—challenged their authority and expertise. After his death in 1930, continental drift was virtually ignored.

Over the next few decades, advances in technology led to a better understanding of the geological forces that shape Earth's surface. By the early 1960s, younger geologists were able to explain the mechanism by which the continents moved. The ideas behind continental drift re-emerged as the theory of plate tectonics.

Wegener often took research trips to Greenland to study its climate. By taking core samples of ice, climatologists can learn about the climate of the past.

Plate Tectonics and Earth's Surface

Guiding Questions

- How do Earth's plates move?
- How do Earth's surface features support the theory of plate tectonics?
- What are the products of plate movement at different scales?

Connections

Literacy Integrate With Visuals

Math Reason Quantitatively

MS-ESS2-2

Vocabulary

divergent
boundary
convergent
boundary
transform
boundary

Academic Vocabulary

theory

 VOCABULARY APP

Practice vocabulary on a mobile device.

Quest CONNECTION

Consider how the activity at plate boundaries could be related to the formation and behavior of Mount Rainier.

 **Connect It**

✏️ **Identify where the Himalayan Mountains are and circle them.**

Predict Scientists are measuring Mount Everest to determine whether its height has changed. Why would the Himalayas be getting taller?

....

....

....

The Theory of Plate Tectonics

With observations of many geologists in the 1950s and 1960s, particularly of the features of the ocean floor, the ideas behind continental drift re-emerged as the **theory** of plate tectonics. This theory states that Earth's lithosphere—the crust and upper part of the mantle—is broken up into distinct plates. The plates are puzzle-like pieces that are in slow, constant motion relative to each other due to forces within the mantle. The theory explains the specific patterns of motion among the plates, including the different types of boundaries where they meet and the events and features that occur at their boundaries (**Figure 1**). The term *tectonic* refers to Earth's crust and to the large-scale processes that occur within it.

HANDS-ON LAB

Investigate the role of stress in changing Earth's surface.

Academic Vocabulary

In science, the term *theory* is applied only to ideas that are supported by a vast, diverse array of evidence. How is the term used in everyday life?

....

....

....

....

....

....

Plate Tectonics Give Rise to the Himalayas

Figure 1 The tallest mountains on Earth, K2 and Mount Everest, are part of the Himalayas. When the landmass that is now known as India collided with Asia, these mountains began to form.

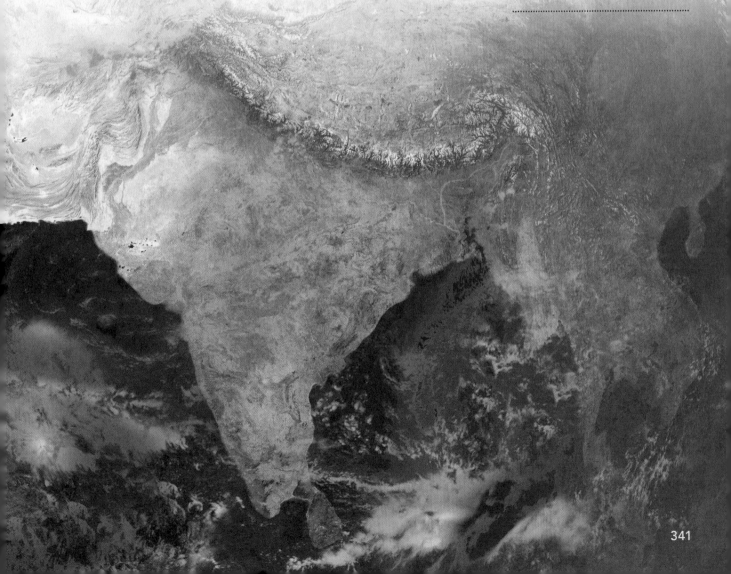

Convection Currents

Figure 2 In a pot of boiling water, warmer water rises and cooler water sinks to fill the void. This movement creates convection currents in the pot of water.

Convection Drives Plate Motions The tectonic plates move because they are part of convection currents in the mantle. You may recall that convection is a cyclical movement of fluid driven by temperature differences at the top and bottom, such as cold water sinking from the surface and warm water rising from below (**Figure 2**). Convection occurs in the mantle where solid rock flows in slow-moving currents. These currents are responsible for moving the continents great distances across Earth's surface, even if they move at speeds too slow to be noticed.

Types of Crust
Plates consist of one or two types of crust. Oceanic crust is the dense type of crust that is found at the bottom of the ocean (**Figure 3**). Some plates, such as the Pacific Plate, consist entirely of oceanic crust. The other type of crust is called continental crust. It is less dense than oceanic crust and is almost always thicker. As a result, the surfaces of continents are above sea level.

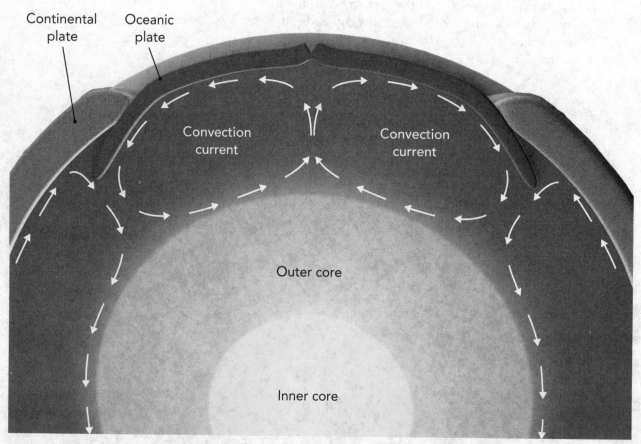

Oceanic and Continental Crust

Figure 3 The very dense crust of the ocean floor is oceanic crust. Crust that is less dense can be thick enough that it's above sea level. Continental crust gets its name from the fact that the surfaces of continents are mostly above sea level.

Interpret Visuals ✏ Use the directions in which the convection currents are moving in the figure to draw in arrows indicating the direction of the oceanic plates.

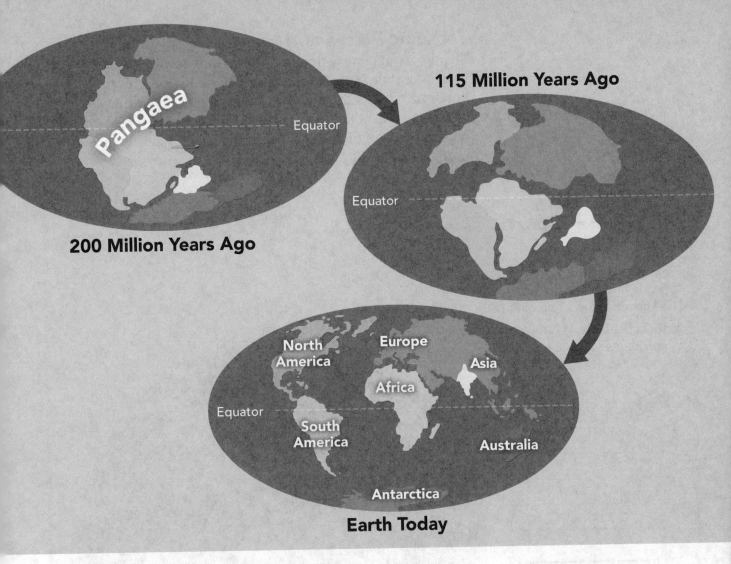

Pangaea

Equator

200 Million Years Ago

115 Million Years Ago

Equator

North America

Europe

Asia

Africa

Equator

South America

Australia

Antarctica

Earth Today

Plate Motions Over Time Scientists use satellites to measure plate motions precisely. The plates move very slowly—about 1 to 10 centimeters per year. The North American and Eurasian plates, named for the continents they carry, move apart at a rate of 1 to 2 centimeters per year, or about as fast as your fingernails grow. Because the plates have been moving for billions of years, they have moved great distances.

Over time, the movement of Earth's plates has greatly changed the locations of the continents and the size and shape of the ocean basins. Long before Pangaea existed, over billions of years, other supercontinents had formed and split apart. Pangaea itself formed when Earth's landmasses moved together about 350 to 250 million years ago. Then, about 200 million years ago, Pangaea began to break apart (**Figure 4**).

☑ **READING CHECK** **Draw Conclusions** When might the continents we know today form a new supercontinent?

....

200 Million Years of Plate Motions

Figure 4 It has taken the continents about 200 million years to move to their present locations, since the breakup of Pangaea.

Interpret Visuals 🖉
Label the landmasses from 115 million years ago with the present-day names of landmasses, as shown on the "Earth Today" map.

 **INTERACTIVITY**

Compare the relative rates of motion of different plates.

Tectonic Plates and the "Ring of Fire"

The theory of plate tectonics predicts that earthquakes and volcanoes should occur at plate boundaries, and that some landforms, such as mountain ranges, should mark the plate boundaries. For example, many volcanic eruptions and earthquakes occur at the edges of the Pacific Plate (**Figure 5**), that lies under the Pacific Ocean.

Model It

Ring of Fire

Figure 5 Because the region around the Pacific Ocean is prone to volcanic activity and earthquakes, it is known as the "Ring of Fire."

1. **Interpret Maps** Why do so many volcanoes seem to occur on coastlines of the Pacific Ocean?

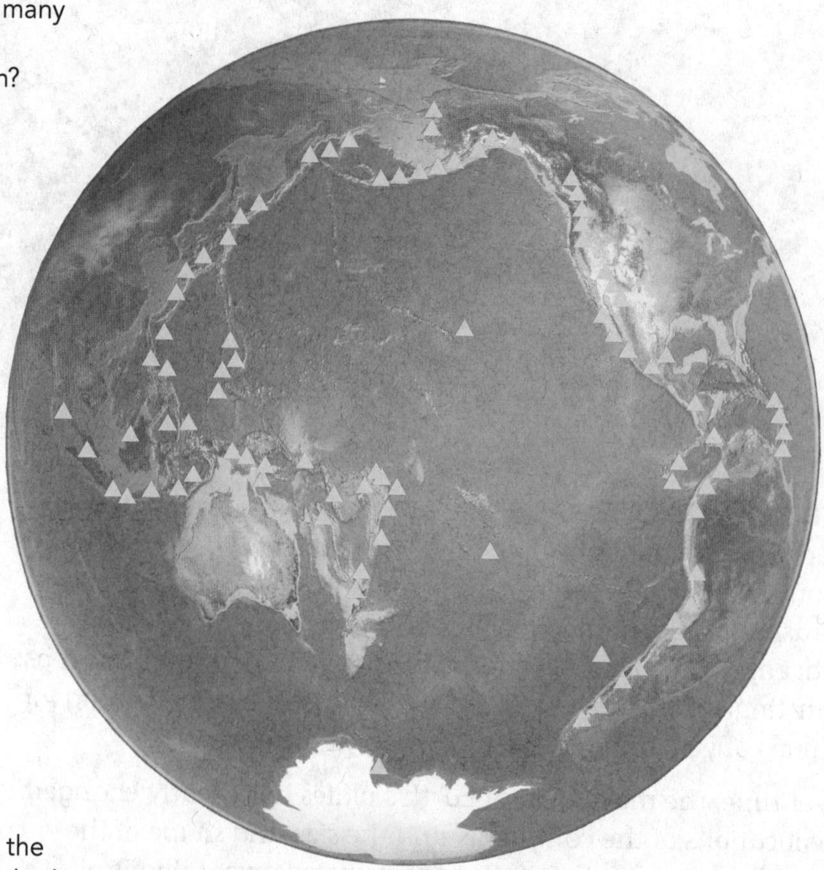

....

....

....

....

....

....

▲ Volcanoes

2. **Use Models** ✎ According to the theory of plate tectonics, how do the locations of volcanoes compare with plate boundaries? On **Figure 5,** draw the edges of the different plates, including the Pacific Plate. Use **Figure 6** to help you.

3. **Explain** Describe how the symbols on the map guided your mark-up of the map.

....

....

Plate Map

Figure 6 🖊 Earth scientists have identified the different tectonic plates, many of which are named for the continents they carry. The boundaries have been identified as convergent, divergent, or transform. Relative plate movements at some of the boundaries are indicated with red arrows. Using the map key as a reference, add the arrows that are missing in the circles provided.

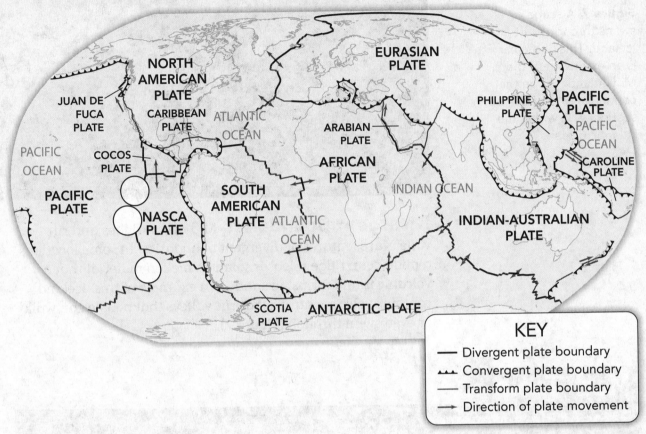

KEY
— Divergent plate boundary
⩜⩜⩜ Convergent plate boundary
— Transform plate boundary
→ Direction of plate movement

Plate Boundaries

Earth's plates meet and interact at boundaries. Along each boundary, plates move in one of three ways. Plates move apart, or diverge, from each other at a **divergent boundary** (dy VUR junt). Plates come together, or converge, at a **convergent boundary** (kun VER junt). Plates slip past each other along a **transform boundary**. The interactions of plates at boundaries produce great changes on land and on the ocean floor. These changes include the formation of volcanoes, mountain ranges, and deep-ocean trenches. Earthquakes and the triggering of tsunamis are also more common at or near plate boundaries. **Figure 6** depicts the major tectonic plates and the types of boundaries between them.

✅ **READING CHECK** **Integrate With Visuals** Which of the plates from the map would be a good starting point for a diagram that summarizes the different boundaries? Why?

....

....

Literacy Connection

Integrate With Visuals
In your science notebook, draw sketches of the different interactions at plate boundaries. Work toward a visual presentation that summarizes the plate boundaries in a single diagram.

👆 **INTERACTIVITY**

Explore surface features associated with plate movement at different locations around the world.

VIDEO

Learn about the tectonic plate boundary types.

Iceland

Figure 7 A scuba diver swims through a rift in Iceland. This particular rift is an extension of the Mid-Atlantic Ridge that continues to produce new seafloor and widen the Atlantic Ocean.

Divergent Boundaries Mid-ocean ridges and rift valleys are features of divergent boundaries. In some locations, a mid-ocean ridge releases so much molten material that a volcanic island forms. Iceland is an example of this. Iceland contains volcanoes as well as rift valleys that people can walk or even swim through (**Figure 7**).

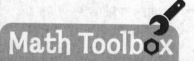

Math Toolbox

Rates of Plate Movement

Earth scientists measure plate movement by using the Global Positioning System (GPS) of satellites. Receivers anchored in Earth's surface receive signals from satellites, and calculate their positions using the time it takes for signals to be received. Over time, changes in those signal times indicate plate movement.

1. **Reason Quantitatively** Evidence from GPS readings suggests that the Mid-Atlantic Ridge spreads about 2.5 cm per year. How fast is the North American Plate moving away from the ridge? Explain your answer.

....

....

....

....

....

....

2. **Calculate** The Pacific Plate moves to the northwest at an average rate of 10 cm per year. Hawaii is in the middle of the Pacific Plate, 6,600 kilometers southeast of Japan, which is on the edge of several adjacent plates. If the Pacific Plate continues to move at the same rate and in the same direction, when will Hawaii collide with Japan? Show your work.

....

....

....

....

Convergent Boundaries

A boundary where two plates collide, or move toward each other, is called a convergent boundary. If two continents collide, then a mountain range is pushed up. This is how the Himalayas formed, and are still being pushed up. What is now India used to be a separate continent that broke away from Antarctica and headed north. It began colliding with Asia more than 60 million years ago, and the edges of the two plates folded like the hoods of two cars in a head-on collision (**Figure 8**). Mount Everest and the rest of the Himalayas are the result.

If one or both plates are oceanic, then subduction occurs. The ocean plate always subducts if it collides with a continent. If two oceanic plates collide, the older, colder, and denser plate usually subducts beneath the younger plate, with an ocean trench marking the plate boundary. As the subducting plate sinks back into the mantle, water that was in the ocean crust rises into the overlying mantle, lowering its melting point. Magma forms and rises up through the overlying plate, producing volcanoes. On land, this results in the formation of volcanic mountains. Mountains can also form as ocean seafloor sediments are scraped onto the edge of the overlying plate, forming a large wedge of rock.

Under the sea, subduction produces undersea volcanoes, also known as seamounts. If they grow tall enough, these volcanoes form a volcanic island chain. This is why there are often chains of volcanic islands where convergent boundaries exist in the ocean.

HANDS-ON LAB

Investigate Explore different plate interactions.

Collision at a Convergent Boundary

Figure 8 When two continental plates collide, their collision can have a crumpling effect on the crust that produces tall mountains, just as when two cars crash in a head-on collision. If one plate is denser, such as a plate of oceanic crust, that denser plate will dive under the other. This can also produce mountains as the overlying plate edge is nudged upward.

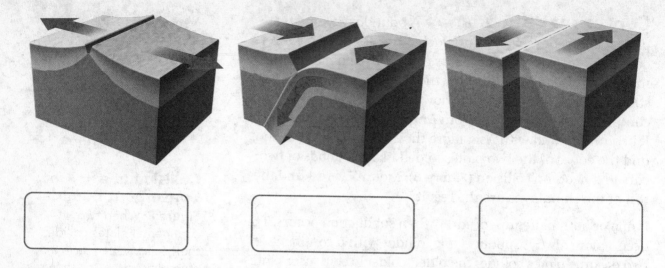

[ ] [ ] [ ]

Types of Plate Boundaries

Figure 9 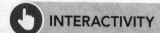 The three types of plate boundaries are modeled here. Label each illustration with the term that describes the boundary.

INTERACTIVITY

Investigate how stress is built up and released at faults.

Transform Boundaries Plates slide past each other at a transform boundary. Earthquakes occur here on faults called transform faults. Bending across a fault occurs when the two sides remain locked together. When enough stress builds up, the fault ruptures and an earthquake occurs. This is what causes earthquakes along transform faults such as the San Andreas Fault in California. In some cases a surface feature (such as a stream or road) that crossed a fault is visibly offset after a major slippage of the plates. Depending on how the plate edges match up, a vertical offset can exist across the fault.

Keep in mind that the tectonic plates of Earth's lithosphere are three-dimensional objects that are moving around a sphere. The shapes of the plates are irregular. This means every plate has some mixture of the different types of boundaries, and at some point the boundaries may change as the plates shrink, grow, collide, slip past each other, subduct, and so on. Interactions among tectonic plates continue to reshape Earth's surface features.

READING CHECK **Summarize Text** What happens at divergent, convergent, and transform boundaries?

....

....

....

1. Identify At what type of plate boundary would you find a rift valley that is growing wider?

....

2. Interpret Visuals Describe what is going on in this diagram.

....

....

....

....

....

3. Predict What other surface feature that is not shown in the diagram could be produced as a result of the process shown?

....

4. Calculate It takes 100,000 years for a plate to move about 2 kilometers. What is that plate's rate of motion in centimeters per year?

....

5. Connect to Nature of Science What does the theory of plate tectonics have that Wegener's hypothesis of continental drift did not have?

....

....

....

....

....

....

Quest CHECK-IN

In this lesson, you learned about the specific mechanisms by which plates move and how interactions of tectonic plates affect Earth's surface.

Infer What's the connection between Mount Rainier and the plate boundaries along the coast of the Pacific Northwest?

....

....

....

INTERACTIVITY

Mount Rainer's Threat

Go online to learn how Mount Rainer and other volcanic mountains in the Cascade Range formed as a result of geologic activity at tectonic plate boundaries.

AUSTRALIA
on the Move

Located on one of the world's fastest moving tectonic plates—the Australian Plate—Australia is moving about 7 centimeters north, and slightly east, each year.

Australia's plate, of course, is not the only moving plate on Earth. But each of the planet's plates moves at a different rate. Most move at a rate of a few centimeters a year. At 7 centimeters a year, Australia is one of the fastest.

In the 1960s, geologists confirmed that tectonic plates move along Earth's mantle. But only recently, with the help of computer modeling, have they come to understand why the plates move at different speeds. As a plate sinks into the mantle at a subduction zone, it pulls along the rest of the plate. It's similar to what happens to all the dishes and glasses on a dinner table when you pull the tablecloth down on one side. The size and structure of the subduction zone influence the strength of this pull. A large plate edge that is descending into the mantle at a large subduction zone would exert more force on the rest of the plate.

Measuring Movement

No one can feel the plates moving. They move only about as fast as your fingernails grow. But the movement adds up. In 50 million years, the Australian Plate could collide with Southeast Asia.

Over time, the continent's movement means that Australia's latitude and longitude on older maps no longer match the actual location of the continent. Maps require corrections to compensate for Australia's movement.

Australia has officially changed its location four times in the last 50 years. At the beginning of 2017, Australia changed its location once again, this time moving it another 1.5 meters (about 5 feet) north.

A Kangaroo's Length
The movement of Australia requires updates to its official location on maps. In 2017, it moved 1.5 meters north. This is about the length of a gray kangaroo.

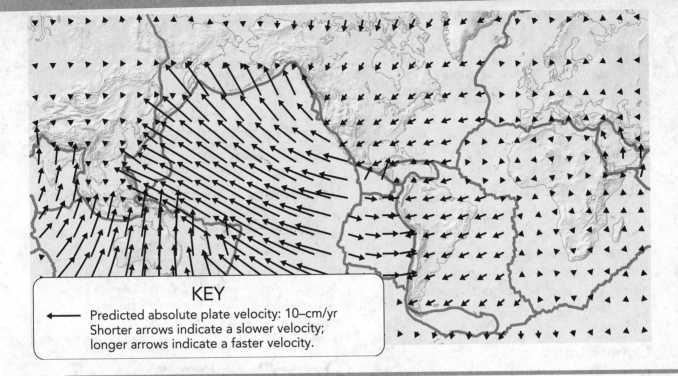

KEY

← Predicted absolute plate velocity: 10–cm/yr
Shorter arrows indicate a slower velocity;
longer arrows indicate a faster velocity.

**Use this map and Figure 6 in Lesson 2 to answer the
following questions.**

1. **Summarize** What factors affect the speed at which a tectonic
   plate moves?

   ....

   ....

2. **Interpret Data** Which plate is moving fastest? Cite evidence to
   justify your answer.

   ....

   ....

3. **Apply Concepts** Would you expect a largely oceanic plate to
   move faster than a largely continental plate? Explain.

   ....

   ....

   ....

   ....

4. **Construct Explanations** The Australian and Pacific plates are
   among the fastest-moving plates. What conclusions can you draw
   about the subduction zone where the Australian Plate meets the
   Pacific Plate? Use evidence from the text and the map to support
   your explanation.

   ....

   ....

Earthquakes and Tsunami Hazards

Guiding Questions

- How do plate movement and stress produce new landforms?
- What are earthquakes and tsunamis, and why do they occur?
- How can the effects of earthquakes and tsunamis be mitigated?

Connections

Literacy Evaluate Media

Math Analyze Graphs

MS-ESS2-2, MS-ESS3-2

Vocabulary

stress
tension
compression
shearing
fault
earthquake
magnitude
tsunami

Academic Vocabulary

scale

VOCABULARY APP

Practice vocabulary on a mobile device.

Quest CONNECTION

Consider how monitoring a volcano for signs of an eruption might be similar to monitoring an area for signs of an earthquake.

Connect It!

✏️ **Circle and label evidence that a tsunami occurred.**

Infer How did the ship come to rest on land?

....

....

....

Stress and Earth's Crust

The movement of Earth's massive tectonic plates generates tremendous force. This force can bend and break the rock of Earth's crust. The force that acts on rock to change its shape or volume is called **stress**. There are three kinds of stress. **Tension** pulls on Earth's crust, stretching the rock to make it thinner, especially at the point halfway between the two pulling forces. **Compression** squeezes rock until it bends or breaks. When compression occurs at a large scale, rock can be folded into mountains. **Shearing** occurs when rock is being pushed in two opposite directions, to the point that it bends or breaks. These types of stress can produce both folds and faults. Movement of Earth's crust around faults can produce destructive earthquakes and, in some cases, tsunamis **(Figure 1)**.

Make Meaning As you go through the lesson, keep notes in your science notebook about how the physical stresses described here are involved in processes that produce earthquakes and tsunamis.

Tsunami Damage
Figure 1 In 2011, a major tsunami engulfed parts of Japan, killing thousands and destroying property.

353

Death Valley

Figure 2 Tension can result in peaks around a sunken valley, such as Death Valley in California.

Normal Fault

A **fault** is a break in the rock of Earth's crust or mantle. Most faults occur along plate boundaries, where stress of one or more types is deforming the rock, leading to changes at Earth's surface (**Figure 2**). The two sides of a fault are referred to as walls. The wall whose rock is over the other is called the hanging wall, and the other is called the footwall. In a normal fault, the hanging wall slips down relative to the footwall (**Figure 3A**). This usually occurs at a divergent plate boundary, where tension is pulling the plates away from each other. If there is a series of normal faults, a slab of crust that falls away can become a valley while the adjacent slabs can become mountains.

Reverse Fault

Compression can produce a reverse fault, in which the hanging wall slides up and over the footwall (**Figure 3B**). The northern Rocky Mountains were gradually lifted by the action at several reverse faults. Reverse faults are common at convergent boundaries.

Strike-Slip Fault

California's San Andreas Fault is a product of shearing. Walls of rock grind past each other in opposite directions, making a strike-slip fault (**Figure 3C**). Transform boundaries are home to strike-slip faults.

☑ READING CHECK **Determine Central Ideas** Pair each fault type with the type of stress that produces it.

....

....

Types of Faults

Figure 3 🖊 The three types of faults are shown here. Complete diagrams A and B by labeling the hanging walls and footwalls. In Diagram C, draw arrows to indicate the direction of shearing force and the movement along the fault.

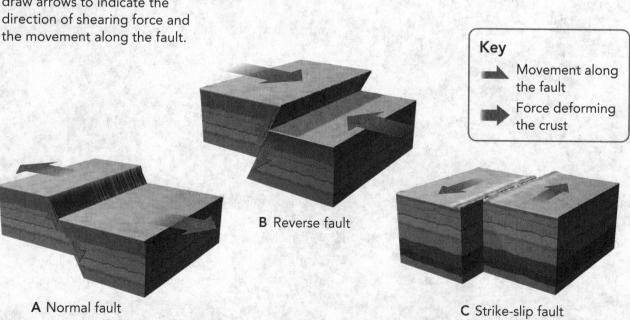

Key

➡ Movement along the fault

➡ Force deforming the crust

A Normal fault

B Reverse fault

C Strike-slip fault

Valleys and Mountains

Figure 4 As tension pulls rock apart along normal faults, some blocks fall, leaving others elevated. Over time, the resulting mountains weather.

Rift valley

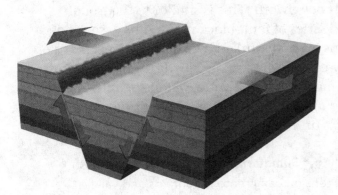

Fault-block mountains

Key

 Movement along the fault

 Force deforming the crust

New Landforms From Plate Movement

Over millions of years, the forces of plate movement can change a flat plain into folded mountains, fault-block mountains, and other dramatic features of Earth's surface.

Tension and Normal Faults

To see how tension and normal faults produce mountains, we need to zoom out and look at a series of at least two normal faults. Where two plates move away from each other, tension forms numerous faults that run parallel to each other over a wide area. A wedge of rock that has hanging walls at both faults drops down as tension pulls the adjacent footwalls away to form a rift valley (**Figure 4**). This leaves the other blocks higher up, as mountains. Mountains built this way are called fault-block mountains.

Folding

Compression within a plate causes the crust to deform without breaking. Folds are bends in rock that form when compression shortens and thickens Earth's crust. Folds may be centimeters across or they may span many kilometers. The folds are often most visible and obvious when the rock is layered. When folding occurs on a large **scale,** folds that bend upward become mountains and folds that bend downward become valleys.

Academic Vocabulary

The processes of plate tectonics occur at different scales of time and space. List some different terms that are used to describe distance and time at vastly different scales.

....

....

....

355

Folded Mountain

Figure 5 Formations at the Hong Kong UNESCO Global Geopark reveal distinct folding patterns.

Anticlines and Synclines A fold in rock that bends upward into an arch is called an anticline (AN tih klyn). This may resemble the crest of a wave, as seen in **Figure 5**. Weathering and erosion have shaped many large-scale anticlines into mountains. The height of an anticline is exaggerated by the valley-like syncline (SIN klyn), which is a fold that bends downward. This is similar to the trough of a wave. Like a series of fault-block mountains, a series of folded mountains is often marked by valleys between rows of mountains. Viewed at a large scale, a wide area of compressed crust may have mountains and valleys made of anticlines and synclines (**Figure 6**), while the large-scale folds may themselves contain their own anticlines and synclines.

✓ READING CHECK Summarize Text Describe how both compression and tension can create mountains and valleys.

....

....

....

....

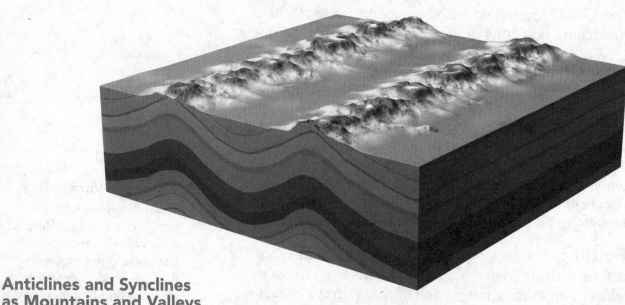

Anticlines and Synclines as Mountains and Valleys

Figure 6 ✏ Label the anticlines and synclines in the diagram.

Identify Limitations How does this figure oversimplify how compression produces folds in Earth's crust?

....

....

....

Earthquakes

Some plate interactions are gradual, quiet, and almost imperceptible. Others can be sudden, violent, loud, and destructive. At some faults, the plates may grind to a halt and remain stuck in place for years. Stress builds up until the plates lurch into motion, releasing a great amount of energy. The shaking and trembling that results from this plate movement is an **earthquake**. Some of the energy released in an earthquake is in the form of seismic waves.

HANDS-ON LAB

иInvestigate Analyze data and interpret patterns to predict future earthquakes.

Seismic Waves Similar to sound waves, seismic waves are vibrations that travel through Earth carrying energy released by various processes, such as earthquakes, ocean storms, and volcanic eruptions. There are three types of seismic waves, as shown in **Figure 7**. The waves begin at the earthquake's focus, where rock that was under stress begins to break or move. Waves may strike quickest and with the most energy at the point on Earth's surface directly above the earthquake's focus, called the epicenter. But seismic waves also move in all directions, through and across Earth's interior and surface. When seismic waves pass from one material to another, they can change speeds and directions.

P and S Waves

Figure 7 🖉 The motion of particles in Earth's surface is shown for P waves and S waves. Draw the particle motion for the surface waves.

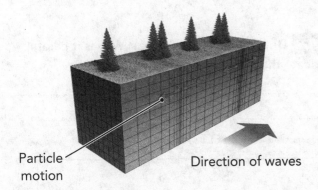

Particle motion   Direction of waves

P waves, short for primary waves, travel the fastest. They are the first to arrive at a location on Earth's surface. P waves compress and expand the ground.

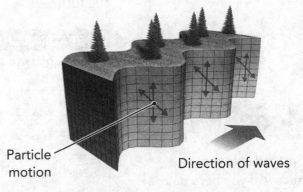

Particle motion   Direction of waves

S waves, short for secondary waves, travel more slowly so they arrive after P waves. S waves can move the ground side to side or up and down, relative to the direction in which they travel.

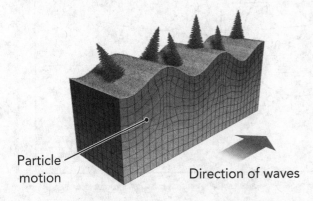

Particle motion   Direction of waves

Surface waves can form when P waves and S waves reach Earth's surface. The result can be a kind of rolling motion, like ocean waves, where particles move in a pattern that is almost circular. Surface waves damage structures on the surface.

Seismogram

Figure 8 The surface waves that travel along Earth's surface usually have the largest amplitudes and therefore cause the most damage.

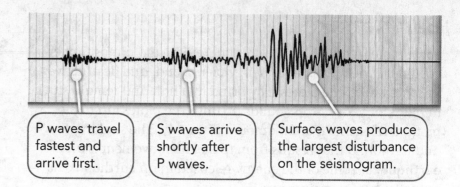

P waves travel fastest and arrive first.

S waves arrive shortly after P waves.

Surface waves produce the largest disturbance on the seismogram.

INTERACTIVITY

Analyze seismic waves to locate an earthquake.

Seismographs Seismic waves produced by earthquakes are measured by a device called a seismograph, or seismometer. This device converts the energy in the different waves to a visual called a seismogram **(Figure 8)**. The seismogram shows the timing of the different seismic waves, with the relatively gentle P and S waves arriving first, followed by surface waves with larger amplitudes. The amplitudes, or heights, of the waves on a seismogram are used to quantify the size of the earthquake.

When an earthquake occurs, geologists use data from seismograph stations in different locations to pinpoint the earthquake's epicenter **(Figure 9)**. Locating the epicenter helps geologists to identify areas where earthquakes may occur in the future.

READING CHECK **Determine Central Ideas** Why is it helpful for geologists to locate the epicenters of earthquakes?

....

....

Model It

Triangulation

Figure 9 If you have data from three seismograph stations, you can locate the precise location of an earthquake's epicenter. The center of each circle is the location of a station. The radius of each circle is the distance from the epicenter. The point where the three circles overlap is the location of the epicenter.

Analyze Data Draw an X on the map to indicate the epicenter of the earthquake.

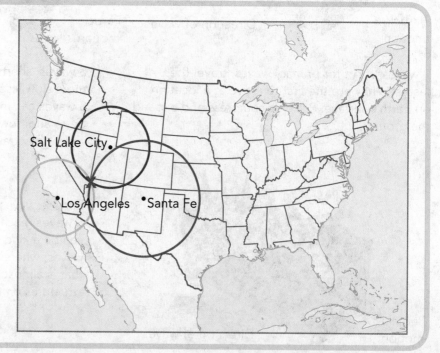

Finding an Epicenter

Geologists are trying to locate the epicenter of an earthquake. The data table below shows the arrival times of seismic waves at three different stations across Earth's surface. Use the graph to answer the questions.

Station	P Wave Arrival Time	S Wave Arrival Time	Distance from Epicenter (km)
A	4 mins, 6 s	7 mins, 25 s	
B	6 mins, 58 s	12 mins, 36 s	
C	9 mins, 21 s	16 mins, 56 s	

1. **Analyze Graphs** ✏ Use the graph to determine the distance of each station from the epicenter. Record the distances in the table.

2. **Interpret Graphs** If another station is 5,000 km from the epicenter of the earthquake, about how long after the start of the earthquake would the S waves have arrived at this station?

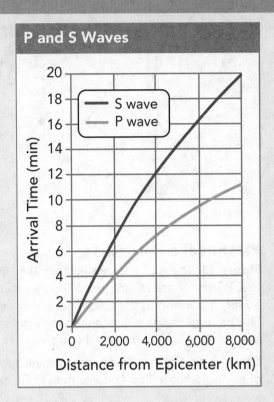

P and S Waves

— S wave
— P wave

Arrival Time (min) vs. Distance from Epicenter (km)

Magnitude An earthquake's **magnitude** is a single number that geologists use to assign to an earthquake based on the earthquake's size. The size of an earthquake is usually measured using the moment magnitude scale, which is a measure of the energy released. Each whole-number increase in this scale represents a roughly 32-fold increase in energy. So, the seismic waves of a magnitude-9 earthquake are 10 times larger than for a magnitude-8 earthquake. The energy released, however, is 32 times greater **(Figure 10)**.

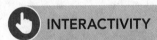

INTERACTIVITY

Explore technologies that help make buildings earthquake resistant.

Magnitude	Location	Date
9.2	Sumatra	2004
9.0	Japan	2011
7.9	China	2008
7.9	Nepal	2015
7.0	Haiti	2010

Earthquake Magnitude

Figure 10 The table shows the moment magnitudes of some large earthquakes.

Analyze Data How much more energy was released by the earthquake in China than the one in Haiti?

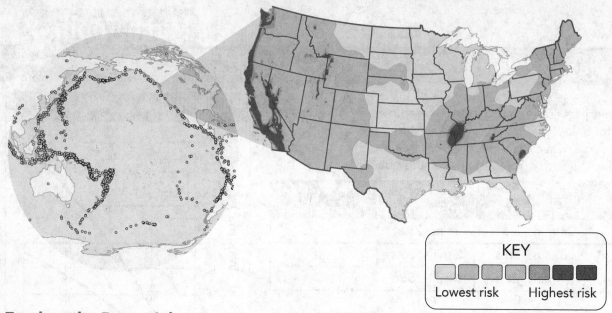

KEY

Lowest risk   Highest risk

Earthquake Potential

Figure 11 The globe shows earthquakes occurring from 2007 to 2017 that were magnitude 6.0 or greater. The U.S. Geological Survey has mapped the risk of earthquakes in the United States. On the map, beige indicates the lowest risk of earthquakes occurring, while purple indicates the highest risk.

Cause and Effect What do you think accounts for the higher risk of earthquakes in Los Angeles than in Chicago?

....

....

Literacy Connection

Evaluate Media ✏️
Identify an area of the U.S. earthquake risk map in **Figure 11** that does not fit the pattern of earthquake occurrences described on this page. Circle the area.

👆 **INTERACTIVITY**

Help determine the best location for a new stadium in an earthquake zone.

Earthquake Risks and Tsunamis

The "Ring of Fire" around the Pacific Ocean is where many of the world's earthquakes occur. There are many plate boundaries around the Pacific, including convergent and transform boundaries where stress builds up. Because the west coast of the United States, including Alaska, is on the edge of several boundaries, the western states have a much higher risk of experiencing an earthquake than other regions of the U.S., as shown in **Figure 11**. Earthquakes themselves can cause tremendous damage, but if they occur near or below the ocean floor they can produce another type of disaster.

Ocean Floor Uplift When an area of Earth's crust moves during an earthquake, it can force anything above it to move as well. For example, an area of off-shore ocean floor that has been stressed for years at a convergent plate boundary can suddenly pop up, thrusting up the ocean water above it. Depending on how the water is moved, a tsunami may form.

A **tsunami** is a wave or series of waves produced by an earthquake or landslide. Unlike typical ocean waves formed by the wind, tsunami waves can involve the entire water column—every drop between the surface and the ocean floor—and this means they can carry tremendous energy and can be highly destructive **(Figure 12)**. In 2004, hundreds of thousands of people lost their lives due to a tsunami that struck Indonesia, Thailand, Sri Lanka, and other coastal nations around the Indian Ocean. That tsunami travelled across the Indian Ocean at a speed of 800 kilometers per hour.

Landslides Ocean floor uplift is one cause of tsunamis. Landslides are another. In both cases, some kind of displacement of water occurs, setting the tsunami in motion. In 1958, an earthquake triggered a landslide on a mountainside on the shore of Lituya Bay, Alaska. About 30 million cubic meters of rock tumbled into the water at one end of the bay, producing a tsunami that swept across the bay and splashed as high as 524 meters up along the steep shoreline **(Figure 13)**.

✔ READING CHECK How can an earthquake or landslide produce a tsunami?

....

....

....

A Wall of Water
Figure 12 A tsunami does not always look like a wave. In some cases it is more like a sudden, massive rise in sea level, which simply floods low-lying areas.

Tsunami Hazards
Figure 13 ✏ The site of the rockslide that produced the tsunami in Lituya Bay is marked by the circle. Draw lines to indicate where the water splashed up and tore away plants and sediment from the bay's shore.

☑ LESSON 3 Check

MS-ESS2-2, MS-ESS3-2

1. Identify Which type of stress on Earth's crust can make a slab of rock shorter and thicker?

....

2. Cause and Effect How do mountains and valleys form through folding?

....

....

....

....

....

3. Explain You hear about a magnitude 8.0 earthquake on the news. Someone says "That doesn't sound too bad. An 8.0 is just one more than the 7.0 we had here last year." Explain why that's not the right way to think about the moment magnitude scale.

....

....

....

....

4. Infer A news bulletin reports a powerful earthquake 200 kilometers off the coast of California. Hours later, there's no sign of any tsunami anywhere on the West Coast. Why not?

....

....

....

....

5. Summarize Describe the roll that stress plays in the production of earthquakes and tsunamis.

....

....

....

....

....

....

....

Quest CHECK-INS

In this lesson, you learned about the connection between plate tectonics and features and events at Earth's surface, including mountains and earthquakes.

Evaluate How can monitoring Earth for seismic activity near plate boundaries be useful in monitoring volcanoes?

....

....

....

....

....

👆 **INTERACTIVITY**

Monitoring a Volcano

Go online to practice several data collection and analysis techniques to monitor a volcano and predict an eruption.

DESIGNING TO PREVENT
Destruction

▶ VIDEO

Watch how underwater earthquakes displace water.

How do you design buildings that can withstand the forceful waves of a tsunami? You engineer it!

The Challenge: To construct tsunami-safe buildings.

Phenomenon A seafloor earthquake can displace water above it, causing a tsunami to form. When the tsunami reaches land, giant waves cause widespread destruction.

Because parts of the United States are at risk for tsunamis, U.S. engineers have developed new building standards to save lives. They studied new design concepts. Strong columns enable buildings to stand, even when battered by tons of water and debris. Exits on upper floors allow people to get out when lower floors are flooded.

To develop standards, engineers visited Japan, where an earthquake and tsunami in 2011 caused terrible losses of life and property. The engineers also used wave research to model tsunamis and their impact on buildings.

These engineers hope that hospitals, schools, and police stations, if built to the new standards, can then provide shelter for people fleeing danger.

It is a challenge to design and engineer structures that can withstand the force of a tsunami. Under the new standards, schools would be built to withstand the force of water and debris.

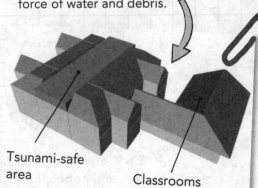

Tsunami-safe area

Classrooms

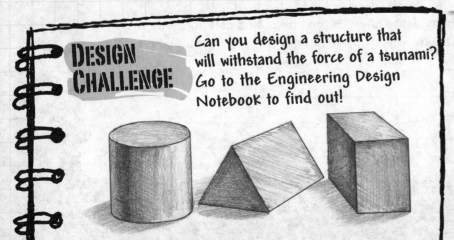

DESIGN CHALLENGE Can you design a structure that will withstand the force of a tsunami? Go to the Engineering Design Notebook to find out!

Volcanoes and Earth's Surface

Guiding Questions

- How is plate tectonics connected to volcanic eruptions and landforms?
- What role does volcanic activity play in shaping Earth's surface?
- What hazards do different types of volcanoes pose?

Connections

Literacy Integrate With Visuals

Math Analyze Proportional Relationships

MS-ESS2-2, MS-ESS3-2

Vocabulary

volcano
magma
lava
hot spot
extinct
dormant

Academic Vocabulary

active
composite

 VOCABULARY APP

Practice vocabulary on a mobile device.

Quest CONNECTION

Think about how Mount Rainier may have been built and how understanding its history and characteristics can help hikers stay safe.

Connect It!

✏️ **Circle and label effects that the volcano in the photo is having on Earth's surface and atmosphere.**

Classify List the effects that you identified in the photo, and categorize them by the Earth system that is affected—hydrosphere, atmosphere, geosphere, biosphere.

....

....

....

....

Volcanoes

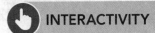
INTERACTIVITY

Explore how an erupting volcano might change Earth's surface.

While active volcanoes are found in a relatively small number of states in the U.S., they have a profound impact on Earth's surface—especially at plate boundaries. Volcanoes add new material to Earth's surface, release gases into the atmosphere, build new islands in the ocean, and shape habitats for organisms. A **volcano** is a structure that forms in Earth's crust when molten material, or magma, reaches Earth's surface. This can occur on land or on the ocean floor. **Magma** is a molten mixture of rock-forming substances, gases, and water from the mantle. Once magma reaches the surface, it is known as **lava**. When lava cools, it forms solid rock.

As with earthquakes, there is a pattern to where volcanoes occur on Earth. Most are found at convergent or divergent plate boundaries, but they can also occur at seemingly random places far from plate boundaries.

Volcanism

Figure 1 The activity of volcanoes is called volcanism. Eruptions that release lava and other matter from Earth's interior can pose hazards to organisms, including humans.

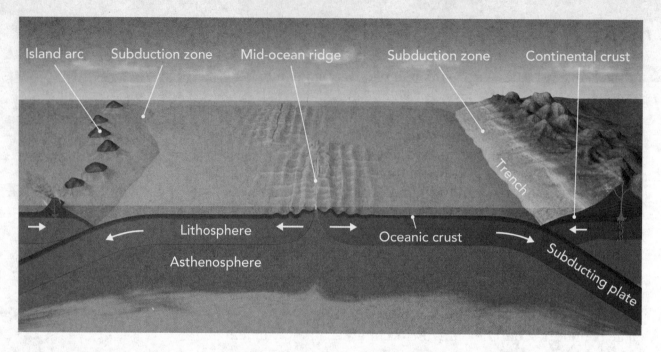

Island arc Subduction zone Mid-ocean ridge Subduction zone Continental crust

Trench

Lithosphere

Oceanic crust

Asthenosphere

Subducting plate

Divergent and Convergent Boundaries

Figure 2 Volcanic activity at plate boundaries can produce volcanoes on continents and volcanic island arcs.

Summarize Describe what is happening on the left side of the diagram, where ash is rising in the air over an active volcano.

....

....

....

....

....

....

....

HANDS-ON LAB

☑**Investigate** Explore moving volcanoes.

Volcanoes and Plate Boundaries

At convergent boundaries, the subduction of an oceanic plate under a continental plate can produce volcanoes along the edge of the continent. Subduction of an oceanic plate under an adjacent oceanic plate can result in a volcanic island arc. At divergent boundaries, molten magma comes through the crust as lava, which quickly hardens into rock, but if the volume of magma is especially large, then a volcanic cone may form. **Figure 2** summarizes these processes.

At Divergent Boundaries
Volcanoes form at divergent boundaries when plates move apart and rock rises to fill the vacant space. Most volcanoes at divergent boundaries occur in the ocean at mid-ocean ridges, so they are never seen. Only in places such as Iceland can you see ocean-ridge volcanoes. Less common are volcanoes like Mt. Kilimanjaro that occur at continental divergent boundaries such as the East African Rift.

At Convergent Boundaries
When a plate dives into the mantle in the process of subduction, trapped water leaves the sinking plate and mixes with the material of the overlying mantle, causing it to melt. The buoyant magma starts to rise toward the surface. If the magma reaches the surface before cooling, a volcano forms. If the overlying plate is part of the ocean floor, the resulting volcano begins to form on the seafloor as a seamount. If it grows large enough to break the ocean surface, it becomes a volcanic island. A whole chain of islands may form when volcanism occurs at multiple spots along the edge of an oceanic plate. This is called a volcanic island arc.

Hot Spot Volcanism In addition to divergent and convergent plate boundaries, there is a third source of volcanoes: hot spots. A **hot spot** is an area where lava frequently erupts at the surface, independent of plate boundary processes. Most hot spots sit atop mantle plumes of hot rock. Hot spot plumes are fixed within the deep mantle. As a plate moves over the plume, a chain of volcanoes is created because older volcanoes keep being carried away from the hot spot. The many islands and seamounts of Hawaii have formed from the westward motion of the Pacific Plate, as is illustrated in **Figure 3**. Another hot spot is found at Yellowstone National Park in Wyoming. The "supervolcano" beneath the park may erupt again someday. During past giant eruptions of Yellowstone, the last one being 640,000 years ago, most of North America was covered with volcanic ash.

☑ READING CHECK **Determine Conclusions** The Aleutian Islands of Alaska occur in a chain near a plate boundary. What type of boundary is it?

....

Model It

Hot Spot Modeling
Figure 3 The Hawaiian Islands have formed from the movement of the Pacific Plate over a hot spot plume.

Integrate With Visuals
✏ Using the diagram as inspiration, design a functioning physical model of how a hot spot makes volcanoes on the ocean crust of a moving plate. Sketch or describe your model in the space here, including details on how it would work.

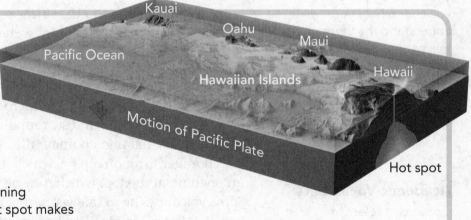

Kauai · Oahu · Maui · Hawaii · Pacific Ocean · Hawaiian Islands · Motion of Pacific Plate · Hot spot

Composite Volcano

Figure 4 🖊 A composite volcano has alternating layers of hardened lava and ash. Complete the diagram by reading the description of the volcano's parts and writing in the missing labels.

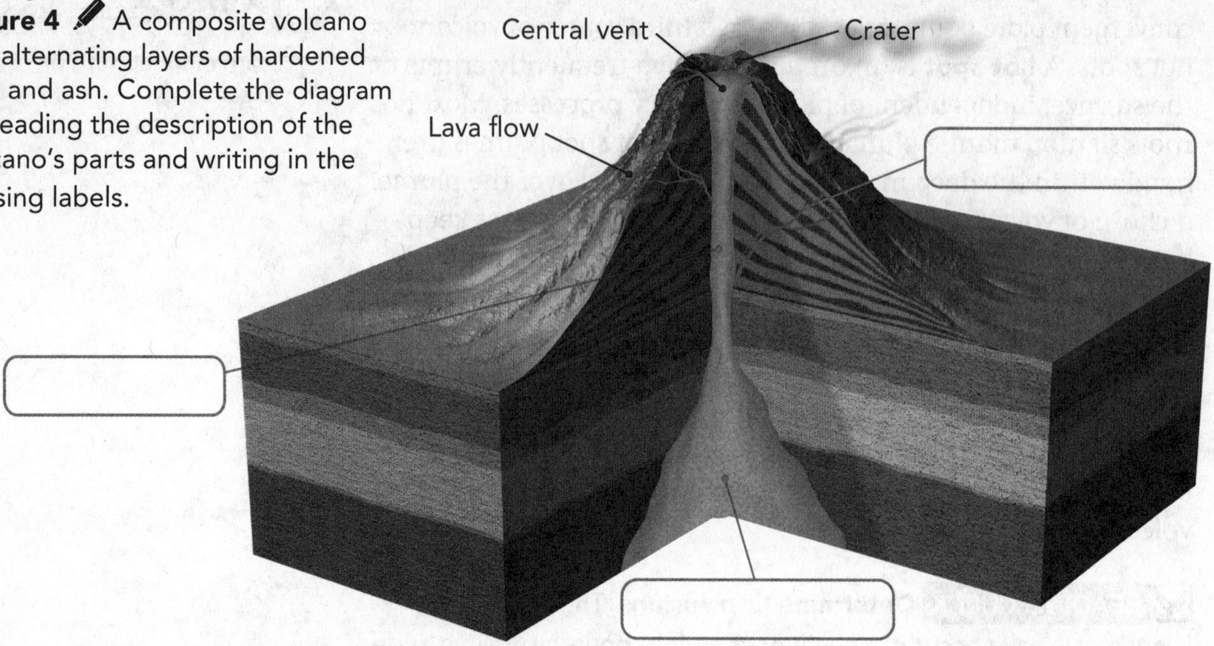

Central vent

Crater

Lava flow

Literacy Connection

Integrate With Visuals
Use the diagram of the volcano to help you understand the text on this page.

Academic Vocabulary

Composite refers to something made of a mixture of different parts or elements. Many manufactured objects are made of composites—blends of different raw materials. How does this help you to understand what a composite volcano is?

....

....

....

....

Volcano Landforms

Magma usually forms in the layer of hot rock in the upper mantle. Because magma is less dense than the rock around it, it cracks on its way up to the surface. Once the magma exits a volcano and is exposed to air or water, it is called lava.

Volcano Parts Inside a volcano (**Figure 4**) is a system of passageways through which magma travels. Below the volcano is a magma chamber, where magma collects before an eruption. The volcano and surrounding landscape may swell slightly as the magma chamber fills. Magma moves up from the chamber through a pipe, which leads to the central vent—an opening at the top, which may be in a bowl-shaped crater. Some volcanoes have side vents, too. When lava flows out from a vent, it begins to cool and harden as it is pulled by gravity down the slope of the volcano. If lava is thrown explosively into the air, it hardens and falls to Earth in different forms. Bombs are large chunks of hardened lava. Cinders are the size of pebbles. The finest particles are called ash. The type of lava-based material that emerges from a new volcano defines the type of volcano that is built.

Volcano Types The volcano in **Figure 4** is a **composite** volcano. Also called a stratovolcano, it is made of alternating layers of lava flows and ash falls. These tend to be cone-shaped and tall. Mount Fuji in Japan is an example of a composite volcano. Other types of volcanic formations are shown in **Figure 5**.

Volcanic Formations

Figure 5 Volcanic activity can result in different landforms.

1. **Compare and Contrast** How are shield volcanoes and lava plateaus similar? How are they different?

....

....

....

2. **Develop Models** ✏ Review the three steps of caldera formation. Finish the sentence to describe the second phase of caldera formation.

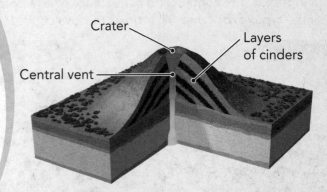

Cinder Cone Volcano If lava emerges from a new vent in Earth's crust as a mix of bombs, ash, and cinders, these materials build up into a cinder cone volcano. The loose, ashy material tends to erode quickly.

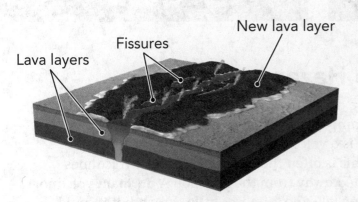

Lava Plateau Lava can flow out of several long cracks in Earth's crust and flood an area repeatedly over many years. Over time, these relatively flat layers of hardened lava build up into a lava plateau.

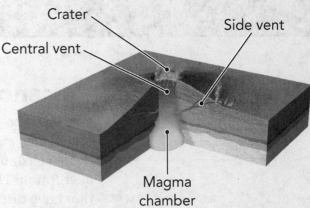

Shield Volcano Some volcanoes have slow, steady eruptions in which lava flows out and builds up over a broad area. Hot spot volcanoes tend to be shield volcanoes, and they can be massive.

Caldera A caldera forms when a volcano collapses on itself.

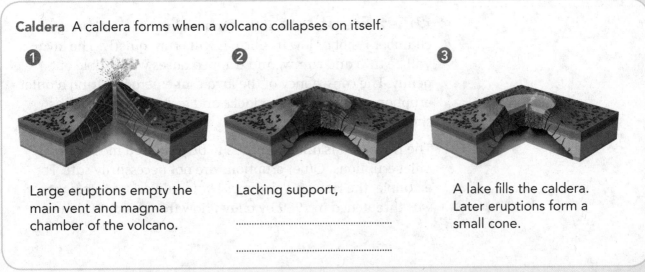

❶ Large eruptions empty the main vent and magma chamber of the volcano.

❷ Lacking support,

....

....

❸ A lake fills the caldera. Later eruptions form a small cone.

369

Lava from Quiet Eruptions

Figure 6 The content and consistency of lava determines the type of rock that will form as the lava cools.

INTERACTIVITY

Explore different volcanic landforms.

Academic Vocabulary

What does it mean if you have an active lifestyle?

....

....

....

Volcano Hazards

Volcanoes pose different hazards to humans and other organisms, mainly through eruptions. An **extinct**, or dead, volcano is a volcano that poses very little threat of eruption. This is often the case with hot-spot volcanoes that have drifted away from the hot spot. A **dormant** volcano is like a sleeping volcano—it poses little threat, but it could reawaken someday. **Active** volcanoes are the more immediate threat. Volcanologists classify eruptions as quiet or explosive. Whether an eruption is quiet or explosive depends in part on the magma's silica content and whether the magma is thin and runny or thick and sticky. Temperature helps determine how runny magma is.

Quiet Eruptions If the magma in a volcano's magma chamber is hot or low in silica, it will erupt quietly. The lava will be thin and runny, and trapped gases will bubble out gently. The consistency of the lava that emerges during a quiet eruption will affect how it looks and feels when it cools, as shown in **Figure 6**.

The Hawaiian Islands continue to be produced mostly by quiet eruptions. Quiet eruptions are not necessarily safe. For example, the Hawaii Volcanoes National Park's visitors center was threatened in 1989 by a lava flow from Mount Kilauea.

Explosive Eruptions Magma that has a lot of silica will erupt more than magma containing little or no silica. High-silica magma is thick and sticky, causing it to build up in a pipe until pressure is so great that it bursts out over the surface. Trapped gases explode out instead of bubbling out gently. An explosion with that much force can hurl lava, ash, cinders, and bombs high into the atmosphere.

Krakatau, a volcano in a large volcanic arc in Indonesia, erupted in 1883. The eruption, depicted in **Figure 7**, was so violent that much of the the visible part of the island collapsed into the sea, producing a tsunami that killed 36,000 people. Gas and debris billowed more than 25 kilometers into the sky, and the sound from the explosion was heard 4,500 kilometers away. So much ash and sulfur dioxide was emitted into the atmosphere by the eruption that global temperatures were cooler for the following five years.

Krakatau Explodes

Figure 7 The eruption of Krakatau was a major disaster in Indonesia, but it affected the entire world as ash and sulfur dioxide entered the atmosphere.

Magma Composition

Magma is classified according to the amount of silica it contains. The less silica the magma contains, the more easily it flows. More silica makes magma stickier and thicker. Trapped gases can't emerge easily, so eruptions are explosive.

1. **Analyze Proportional Relationships** How do the two magma types compare in terms of silica content?

....

....

2. **Infer** Which of the magma types would erupt more explosively? How would knowing the type of magma a volcano produces help nearby communities prepare for eruptions?

....

....

....

....

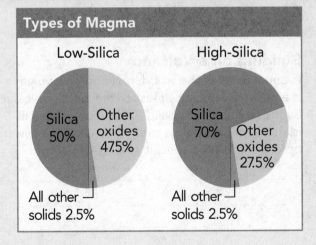

Types of Magma

Low-Silica

Silica 50%
Other oxides 47.5%
All other solids 2.5%

High-Silica

Silica 70%
Other oxides 27.5%
All other solids 2.5%

Measuring Gas Concentration

Figure 8 This device, called a spectrometer, can measure concentrations of volcanic gases by measuring how light passes through them. A high concentration of sulfur dioxide may mean an eruption is likely to occur.

 INTERACTIVITY

Analyze how volcanic activity can change Earth's surface.

Predicting Volcano Hazards Volcanologists use different tools to monitor volcanoes and predict eruptions. The gas emissions from volcanoes can be monitored to check for increases in sulfur dioxide, which may indicate that an eruption is coming **(Figure 8)**. Seismographs can detect rumblings deep inside a volcano that precede an eruption.

Volcanologists can also use devices to measure whether a volcano is swelling as its magma chamber fills up. These devices, called tiltmeters, are like carpenters' levels but much more sensitive. They can detect very slight changes in the tilt of a volcano's slopes. If the tilt increases, it means the volcano is swelling and likely to erupt. Telecommunications technology can transmit the data from these devices to scientists, who can then interpret the data and look for patterns associated with eruptions. They can then notify the public if an eruption is predicted.

☑ READING CHECK **Summarize Text** If the concentration of sulfur dioxide emitted from a volcano increases from less than one part per million (ppm) to 4 ppm, is the volcano more or less likely to erupt soon?

....

....

....

Question It!

Building on a Volcano

In some parts of the world, building on a volcano is a necessity because most of the land is volcanic. Suppose you had to build a home on a volcanic island. What questions would you want to answer before choosing a specific site for construction?

....

....

....

....

....

....

☑LESSON 4 Check

1. **Identify** Runny lava oozes from the vent of a broad, gently-sloping shield volcano. What type of eruption is this?

....

2. **Cause and Effect** Why do volcanoes form at divergent and convergent boundaries?

....
....
....
....
....

3. **Patterns** The Hawaiian Islands formed as the Pacific Plate has moved west-northwest over a hot spot. In which part of the islands would you expect to find the most active volcanoes? What about dormant and extinct volcanoes? Explain.

....
....
....
....
....
....
....

4. **Interpret Data** You are sailing in the South Pacific Ocean, far from any plate boundary. Looming on the horizon is a dark, broad, rounded island with sparse vegetation. A few thin flows of orange lava drip into the sea. Some smoky vapor unfurls from the center of the island. What kind of volcano is this? Explain.

....
....
....
....
....

5. **Summarize** How are volcanic island arcs formed?

....
....
....
....
....
....
....

Quest CHECK-INS

In this lesson, you learned about the connection between plate tectonics and volcanoes.

Evaluate Why is it important to understand the type of volcano Mount Rainier is and the patterns of activity at the nearest plate boundary?

....
....
....

HANDS-ON LAB

Signs of Eruption

Go online to download the lab and identify signs of a volcanic eruption.

☑TOPIC 8 Review and Assess

① Evidence of Plate Motions

MS-ESS2-3

1. Wegener developed the hypothesis that Earth's landmasses had once been fused together, and then slowly broke apart in a process called
A. continental drift.
B. subduction.
C. Pangaea.
D. divergence.

2. Evidence that supported the hypothesis of continental drift included fossils, land features, and
A. ocean currents.
B. solar activity.
C. climate data.
D. presence of bacteria.

3. The zipper-like mountain ranges that run across the floors of the ocean are called
A. tectonic plates.
B. mid-ocean ridges.
C. subduction zones.
D. convergent boundaries.

4. Develop Models 🖊 In the space below, sketch one of the types of stress that affect Earth's crust.

② Plate Tectonics and Earth's Surface

MS-ESS2-2

5. Which of the following explains how Mount Everest formed?
A. The mountain formed from volcanic activity at a divergent boundary.
B. The mountain formed when two tectonic plates collided at a convergent boundary.
C. The mountain formed from volcanic activity at a convergent boundary.
D. The mountain formed as a result of an earthquake when two plates slipped past each other.

6. The circular movement of material in the mantle that drives plate movement is called
A. conduction.
B. subduction.
C. compression.
D. convection.

7. Plates move apart from each other at a
A. divergent boundary.
B. convergent boundary.
C. transform boundary.
D. subduction boundary.

8. Earthquakes often occur along
.... as a result of the buildup of stress.

9. Construct Arguments A local official pledges to have a new highway built over a transform boundary. Explain why this may be a bad idea.

....
....
....
....
....

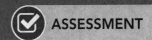
3 Earthquakes and Tsunami Hazards

MS-ESS2-2, MS-ESS3-2

10. The type of stress that pulls on and thins an area of Earth's crust is called
A. torsion.
B. tension.
C. shearing.
D. diverging.

11. When a plate is compressed, it can create anticlines and synclines that can become
A. mountains and valleys.
B. folds and breaks.
C. plateaus and canyons.
D. landmasses and oceans.

12. How much more energy is released by an earthquake with a magnitude of 8.0 on the moment magnitude scale than one with a 6.0 magnitude?
A. 32 times more
B. 64 times more
C. 2 times more
D. 20 times more

13. Explain Phenomena Describe how ocean floor uplift and landslides can cause tsunamis.

....
....
....
....
....
....
....
....

4 Volcanoes and Earth's Surface

MS-ESS2-2, MS-ESS3-2

14. Volcanoes may emerge at long cracks in Earth's crust at .... ridges, on continents near convergent ...., and at random locations away from plate boundaries called ....

15. Cause and Effect What causes volcanoes to form along a mid-ocean ridge?

....
....
....
....
....

16. Explain Phenomena Why are volcanoes often found along both convergent and divergent plate boundaries?

....
....
....
....
....
....
....
....

MS-ESS2-2, MS-ESS3-2

Evidence-Based Assessment

In 2011, a magnitude 9.0 earthquake occurred in the ocean floor off the east coast of Japan. Tsunameter buoys and tide gauges recorded tsunami waves as they crossed the Pacific Ocean. Scientists used the data to predict how large the waves would be and when they would arrive at different locations. The map shown represents the tsunami forecast model for the event, which was used by coastal communities around the Pacific to prepare for local impacts of the tsunami.

Analyze the map of the 2011 tsunami wave forecast. Keep in mind the following information:

- The triangles symbolize specific tsunameter buoys, which measure wave height, or amplitude.

- The numbered contour lines represent how many hours after the earthquake the tsunami waves were forecasted to reach those areas of the ocean.

- Major plate boundaries are are indicated on the map.

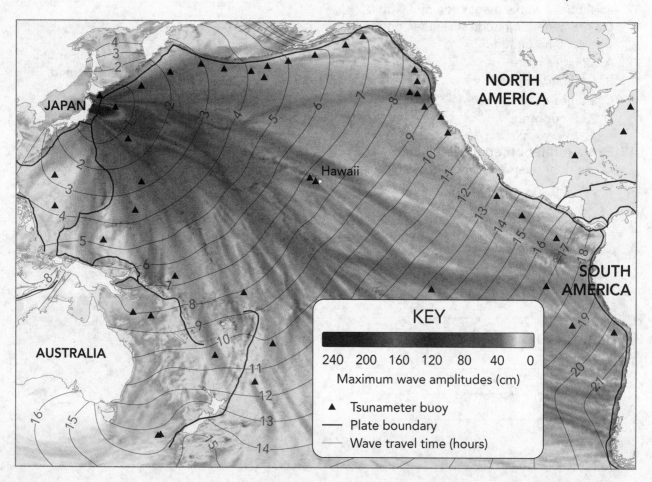

KEY

240 200 160 120 80 40 0
Maximum wave amplitudes (cm)

▲ Tsunameter buoy
— Plate boundary
— Wave travel time (hours)

1. **Analyze Data** According to the data, where was tsunami wave height expected to be greatest?
   A. Australia
   B. Japan
   C. North America
   D. South America

2. **Interpret Data** How many hours after the earthquake were the tsunami waves expected to reach South America?
   A. 9
   B. 23
   C. 7
   D. 19

3. **Use Models** When was a tsunami wave expected to reach Hawaii, and what was the expected wave height?

   ....

   ....

   ....

   ....

   ....

   ....

   ....

   ....

   ....

   ....

   ....

4. **Cause and Effect** Describe how the motion of tectonic plates can result in a tsunami.

   ....

   ....

   ....

   ....

   ....

   ....

   ....

   ....

5. **Construct Explanations** In terms of their usefulness in protecting human lives, why are so many tsunameters placed along coastlines of the Pacific Ocean? Provide two explanations.

   ....

   ....

   ....

   ....

   ....

   ....

   ....

   ....

   ....

   ....

   ....

Quest FINDINGS

Complete the Quest!

Phenomenon Present information on Mount Rainier's history and current geological research, along with your evidence-based argument about whether it is safe to hike and camp there.

Reason Quantitatively What data will help you to predict that Mount Rainier could erupt while you are on a two-week camping trip nearby? Explain.

   ....

   ....

   ....

👆 **INTERACTIVITY**

Reflect on Mount Rainier's Safety

Modeling Sea-Floor Spreading

How can you prevent a major oil spill by **designing** and building a model that **demonstrates** sea-floor spreading?

Background

Phenomenon Imagine you are a marine geologist reviewing a plan to construct a gas pipeline attached to the ocean floor. You notice that part of the pipeline will cross a mid-ocean ridge zone. In this investigation, you will design and build a model that demonstrates sea-floor spreading to show why this plan is not a good idea.

(per group)
- scissors
- transparent tape
- colored marker
- metric ruler
- 2 sheets of unlined letter-sized paper
- manila folder or file
- crayons or colored pencils

Be sure to follow all safety guidelines provided by your teacher. The Safety Appendix of your textbook provides more details about the safety icons.

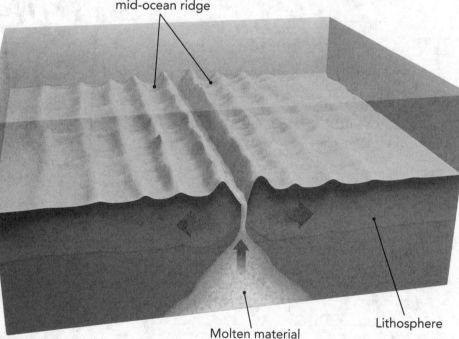

New rock added to each side of the mid-ocean ridge

Molten material

Lithosphere

Design Your Model and Investigation

Discuss with your group why building a pipeline that spans the mid-ocean ridge is a bad idea. Over time, what will happen to the pipeline?

With your group, take a look at the materials. How can you use the materials to construct a model that demonstrates why the pipeline plan is a problem?

HANDS-ON LAB

и**Demonstrate** Go online for a downloadable worksheet of this lab.

Consider the following questions:

- How can you use the manila folder to represent the mantle?

- How can you use the two pieces of plain letter-sized paper to create matching strips of striped sea floor?

- How can you represent the mid-ocean ridge and the subduction zones on either side of the ridge?

Use the space provided to sketch your group's model and write notes for guiding its construction. Have your teacher approve your group's plan, and then construct and demonstrate the model.

Sketch of Model

Design Notes

....

....

....

....

....

....

....

....

....

....

....

....

....

Analyze and Interpret Data

1. **Apply Concepts** Why is it important that your model have identical patterns of stripes on both sides of the center slit?

....

....

....

....

2. **Construct Explanations** Use evidence from your model to support the claim that sea-floor spreading builds two different tectonic plates.

....

....

....

....

3. **Refine Your Solution** Look at the models created by other groups. How are the other solutions different? How might you revise your group's model to better demonstrate sea-floor spreading?

....

....

....

....

4. **Use Models** How could your group revise the model to reinforce the idea that the amount of crust that forms at the mid-ocean ridge is equal to the amount of crust recycled back into the mantle at subduction zones?

....

....

....

....

5. **Infer** How does your model support the claim that building an oil pipeline across a divergent boundary would be a bad idea?

....

....

....

Earth's Surface Systems

How did this rock get its strange shape?

NGSS PERFORMANCE EXPECTATIONS

MS-ESS2-2 Construct an explanation based on evidence for how geoscience processes have changed Earth's surface at varying time and spatial scales.

MS-ESS3-2 Analyze and interpret data on natural hazards to forecast future catastrophic events and inform the development of technologies to mitigate their effects.

HANDS-ON LAB

uConnect Explore how the height and width of a hill affects mass movement.

GO ONLINE
to access your
digital course

 VIDEO

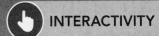 INTERACTIVITY

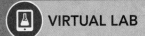 VIRTUAL LAB

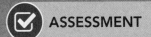 ASSESSMENT

 eTEXT

 APP

The Essential Question

What processes change Earth's surface?

Known as Thor's Hammer, this towering column of rock is a favorite sight at Bryce Canyon National Park in Utah. Hoodoos, or the tall, sedimentary rock spires, are commonly found in high plateau areas and regions of the northern Great Plains, but they are most abundant in Bryce Canyon. How do you think this feature formed?

....

....

....

Quest KICKOFF

How can I design and build an artificial island?

STEM **Phenomenon** One way to expand a city surrounded by water is to make more land. In New York City, the area of lower Manhattan known as Battery Park City was created by civil engineers using soil and rock excavated during the construction of new skyscrapers. But what factors do engineers need to consider when they create new land in water? In this problem-based Quest activity, you will design an artificial island that can withstand nature's forces and that has minimal environmental impact.

 INTERACTIVITY

Ingenious Island

MS-ESS2-2 Construct an explanation based on evidence for how geoscience processes have changed Earth's surface at varying time and spatial scales. **MS-ESS3-2** Analyze and interpret data on natural hazards to forecast future catastrophic events and inform the development of technologies to mitigate their effects.

NBC LEARN ▶ VIDEO

After watching the Quest Kickoff video about how coastal engineers study and reduce coastal erosion, complete the 3-2-1 activity.

3 ways that water changes land

....

....

....

2 ways that wind changes land

....

....

1 way that those changes could be prevented or minimized

....

....

Quest CHECK-IN

IN LESSON 1

How does weathering affect various materials? Consider the benefits and drawbacks of using different materials for an artificial island.

HANDS-ON LAB

Breaking It Down

Quest CHECK-INS

IN LESSON 2

STEM What criteria and constraints need to be considered when designing your island model to resist erosion over periods of time? Design and build your island model.

HANDS-ON LAB

Ingenious Island: Part I

INTERACTIVITY

Changing Landscapes

Quest CHECK-IN

IN LESSON 3

STEM How resistant is your island model to erosion? Test the effects of the agents of erosion on your model and make improvements.

HANDS-ON LAB

Ingenious Island: Part II

Beachfront properties line one of the "branches" of the Palm Jumeirah in the United Arab Emirates. The palm-shaped artificial island extends into the Persian Gulf off the coast of Dubai. It provides miles of additional shoreline for homes and elaborate hotels.

Quest CHECK-IN

IN LESSON 4
How can wave erosion impact the location of your artificial island? Adjust your design as needed to account for wave erosion.

👆 **INTERACTIVITY**

Breaking Waves

Quest FINDINGS

Complete the Quest!

Present your island model and explain how your design decisions relate to the forces that change Earth's surface.

👆 **INTERACTIVITY**

Reflect on Your Ingenious Island

Guiding Questions

- How does erosion change Earth's surface?
- How does weathering change Earth's surface?
- How does soil form?

Connections

Literacy Write Explanatory Texts

Math Reason Quantitatively

MS-ESS2-2

Vocabulary

uniformitarianism
erosion
mechanical
   weathering
chemical
   weathering
soil
humus

Academic Vocabulary

principle
component

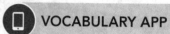 **VOCABULARY APP**

Practice vocabulary on a mobile device.

Quest CONNECTION

Think about what criteria need to be considered when designing an island to resist erosion.

Connect It!

✎ **The Wave is a stunning dip in Earth's surface. Draw an arrow showing where the material originally covering the Wave would have begun.**

Construct Explanations What processes have broken apart and carried off the many layers of solid rock that covered the Wave for millions of years?

....

....

Breaking Down Earth's Surface

Even the hardest rocks wear down over time on Earth's surface. Natural processes, such as the one that produced the Wave in **Figure 1**, break down rocks and carry the pieces away. Geologists make inferences about what processes shaped Earth's surface in the past based on the **principle** of **uniformitarianism** (yoon uh form uh TAYR ee un iz um). This principle states that the geologic processes that operate today also operated in the past. Scientists infer that ancient landforms and features formed through the same processes they observe today and will continue to do so in the future.

The processes of weathering and **erosion** (ee ROH zhun) work together to change Earth's surface by wearing down and carrying away rock particles. The process of weathering breaks down rock and other substances. Heat, cold, water, ice, and gases all contribute to weathering. Erosion involves the removal of rock particles by wind, water, ice, or gravity.

Weathering and erosion work continuously to reshape Earth's surface. The same processes that wear down mountains also cause bicycles to rust, paint to peel, and sidewalks to crack. Weathering and erosion can take millions of years to break down and wear away huge mountains, or they can take seconds to carry rock away in an avalanche. These processes started changing Earth's surface billions of years ago and they continue to do so.

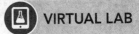 **VIRTUAL LAB**

Explore one factor that affects the time it takes weathering to occur.

Academic Vocabulary

Describe another principle you follow in science or in your everyday life.

....

....

....

Determine Meaning

How has weathering or erosion affected you? In your science notebook, describe an example of weathering or erosion you observed and any impact it had on you or your community.

Riding the Rock Wave

Figure 1 Known as the Wave, this sandstone dip in Earth's surface in Northern Arizona was buried beneath solid rock for millions of years.

Figure 2 Label each photo with an agent of mechanical weathering.

Construct Explanations How might more than one agent of mechanical weathering operate in the same place?

....

....

....

....

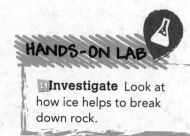

HANDS-ON LAB

Investigate Look at how ice helps to break down rock.

Weathering Earth's Surface

The type of weathering in which rock is physically broken into smaller pieces is called **mechanical weathering**. A second type of weathering, called chemical weathering, also breaks down rock. **Chemical weathering** is the process that breaks down rock through chemical changes.

Mechanical Weathering

Rocks that are cracked or split in layers have undergone mechanical weathering. Mechanical weathering usually happens gradually, over very long periods of time. Mechanical weathering, as part of erosion, can eventually wear away whole mountains.

The natural agents of mechanical weathering include freezing and thawing, release of pressure, plant growth, actions of animals, and abrasion, as shown in **Figure 2**. Abrasion (uh BRAY zhun) refers to the wearing away of rock by rock particles carried by water, ice, wind, or gravity. Human activities, such as mining and farming, also cause mechanical weathering.

Through mechanical weathering, Earth systems interact and shape the surface. For example, the geosphere (rocks) interacts with the hydrosphere (water, ice) during frost wedging. Frost wedging occurs when water seeps into cracks in rocks and expands as it freezes. Wedges of ice in rocks widen and deepen cracks. When the ice melts, water seeps deeper into the cracks. With repeated freezing and thawing, the cracks slowly expand until pieces of rock break off.

Chemical Weathering
Chemical weathering often produces new minerals as it breaks down rock. For example, granite is made up of several minerals, including feldspars. Chemical weathering causes the feldspar to eventually change to clay minerals.

Water, oxygen, carbon dioxide, living organisms, and acid rain cause chemical weathering. Water weathers some rock by dissolving it. Water also carries other substances, including oxygen, carbon dioxide, and other chemicals, that dissolve or break down rock.

The oxygen and carbon dioxide gases in the atmosphere cause chemical weathering. Rust forms when iron combines with oxygen in the presence of water. Rusting makes rock soft and crumbly and gives it a red or brown color. When carbon dioxide dissolves in water, carbonic acid forms. This weak acid easily weathers certain types of rock, such as marble and limestone.

As a plant's roots grow, they produce weak acids that gradually dissolve rock. Lichens—plantlike organisms that grow on rocks—also produce weak acids.

Humans escalate chemical weathering by burning fossil fuels. This pollutes the air and results in rainwater that is more strongly acidic. Acid rain causes very rapid chemical weathering of rock.

☑ READING CHECK **Summarize Text** How are the agents of weathering similar and different?

....

....

Literacy Connection
Write Explanatory Texts
An ancient marble statue is moved from a rural location to a highly polluted city. Explain how the move might affect the statue and why you think so.

....

....

....

....

....

....

....

389

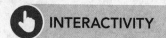

INTERACTIVITY

Find out how weathering rates help with dating.

Rate of Weathering In historic cemeteries, slate tombstones from the 1700s are less weathered than marble tombstones from the 1800s. Why? Some kinds of rocks weather more rapidly than others. The rate at which weathering occurs is determined by the type of rock and the climate.

Type of Rock Rocks wear down slowly if they are made of minerals that do not dissolve easily. Rocks weather faster if they are made of minerals that dissolve easily.

Some rocks weather more easily because they are permeable. A permeable (PUR mee uh bul) material is full of tiny air spaces. The spaces increase the surface area. As water seeps through the spaces in the rock, it carries chemicals that dissolve the rock and removes material broken down by weathering.

Climate Climate is the average weather conditions in an area. Weathering occurs faster in wet climates. Rainfall causes chemical changes. Freezing and thawing cause mechanical changes in cold and wet climates.

Chemical reactions occur faster at higher temperatures. That is why chemical weathering occurs more quickly where the climate is both hot and wet. Human activities, such as those that produce acid rain, also increase the rate of weathering.

Math Toolbox

Comparing Weathered Limestone

The data table shows how much rock was broken down by weathering for two identical pieces of limestone in two different locations.

1. **Construct Graphs**  Use the data to make a double-line graph. Decide how to make each line look different. Be sure to provide a title and label the axes and each graph line.

2. **Reason Quantitatively** As time increases, the limestone thickness (increases/decreases).

3. **Evaluate Data** Limestone A weathered at a (slower/faster) rate than Limestone B.

Weathering Rates of Limestone		
Time (years)	Thickness of Limestone Lost (mm)	
	Limestone A	Limestone B
200	1.75	0.80
400	3.50	1.60
600	5.25	2.40
800	7.00	3.20
1,000	8.75	4.00

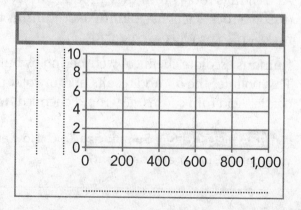

Gravel
2 mm
& larger

Sand
Less than
2 mm

Silt
Less than
0.05 mm

Clay
Less than
0.002 mm

Source: Michigan Technological University

Forming Soil

Have you ever wondered how plants grow on rocks? Plants can grow only when soil begins to form in the cracks. **Soil** is the loose, weathered material on Earth's surface in which plants grow.

Soil Composition Soil is a mixture of rock particles, minerals, decayed organic material, water, and air. The main **components** of soil come from bedrock. Bedrock is the solid layer of rock beneath the soil. Once bedrock is exposed to air, water, and living things, it gradually weathers into smaller and smaller particles.

The particles of rock in soil are classified by size as gravel, sand, silt, and clay. **Figure 3** shows the relative sizes of these particles. A soil's texture depends on the size of the soil particles.

The decayed organic material in soil is called humus. **Humus** (HYOO mus) is a dark-colored substance that forms as plant and animal remains decay. Humus helps to create spaces in soil that are then filled by air and water. It contains nutrients that plants need.

☑ **READING CHECK** **Write Explanatory Texts** Explain how you might determine the rate of weathering on a sample of rock.

....

....

....

....

Soil Particle Size
Figure 3 🖊 The rock particles shown here have been enlarged. On the graph, mark the size of a 1.5-mm particle with an X.

Classify Explain how you would classify that size particle and why.

....

....

....

Academic Vocabulary

What are the similarities between components of a computer and the components of soil?

....

....

....

....

🔘 **INTERACTIVITY**

Learn how minerals affect the colors of sand.

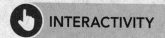
Soil Formation

Soil forms as rock is broken down by weathering and mixes with other materials on the surface. Soil forms constantly wherever bedrock weathers. Soil formation continues over a long period of time, taking hundreds to thousands of years. The same process that forms soil today was also taking place billions of years ago and will continue to form soil in the future.

Gradually, soil develops layers called horizons. A soil horizon is a layer of soil that differs in color, texture, and composition from the layers above or below it. **Figure 4** shows the sequence in which soil horizons form.

Soil and Organisms

Recall that organisms are part of Earth's biosphere. Many organisms live in soil and interact with the geosphere. Some soil organisms aid in the formation of humus, which makes soil rich in the nutrients that plants need. Other soil organisms mix the soil and make spaces in it for air and water.

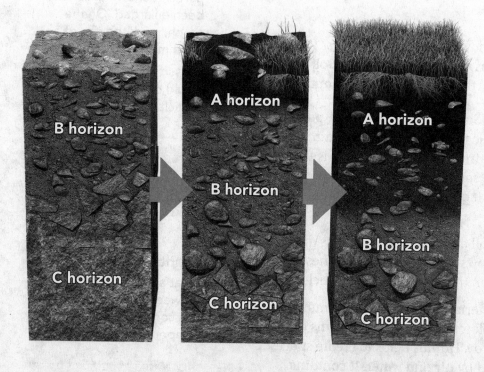

A horizon
The A horizon is made up of topsoil, a crumbly, dark brown soil that is a mixture of humus, clay, and minerals. Topsoil forms as plants add organic material to the soil, and plant roots weather pieces of rock.

B horizon
The B horizon, often called subsoil, usually consists of clay and other particles of rock, but little humus. It forms as rainwater washes these materials down from the A horizon.

C horizon
The C horizon forms as bedrock begins to weather. The rock breaks up into small particles.

Soil Horizons

Figure 4 Soil horizons form in three main steps.

1. **Interpret Diagrams** ✏ Underline the soil horizon that contains the most organic matter.

2. **Evaluate Quantity** In what climates would you expect soil to form fastest? Why?

....

....

Forming Humus Dead leaves, roots, and other plant materials contribute most of the organic remains that form humus. Humus forms in a process called decomposition carried out by a combination of decomposers including fungi, bacteria, worms, and other organisms. Decomposers break down the remains of dead organisms into smaller pieces through the process of chemical digestion. This material then mixes with the soil as nutrient-rich humus where it can be used by living plants.

Mixing the Soil Earthworms and burrowing mammals mix humus with air and other materials in soil, as shown in **Figure 5**. As earthworms eat their way through the soil, they carry humus down to the subsoil and from the subsoil up to the surface. These organisms increase the soil's fertility by dispersing organic matter throughout the soil. Mammals such as mice, moles, and prairie dogs break up hard, compacted soil and mix humus with it. Animal wastes contribute nutrients to the soil as well.

☑ READING CHECK **Integrate With Visuals** Review the information and illustrations in **Figure 4**. How is weathering related to soil formation?

....

....

....

Organisms Impact Soil
Figure 5 Earthworms and chipmunks break up hard, compacted soil, making it easier for air and water to enter the soil.

1. Synthesize Information Besides breaking up and mixing soil, the (earthworm/chipmunk) is also a decomposer.

2. Apply Concepts As these organisms change the soil, which Earth systems are interacting?

....

....

Model It ✏️

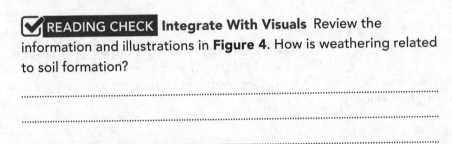

Bedrock .... Topsoil

From Rock to Soil

Figure 6 The illustrations show bedrock and topsoil rich in humus.

1. Develop Models ✏️ In the empty boxes, draw the processes that help to change the bedrock into soil. Label the processes in each drawing. Include at least two processes that involve organisms.

2. Use Models The topsoil represents the (A/B/C) horizon.

393

☑LESSON 1 Check

MS-ESS2-2

1. **Describe** How does erosion affect Earth's surface?

....

....

....

....

2. **Synthesize Information** Give examples of how water can wear down Earth's surface over a short time period and a very long time period.

....

....

....

....

....

3. **Compare and Contrast** Compare and contrast mechanical weathering and chemical weathering.

....

....

....

....

....

4. **Write Explanatory Text** A community group needs advice on choosing rock for a city park monument that will last a long time. Explain the factors that would likely affect how long the monument lasts.

....

....

....

....

....

....

....

....

5. **Apply Concepts** How did organisms change the soil in North America over millions of years? Cite evidence to support your answer.

....

....

....

....

....

Quest CHECK-IN

In this lesson, you learned how weathering and erosion change Earth's surface. You also discovered how soil forms.

Use Models How can modeling the effects of weathering on different materials help you to design your island?

....

....

....

....

HANDS-ON LAB

Breaking It Down

Investigate what constraints need to be considered when designing an island to resist long-term erosion.

GROUND SHIFTING ADVANCES:
Maps Help Predict

🖐 **INTERACTIVITY**

Learn about the causes of landslides and predict where they might occur.

Do you know what happens after heavy rains or earthquakes in California? There are landslides. Engineers look for patterns to determine how and where they can happen.

The Challenge: To protect highways and towns from landslides.

Phenomenon Evaluating hazards is one way to prepare for natural disasters. In the early 1970s, the California Geological Survey (CGS) began drawing up "Geology for Planning" maps. Its goal was to create maps showing areas all over the state where natural hazards, such as wildfires and landslides, were most likely to occur. Engineers and city planners could then use the maps to prepare for, or possibly prevent, natural disasters.

In 1997, the Caltrans Highway Corridor Mapping project began. Caltrans stands for California Department of Transportation. Caltrans engineers set out to map all known sites of landslides, as well as unstable slopes along the major interstate highways. Most of the landslide sites were along highways that wind through California's mountains. Using these maps, engineers have installed sensitive monitoring equipment to help predict future landslides.

Landslides destroy roadways, cut people off from access to vital services, and disrupt local economies.

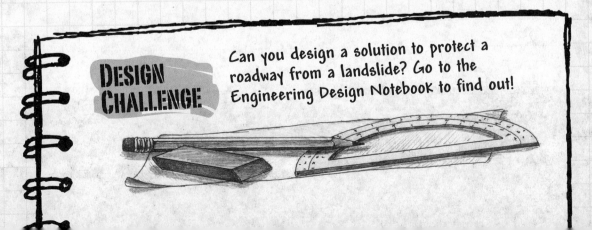

DESIGN CHALLENGE

Can you design a solution to protect a roadway from a landslide? Go to the Engineering Design Notebook to find out!

Erosion and Deposition

Guiding Questions

- What processes change Earth's surface?
- How does mass movement change Earth's surface?
- How does wind change Earth's surface?

Connections

Literacy Integrate With Visuals

Math Analyze Quantitative Relationships

MS-ESS2-2, MS-ESS3-2

Vocabulary

sediment
deposition
mass movement
deflation
sand dune
loess

Academic Vocabulary

similar
significant

 VOCABULARY APP

Practice vocabulary on a mobile device.

Quest CONNECTION

As you design and build a model of your island, consider the effects of erosion and deposition.

Connect It !

✏ **Circle the change shown in the photo, then draw an arrow to show the direction of the rocks' movement.**

Interpret Photos How has Earth's surface changed in this photo?

....

....

Predict What natural processes do you think caused the change you observe?

....

....

Changing Earth's Surface

Have you ever watched water carry away bits of gravel and soil during a rainstorm? If so, you observed erosion. Recall that erosion is a process that moves weathered rock from its original location. Gravity, water, ice, and wind are all agents of erosion.

The process of erosion moves material called **sediment**. Sediment may consist of pieces of rock or soil, or the remains of plants and animals.

Deposition occurs where the agents of erosion deposit, or lay down, sediment. Like erosion, deposition changes the shape of Earth's surface. You may have watched an ant carry away bits of soil and then put the soil down in a different location to build an ant hill. The ant's activity is **similar** to erosion and deposition, which involves picking up, carrying away, and putting down sediment in a different place.

Weathering, erosion, transportation, and deposition act together in a continuous cycle that wears down and builds up Earth's surface. As erosion wears down a mountain in one place, deposition builds up a new landform in another place. Some changes happen over a large area, while others occur in a small space. Some happen slowly over thousands or millions of years, and others take only a few minutes or seconds, such as the rockslide shown in **Figure 1**. No matter how large or fast the changes, the cycle of erosion and deposition is continuous. The same changes that shaped Earth's surface in the past still shape it today and will continue to shape it in the future.

Academic Vocabulary

Using two things you can observe right now, write a sentence describing how they are similar.

....

....

....

....

Literacy Connection

Integrate With Visuals
In the third paragraph of the text, underline a statement that is supported by evidence in the photograph.

Moving Rock

Figure 1 The sudden change in the appearance of this hillside was caused by the natural movement of rock.

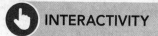
Mass Movement

If you place a ball at the top of a hill, with a slight push the ball will roll down the hill. Gravity pulls the ball downward. Gravity is also the force that moves rock and other materials downhill.

Gravity causes **mass movement**, one of several processes that move sediment downhill. Mass movement can be rapid or slow. Erosion and deposition both take place during a mass movement event. The different types of mass movement include landslides, mudflows, slumps, and creep (**Figure 2**).

A mass movement may be caused by a natural disaster, such as a flood, earthquake, or hurricane. Natural disasters can dramatically and suddenly change Earth's surface. Scientists make maps of past mass movements in a region to better understand their hazards. Such maps help scientists to identify patterns and predict where future mass movement is likely to occur in order to prevent human casualties.

☑ READING CHECK **Integrate With Visuals** Read and think about the information relating to different kinds of mass movement. Which type of mass movement do you think is least dangerous? Why?

....

....

Mass Movement

Figure 2 Different types of mass movement have different characteristics.

1. **Develop Models** ✏ Draw arrows on each image of mass movement to show the direction that material moves.

2. **Identify Patterns** What pattern(s) can you identify among the types of mass movement?

....

....

Landslides

A landslide occurs when rock and soil slide quickly down a steep slope. Some landslides contain huge masses of rock, while others contain only small amounts of rock and soil. Often caused by earthquakes, landslides occur where road builders have cut highways through hills or mountains, leaving behind unstable slopes.

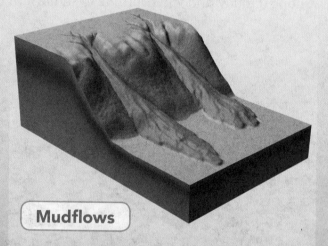

Mudflows

A mudflow is the rapid downhill movement of a mixture of water, rock, and soil. Mudflows often occur after heavy rains in a normally dry area. In clay-rich soils with a high water content, mudflows may occur even on very gentle slopes. Under certain conditions, clay-rich soil suddenly behaves as a liquid and begins to flow.

Math Toolbox

Major Landslides and Mudflows

Landslides and mudflows are a problem in all 50 states and all around the world. Annually in the United States, landslides cause $1 billion to $2 billion in damage and about 25 deaths. But some catastrophic mass movements in other countries have killed more than 100,000 people.

1. **Use Proportional Relationships** What proportion of the landslides were caused by earthquakes?

....

2. **Analyze Quantitative Relationships** Which process caused the most landslides? Which caused the fewest landslides?

....

Major Landslides and Mudflows of the 20th Century

Year	Location	Cause
1919	Java, Indonesia	volcanic eruption
1920	Ningxia, China	earthquake
1933	Sichuan, China	earthquake
1949	Tadzhikistan	earthquake
1958	Japan	heavy rains
1970	Peru	earthquake
1980	Washington, USA	earthquakes
1983	Utah, USA	heavy rain and snowmelt
1985	Colombia	volcano
1998	Central America	hurricane rains

Slumps

In a slump, a mass of rock and soil suddenly slips down a slope. Unlike a landslide, the material in a slump moves down in one large mass. It looks as if someone pulled the bottom out from under part of the slope. A slump often occurs when water soaks the bottom of clay-rich soil.

Creep

Creep is the very slow downhill movement of rock and soil. It can even occur on gentle slopes. Creep often results from the freezing and thawing of water in cracked layers of rock beneath the soil. Even though it occurs slowly, you can see the effects of creep in vertical objects such as telephone poles and tree trunks. Creep may tilt these objects at unusual angles.

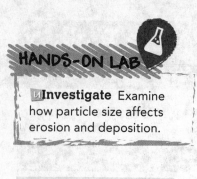

Academic Vocabulary

Describe a significant change in weather from the winter to the summer.

....

....

....

Erosion and Deposition by Wind

Recall that wind, or moving air, is an agent of erosion and deposition. Through these processes, wind wears down and builds up Earth's surface.

Wind Erosion Wind can be a **significant** agent in shaping the land in areas where there are few plants to hold the soil in place. In a sandstorm, strong winds pick up large amounts of sediment and loose soil and transport it to new locations.

Deflation Wind causes erosion mainly by **deflation**, the process by which wind removes surface materials. You can see the process of deflation in **Figure 3**. When wind blows over the land, it picks up the smallest particles of sediment, such as clay and silt. Stronger, faster winds pick up larger particles. Slightly larger particles, such as sand, might skip or bounce for a short distance. Strong winds can roll even larger and heavier sediment particles. In deserts, deflation can create an area called desert pavement where smaller sediments are blown away, and larger rock fragments are left behind.

Abrasion Wind, water, and ice carry particles that rub or scrape against exposed rock. As particles move against the rock, friction wears away the rock by the process of abrasion.

Wind Erosion and Deflation

Figure 3 Wind causes deflation by moving surface particles in three ways.

1. **Patterns** ✏ In each circle, draw the size of particles that would be moved by the wind.

2. **Construct Explanations** How does a particle's size affect how high and far it travels?

....

....

....

3. **Interpret Diagrams** Complete each sentence to the right with one of the following words: Fine, Medium, Large.

Fine particles   Medium particles   Large particles

.... particles are carried through the air.

.... particles skip or bounce.

.... particles slide or roll.

Wind Deposition All the sediment picked up by wind eventually falls to the ground. This happens when the wind slows down or encounters an obstacle. Wind deposition may form sand dunes and loess deposits.

Sand Dunes When wind meets an obstacle, such as a clump of grass, the result is usually a deposit of windblown sand called a **sand dune**. **Figure 4** shows how wind direction can form different dunes. The shape and size of sand dunes is determined by the direction of the wind, the amount of sand, and the presence of plants. This same process changed Earth's surface billions of years ago, just as it does today. You can predict how wind deposition will affect the surface in the future. You can see sand dunes on beaches and in deserts where wind-blown sediment builds up. Sand dunes also move over time because the sand shifts with the wind from one side of the dune to the other. Sometimes plants begin growing on a dune, and the roots help to anchor the dune in one place.

Loess Deposits The wind drops sediment that is finer than sand but coarser than clay far from its source. This fine, wind-deposited sediment is **loess** (LOH es). There are large loess deposits in central China and in states such as Nebraska, South Dakota, Iowa, Missouri, and Illinois. Loess helps to form soil rich in nutrients. Many areas with thick loess deposits are valuable farmlands.

☑ **READING CHECK Cite Textual Evidence** What factors affect wind erosion and deposition?

....

....

Question It!

Moving Sand Dunes

Sand dunes keep drifting and covering a nearby, busy parking lot.

Define the Problem State the problem that needs to be solved in the form of a question.

....

....

Develop Possible Solutions Describe two possible solutions to the problem. Explain why each would solve the problem.

....

....

....

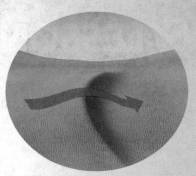

Crescent-shaped dune

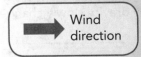

Wind direction

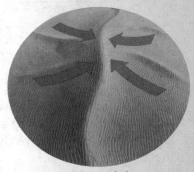

Star-shaped dunes

Dune Formation

Figure 4 Sand dunes form and change shape as the wind deposits sand.

1. **Predict** ✏ Draw a line to show how the ridge of the crescent-shaped dune will likely shift over time.

2. **Explain** Why do these dunes have different shapes?

....

....

....

INTERACTIVITY

Explore fast and slow changes to Earth's surface.

1. Classify Which kinds of mass movement happen quickly?

....

....

2. Describe Describe a way in which deposition by gravity slowly changes Earth's surface.

....

....

....

....

....

3. Patterns Explain how the wind both builds up and wears down Earth's surface in a desert. Give examples of features that result from these processes.

....

....

....

....

....

....

4. Construct an Explanation Explain why a scientist may make a map of the location of landslides in a certain area.

....

....

....

....

....

....

5. Interpret Data Two towns are located in the same dry region. Town X has steeper slopes than Town Y. Town Y gets heavier than normal rain for several days while Town X remains dry. Which town is more likely to experience mass movement in the near future? Explain your answer.

....

....

....

....

Quest CHECK-INS

In this lesson, you learned how gravity causes erosion and deposition. You also learned how wind causes erosion and deposition.

Refine Your Solution What are some ways that the effects of erosion can be mitigated in your design for the artificial island?

....

....

....

....

HANDS-ON LAB

Ingenious Island, Part I

👆 INTERACTIVITY

Changing Landscapes

Do the hands-on lab to test your island's resistance to erosion by surface water.

Go online to explore how landscapes can be changed.

CAREERS
Civil Engineer

Civil Engineers
SAVE THE DAY!

Who put the civil in civilization? Engineers! Civil engineers are responsible for all the works that benefit the citizens of a society. After a natural disaster, civil engineers get involved in reconstruction efforts.

Think of the networks and systems we rely on every day—roadways, train tracks, cell phone towers, the electrical grid, and gas lines. Consider the cities built on filled-in swamp or a town built over rough terrain. Think of all the bridges connecting two sides of a river—even one as wide as the Mississippi. Civil engineers and the construction workers they guided made all of this possible.

Whether planning a new road or bridge, civil engineers must take into account the forces that change Earth's surface. Water and wind erosion, for example, have serious effects on roadways and can cause costly damage. A civil engineer's job is to determine how to build the road in a way that minimizes nature's potentially damaging effects.

If you want to be a civil engineer, you'll need to study science and math. You'll also need to develop your imagination, because solutions require creativity as well as analytical thinking.

▶ **VIDEO**

Watch what's involved in being a civil engineer.

MY CAREER

Type "civil engineer" into an online search engine to learn more about this career.

Civil engineers survey and measure the surface of Earth. The data they collect are used to plan construction projects such as this bridge.

③ Water Erosion

Guiding Questions

- How does moving water change Earth's surface?
- What landforms form from water erosion and deposition?
- How does groundwater change Earth?

Connection

Literacy Cite Textual Evidence

MS-ESS2-2

Vocabulary

runoff
stream
tributary
flood plain
delta
alluvial fan
groundwater

Academic Vocabulary

develop
suggest

 VOCABULARY APP

Practice vocabulary on a mobile device.

Quest CONNECTION

Think about how other types of erosion might impact your island design.

Connect It!

🖊 **Draw a line showing where Niagara Falls may have been in the past.**

Construct Explanations How do you think Niagara Falls formed?

....

....

....

Apply Scientific Reasoning What do you think this waterfall and all other waterfalls have in common?

....

How Water Causes Erosion

Erosion by water doesn't start with a giant waterfall, such as the one in **Figure 1**. It begins with a little splash of rain. Some rainfall sinks into the ground, where it is absorbed by plant roots. Some water evaporates, while the rest of the water runs off over the land surface. Moving water of the hydrosphere is the primary agent of the erosion that shaped Earth's land surface, the geosphere, for billions of years. It continues to shape the surface today in small and large ways.

Runoff As water moves over the land, it picks up and carries sediment. This moving water is called **runoff**. When runoff flows over the land, it may cause a type of erosion called sheet erosion, where thin layers of soil are removed. The amount of runoff in an area depends on five main factors. The first factor is the amount of rain an area gets. A heavy or lengthy rainfall can add water to the surface more quickly than the surface can absorb it. A second factor is vegetation. Grasses, shrubs, and trees reduce runoff by absorbing water and holding soil in place. A third factor is the type of soil. Different types of soils absorb different amounts of water. A fourth factor is the shape of the land. Runoff is more likely to occur on steeply sloped land than on flatter land. Finally, a fifth factor is how people use land. For example, pavement does not absorb water. All the rain that falls on it becomes runoff. Runoff also increases when trees or crops are cut down, because this removes vegetation from the land.

Factors that reduce runoff also reduce erosion. Even though deserts have little rainfall, they often have high runoff and erosion because they have few plants and thin, sandy soil. In wet areas, such as rain forests and wetlands, runoff and erosion may be low because there are more plants to protect the soil.

INTERACTIVITY

Locate evidence of water erosion and determine why it happened.

Literacy Connection

Cite Textual Evidence As you read the second paragraph, number the factors that affect runoff.

Taking the Plunge
Figure 1 The powerful Niagara River plunges more than 50 meters from the highest point of Niagara Falls. Here, the hydrosphere (river) interacts with the geosphere (land) and shapes Earth's surface.

HANDS-ON LAB

☑**Investigate** Trace the paths raindrops can follow after hitting the ground.

Stream Formation Gravity causes runoff and the sediment it carries to flow downhill. As runoff moves across the land, it flows together to form rills, gullies, and streams, as shown in **Figure 2**.

Rills and Gullies As runoff travels, it forms tiny grooves in the soil called rills. Many rills flow into one another to form a gully. A gully is a large groove, or channel, in the soil that carries runoff after a rainstorm. As water flows through gullies, it picks up and moves sediment with it, thus enlarging the gullies through erosion.

Streams and Rivers Gullies join to form a stream. A **stream** is a channel along which water is continually flowing down a slope. Unlike gullies, streams rarely dry up. Small streams are also known as creeks or brooks. As streams flow together, they form larger bodies of flowing water called rivers.

Tributaries A **tributary** is a stream or river that flows into a larger river. For example, the Missouri and Ohio rivers are tributaries of the Mississippi River. A drainage basin, or watershed, is the area from which a river and its tributaries collect their water.

☑READING CHECK **Integrate With Visuals** Review the information in paragraph 2 and in **Figure 2**. How does the amount of water change as it moves from rills and gullies to streams?

....

....

Stream Formation

Figure 2 ✏ In the diagram, shade only the arrows that indicate the direction of runoff flow that causes erosion.

Reason Quantitatively How will the depth of the channel likely change with further erosion?

....

....

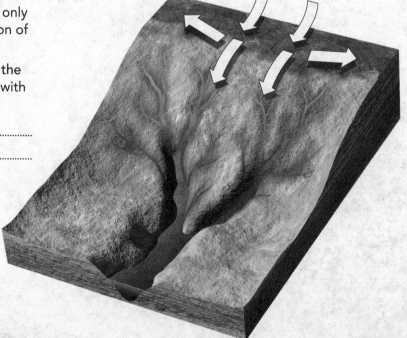

Waterfalls

Figure 3 Waterfalls form where rivers erode hard and soft rock layers at different rates.

1. Interpret Diagrams The rock at the top of the waterfall erodes at a (slower/faster) rate than the rock below it.

2. Predict How do you think erosion will change this waterfall in the next 100 years?

....

....

....

....

....

Water Erosion and Deposition Change Earth's Surface

Some landforms result from erosion by rivers and streams, while others result from deposition. Still other landforms are created from a combination of these processes. Erosion by water removes particles on Earth's surface, while deposition by water builds it up.

Water Erosion Many rivers begin on steep mountain slopes as flowing rain water or melted snow. This running water starts out fast-flowing and generally follows a straight, narrow course. The steep slopes along the river erode rapidly, resulting in a deep, V-shaped valley. As a river flows to the sea, it forms other features such as waterfalls, flood plains, meanders, and oxbow lakes.

Waterfalls Waterfalls, as shown in **Figure 3,** erode soft rock, leaving a ledge made up of hard, slowly eroding rock. Eventually a waterfall develops along the ledge where the softer rock has worn away. Rushing water and sediment can cause further erosion at the base of the waterfall. Rough water rapids also occur where a river tumbles over hard rock, wearing away the supporting rock base and leaving the rock above it unsupported.

Flood Plains Lower down on its course, a river usually flows over more gently sloping land. The river spreads out and erodes the land along its side, forming a wide river valley. The flat, wide area of land along a river is a **flood plain**. During a flood or a rainy season, a river overflows its banks and flows onto the flood plain. As the flood water retreats, it deposits sediment. This gradually makes the soil of a flood plain rich in nutrients.

What things did you develop in science class this year? Name two examples.

....

....

....

▶ VIDEO

Explore landforms caused by water erosion.

Meanders A river often **develops** meanders where it flows through easily eroded rock or sediment. A meander is a loop-like bend in the course of a river. A meandering river erodes sediment from the outer bank and deposits the sediment on the inner bank farther downstream. The water flows faster in the deeper, outer section of each bend, causing more erosion. Over time, a meander becomes more curved.

Flood plains also follow the meander as sediment erodes more of the land to the side of the river. Here, the river's channel is often deep and wide. For example, the southern stretch of the Mississippi River meanders on a wide, gently sloping flood plain.

Oxbow Lakes Sometimes a meandering river forms a feature called an oxbow lake. An oxbow lake occurs when a meander develops such a large loop that the bends of the river join together. Sediment deposits block the ends of the bends, cutting off the river flow. Oxbow lakes are the remains of the river's former bend, seen in **Figure 4**.

☑ READING CHECK **Cite Textual Evidence** What evidence supports the idea that a floodplain is formed by erosion and deposition?

....

....

....

Model It !

Oxbow Lakes

Figure 4 A meander may gradually form an oxbow lake.

Develop Models ✏ Draw steps 2 and 4 to show how an oxbow lake forms. Then describe step 4.

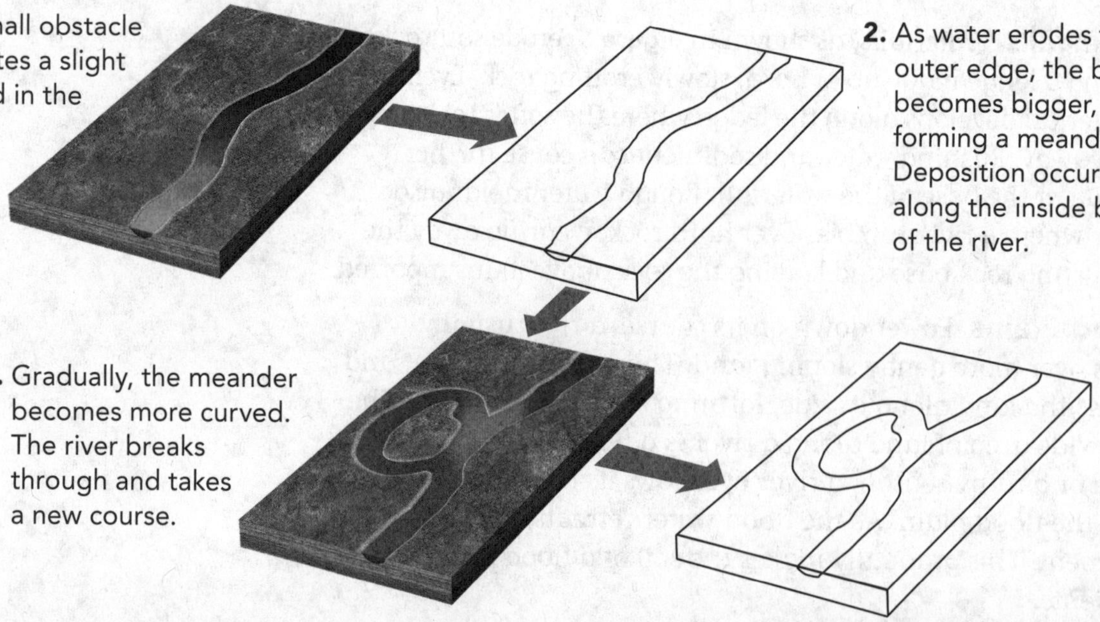

1. A small obstacle creates a slight bend in the river.

2. As water erodes the outer edge, the bend becomes bigger, forming a meander. Deposition occurs along the inside bend of the river.

3. Gradually, the meander becomes more curved. The river breaks through and takes a new course.

4. ....

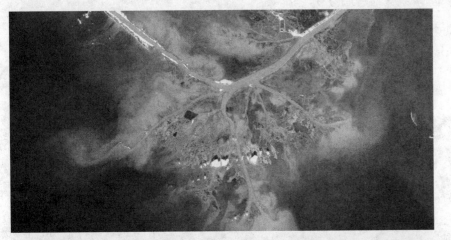

Delta and Alluvial Fan
Figure 5 ✏ Draw arrows to show the direction in which water carries sediment to each landform.

Interpret Photos Record your observations about deltas and alluvial fans.

....
....
....
....
....
....

Water Deposition Any time moving water slows, it deposits some of the sediment it carries. First, larger rocks stop rolling and sliding as fast-moving water starts to slow down. Then, finer and finer particles fall to the river's bed as the water flows even more slowly. In this way, water deposition builds up Earth's surface and produces landforms such as deltas and alluvial fans.

Deltas Eventually, a river flows into a body of water, such as an ocean or a lake. Because the river water no longer flows downhill, the water slows down. At this point, the sediment in the water drops to the bottom. Sediment deposited where a river flows into an ocean or lake builds up a landform called a **delta**. Some deltas are arc-shaped, while others are triangular. The delta of the Mississippi River, shown in **Figure 5**, is an example of a type of delta called a "bird's foot" delta.

Alluvial Fans When a stream flows out of a steep, narrow mountain valley, it suddenly becomes wider and shallower. The water slows down and deposits sediments in an **alluvial fan**. An alluvial fan is a wide, sloping deposit of sediment formed where a stream leaves a mountain range. As its name **suggests**, this deposit is shaped like a fan.

Academic Vocabulary
Suggest means "to mention as a possibility." Use *suggest* in a sentence.

....
....
....
....

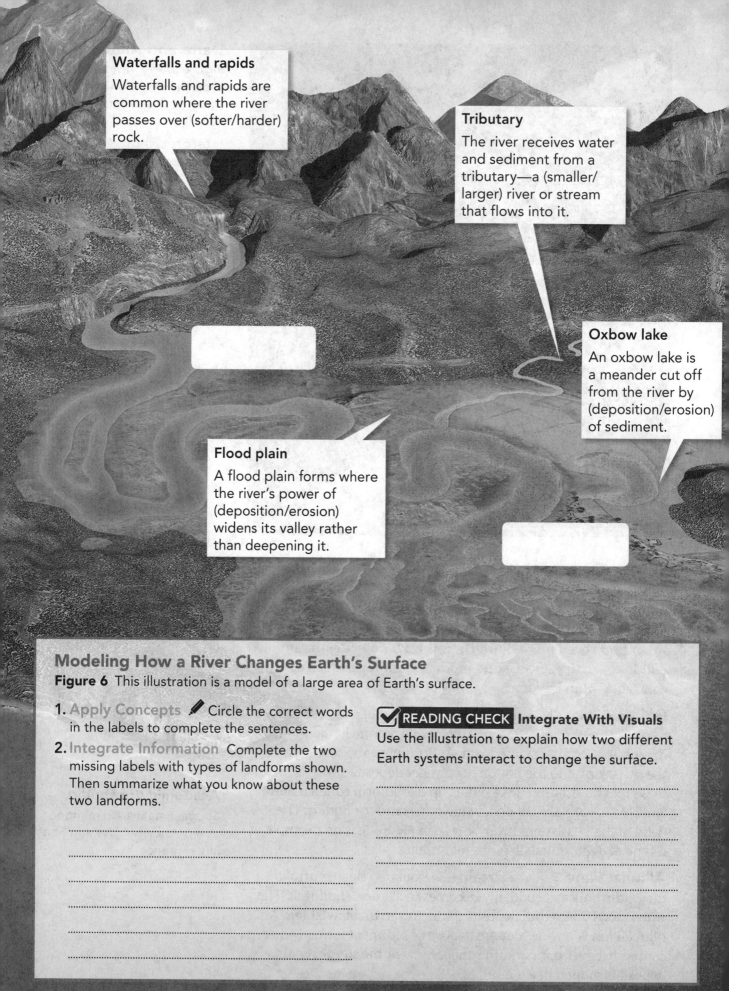

Waterfalls and rapids
Waterfalls and rapids are common where the river passes over (softer/harder) rock.

Tributary
The river receives water and sediment from a tributary—a (smaller/larger) river or stream that flows into it.

Oxbow lake
An oxbow lake is a meander cut off from the river by (deposition/erosion) of sediment.

Flood plain
A flood plain forms where the river's power of (deposition/erosion) widens its valley rather than deepening it.

Modeling How a River Changes Earth's Surface

Figure 6 This illustration is a model of a large area of Earth's surface.

1. **Apply Concepts** ✏ Circle the correct words in the labels to complete the sentences.

2. **Integrate Information** Complete the two missing labels with types of landforms shown. Then summarize what you know about these two landforms.

....

....

....

....

....

✓ **READING CHECK** **Integrate With Visuals**
Use the illustration to explain how two different Earth systems interact to change the surface.

....

....

....

....

....

Groundwater Changes Earth's Surface

When rain falls and snow melts, some water soaks into the ground. It trickles into cracks and spaces in layers of soil and rock. **Groundwater** is the term geologists use for this underground water. Like moving water, groundwater changes the shape of Earth's surface.

Groundwater Erosion Groundwater causes erosion by chemical weathering. In the atmosphere, rain water combines with carbon dioxide to form a weak acid called carbonic acid, which can break down limestone. Groundwater may also become more acidic as it flows through leaf debris at the surface. When groundwater flows into cracks in limestone, some of the limestone dissolves and gets carried away. This process gradually hollows out pockets in the rock. Over time, large underground holes, called caves or caverns, develop.

Groundwater Deposition The action of carbonic acid on limestone can also result in deposition. Water containing carbonic acid and calcium drips from a cave's roof. Carbon dioxide escapes from the solution, leaving behind a deposit of calcite. A deposit that hangs like an icicle from the roof of a cave is known as a stalactite (stuh LAK tyt). On the floor of the cave, a cone-shaped stalagmite (stuh LAG myt) builds up as water drops from the cave roof (**Figure 7**).

 Write About It How does groundwater form caves? In your science notebook, write entries for a tourist brochure for a cave, explaining to visitors how the cave and its features formed through erosion and deposition.

INTERACTIVITY

Explore erosion caused by groundwater.

Groundwater Erosion and Deposition

Figure 7 On the photo, draw a line from each label to the formation it names.

Construct Explanations How do deposition and erosion shape caves? Outline your ideas in the table.

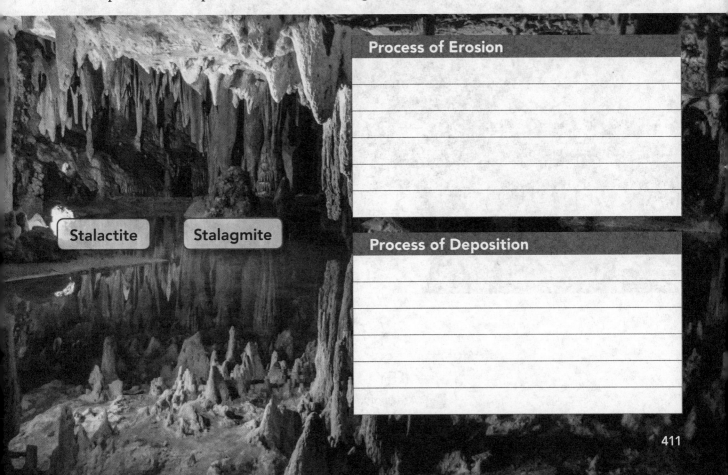

Stalactite   Stalagmite

Process of Erosion

Process of Deposition

411

Karst Topography

Figure 8 This sinkhole formed in a day in Winter Park, Florida, in 1981. What was the cause of the sinkhole?

....

1. **Interpret Diagrams** 🖉 Circle the state that has the most karst topography.

2. **Interpret Diagrams** Identify two states that have very little karst topography.

....

Karst Topography

In rainy regions such as Florida where there is a layer of limestone near the surface, groundwater erosion can significantly change the shape of Earth's surface. Deep valleys and caverns commonly form. If the roof of a cave collapses because of limestone erosion, the result is a depression called a sinkhole. This type of landscape is called karst topography.

The formation of karst topography happens over small to large areas and over short to very long time periods. Groundwater erosion starts with a single drop of water that dissolves a microscopic amount of limestone in seconds. After 100 years, groundwater might deposit 1 or 2 cm of calcite on the roof of a cave. Erosion might take thousands to millions of years to form a deep valley or huge cave system hundreds of kilometers long. The roof of a cave may very slowly erode over hundreds of years, but collapse within minutes to form a small or large sinkhole, as shown in **Figure 8**.

✓ **READING CHECK** **Summarize** How does groundwater cause karst topography?

....

....

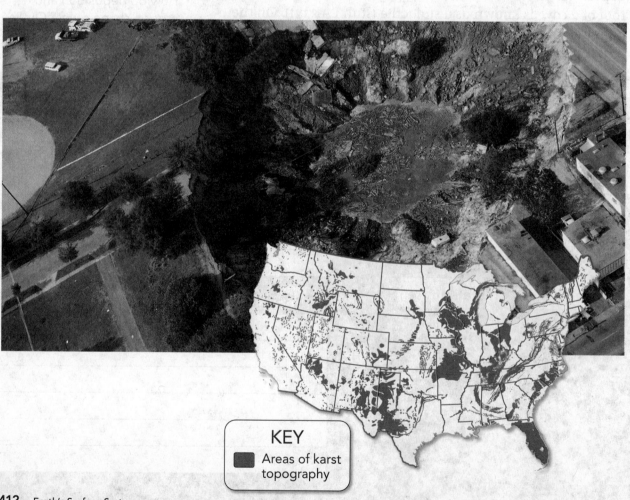

KEY
■ Areas of karst topography

MS-ESS2-2

1. **Identify** What are two features that result from deposition by groundwater?

....

....

2. **Explain** How does a meander form by erosion and deposition?

....

....

....

....

....

3. **Describe** Identify and describe a landform that results from water wearing down Earth's surface.

....

....

....

....

....

4. **Predict** How will Niagara Falls most likely change naturally in the future?

....

....

....

....

....

5. **Construct a Solution** Suggest two things a property owner could do to reduce water erosion on soil-covered land that has a steep slope.

....

....

....

....

....

....

....

....

Quest CHECK-IN

In this lesson, you learned how water on Earth's surface causes erosion and deposition. You also found out how groundwater causes erosion and deposition.

Evaluate Your Solution Why is it important to take different types of erosion and deposition into account when designing an artificial island?

....

....

....

....

....

HANDS-ON LAB

Ingenious Island: Part II

Investigate how you can use a model to test the effects of the agents of erosion on your artificial island.

Water table

Sand and Clay

Cavity

Limestone

When a cavity forms in limestone below the ground, a sinkhole can form when the ground eventually collapses into the cavity.

Buyer Beware!

It may sound like something out of a science fiction movie, but the United States is home to monsters that can destroy a roadway or swallow an entire house in a single gulp. They're known as sinkholes.

Geologic Hazards

Sinkholes come in all sizes—from an area the size of a small carpet and 30 centimeters deep to an area spreading over hundreds of acres and several hundreds of meters deep. The size of a sinkhole depends on the surrounding land features. Collapse sinkholes, for example, tend to happen in regions with clay sediments on top of limestone bedrock. As their name suggests, collapse sinkholes form quickly. The ceiling of an underground cavity suddenly gives way, and everything on the surface above that cavity collapses down into it.

In addition to the natural processes, such as heavy rainfall or extreme drought, that form sinkholes, human activities can have an impact. As we turn more of the countryside into housing developments, more people are living in areas prone to sinkholes. As we develop land, we use more water. Overuse of the groundwater, digging new water wells, or creating artificial ponds of surface water can all increase the chances of sinkhole formation.

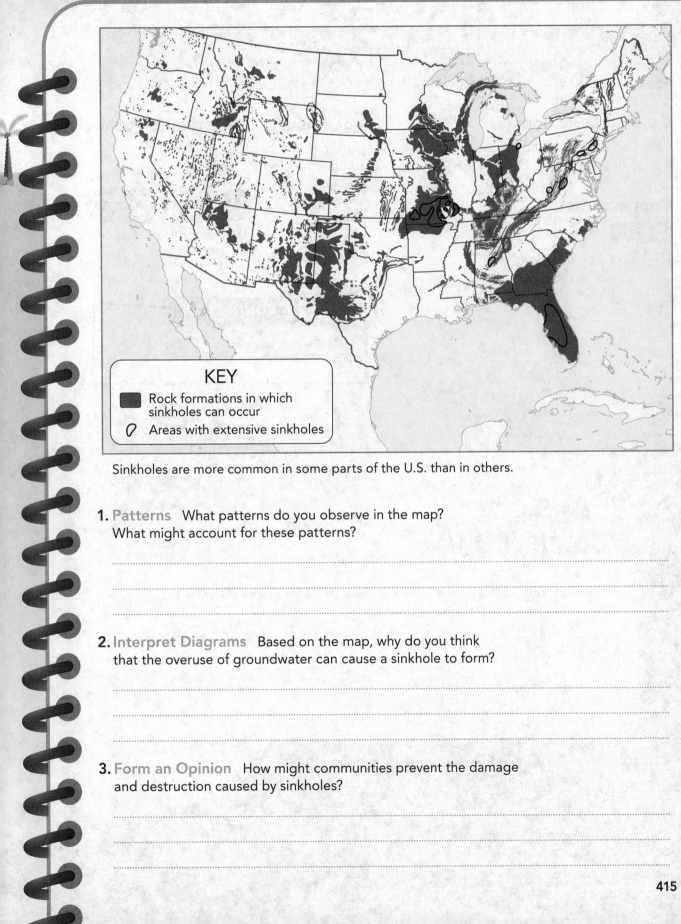

KEY

■ Rock formations in which sinkholes can occur

∅ Areas with extensive sinkholes

Sinkholes are more common in some parts of the U.S. than in others.

1. **Patterns** What patterns do you observe in the map? What might account for these patterns?

_____

_____

_____

2. **Interpret Diagrams** Based on the map, why do you think that the overuse of groundwater can cause a sinkhole to form?

_____

_____

_____

3. **Form an Opinion** How might communities prevent the damage and destruction caused by sinkholes?

_____

_____

_____

LESSON
4 Glacial and Wave Erosion

Guiding Questions

- How do glaciers change Earth's surface?
- How do waves change Earth's surface?

Connections

Literacy Write Informative Texts

Math Reason Abstractly

MS-ESS2-2

Vocabulary

glacier
continental glacier
ice age
valley glacier
plucking
till
longshore drift

Academic Vocabulary

interaction
impact

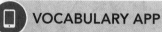 **VOCABULARY APP**

Practice vocabulary on a mobile device.

Quest CONNECTION

Consider how wave erosion impacts the location of your island.

Connect It!

✎ **Look closely at the image of the glacier. Draw an arrow showing the direction in which the glacier is flowing.**

Apply Scientific Reasoning How do you think this giant mass of ice changes Earth's surface?

....

....

Glaciers Change Earth's Surface

If you were to fly over Alaska, you would see snowcapped mountains and evergreen forests. Between the mountains and the Gulf of Alaska, you would also see a thick, winding mass of ice. This river of ice in **Figure 1** is a glacier. Geologists define a **glacier** (GLAY shur) as any large mass of ice that moves slowly over land.

Glaciers occur in the coldest places on Earth. That's because they can form only in an area where more snow falls than melts. Layers of snow pile on top of more layers of snow. Over time, the weight of the layers presses the particles of snow so tightly together that they form a solid block of ice.

Glaciers are part of the cryosphere (KRI oh sfear), which includes all the frozen water on Earth. As glaciers move slowly over land, the cryosphere interacts with the rocky upper layer of the geosphere that is known as the lithosphere. This **interaction** changes Earth's surface through weathering, erosion, and deposition. When the ice of the cryosphere melts, it becomes part of the hydrosphere.

HANDS-ON LAB

Examine how glaciers move across Earth's surface.

Academic Vocabulary

Describe an interaction you observed and one you took part in. Be sure to identify the people and things involved in the interaction.

....

....

....

....

....

Giant Bulldozer of Ice

Figure 1 Like a slow-moving bulldozer, Alaska's Bering Glacier, the largest glacier in North America, plows across Earth's surface.

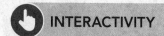
Continental Glaciers

A **continental glacier** is a glacier that covers much of a continent or large island. It can spread out over millions of square kilometers and flow in all directions. Today, continental glaciers cover about 10 percent of Earth's land, including Antarctica and most of Greenland.

During **ice ages**, continental glaciers covered larger parts of Earth's surface. The glaciers gradually advanced and retreated several times, changing the shape of Earth's surface each time.

Valley Glaciers

A **valley glacier** is a long, narrow glacier that forms when snow and ice build up in a mountain valley. High mountains keep these glaciers from spreading out in all directions, and gravity pulls the glacier downhill. Valley glaciers usually move slowly down valleys that have already been cut by rivers. Sometimes a valley glacier can experience a surge, or a quick slide, and move about 6 kilometers in one year. Alaska's Bering Glacier, shown in **Figure 1**, is a valley glacier.

Math Toolbox

Comparing Glacier Thickness

The graph shows the cumulative mass balance of a set of glaciers observed by scientists from 1945 to 2015. The cumulative mass balance is the total amount of ice the glaciers have gained or lost since 1945. The curve is always negative, so the glaciers have lost ice since 1945. The slope of the curve (how steep it is) shows how fast or slow the glaciers are losing ice.

1. **Reason Abstractly** What does a flat slope indicate? What does a steep slope indicate?

....

....

....

....

2. **Interpret Graphs** According to the data, the reference glaciers have melted and lost ice in every decade. In which decade did the glaciers lose ice slowest? In which decade did they lose ice quickest?

....

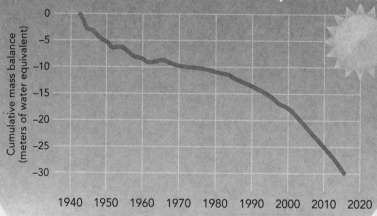

Average Cumulative Mass Balance of "Reference" Glaciers Worldwide, 1945–2015

Cumulative mass balance (meters of water equivalent)

Source: World Glacier Monitoring Service, 2016

Glacial Erosion

The movement of a glacier slowly changes the land beneath it. The two processes by which glaciers erode the land are plucking and abrasion.

As a glacier flows over the land, it picks up rocks in a process called **plucking**. The weight of the ice breaks rocks into fragments that freeze to the bottom of the glacier. Then the rock fragments get carried with the glacier, as shown in **Figure 2**. Plucking leaves behind a jagged landscape.

Many rocks remain embedded on the bottom and sides of the glacier, and the glacier drags them across the land much like sandpaper in a process called abrasion. Land is worn away and deep gouges and scratches form in the bedrock.

For most glaciers, advancing, retreating, and eroding the land are very slow events. It can take years for scientists to observe any change in a glacier or its effects. Sometimes, however, glaciers move unusually fast. In 2012, scientists determined that a glacier in Greenland advanced up to 46 meters per day, faster than any other glacier recorded.

Although glaciers move and work slowly, they are a major force of erosion. They can take years to carve tiny scratches in bedrock. They can also carve out huge valleys hundreds of kilometers long over thousands of years. Through slow movement and erosion, glaciers dramatically change the shape of large areas of Earth's surface.

Glacial Erosion

Figure 2 Glaciers wear down Earth's surface by plucking and abrasion.

1. **Interpret Diagrams** Draw an arrow in the diagram to show the direction in which the ice is moving. Draw an X where you think abrasion is occurring. Draw a circle where plucking is happening.

2. **Construct Explanations** In your own words, describe the glacial erosion taking place in the diagram.

....

....

....

....

....

....

419

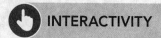

INTERACTIVITY

Examine water's effect on glaciers.

Glacial Deposition

A glacier carries large amounts of rock and soil as it erodes the land in its path. As the glacier melts, it deposits the sediment it eroded from the land, creating various landforms, detailed in **Figure 3**. These landforms remain for thousands of years after the glacier has melted. The mixture of sediments that a glacier deposits directly on the surface is called **till**, which includes clay, silt, sand, gravel, boulders, and even rock ground so finely it is called rock flour.

Moraine The till deposited at the edges of a glacier forms a ridge called a moraine. Lateral moraines are deposits of sediment along the sides of a glacier. A terminal moraine is the ridge of till that is dropped at the farthest point reached by a glacier.

Landforms of Glacial Erosion and Deposition

Figure 3 Glacial erosion and deposition wear down and build up Earth's surface, producing landforms.

Classify ✏ In the model of a landscape shaped by glaciers, identify the features of erosion and deposition. In the circles, write *E* for erosion and *D* for deposition.

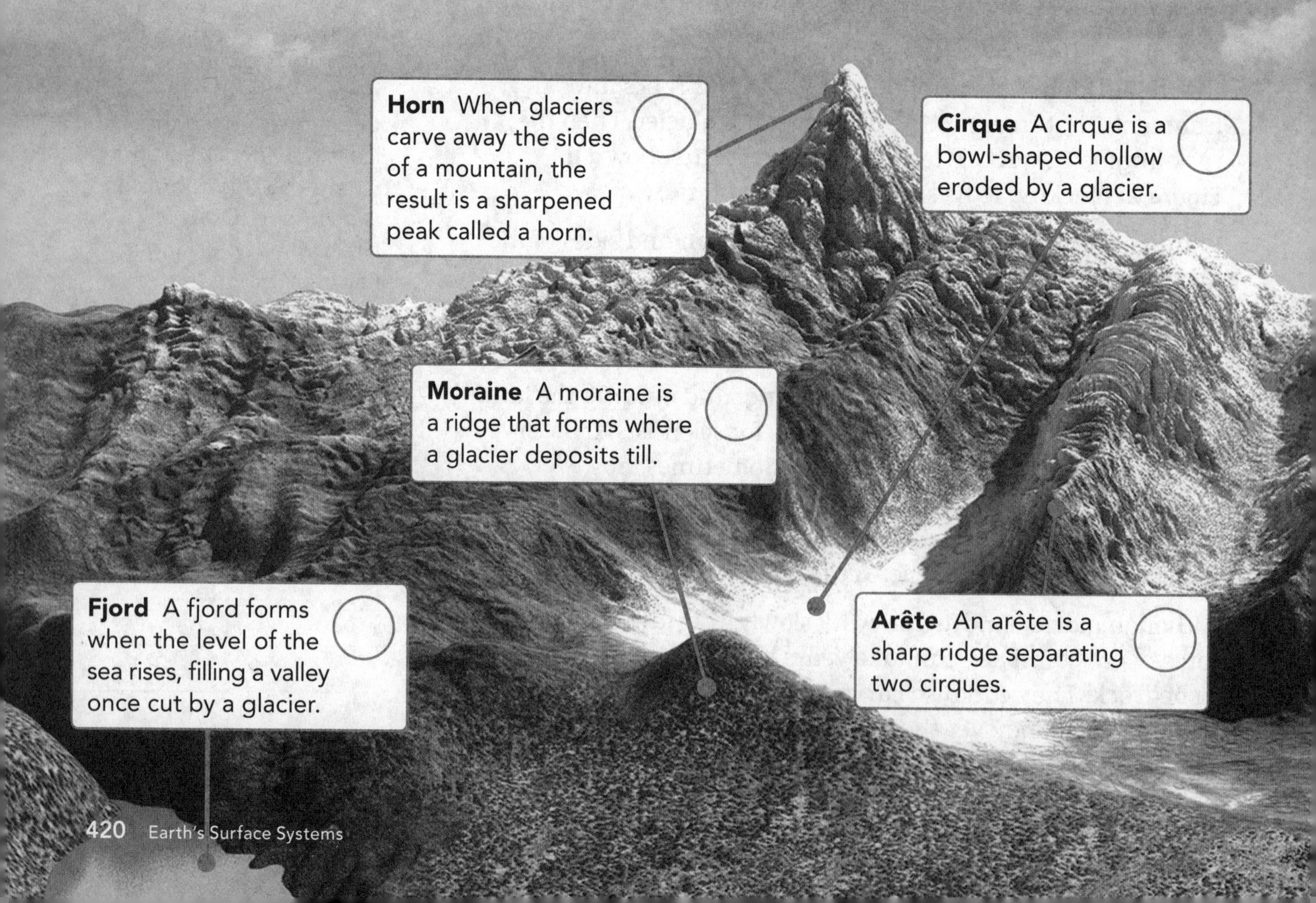

Horn When glaciers carve away the sides of a mountain, the result is a sharpened peak called a horn.

Cirque A cirque is a bowl-shaped hollow eroded by a glacier.

Moraine A moraine is a ridge that forms where a glacier deposits till.

Fjord A fjord forms when the level of the sea rises, filling a valley once cut by a glacier.

Arête An arête is a sharp ridge separating two cirques.

Kettle Retreating, or melting, glaciers also create features called kettles. A kettle is a steep-sided depression that forms when a chunk of ice is left in glacial till. When the ice melts, the kettle remains. The continental glacier of the last ice age left behind many kettles. Kettles often fill with water, forming small ponds or lakes called kettle lakes. Such lakes are common in areas such as Wisconsin that were once covered with glaciers.

✓ READING CHECK **Write Informative Texts** What are the effects of glacial deposition?

....

....

....

....

U-Shaped valley A flowing glacier scoops out a U-shaped valley.

Kettle lake A kettle lake forms when a depression left in till by melting ice fills with water.

Model It !

Develop Models ✏ In the space provided, draw part of the same landscape to show what the surface looked like before glacial erosion and deposition.

Waves Change Earth's Surface

Like glaciers, waves change Earth's surface. The energy in most waves comes from the wind. Stronger winds cause larger waves. The friction between the wave and the ocean floor slows the wave. Then the water breaks powerfully on the shore. This forward-moving water provides the force that changes the land along the shoreline.

Wave Erosion Waves shape the coast through weathering and erosion by breaking down rock and moving sand and other sediments. Large waves can hit rocks along the shore with great force, or **impact**. Over time, waves can enlarge small cracks in rocks and cause pieces of rock to break off. Waves also break apart rocks by abrasion. As a wave approaches shallow water, it picks up and carries sediment, including sand and gravel. When the wave hits land, the sediment wears away rock like sandpaper slowly wearing away wood.

Waves approaching the shore gradually change direction as different parts of the waves drag on the bottom, as shown in **Figure 4**. The energy of these waves is concentrated on headlands. A headland is a part of the shore that extends into the ocean. Gradually, soft rock erodes, leaving behind the harder rock that is resistant to wave erosion. But over time, waves erode the headlands and even out the shoreline.

Academic Vocabulary

How might you use the word *impact* in everyday life? Write a sentence using the word.

....

....

....

....

....

Headland Erosion

Figure 4 Wave erosion wears away rock to form headlands.

1. **Interpret Diagrams** ✏ Shade in the arrows that indicate where waves concentrate the greatest amount of energy.

2. **Predict** ✏ Draw a line to show how continued erosion will change the shoreline.

3. **Use Models** How does this model help you understand a system or process of change?

....

....

....

....

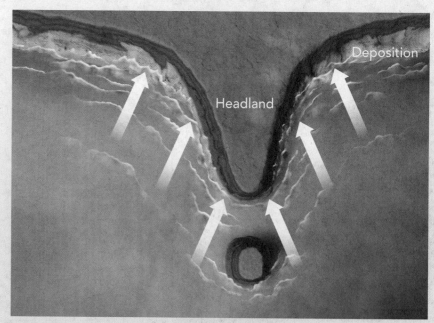

Deposition

Headland

Landforms Formed by Wave Erosion

Figure 5 ✏ Identify and label the landforms in the photo.

Landforms Formed by Wave Erosion When an ax strikes the base of a tree trunk, the cut gets bigger and deeper with each strike. Similarly, when ocean waves hit a steep, rocky coast, they erode the base of the land. Waves erode the softer rock first. Over time, the waves may erode a hollow notch in the rock called a sea cave. Eventually, waves may erode the base of a cliff so much that the cliff collapses. The rubble is washed out by wave action and the result is a wave-cut platform at the cliff's base, which is all that remains of the eroded cliff. A sea arch is another feature of wave erosion that forms when waves erode a layer of softer rock that underlies a layer of harder rock. If an arch collapses, a pillar of rock called a sea stack may result.

Wave erosion changes Earth's surface at different rates. Sometimes it changes the land quickly. During a single powerful storm with strong winds that form high-energy waves, part of a cliff or sea stack may crumble. Waves may pick up and carry away large amounts of sediment along a shore. In general, waves erode rock slowly, cutting cliffs and headlands back centimeters to meters in a year. Waves may take hundreds to thousands of years to wear away headlands and even out shorelines.

✓ **READING CHECK** **Write Explanatory Texts** Reread the text. Then explain how you think a sea cave might become a sea arch.

....

....

Literacy Connection

Write Informative Texts
As you read, think about how you could help another student understand the concepts. Then, in your own words, describe how waves cause erosion.

....

....

....

....

....

....

....

....

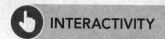

Wave Deposition Deposition occurs when waves lose energy and slow down, causing the water to drop the sediment it carries. Waves change the shape of a coast when they deposit sediment and form landforms.

Landforms Formed by Wave Deposition A beach is an area of wave-washed sediment along a coast. The sediment deposited on beaches is usually sand. Some beaches are made of coral or seashell fragments piled up by wave action. Florida has many such beaches.

Waves usually hit the beach at an angle, creating a current that runs parallel to the coastline. As waves repeatedly hit the beach, some of the sediment gets carried along the beach with the current, in a process called **longshore drift**.

Longshore drift also builds up sandbars and creates barrier islands. Sandbars are long ridges of sand parallel to the shore. A spit is an extended part of a beach that is connected by one end to the mainland. A barrier island forms when waves pile up large amounts of sand above sea level, forming a long, narrow island parallel to the coast. Barrier islands are found in Florida and numerous other places along the Atlantic coast of the United States. Barrier islands are constantly changing from wave erosion and deposition that occur during hurricanes and other storms.

☑ READING CHECK **Translate Information** Use the information in the text and **Figure 6** to determine how the coastline might change if large amounts of sand built up higher than sea level as a result of storm deposition.

Landforms Formed by Wave Deposition

Figure 6 ✎ On the diagram, draw arrows and label them to show the direction of longshore drift and the flow of sediment from the river to the sea.

Beach

Spit

Sandbar

MS-ESS2-2

1. Identify What are three landforms formed by wave deposition?

....

....

....

....

....

2. Construct Explanations How are the ways in which glaciers and waves wear down Earth's surface similar?

....

....

....

....

....

....

....

3. Predict A valley in the Rocky Mountains contains a glacier. How might the glacier change this valley in the future?

....

....

....

....

....

....

....

....

4. Develop Models 🖊 Draw and label diagrams to show how a sea arch might form from a headland.

Quest CHECK-IN

In this lesson, you discovered how erosion and deposition by glaciers change Earth's surface. You also learned how erosion and deposition by waves change Earth's surface.

Evaluate Your Solution Why is it important to consider the effects of wave erosion and deposition when designing an artificial island?

....

....

....

....

👆 INTERACTIVITY

Breaking Waves

Go online to examine how wave erosion might impact the location of your island, and adjust your design as needed.

☑TOPIC 9 Review and Assess

1 Weathering and Soil

MS-ESS2-2

1. How does acid rain cause weathering?
   A. through abrasion
   B. through oxidation
   C. by dissolving rock
   D. by carrying rock away

2. Mechanical weathering breaks some limestone into pieces. What effect would this have on chemical weathering of the limestone?
   A. Chemical weathering would stop occurring.
   B. Chemical weathering would remain the same.
   C. Chemical weathering would occur at a slower rate.
   D. Chemical weathering would occur at a faster rate.

3. The process of .... is an example of .... weathering in which rock splits through repeated freezing and thawing.

4. **Integrate Information** ✏ Draw a diagram of the A, B, and C horizons of soil. Label the horizons and describe the processes that formed each layer. Include examples of weathering in your description.

   ....
   ....
   ....
   ....
   ....
   ....

2 Erosion and Deposition

MS-ESS2-2, MS-ESS3-2

5. Which change occurs as a result of wind slowing down?
   A. erosion
   B. deposition
   C. chemical weathering
   D. mechanical weathering

6. How are erosion and deposition alike?
   A. Both change Earth's surface over time.
   B. Both build up Earth's surface quickly.
   C. Both wear down Earth's surface slowly.
   D. Neither changes Earth's surface.

7. Which type of mass movement occurs rapidly when a single mass of soil and rock suddenly slip downhill?
   A. creep
   B. landslide
   C. mudslide
   D. slump

8. Deposition by .... causes sand .... to form.

9. **Construct Explanations** A scientist observes that over several decades, fence posts placed in soil on a slope became tilted. Have erosion, deposition, or both occurred in this area? Use evidence to explain how you know.

   ....
   ....
   ....
   ....
   ....
   ....
   ....

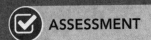

3 Water Erosion

MS-ESS2-2

10. Which landform develops as a result of river deposition?

A. cave

B. delta

C. stalactite

D. waterfall

11. Which of the following processes causes sinkholes to form?

A. erosion of sediment by runoff

B. deposition of sediment by a river

C. deposition of calcite by groundwater

D. erosion of limestone by groundwater

12. Sediments get deposited in an alluvial fan because ....

....

13. Develop Models ✏ Complete the flow chart to model a process that changes Earth's surface. Be sure to give the model a title.

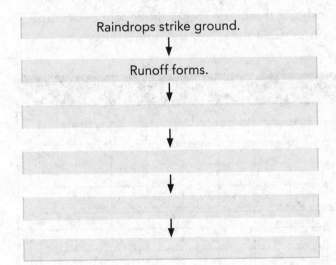

Raindrops strike ground.

↓

Runoff forms.

↓

↓

↓

4 Glacial and Wave Erosion

MS-ESS2-2

14. Which term describes sediment of mixed sizes deposited directly by a glacier?

A. kettle

B. loess

C. slump

D. till

15. How does longshore drift affect Earth's surface?

A. Rivers carry sediment to the ocean.

B. Rock cliffs break apart from impact.

C. Sediment moves down a beach with the current.

D. Waves concentrate their energy on headlands.

16. Which landform is created as a direct result of waves slowly eroding rocks?

A. beach

B. sandbar

C. sea stack

D. spit

17. Glaciers erode Earth's surface through the processes of .... and ....

18. Cite Evidence You are in a mountain valley studying a glacier. How could you use local landforms to tell whether the glacier is advancing or retreating?

....

....

....

....

....

....

MS-ESS2-2, MS-ESS3-2

Evidence-Based Assessment

A team of researchers is studying a massive landslide that occurred on the scenic stretch of California's coast known as Big Sur on May 20, 2017. Millions of tons of rock and dirt collapsed down a seaside slope onto the highway and spilled into the sea.

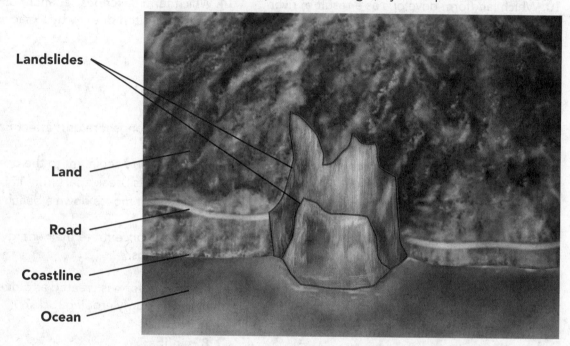

Landslides

Land

Road

Coastline

Ocean

To understand what happened in Big Sur, researchers are analyzing average winter precipitation data collected over a thirty-year period. The data is displayed in the graph. The solid line across the middle of the graph marks the mean, or average, winter precipitation for California over the entire thirty-year period.

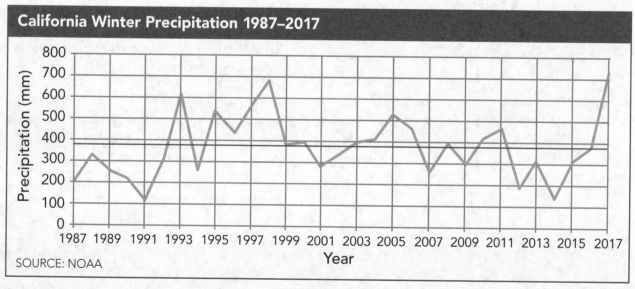

California Winter Precipitation 1987–2017

SOURCE: NOAA

1. **Analyze Data** How much precipitation did California receive in the winter prior to the May 20 landslide of 2017?
   A. 710 mm   **B.** 390 mm
   C. 520 mm   **D.** 800 mm

2. **Interpret Data** How would you describe California's precipitation in the five winters prior to 2017? Select all the statements that apply.
   ☐ It was above average for the five winters.
   ☐ It was below average for four winters, and average for one.
   ☐ It was below average for the five winters.
   ☐ It was mostly above average.
   ☐ It was mostly below average.
   ☐ It was above average for four winters, and below average for one.

3. **Cite Evidence** In the image of the coast at Big Sur, what are three visible indications that a large landslide occurred?

   ....

   ....

   ....

   ....

   ....

   ....

   ....

4. **Predict** How do you think weathering and erosion will affect the base of the deposited sediment, which is in the ocean? How will this affect the coastline in the future?

   ....

   ....

   ....

   ....

   ....

   ....

   ....

5. **Construct Explanations** What do you think is the connection between the precipitation in the winter of 2017 and the landslide?

   ....

   ....

   ....

   ....

   ....

   ....

   ....

   ....

Quest FINDINGS

Complete the Quest!

Phenomenon Reflect on how changes to Earth's surface will impact an artificial island. Then, prepare and deliver an oral or written presentation explaining your island design and your model.

Analyze Systems What are three things you learned about the processes that shape Earth's surface that helped you to design your artificial island?

....

....

....

....

....

....

....

👆 **INTERACTIVITY**

Reflect on Your Ingenious Island

429

Materials on a Slope

How can you use a **model** to determine the likelihood of **mass movement**?

Background

Phenomenon Geoscience processes such as rapid mass movement result in large amounts of sediment moving down hillsides.

In this investigation, you will work as part of a landslide monitoring team. You will develop and use a model to explore the relationship between the height and width of a hill. You will gain understanding about how these factors affect the hill's stability and the likelihood that mass movement will occur.

Safety

Be sure to follow all safety guidelines provided by your teacher. The Safety Appendix of your textbook provides more details about the safety icons.

Materials

(per group)

- tray (about 15 cm × 45 cm × 60 cm)
- several sheets of white paper
- masking tape
- cardboard tube
- spoon or paper cup
- dry sand (500 mL) in container
- wooden skewer
- metric ruler
- pencil or crayon
- graph paper

Landslides are destructive events that not only damage roadways and buildings, but also result in the loss of life.

Plan Your Investigation

HANDS-ON LAB

Demonstrate Go online for a downloadable worksheet of this lab.

☐ Use the metric ruler to mark off centimeters across the length of the paper. Take the tray provided by your teacher and use the paper to cover its interior surface. Secure the paper with tape. In the middle of the tray, stand the cardboard tube upright. Use a spoon or cup to fill the tube with sand.

☐ When the tube is nearly full, slowly and steadily pull the tube straight up so that the sand falls out of the bottom and forms a cone-shaped hill. Use different quantities of sand and observe the shapes and sizes of the sand hills created.

☐ Using the materials provided by your teacher, design an investigation to explore the relationship between the height and width of a sand hill. Determine how many sand hills you will create in your investigation.

☐ Then use the space provided to outline your procedure. Have your teacher review and approve your procedure, and then conduct your investigation. Create a data table to record your data about the heights and widths of the sand hills your group models.

Design Your Procedure

Data Table

Analyze and Interpret Data

1. **Analyze Data** Study your data table. What patterns do you notice in your data?

....

....

2. **Use Evidence** What do your data suggest about the relationship between the height and width of a sand hill?

....

....

....

3. **Identify Limitations** What are the advantages of using the sand hill model in this investigation? What are the limitations of using the model?

....

....

....

....

....

....

4. **Use Models** How is your sand hill model similar to and different from a natural hill that undergoes mass movement?

....

....

....

....

5. **Construct Explanations** How could you apply the results of your investigation to help assess the likelihood of and forecast future mass movement events such as landslides? Use evidence from your investigation to support your explanation.

....

....

....

....

Living Things in the Biosphere

NGSS PERFORMANCE EXPECTATIONS

MS-LS1-1 Conduct an investigation to provide evidence that living things are made of cells; either one cell or many different numbers and types of cells.

MS-LS1-2 Develop and use a model to describe the function of a cell as a whole and ways parts of cells contribute to the function

MS-LS1-3 Use argument supported by evidence for how the body is a system of interacting subsystems composed of groups of cells.

MS-LS4-2 Apply scientific ideas to construct an explanation for the anatomical similarities and differences among modern organisms and between modern and fossil organisms to infer evolutionary relationships.

HANDS-ON LAB

u**Connect** Expand your knowledge of what might be an animal.

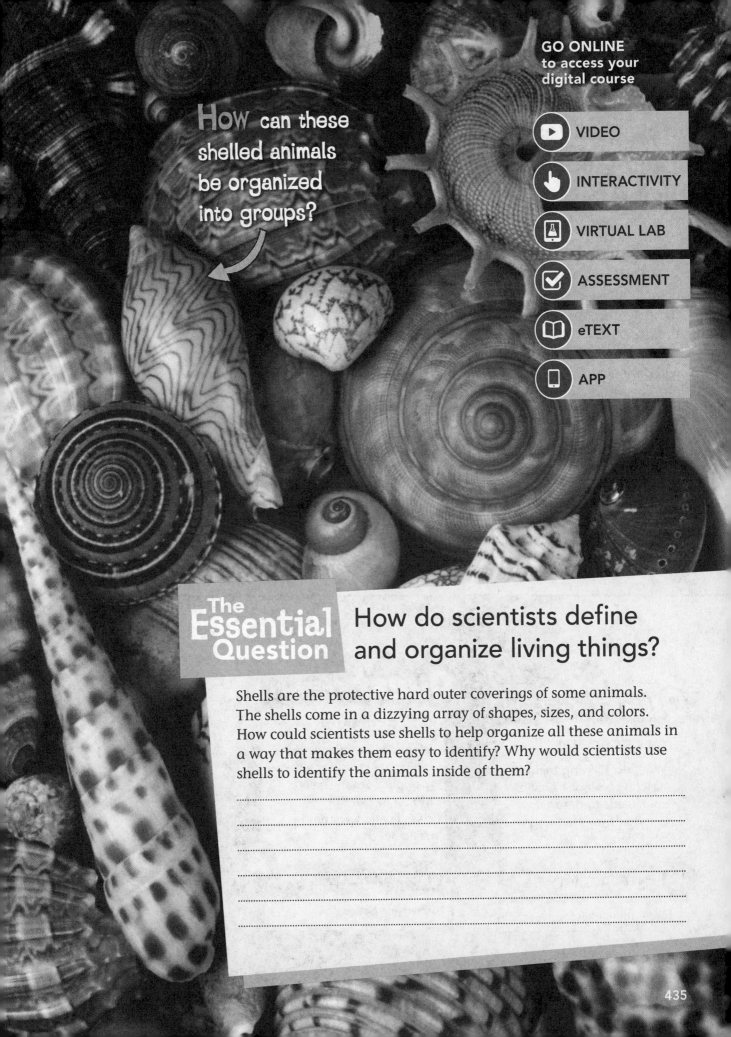

How can these shelled animals be organized into groups?

GO ONLINE
to access your
digital course

▶ VIDEO

👆 INTERACTIVITY

⏲ VIRTUAL LAB

☑ ASSESSMENT

📖 eTEXT

📱 APP

The Essential Question

How do scientists define and organize living things?

Shells are the protective hard outer coverings of some animals. The shells come in a dizzying array of shapes, sizes, and colors. How could scientists use shells to help organize all these animals in a way that makes them easy to identify? Why would scientists use shells to identify the animals inside of them?

....

....

....

....

....

....

Quest KICKOFF

How can you design a field guide to organize living things?

Phenomenon A 2011 scientific study estimates that there are around 8.7 million, plus or minus 1.3 million, species on our planet. Guess how many species have actually been identified! About two million. To identify these new organisms, taxonomists look at characteristics. Taxonomy is the branch of science that classifies organisms. In this problem-based Quest activity, you will design a field guide to help people identify the different organisms they may see at a nature center. By applying what you learn in each lesson, digital activity, or hands-on lab, you will gather key Quest information. With this information, you will develop your field guide in the Findings activity.

NBC LEARN ▶ VIDEO

After watching the Quest Kickoff video about discovering and categorizing organisms, choose two organisms that you observe in your daily life. Complete the Venn diagram by describing what makes them similar and different.

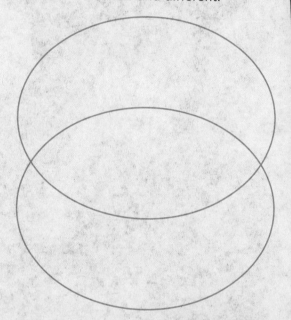

 INTERACTIVITY

Sort Out Those Organisms

MS-LS4-2 Apply scientific ideas to construct an explanation for the anatomical similarities and differences among modern organisms and between modern and fossil organisms to infer evolutionary relationships.

Quest CHECK-IN

IN LESSON 1

What do all living things have in common? Analyze specimens to determine whether they are living or nonliving.

 INTERACTIVITY

Under the Microscope

Quest CHECK-IN

IN LESSON 2

What characteristics do biologists consider when grouping organisms? Model a scientific classification system using seeds.

HANDS-ON LAB

Classifying Seeds

Quest CHECK-IN

IN LESSON 3

What distinguishes unicellular and multicellular organisms? Classify organisms based on their characteristics as unicellular or multicellular.

INTERACTIVITY

Discovering Rainforest Organisms

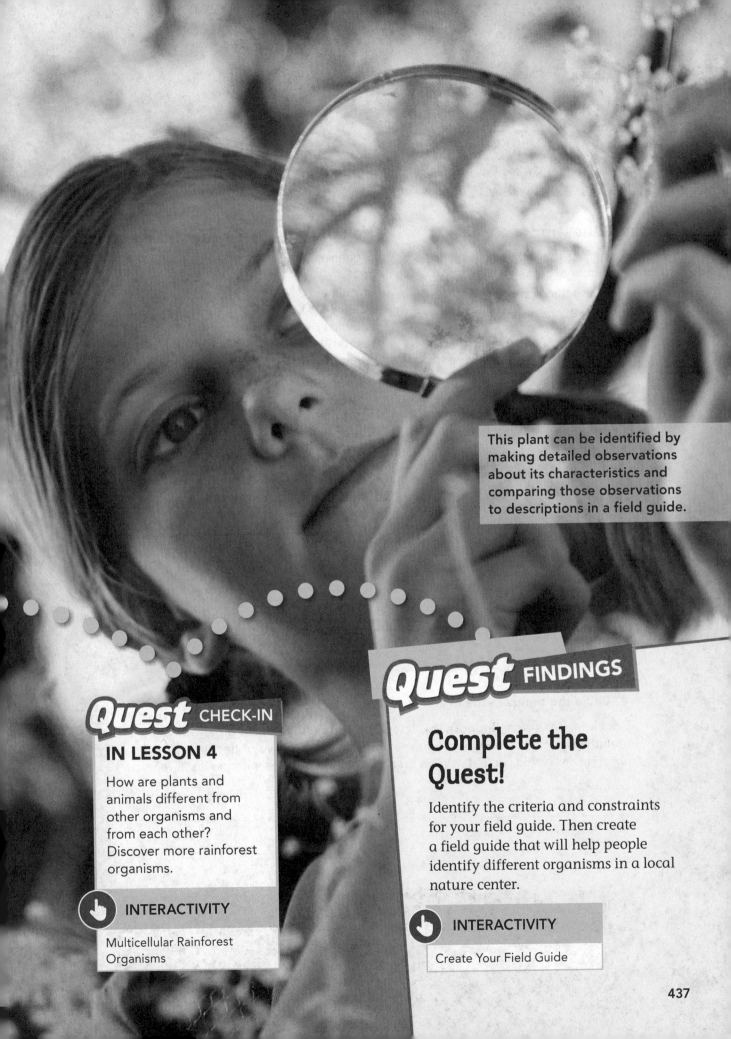

This plant can be identified by making detailed observations about its characteristics and comparing those observations to descriptions in a field guide.

Quest CHECK-IN

IN LESSON 4

How are plants and animals different from other organisms and from each other? Discover more rainforest organisms.

👆 **INTERACTIVITY**

Multicellular Rainforest Organisms

Quest FINDINGS

Complete the Quest!

Identify the criteria and constraints for your field guide. Then create a field guide that will help people identify different organisms in a local nature center.

👆 **INTERACTIVITY**

Create Your Field Guide

① Living Things

Guiding Questions

- What evidence is there that all living things are made of cells?
- Where do living things come from?
- What do living things need to stay alive, grow, and reproduce?

Connection

Literacy Gather Information

MS-LS1-1

Vocabulary

organism
cell
unicellular
multicellular
stimulus
response
spontaneous
  generation
homeostasis

Academic Vocabulary

characteristics

 VOCABULARY APP

Practice vocabulary on a mobile device.

Quest CONNECTION

Consider how the characteristics of living things are important when creating a field guide.

Connect It!

✏ **Circle the things in the image that appear to be living.**

Conduct Research Suppose you scraped off some of the pale green stuff from the tree bark. How would you know whether it was alive or not? What observations would you note? What tests could you do to see whether it's alive?

....

....

....

Characteristics of Living Things

An **organism** is any living thing. It could be a horse, a tree, a mushroom, strep bacteria, or the lichens (LIE kins) in **Figure 1**. Some organisms are familiar and obviously alive. No one wonders whether a dog is an organism. Other organisms are a little harder to distinguish from nonliving things. Lichens, for example, can be very hard and gray. They don't seem to grow much from year to year. How can we separate living from nonliving things? The answer is that all organisms share several important **characteristics**:

- All organisms are made of cells.

- All organisms contain similar chemicals and use energy.

- All organisms respond to their surroundings.

- All organisms grow, develop, and reproduce.

HANDS-ON LAB

Explore what makes a living thing alive.

Academic Vocabulary

A *characteristic* is a feature that helps to identify something. How would you describe the characteristics of a good movie or book?

....

....

....

....

Still Life with Lichens
Figure 1 Lichens blend in with the trees.

Characteristics of Living Things

Figure 2 All living things share certain characteristics.

Determine Conclusions What is the one characteristic that all living things and only living things have in common?

....

....

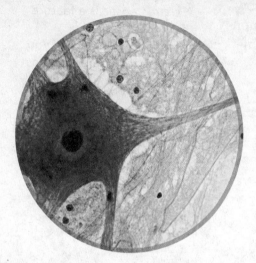

Cellular Organization All living things are made of smaller living units called cells. **Cells** are the basic unit of structure and function in living things. In a single-celled or **unicellular** organism, one cell carries out the functions necessary to stay alive. Organisms consisting of many cells are **multicellular**. You are a multicellular organism with trillions of cells specialized to do certain tasks. The nerve cell shown here sends electrical signals throughout your body. It may signal you to let go of something hot or to take a step. In a multicellular organism, all cells work together to keep the organism alive.

The Chemicals of Life All substances, including living cells, are made of chemicals. The most common chemical in cells is water, which is essential for life. Other chemicals, called carbohydrates (kahr boh HY drayts) provide the cell with energy. Proteins and lipids are chemicals used in building cells, much as wood and bricks are used to build schools. Finally, nucleic (noo KLEE ik) acids provide chemical instructions that tell cells how to carry out the functions of life. You've probably heard of DNA, deoxyribonucleic acid, but did you know what it looks like? The nucleic acid DNA directs the actions of every cell in your body.

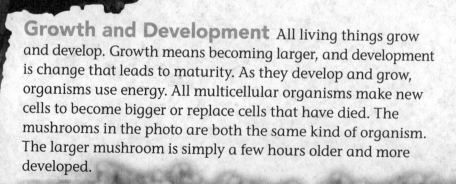

Growth and Development All living things grow and develop. Growth means becoming larger, and development is change that leads to maturity. As they develop and grow, organisms use energy. All multicellular organisms make new cells to become bigger or replace cells that have died. The mushrooms in the photo are both the same kind of organism. The larger mushroom is simply a few hours older and more developed.

Response to Surroundings Have you ever touched the palm of a baby's hand? If so, you may have observed the baby's fingers curl to grip your fingertip. The baby's grip is a natural reflex. Like a baby's curling fingers, all organisms react to changes in their surroundings. Any change or signal in the environment that can make an organism react in some way is called a **stimulus** (plural *stimuli*). Stimuli include changes in light, sound, flavors, or odors. An organism reacts to a stimulus with a **response**—an action or a change in behavior. Responding to stimuli helps the baby and all other organisms to survive and function.

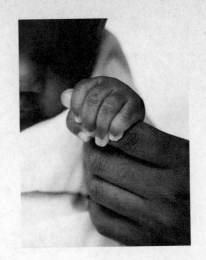

Reproduction Organisms reproduce to create offspring that are similar to the parent or parents. Some organisms reproduce asexually, creating an identical offspring with only one parent. One example is the young hydra (HY druh) budding off the parent hydra in the image. Mammals, birds, and most plants reproduce sexually. In sexual reproduction, two parents combine their DNA to create an offspring with a mix of both parents' characteristics.

Energy Use All organisms need energy to power their cells. Within an organism's cells, chemical reactions break down materials to get energy. Some organisms, called producers, can get energy from sunlight in a process known as photosynthesis, while other producers use different chemicals in their environment to make energy. Other organisms, called consumers, get energy by eating other living things. The shrew pictured here must eat more than its own weight in food every day. A shrew can starve to death if it goes five hours without eating!

HANDS-ON LAB

☑ **Investigate** Identify structures found in the cells of living things.

Life Produces More Life

Every spring, wildflowers seem to pop up out of the ground from nowhere. Do the plants sprout directly from rocks and soil? No, we know that the new plants are reproduced from older plants. Four hundred years ago, however, people believed that life could appear from nonliving material. For example, when people saw flies swarming around spoiled meat, they concluded that the meat produced the flies. The mistaken idea that living things arise from nonliving sources is called **spontaneous generation**. It took hundreds of years and many experiments to convince people that spontaneous generation does not occur.

Redi's Experiment In the 1600s, an Italian doctor named Francesco Redi helped to prove spontaneous generation wrong. Redi investigated the source of the maggots that develop into adult flies on rotting meat. Redi performed a controlled experiment so he was certain about the cause of the results. In a controlled experiment, a scientist carries out two or more tests that are identical in every way except one. As shown in **Figure 3**, Redi set up two jars in the same location with meat in them. Then Redi changed just one variable in his experiment and watched to see what would happen.

Redi's Experiment
Figure 3 Redi showed that meat did not cause the spontaneous generation of flies.

Relate Text to Visuals Read the steps below. Then sketch steps 2 and 3.

Step 1 Redi placed meat in two identical jars. He covered one jar with a cloth that let in air, the control in the experiment.

Step 2 After a few days, Redi saw maggots (young flies) on the decaying meat in the open jar.

Step 3 Redi reasoned that flies had laid eggs on the meat in the open jar. The eggs hatched into maggots.

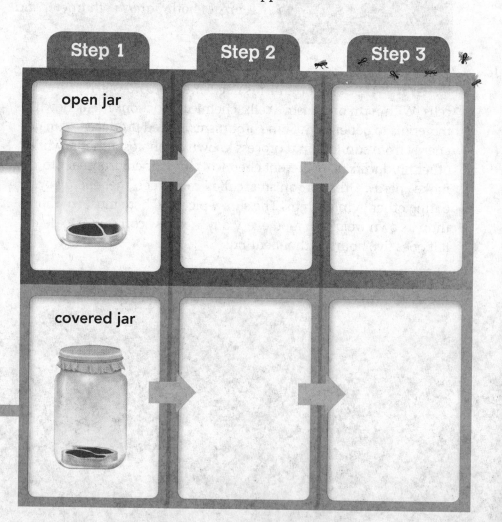

Pasteur's Experiment Even after Redi's experiment, many people continued to believe in spontaneous generation. Almost 200 years after Redi's experiment, French chemist Louis Pasteur (pah STUHR) decided to put spontaneous generation to the test. In his experiment, Pasteur used a control group. A control group is exposed to the same factors as the experimental group, except that it is not exposed to the variable being tested. **Figure 4** shows the experiment that convinced the scientific community that spontaneous generation was just a myth.

☑ READING CHECK **Gather Information** How did both the Redi and Pasteur experiments prove there was no such thing as spontaneous generation?

....

....

....

Pasteur's Experiment
Figure 4 Pasteur carefully controlled his experiment.

1. Relate Text to Visuals ✏ Draw and label the flasks in steps 2 and 3. Label the control and experimental flasks.

2. Draw Conclusions What did the bacterial growth in Step 3 confirm for Pasteur?

....

....

....

Step 1
Pasteur put clear broth into flasks with curved necks. The necks let in air but kept out bacteria. He boiled the broth in the flasks to kill all bacteria present.

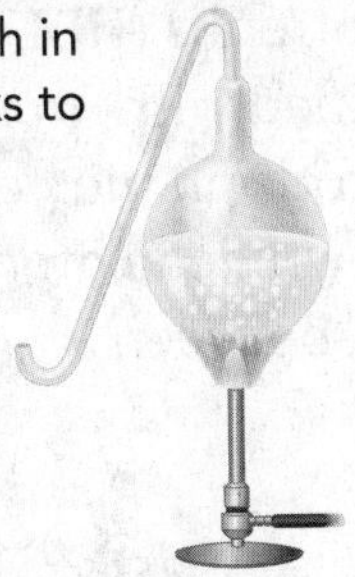

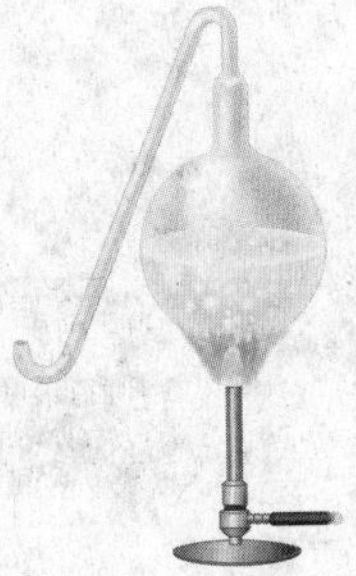

....

....

Step 2
The boiled broth remained clear. Pasteur then set some of the flasks aside, just as they were.

Pasteur broke the curved necks off the other flasks. Bacteria from the outside air were able to enter these flasks.

Step 3
The broth in these flasks remained clear. Pasteur concluded that bacteria could not arise from the broth.

The broth in the broken flasks became cloudy, showing bacterial growth.

Literacy Connection

Gather Information
Use multiple print and online sources to gather information about the special properties of water. Can you find a good substitute for water?

Needs of Living Things

Though it may seem surprising, pine trees, worms, and all other organisms have the same basic needs as you do. All living things must satisfy their basic needs for water, food, living space, and homeostasis.

Water All living things depend on water for their survival. In fact, some organisms can live only for a few days without water. All cells need water to carry out their daily functions. Many substances dissolve easily in water. Once food or other chemicals are dissolved, they are easily transported around the body of an organism. About half of human blood is made of water. Our blood carries dissolved food, waste, and other chemicals to and from cells. Also, many chemical reactions that take place in cells require water.

Food All living things consume food for energy. Some organisms, such as plants, capture the sun's energy and use it to make food through the process of photosynthesis. Producers are organisms that make their own food. Producers are also called autotrophs (AW toh trohfs). *Auto-* means "self" and *-troph* means "feeder." Autotrophs use the sun's energy to convert water and a gas into food.

Autotrophs and Heterotrophs

Figure 5 Every organism has to eat!

Apply Concepts ✏ Write whether each organism is an autotroph or a heterotroph in the space provided.

Every organism that can't make its own food must eat other organisms. Consumers are organisms that cannot make their own food. Consumers are also called heterotrophs (HET uh roh trohfs). *Hetero-* means "other," so combined with *-troph* it means "one that feeds on others." A heterotroph may eat autotrophs, other heterotrophs, or break down dead organisms to get energy. **Figure 5** shows an interaction between autotrophs and heterotrophs.

Crocodile

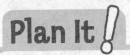

Plan It

Can a Person Be an Autotroph?

Shelby and Michaela are learning about organisms. Shelby says she is sometimes an autotroph because she makes her own food after school, a bowl of cut fruit.

Explain Phenomena How can Michaela prove to Shelby that she is not an autotroph? What could she do to help Shelby investigate what an autotroph is?

....

....

....

Space All organisms need a place to live—a place to get food and water and find shelter. Whether an organism lives in the savanna, as shown in **Figure 5**, or the desert, its surroundings must provide what it needs to survive. Because there is a limited amount of space on Earth, some organisms compete for space. Trees in a forest, for example, compete with other trees for sunlight. Below ground, their roots compete for water and minerals. If an organism loses its living space, it must move to a new place or it may die.

☑ **READING CHECK** **Cite Textual Evidence** Why do living things need water, food, and space to live?

....

....

....

Tick

Zebra

Grass

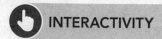

INTERACTIVITY

Examine why an object that has a few characteristics of living things is not living.

Homeostasis

When you go outside on a freezing cold day, does your body temperature fall below freezing as well? Of course not! Your body is able to keep the temperature of your insides steady even when outside conditions change. Shivering, moving to a warmer place, and putting on more clothes all help you to stay warm. The maintenance of stable internal conditions is called **homeostasis** (hoh mee oh STAY sis). All organisms maintain homeostasis to stay alive.

Organisms have many different methods for maintaining homeostasis. The methods depend on the challenges faced by the organism. Consider the marine iguana, pictured in **Figure 6**. Marine iguanas feed underwater in the ocean and swallow a lot of salty water. To maintain homeostasis, the iguanas need a way to get rid of the extra salt. In a human, extra salt would be removed in sweat, tears, or urine. The iguana has a different way of maintaining homeostasis. Iguanas produce very salty liquid that comes out near their noses. Frequent sneezing clears the salty liquid away. Homeostasis is maintained!

✓ READING CHECK **Determine Central Ideas** The paws of the arctic fox are covered in thick fur. How does this help the fox maintain homeostasis?

....

....

....

....

Salty Sneezes

Figure 6 As they eat underwater plants, marine iguanas maintain homeostasis by sneezing out salty liquid.

Apply Concepts Which basic need is an iguana meeting by feeding on underwater plants?

....

....

☑ LESSON 1 Check

MS-LS1-1

1. Apply Concepts Name two autotrophs and two heterotrophs that live near your home.

....

....

2. Use Models ✏ Draw a diagram showing all the things that an organism needs to survive. Label the drawing to show how the organism can meet its needs right where it lives.

3. Identify Variables A student is designing a controlled experiment to test whether the amount of water that a plant receives affects its growth. Which factors should the student hold constant and which variable should the student change?

....

....

....

....

4. Construct an Explanation What sort of evidence can you use to show that all living things grow and develop?

....

....

....

....

....

....

....

....

....

....

....

Quest CHECK-IN

In this lesson, you learned about the characteristics of living things and where living things come from. You also learned about what living things need to grow, stay alive, and reproduce.

Evaluate Your Plan What are your plans for your field guide? How will you use the characteristics of living things to identify and categorize different organisms?

....

....

....

....

....

👆 INTERACTIVITY

Under the Microscope

Go online to observe different objects and determine whether they are living or nonliving.

The TOUGH and *Tiny* TARDIGRADE

Imagine being shrunk to the size of the period at the end of this sentence and getting plopped down in a bed of moss. You just might run into a tardigrade as big as you. Sort of cute, right? No wonder they're nicknamed the water bear.

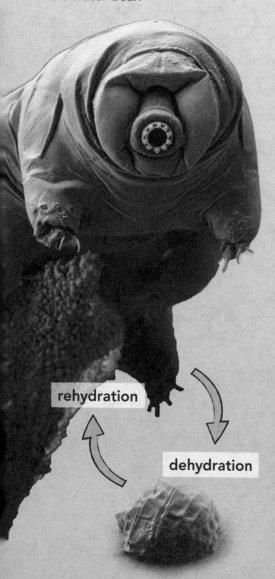

rehydration

dehydration

All living things need water, a safe temperature range, and the right pressure to sustain functioning cells. But one microscopic organism called a tardigrade defies all those rules. Tardigrades survive the most extreme conditions on Earth.

How do they do it? Tardigrades dehydrate themselves. They shed 95 percent of the water in their bodies. Life comes to a nearly complete halt in the dried-out tardigrade. Studies suggest that tardigrades produce proteins and sugars that help to protect their cells while they are dehydrated. Add water and the tardigrade rehydrates and bounces back to life. Scientists study tardigrades to learn more about the activities inside cells that enable animals to develop and survive.

Extreme Temperatures

Tardigrades have been found in conditions ranging from polar waters to bubbling hot springs. In one lab experiment, they even survived at an unimaginable –272°C (–458°F). And they withstood temperatures well over boiling, too.

Intense Pressure

If you stood in the very deepest part of the ocean, the pressure would crush you flat. But tardigrades? They can withstand *six times* that pressure. In the vacuum of space where there's almost no pressure, your insides would start to expand until your body exploded like a balloon. But tardigrades toured outer space for ten days and came back to Earth unharmed.

Radiation

In high doses, radiation damages cells and destroys DNA. Humans can withstand only very small doses (measured in Grays, or Gy), but tardigrades can survive 5,000 Gy or more. With their ability to protect their cells from these extremes, you'd think tardigrades would live in the wildest places on Earth. But they prefer to live in the water, or in damp places, such as among wet leaves and in moist soil.

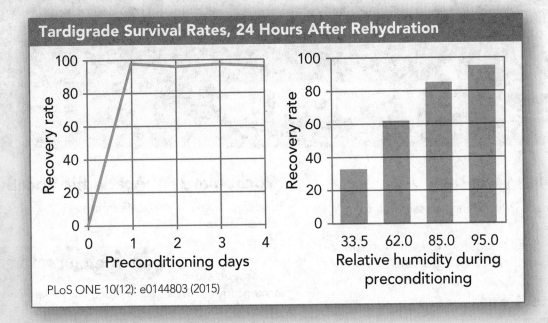

Tardigrade Survival Rates, 24 Hours After Rehydration

PLoS ONE 10(12): e0144803 (2015)

Tardigrades are exposed to different amounts of humidity (or moisture) before dehydrating. This is called preconditioning. The graphs show results from an experiment that tested whether preconditioning was necessary. The bar graph above shows the results of changing the amount of humidity in the air during preconditioning. The recovery rate is the percent of tardigrades who survive the transition from dehydration to rehydration.

1. **Analyze Properties** When you think of the common characteristics that all living things share, which one stands out the most in this experiment?

....

2. **Evaluate Data** What does the bar graph above suggest about the effects of relative humidity during preconditioning?

....

....

3. **Predict** What do you think the data would look like if the relative humidity were 45 percent?

....

....

....

4. **Synthesize Information** Why might humidity be helpful to a tardigrade?

....

....

....

② Classification Systems

Guiding Questions

- How are living things classified into groups?
- How does the theory of evolution support the classification of organisms?

Connections

Literacy Assess Sources

Math Write an Expression

MS-LS4-2

Vocabulary

species
classification
genus
binomial
  nomenclature
taxonomy
domain
evolution
convergent
  evolution

Academic Vocabulary

determine

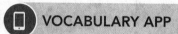 **VOCABULARY APP**

Practice vocabulary on a mobile device.

Quest CONNECTION

Think about how a classification system might be used to organize different organisms in your field guide.

Connect It!

✎ **Draw arrows and label parts of the organism that help you to identify it.**

Make Observations What kind of living thing do you think this is?

....

....

....

Classifying Organisms

It is estimated that there are approximately 8.7 million species of organisms on the planet, with thousands more discovered each day. A **species** is a group of similar organisms that can mate with each other and produce offspring that can also mate and reproduce. Biologists place similar organisms into groups based on characteristics they have in common. **Classification** is the process of grouping things based on their similarities. To classify the organism in **Figure 1**, you'd first need to know about its characteristics. Then you could figure out which group it belonged to.

Linnaean Naming System In the 1730s, biologist Carolus Linnaeus arranged organisms in groups based on their observable features. Then he gave each organism a two-part scientific name. The first word in the name is the organism's **genus**, a group of similar, closely-related organisms. The second word is the species and might describe where the organism lives or its appearance. This system in which each organism is given a unique, two-part scientific name that indicates its genus and species is known as **binomial nomenclature**. Today, scientists still use this naming system that classifies organisms according to their shared characteristics.

HANDS-ON LAB

Organize items based on similar characteristics.

Write About It Pick a favorite animal or plant. What is it that you find most interesting? In your science notebook, describe its characteristics.

Animal, Vegetable, or Mineral?
Figure 1 Some organisms are much harder to classify than others!

Literacy Connection

Assess Sources Books become outdated and the Internet is full of incorrect information. If you need an accurate answer to a scientific question, where would you look? Whom could you ask for help?

....

....

....

....

....

Taxonomy The scientific study of how organisms are classified is called **taxonomy** (tak SAHN uh mee). Scientists use taxonomy to identify the name of an unknown organism or to name a newly discovered organism. For example, if you look closely at the characteristics of the organism in **Figure 1**, you might classify it as a sea slug. It would then be simple to look up sea slugs and find out that they are animals related to slugs and snails. All sea slugs have sensitive tentacles that they use to smell, taste, and feel their way around. They eat other animals by scraping away their flesh. Sea slugs can even gain the ability to sting by eating stinging animals!

Domains In classification of organisms, the broadest level of organization is the **domain**. There are three domains: Eukarya, Archaea, and Bacteria. Eukarya (yoo KA ree uh) includes the familiar kingdoms of plants, animals, and fungi, and a less familiar kingdom, Protista, which has much simpler organisms. Members of Domain Eukarya are called eukaryotes. Eukaryotes have nuclei containing DNA. Domain Archaea (ahr KEE uh) contains a group of one-celled organisms with no nuclei in their cells. Members of Domain Bacteria, like Archaea, have only one cell and no nucleus, but bacteria have different structures and chemical processes from those of Archaea. **Figure 2** shows the levels of classification for Domain Eukarya.

✓READING CHECK **Determine Central Ideas** What do scientists use to determine how organisms are classified in each level? Explain your answer.

....

....

....

Model It !

So Many Levels of Classification!

There are ways to memorize a long list of terms so that you can remember them months or even years later. A mnemonic (nee MON ic) can help you memorize a list of terms in order. To create one type of mnemonic, you compose a sentence from words that start with the first letter of each term in the list. One popular mnemonic for levels of classification is: "<u>D</u>ear <u>K</u>ing <u>P</u>hilip <u>C</u>ome <u>O</u>ver <u>F</u>or <u>G</u>ood <u>S</u>paghetti." In the space, devise your own mnemonic to help you remember the levels of classification.

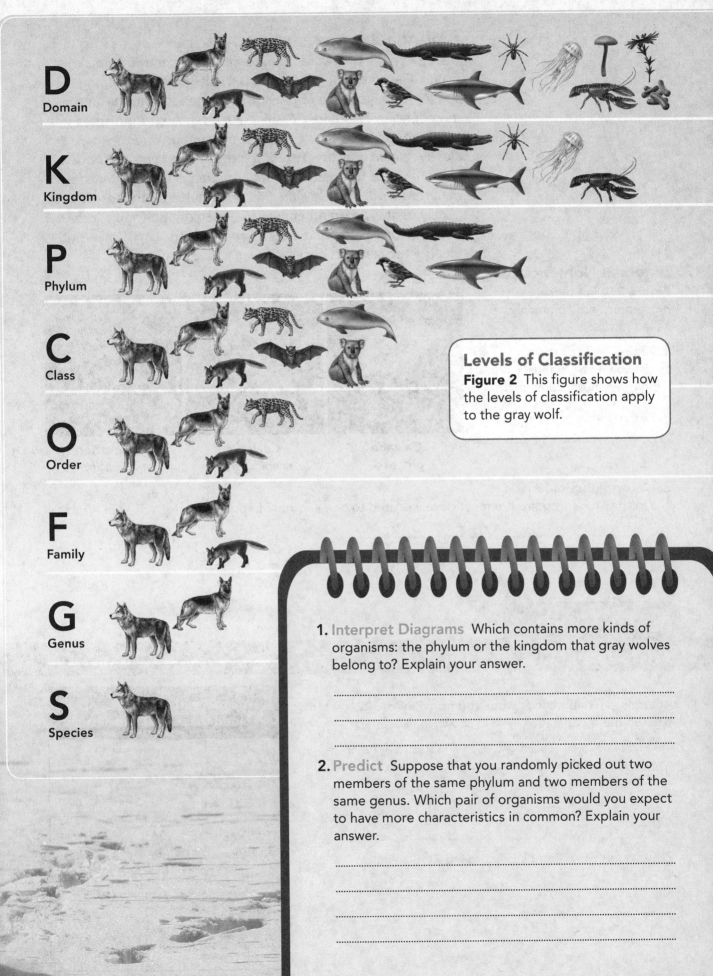

D
Domain

K
Kingdom

P
Phylum

C
Class

O
Order

F
Family

G
Genus

S
Species

Levels of Classification
Figure 2 This figure shows how the levels of classification apply to the gray wolf.

1. **Interpret Diagrams** Which contains more kinds of organisms: the phylum or the kingdom that gray wolves belong to? Explain your answer.

....

....

....

2. **Predict** Suppose that you randomly picked out two members of the same phylum and two members of the same genus. Which pair of organisms would you expect to have more characteristics in common? Explain your answer.

....

....

....

....

453

Binomial Nomenclature As explained at the start of this lesson, the first word in an organism's scientific name is its genus. The genus (plural *genera*) is a classification grouping of similar, closely related organisms. Each genus contains one or more species. The more classification levels two organisms share, the more characteristics they have in common and the more closely related they are. **Figure 3** shows a giant puffball mushroom found in the genus *Calvatia*. Another closely related kind of puffball is also in *Calvatia*. Still other puffballs that are not as closely related are in other genera. The giant puffball's species name, *gigantea*, describes its size. Together, the two words that identify the genus and species form the scientific name.

Binomial Nomenclature

Figure 3 All of these mushrooms are commonly called puffballs.

1. Make Observations
List some characteristics that all three mushrooms share.

....

....

....

Calvatia gigantea **Calvatia craniiformis** **Lycoperdon echinatum**

2. Determine Similarities
Which two mushrooms are most closely related to one another? Explain.

....

....

Math Toolbox

Aristotle and Classification

Aristotle, a Greek scholar who lived from 384 to 322 BCE, created the classification system shown in the table.

1. Write an Expression ✐ Use variables to write an expression to find the percentage of animals that swim. Then, complete the table.

....

....

2. Classify How did Aristotle organize the animals?

....

....

Animals with blood that...	Percentage of animals
fly	22%
walk, run, or hop	46%
swim	

Scientific Names A complete scientific name is written in italics. The first letter in the first word is capitalized. You will notice that most scientific names use Latin. Linnaeus used Latin in his naming system because it was the common language used by all scientists. **Figure 4** shows how using different common names for the same organism can get confusing. Scientists also use taxonomic keys, as shown in **Figure 5**, to help name and identify organisms.

☑ **READING CHECK** **Determine Meaning** How are scientific names written?

....

....

Confusing Common Names

Figure 4 Is this a firefly, a lightning bug, a glowworm, or a golden sparkler? Different names are used in different parts of the country. Luckily, this insect has only one scientific name, *Photinus pyralis*.

Predict What characteristic of the insect do you think scientists used to give it the species name *pyralis*?

....

....

Using a Taxonomic Key

Figure 5 While on a hike, you find an organism with eight legs, two body regions, claw-like pincers, and no tail. Use the key.

1. Interpret Diagrams How many different organisms can be identified using this key?

....

2. Analyze Properties Use the taxonomic key to identify the organism you observed on your hike.

....

HANDS-ON LAB

Use a taxonomic key to identify an unknown pest.

Taxonomic Key			
Step		**Characteristics**	**Organism**
1	1a.	Has 8 legs	Go to Step 2.
	1b.	Has more than 8 legs	Go to Step 3.
2	2a.	Has one oval-shaped body region	Go to Step 4.
	2b.	Has two body regions	Go to Step 5.
3	3a.	Has one pair of legs on each body segment	Centipede
	3b.	Has two pairs of legs on each body segment	Millipede
4	4a.	Is less than 1 millimeter long	Mite
	4b.	Is more than 1 millimeter long	Tick
5	5a.	Has clawlike pincers	Go to Step 6.
	5b.	Has no clawlike pincers	Spider
6	6a.	Has a long tail with a stinger	Scorpion
	6b.	Has no tail or stinger	Pseudoscorpion

Evolution and Classification

When Linnaeus was alive, people thought that species never changed. This point of view changed when Charles Darwin developed a new idea in the 1830s. Darwin was an Englishman. He sailed around the world for five years observing nature and collecting samples of fossils and animals. During the voyage, he was fascinated by the relationships between modern species and ancient types, as shown in **Figure 6**. Darwin was one of the first scientists to understand **evolution**, or the process of change over time. He concluded that all modern species developed from earlier kinds of life through natural selection. Natural selection is the idea that some individuals are better adapted to their environment than others. The better-adapted individuals are more likely to survive and reproduce than other members of the same species.

Common Ancestry Evolution by natural selection is the organizing principle of life science. Evidence from thousands of scientific investigations supports the idea of evolution. As understanding of evolution increased, biologists changed how they classify species. Scientists now understand that certain organisms may be similar because they share a common ancestor and an evolutionary history. The more similar the two groups are, in fact, the more recent their common ancestor.

1.75 million years ago (mya)

Pakicetus, land-dwelling, four-footed mammal

4.15 mya

Ambulocetus, "walking whale," mammal lived both on land and in water

4.5 mya

Dorudon, "spear tooth," water-dwelling mammal

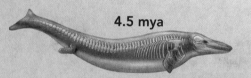

2.2 mya

Odontocetus, modern "toothed whale"

Evolution of the Dolphin

Figure 6 Darwin compared ancient and modern species to develop his theory of evolution by natural selection. Skeletons of dolphin ancestors show how the species evolved.

Form a Hypothesis Why do you think the ancient ancestor of the dolphin became a water-dwelling animal?

....

....

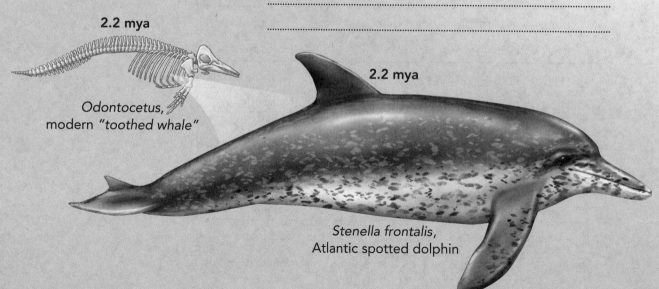

2.2 mya

Stenella frontalis, Atlantic spotted dolphin

Figure 7 These three organisms evolved a similar characteristic over time.

1. Identify ✏ Circle the characteristic that the three organisms share.

2. Form a Hypothesis Why did the same characteristic evolve?

....

....

....

....

Evolutionary Relationships Scientists **determine** the evolutionary history of a species by comparing the structures of organisms. Scientists also compare the genetic information contained in the DNA of organisms' cells. Sometimes, unrelated organisms that live in similar environments evolve similar characteristics, as shown in **Figure 7**. Sharing common characteristics, however, does not necessarily mean that organisms are closely related. The process by which unrelated organisms evolve similar characteristics is called **convergent evolution**. When scientists discovered convergent evolution, they had to change the placement of organisms within the classification system. Because scientific research leads to discovery and new knowledge, scientists sometimes reclassify organisms to account for new evidence. In this sense, the system of classification also evolves.

Academic Vocabulary

To determine is to find out an answer by doing research. When have you determined the answer to an important question?

....

....

....

....

☑ READING CHECK **Assess Sources** Suggest one reliable source of information about Charles Darwin. What makes this source reliable?

....

....

....

☑ LESSON 2 Check

1. Draw Conclusions What can you conclude about two organisms that can mate and produce fertile offspring?

....

2. Distinguish Relationships Use the chart. Which two species are most closely related? How do you know? Which species is the least related to the other three? Explain.

Some Types of Trees				
Common Name	Kingdom	Family	Genus	Species
Bird cherry	Plants	Rosaceae	*Prunus*	avium
Flowering cherry	Plants	Rosaceae	*Prunus*	serrula
Smooth-leaved elm	Plants	Ulmaceae	*Ultima*	minor
Whitebeam	Plants	Rosaceae	*Sorbus*	aria

....

....

....

....

....

3. Determine Similarities How are evolution and classification related?

....

....

....

4. Summarize How did Darwin's discoveries change scientists' understanding of species?

....

....

....

....

....

5. Evaluate Claims A friend claims her pet ferret is descended from the wild polecat. You want to learn more about this ferret ancestor. An online search shows several different kinds of polecats. How could you figure out which one is the ferret ancestor?

....

....

....

....

Quest CHECK-IN

In this lesson, you learned how scientists classify living things based on shared characteristics.

Identify Limitations What are some limitations of using a classification system to categorize living things?

....

....

....

....

HANDS-ON LAB

Classifying Seeds

Go online for a downloadable worksheet of this lab. Model a scientific classification system using seeds. Then brainstorm ideas for how you might use classification in your field guide.

MS-LS4-2

Classification:
What's a Panda?

What's in a name? In the Linnaean classification system, an animal's name tells what species it is. And with millions of species on Earth, this naming system comes in handy.

The naming system is based on observable physical characteristics—an animal's coloration, number of legs, the shape of its wings, and so on. But with today's technology, scientists can now classify animals from the inside out, by using their DNA.

DNA has helped scientists to figure out pandas, which have posed quite a puzzle. *Giant* pandas share a lot of physical traits with bears—their shape, size, shaggy fur, and lumbering movement. But smaller *red* pandas have more in common with raccoons. So what exactly is a "panda"?

Recent DNA studies show that giant pandas and red pandas are not closely related after all. Giant pandas share more DNA with bears and have been classified in the bear family (*Ursidae*). Red pandas, however, didn't make the cut. They're not bears, and, currently, they're not raccoons either. For now, they are classified in their own family, *Ailuridae*. But with further DNA evidence, this could change. Until then, the red panda is an animal unto itself.

MY DISCOVERY

Is a red panda a raccoon? The evidence points in different directions, and scientists are still debating. Read up on these animals and see what you think.

The red panda has a bushy, ringed tail, much like a raccoon's.

Are giant pandas really bears? DNA evidence reveals the answer.

459

Viruses, Bacteria, Protists, and Fungi

Guiding Questions

- What are all living things made of?
- What are the characteristics of viruses, bacteria, protists, and fungi?
- How do viruses, bacteria, protists, and fungi interact with nature and people?

Connections

Literacy Cite Textual Evidence

Math Analyze Relationships

MS-LS1-1

Vocabulary

virus
host
vaccine
bacteria
protist
parasite

Academic Vocabulary

resistant

 VOCABULARY APP

Practice vocabulary on a mobile device.

Quest CONNECTION

Think about how you could compare and contrast unicellular and multicellular organisms. How could this information help you to design a better field guide?

Connect It!

✎ **Write a checkmark on one individual of each kind of living thing you see.**

Make Observations Describe the different types of organisms you see.

....

....

Reason Why might it be unwise to drink water straight from a pond?

....

....

Microorganisms

When people think of organisms, they picture plants or animals. Yet many of the organisms we come in contact with every day are so small that you need a microscope to see them. These microorganisms are vital for the survival of all plants and animals. **Figure 1** shows some amazing microbes living in a single drop of pond water.

Protists are classified in Domain Eukarya and are simpler than the plants, animals, and fungi they are grouped with. However, organisms in Domains Archaea and Bacteria are less complex than protists. Archaea and bacteria are unicellular microorganisms that do not have a nucleus. These microorganisms are classified in different domains because of their different characteristics.

Many archaea live in extreme conditions and make food from chemicals. You might find archaea in hot springs, very salty water, or deep underground. Archaea is a great example of how science is always changing. The domain Archaea was only proposed by taxonomists in 1977!

Bacteria have different structures and chemical processes than archaea do. Some bacteria are autotrophs, meaning they can make their own food. Other bacteria are heterotrophs who must find their food. Still other types of bacteria are decomposers that absorb nutrients from decaying organisms. Bacteria are found in soil, water, and air. In fact, bacteria are found everywhere, even inside you.

✓ **READING CHECK** **Determine Central Ideas** If you had a powerful microscope, how could you determine whether a cell was from a eukaryote?

....

....

....

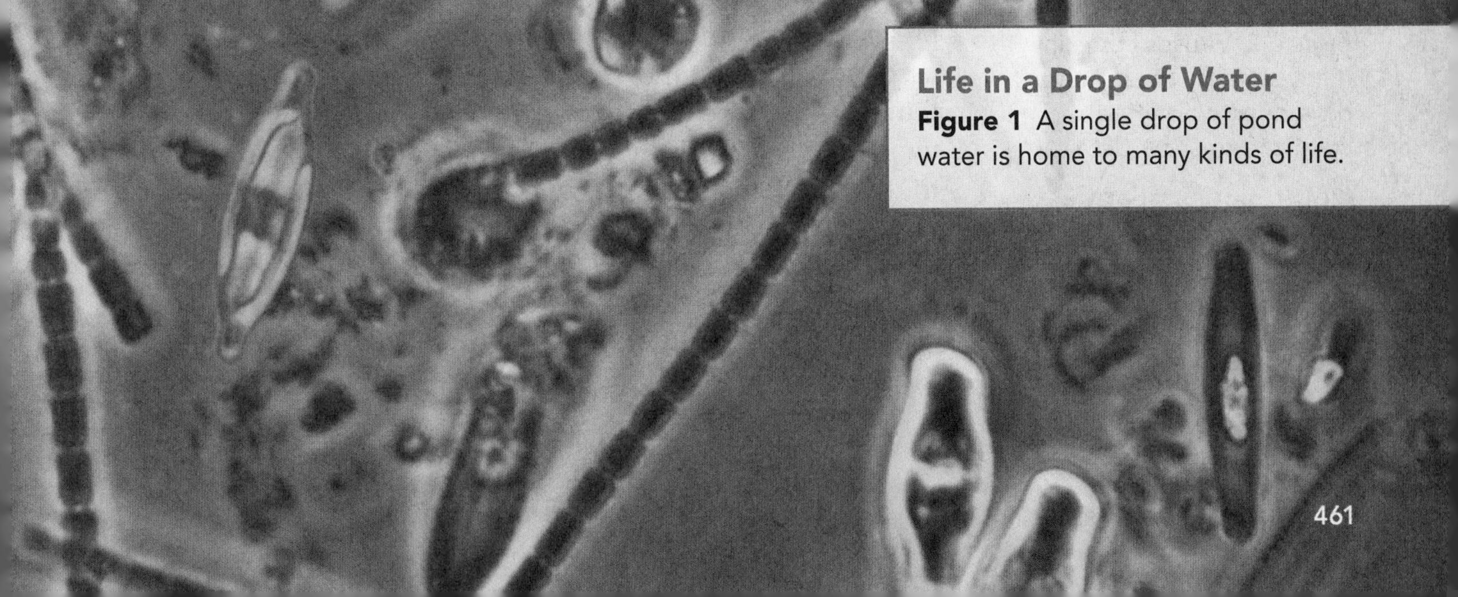

Life in a Drop of Water

Figure 1 A single drop of pond water is home to many kinds of life.

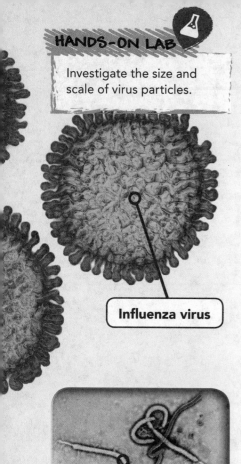

Influenza virus

Ebola virus

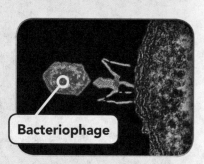

Bacteriophage

Viral Variety

Figure 2 Viruses come in many shapes. These images have been magnified and colorized to show details.

Determine Similarities
✏ Circle the virus that most closely resembles a cell. Explain your choice.

....

....

Viruses

You may have noticed that viruses were not included in the domains of living things. That's because viruses are not alive. A **virus** is a tiny, nonliving particle that enters and then reproduces inside a living cell. They lack most of the characteristics of living things. Some viruses may look like cells, but they are not cells. Viruses cannot reproduce on their own. Instead, they cause the cells they enter to reproduce more viruses. Viruses do not use food for energy or to grow. They also do not respond to their surroundings or produce wastes.

Shapes and Names Viruses can be round or shaped like bricks, threads, or bullets. Some viruses even have complex, robot-like shapes, as shown in **Figure 2**. Viruses are so small that they are measured in units called nanometers (nm), or one billionth of a meter. The common cold virus is 75 nm in diameter. The diameter of a red blood cell—7,500 nm—is much larger. Scientists name some viruses after the disease they cause or after the area where they were discovered.

Reproduction A virus is very small and simple. All viruses contain genetic material with a protein coating. The genetic material contains chemical instructions for making more copies of the virus. To reproduce, a virus attaches itself to a host cell, as shown in **Figure 3**. A **host** is an organism that provides a source of energy or a suitable environment for a virus to live. The virus either enters the cell or injects its genetic material into the host cell. Inside the host cell, the virus's genetic material takes over and forces the cell to make more copies of the virus! Finally, the host cell bursts open, releasing many new viruses which then infect other healthy cells, repeating the process.

Disease Many copies of a virus attacking your cells at once may cause a disease. Some viral diseases are mild, such as the common cold. Other viral diseases can produce serious illnesses. Viruses spread quickly and attack the cells of nearly every kind of organism. Fortunately, scientists have developed vaccines to prevent many dangerous viral diseases. A **vaccine** is a substance used in vaccination that consists of pathogens, such as viruses, that have been weakened or killed but can still trigger the body to produce chemicals that destroy the pathogens. **Figure 4** shows the vaccination process.

☑ READING CHECK **Distinguish Facts** What makes viruses so dangerous and vaccines so important?

....

....

Virus Invasion!

Figure 3 A cell invaded by a virus becomes a kind of zombie. All the cell's energy goes into making more and more new viruses.

Draw Conclusions Which came first: viruses or living organisms? Explain.

....

....

....

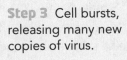

VIRUS

HOST CELL

Step 1 Virus injects genetic material into host cell.

Step 2 Cell makes copies of virus.

Step 3 Cell bursts, releasing many new copies of virus.

The virus that causes a disease is isolated. The virus is then damaged by heat, and a vaccine is prepared from it.

After being injected with a vaccine, the body prepares defenses against the virus.

The body can now resist infection by the disease-causing virus.

Vaccine Protection

Figure 4 Vaccinations can prevent measles and other viral diseases.

Construct Explanations Why is it important to use a weakened virus in a vaccine?

....

....

....

Math Toolbox

A Viral Epidemic

When a virus sickens many people at the same time within a limited geographic area, the outbreak is called an epidemic. During the 2014–2015 Ebola epidemic in West Africa, people began to get sick faster and faster beginning in May. There were about 375 new Ebola cases at the beginning of June. By July first, there were about 750 new cases.

1. **Analyze Relationships** Explain the relationship between the number of cases reported and time.

....

2. **Write an Expression** Find the number of new cases expected by September. Use an expression to plot the number of new cases for both September and October on the graph. Then finish drawing the line.

....

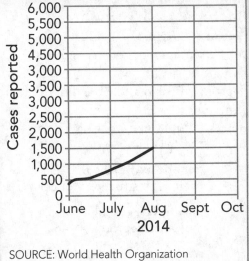

Ebola Cases in West Africa, 2014

Cases reported — 2014

SOURCE: World Health Organization

463

Figure 5 The shape of a bacteria helps a scientist to identify it.

Apply Concepts Label the shape of each bacteria.

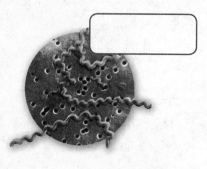

Bacteria

If life were a movie, bacteria would be both villains and heroes. Bacteria would also make up most of the supporting cast. Bacteria make up the great majority of organisms on Earth. Bacteria are very small; millions can fit into the period at the end of this sentence. The smallest bacteria are about the size of the largest viruses. Most bacteria are one of three basic shapes: ball, rod, or spiral. You can see some of these shapes in **Figure 5**. The shape of the cell helps scientists identify the type of bacteria.

Infectious Bacteria You have probably heard of *E. coli*, *Streptococcus* ("strep throat"), and *Staphylococcus* ("staph"). They are types of infectious, or disease–causing, bacteria. Someone can become infected when the bacteria enter the person's body. The bacteria then grow and multiply quite quickly. Because these bacteria give off toxins (dangerous chemicals that damage surrounding cells and tissues), they can cause serious infections. Luckily, fewer than one percent of bacteria are actually infectious.

Bacterial Cell Structures Bacteria are single-celled organisms, also known as prokaryotes, that lack a nucleus. Each cell is a separate living organism that performs all the functions needed for life. **Figure 6** shows the structure of a typical bacterial cell. Bacteria have cell walls that protect them from attacks and keep them from drying out. Inside the cell wall is a cell membrane. The cell membrane controls what substances pass into and out of the cell. Some bacteria have structures attached to the cell wall that help them move around. Flagella whip around like propellers to drive some bacteria toward their food.

Model It !

Bacterial Cell Structures

Figure 6 Structures in a bacterial cell help them function and survive.

Develop Models ✎ Use the descriptions below to label the structures.

cytoplasm everything inside the cell membrane

genetic material string-like chemical instructions for cell

pili tiny hairs that help cell move and reproduce

ribosomes round structures where proteins are made

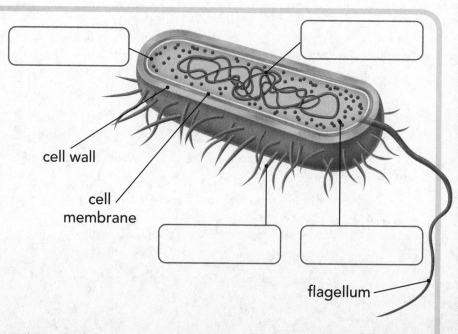

cell wall

cell membrane

flagellum

Obtaining Food Some bacteria make their own food from sunlight, like plants do. Other bacteria create food from chemicals. Chemicals from underwater volcanoes feed the bacteria in **Figure 7**. A third group of bacteria take in food through their cell walls. Food for these bacteria could be milk, sugar, meat, or dead cells. Your digestive system is a good home for bacteria! Some bacteria use the energy from food to make poisonous chemicals called toxins. Toxins cause the pain and sickness you feel when you get food poisoning.

Survival Bacteria cannot move fast. They cannot escape intense heat or hunt for food. In harsh conditions, some bacteria survive by sheltering in place. A thick-walled shell forms around genetic material and cytoplasm, forming a tough endospore. The endospore can grow back into a full cell when conditions improve.

Bacterial Reproduction Bacteria also keep ahead of predators by reproducing rapidly. Even if predators eat some individual bacteria, there are always more. Bacterial reproduction is shown in **Figure 8**. Most bacteria reproduce asexually by growing and then dividing into two identical cells. Asexual reproduction in bacteria is called binary fission.

Bacteria can also pass genetic material to a neighboring bacteria through conjugation. Conjugation occurs when two bacteria cells come together and exchange genetic material. Conjugation does not produce more bacteria, but it does allow genetic information to spread. For example, one bacterial cell could be **resistant** to antibiotics. The antibiotic-resistant cell could pass the resistance on to other bacteria by conjugation. Soon, the whole bacteria population can become resistant and the antibiotic will stop working.

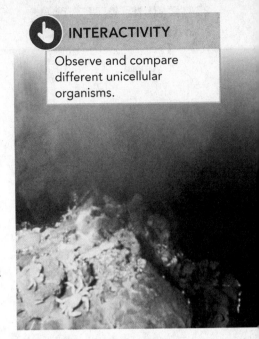

INTERACTIVITY

Observe and compare different unicellular organisms.

Undersea Mystery
Figure 7 These "rocks" are layers of bacteria that have grown up around the mouth of the seafloor volcano.

Academic Vocabulary

Resistant means able to work against or hold off an opposing force. When have you been resistant?

....

....

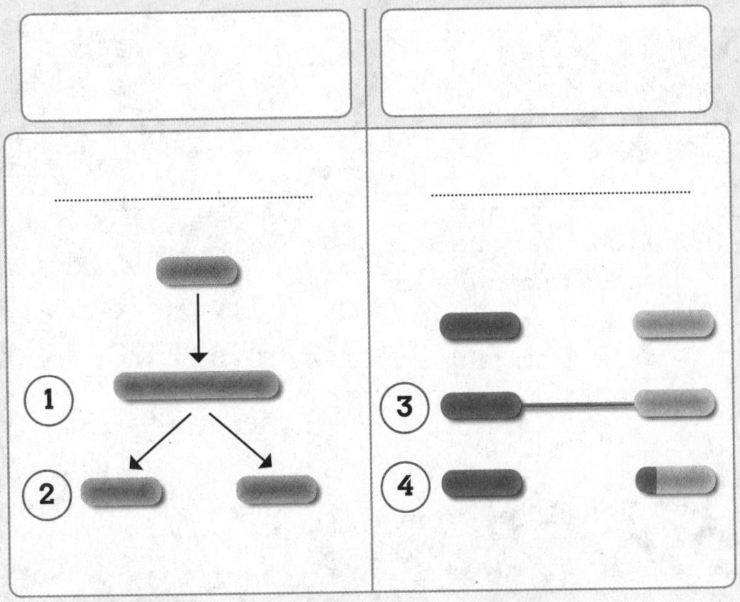

Bacterial Reproduction
Figure 8 🖉 Label the diagram with these terms: asexual reproduction, binary fission, conjugation, and transfer of genetic material. Then, match the number in the diagram to the step it describes below.

_____ Cells separate; one now has some genetic information from the other cell.

_____ Cell splits into two identical cells.

_____ Cell grows larger before dividing.

_____ One cell passes some of its genetic information to another cell.

1

2

3

4

465

Literacy Connection

Cite Textual Evidence
Would you classify bacteria as harmful or helpful? Explain.

....

....

....

....

....

The Many Roles of Bacteria

Figure 9 🖊 Bacteria do other things besides make people sick. They have many important roles in nature and human life. There are many ways we interact with bacteria. Circle or highlight one or more examples of harmful bacteria.

☑ **READING CHECK Cite Textural Evidence** According to what you have read, how do bacteria protect their genetic material and cytoplasm during harsh conditions?

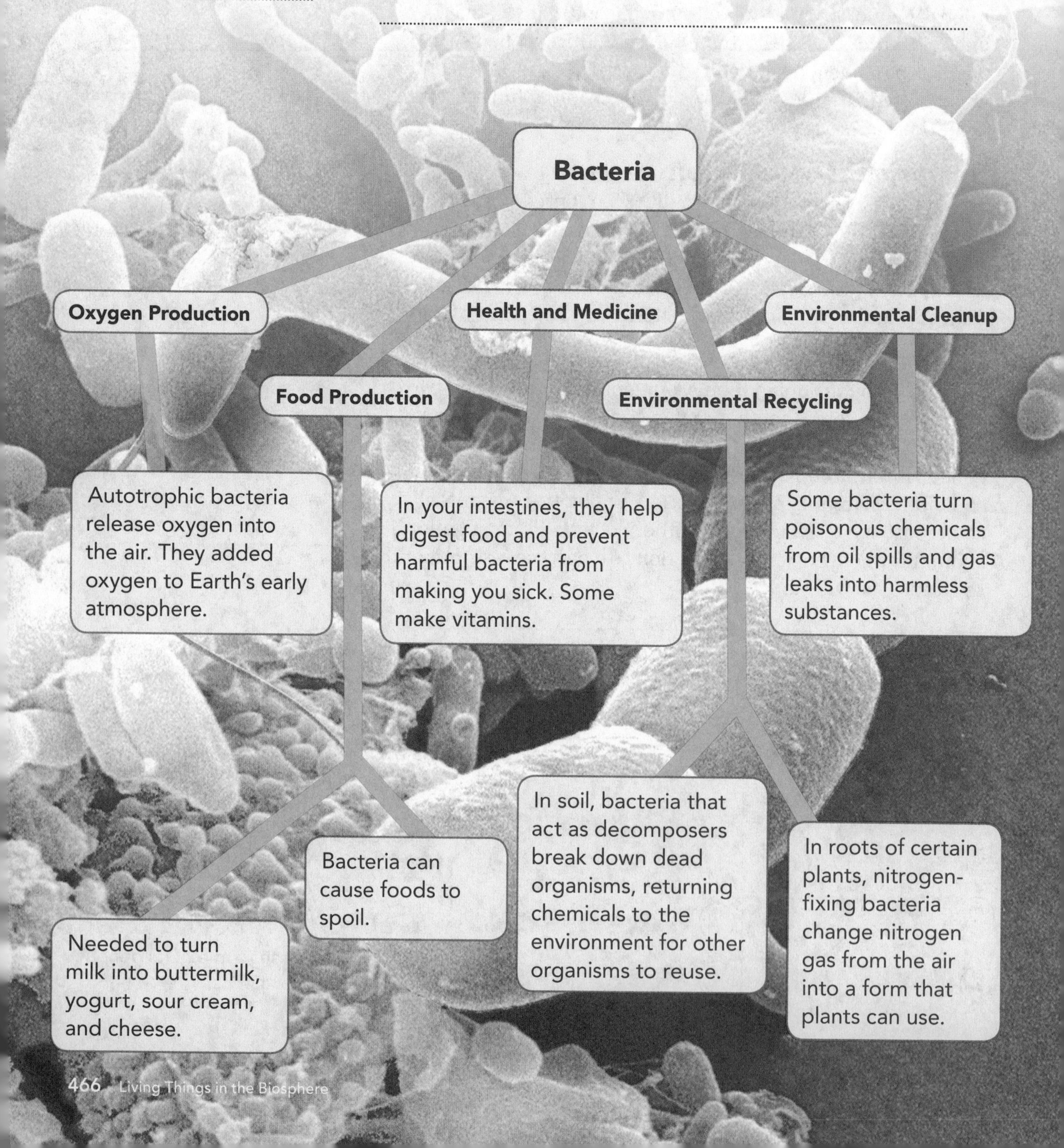

....

....

....

Bacteria

Oxygen Production

Health and Medicine

Environmental Cleanup

Food Production

Environmental Recycling

Autotrophic bacteria release oxygen into the air. They added oxygen to Earth's early atmosphere.

In your intestines, they help digest food and prevent harmful bacteria from making you sick. Some make vitamins.

Some bacteria turn poisonous chemicals from oil spills and gas leaks into harmless substances.

Bacteria can cause foods to spoil.

In soil, bacteria that act as decomposers break down dead organisms, returning chemicals to the environment for other organisms to reuse.

In roots of certain plants, nitrogen-fixing bacteria change nitrogen gas from the air into a form that plants can use.

Needed to turn milk into buttermilk, yogurt, sour cream, and cheese.

Protists

Protists are eukaryotic organisms that cannot be classified as animals, plants, or fungi. **Figure 10** shows that protists have a wide range of characteristics. All protists live in moist environments and are common where humans interact. Most protists are harmless, but some can cause illness or disease. Most harmful protists are **parasites**, organisms that benefit from living with, on, or in a host. Drinking water contaminated with these protists can cause fever, diarrhea, and abdominal pain. For example, a person can become ill after drinking water containing the protist *Giardia*. The protist attaches itself to the small intestine, where it takes in nutrients and prevents those nutrients from entering the human. The person gets ill from the disease giardiasis. Another parasitic protist travels with a mosquito. When a mosquito that is carrying the protist *Plasmodium* bites a human, the protist infects the red blood cells, causing malaria.

✓ READING CHECK **Cite Textual Evidence** Tasha and Marco examine a cell through a microscope. Tasha suggests that the cell is a protist. Marco thinks it might be a bacterium. What evidence would prove Tasha right?

....

....

HANDS-ON LAB

u**Investigate** Discover unicellular and multicellular organisms in pond water.

Diversity of Protists

Figure 10 Protists are classified in Domain Eukarya and Kingdom Protista. The three separate types are shown in the table below.

Identify Use information in the chart to identify the three photos of protists below. Write the name of each type of protist in the space provided.

	Animal-like Protists	**Plant-like Protists**	**Fungi-like Protists**
Food	Heterotrophs	Autotrophs; some also heterotrophs	Heterotrophs
Features	Unicellular	Unicellular or multicellular	Unicellular, but often live in colonies
Movement	Free-swimming	Free-swimming or attached	Move during some part of life cycle
Reproduction	Asexual and sexual	Sexual and asexual	Asexual
Examples	Amoebas: surround and trap food particles Giardia: common parasite, has eight flagella	Red algae: seaweeds people eat, known as nori Dinoflagellates: glow in the dark	Slime molds: brightly colored, grow in garden beds Water molds: attack plants, such as crops

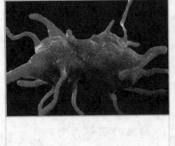

Reflect Think back to a time when you or someone you know had a fungal infection. What symptoms did the infection cause? What made the infection go away?

Fungi

What's the largest organism ever to exist on Earth? Good guesses would be a dinosaur, a blue whale, or a giant tree. These are wrong. The biggest living thing is a honey fungus colony growing under a forest in Oregon. The colony is larger than a thousand football fields! Like all other fungi, the honey fungus has eukaryotic cells with cell walls. Fungi are heterotrophs that feed by absorbing food through their cell walls. Most of the honey fungus is unseen underground. The cells of fungi are arranged into hyphae, or threadlike tubes. Hyphae, like those shown in **Figure 11**, give fungi structure and allow them to spread over large areas. Hyphae also grow into food sources and release chemicals. Food is broken down by the chemicals and then absorbed by the hyphae. Some fungi act as decomposers and consume dead organisms, while others are parasites that attack living hosts.

Fungal Reproduction
Fungi occasionally send up reproductive structures called fruiting bodies. Some fruiting bodies are the familiar mushrooms that you eat or see growing in damp environments. Fruiting bodies produce spores that are carried by wind or water to new locations. Each spore that lands in the right conditions can then start a new fungal colony. Fungi can also reproduce sexually when hyphae from two colonies grow close together and trade genetic information.

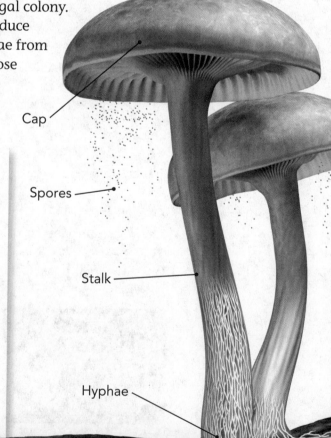

Cap

Spores

Stalk

Hyphae

Structure of a Honey Mushroom
Figure 11 The part of a mushroom you can see above ground is tiny compared to the network of hyphae underground.

Hypothesize What is a possible relationship between the fungus and the tree root?

....

....

☑ **READING CHECK Determine Central Ideas** What is the purpose of fungal spores?

....

....

Roles of Fungi

Roles of Fungi Fungi come in many forms and have varying lifestyles. We depend on fungi for many services. **Figure 12** explores some of the ways that fungi are helpful and harmful. At the same time, fungi can destroy our property and food and make us sick. You've probably heard of *athlete's foot* and *ringworm*. These are both common rashes—mild skin infections caused by fungi in the environment. They are easily treated. Some fungi, however, can cause serious diseases. In fact, more people die each year from fungal infections than from malaria and certain common cancers. There are no vaccines to prevent fungal infections.

INTERACTIVITY

Use research to develop medicine needed for someone that is ill.

Fungi: Friend or Foe?

Figure 12 ✏ Circle or highlight evidence of harm in the image descriptions.

1. **Analyze Systems** Why would a fungus growing on a rock need a partner to provide it food?

....

....

2. **Construct Explanations** Why would fungi be better than seeds at absorbing water?

....

....

Mycorrhiza

Grows around plant seeds and roots.

Brings water to plant and eats plant sugars.

Helps plants grow.

Penicillium Mold

Grows on food products.

Spoils food.

Produces chemicals used in antibiotics.

Some produce poisons or cause allergic reactions.

Shiitake Mushroom

Grows on and consumes dead logs.

Provides nutritious food.

Breaks down dead wood and makes nutrients available for living things.

Lichen

Forms partnership with autotrophic algae or bacteria.

Provides water, shelter, and minerals, while partner provides food.

Produces chemicals used in dyes, perfumes, and deodorant.

Provides food for animals in harsh environments.

Yeast

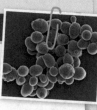

Eats carbohydrates, turning them into alcohols and carbon dioxide.

Helps to bake bread and make beverages.

Causes diaper rash and yeast infections.

Destroys stored foods.

Fungi Files

469

MS-LS1-1

1. Apply Concepts What is unique about parasites?

....

....

....

2. Identify What are three ways that fungi interact with other kinds of living things?

....

....

....

3. Construct Arguments Could you have two or more viral infections at the same time? Explain, using evidence to support your argument.

....

....

....

....

....

4. Use Scientific Reasoning Which of these taxonomic groups are most closely related: Fungi, Archaea, Bacteria, Protista? Explain.

....

....

....

....

5. Develop Models ✏ Draw a Venn Diagram to compare and contrast two types of infectious agents.

Quest CHECK-IN

In this lesson, you learned about the characteristics of viruses, bacteria, protists, and fungi. You also discovered how some of these living and nonliving things interact with nature and people.

Integrate Information When developing a classification system, do you think identifying similarities or identifying differences is more helpful? Explain.

....

....

....

INTERACTIVITY

Discovering Rainforest Organisms

Go online to classify organisms as unicellular or multicellular.

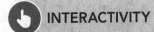

A Disease Becomes a Cure

Viruses make you sick when they work their way into healthy cells. They can do serious damage as a result. But some scientists are taking advantage of a virus's ability to invade cells to make people better.

The Challenge: To use viruses to deliver targeted therapy to cells.

Phenomenon Cancer therapies battle cancer cells, but they often damage healthy cells in the process. This can lead to serious side effects, from severe nausea to hair loss. Scientists are looking for better methods to target diseased cells while leaving healthy ones alone.

To tackle this problem, scientist James Swartz looked to nature for inspiration. Viruses, he realized, are great at targeting specific cells. He and his team re-engineered a virus by removing the disease-causing properties, leaving a hollow shell that might carry medicine inside. Next, they altered the spiky surface of the virus and attached tiny "tags" to it. The tags send the virus to sick cells to deliver medicine.

Swartz and his team still have to do a lot of research and testing to see whether this improved delivery system works. If it does, they'll have engineered a virus that works in reverse—infecting you with medicine rather than disease.

INTERACTIVITY

Explore how viruses are engineered to solve problems.

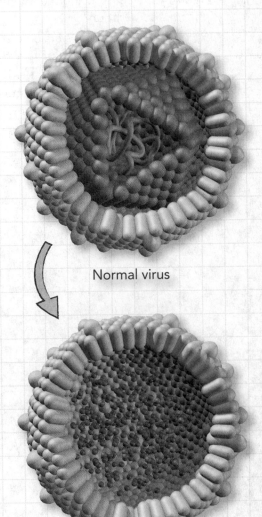

Normal virus

Re-engineered virus

The redesigned protein coat in the middle section of this virus removed the disease-causing properties, leaving the protein able to carry medicine. The spiky virus surface contains tags to direct the virus to the correct cells.

DESIGN CHALLENGE Can you engineer a virus to perform a specific function? Go to the Engineering Design Notebook to find out!

littleBits™

④ Plants and Animals

Guiding Questions

- What makes animals and plants different in form and function?
- Which special structures inside plant and animal cells determine an organism's characteristics?
- How do similar cells work together to help plants and animals function?
- Which traits are unique to animals?

Connection

Literacy Gather Information

MS-LS1-1, MS-LS1-2, MS-LS1-3

Vocabulary

tissue
vascular plants
nonvascular
 plants
vertebrates
invertebrates
organ
mammals

Academic Vocabulary

symmetry

 VOCABULARY APP

Practice vocabulary on a mobile device.

Quest CONNECTION

Gather information on the differences between unicellular organisms and multicellular organisms to include in your field guide.

Connect It!

✏ **Circle a plant and place a square around an animal.**

Determine Differences What characteristics of each organism helped you identify it as either a plant or an animal?

....

....

....

....

Form and Function

The plants and animals you see in **Figure 1**, along with protists and fungi, are all classified in Domain Eukarya. As eukaryotes, they share some characteristics. They are all made of one or more cells, and each cell contains a nucleus with DNA. However, they also have characteristics that set them apart, such as how they get energy and move around. These differences are what separate plants into Kingdom Plantae and animals into Kingdom Animalia.

All living things need water and food for energy. Plants are autotrophs, or producers. They use photosynthesis to make their own food. Plant cells have specialized structures that make food. Animals are heterotrophs, or consumers. They get food by eating other organisms. Animals have specialized body structures that break down food they consume.

Mobility, the ability to move around, also separates plants and animals. To get food, animals need to move around. Structures such as legs, fins, and wings allow movement from one place to another. Because most plants are anchored to the ground, they cannot move around.

✓ **READING CHECK** **Summarize Text** Why are plants and animals placed in different kingdoms?

....

....

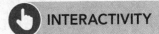
INTERACTIVITY

Explore the different types of cells that make up multi-cellular organisms.

Plants and Animals
Figure 1 Plants and animals are classified in the same domain, but their differences place them in two separate kingdoms.

HANDS-ON LAB

Investigate Discover where land plants come from.

Plant Cell Features

Figure 2 Plants need specialized structures to carry out their life functions. Label the stoma, cell wall, chloroplast, and vacuole. Then list the function of each part. Finally, circle where the chlorophyll is located.

Characteristics of Plants

All land plants are multicellular. In addition, nearly all plants are autotrophs. DNA analysis has led some scientists to classify green algae as part of the Kingdom Plantae. Almost all algae are single-celled organisms and live in the water. All plants undergo photosynthesis to make food. Plants take in carbon dioxide, water, and sunlight to produce food (and oxygen as a by-product). Specialized structures, called stomata, are located on each leaf (**Figure 2**). Each stoma (plural: stomata) is a small opening on the underside of a leaf through which oxygen, water, and carbon dioxide can move. It also prevents water loss.

Plant cells have specialized structures that serve specific functions. Look at the plant cell in **Figure 2**. Surrounding the plant cell is a strong rigid cell wall, which is used for structural support and protection. The largest structure inside the cell is the vacuole. It stores water, wastes, and food. The chloroplasts, which look like green jellybeans, are the cell structures where food is made. Chloroplasts contain a green pigment called chlorophyll that absorbs sunlight, the energy that drives photosynthesis.

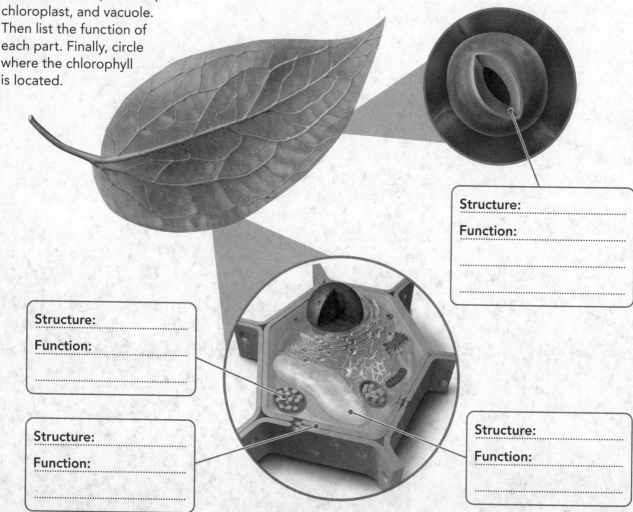

Structure: ....

Function: ....

....

Structure: ....

Function: ....

....

Structure: ....

Function: ....

....

Structure: ....

Function: ....

....

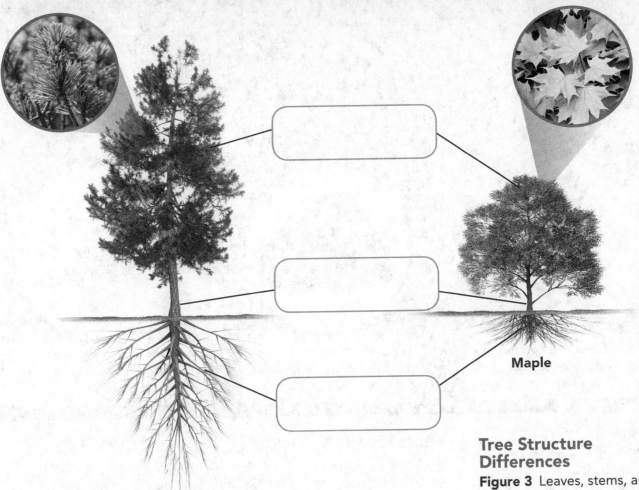

Red Pine

Maple

Plant Structure Think about the aquatic plants you identified in **Figure 1**. To make food, they need water and sunlight. But land plants need special structures to get the water they need to make food. There are three main parts to a land plant: leaves, stem or branch, and roots. A leaf has two functions: to capture light energy and gas exchange. The stem provides support and stores food for the plant. The stem is where leaves, flowers, cones, and buds grow. Stems also connect roots to leaves, so that leaves can get the water they need to carry out photosynthesis. The roots of trees have three major functions. First, roots absorb water and nutrients from the ground. Second, roots anchor the plant to the ground. Third, roots store food and nutrients. See if you can identify the different tree structures in **Figure 3**.

☑ READING CHECK **Cite Textual Evidence** What is the function of the stem on a plant?

....

....

Tree Structure Differences

Figure 3 Leaves, stems, and roots are all adaptations that help land plants survive.

1. **Identify Knowns** 🖉 Label the roots, stem, and leaves in the diagram.

2. **Determine Differences** Explain any differences in the trees' structures.

....

....

....

....

....

....

Beech Trees are seed plants that produce beechnuts and can grow to a height of 35 m.

Moss are seedless plants that do not typically grow taller than 10 cm.

Ferns are seedless plants that range in height from less than 1 cm to 25 m.

Plants

Figure 4 ✎ Some plants have vascular tissue to transport water, food, and minerals. Circle two different types of vascular plants in the picture.

Vascular Plants

Tall, short, large, or small, plants are made up of many cells. A group of similar cells that perform a specific function are called **tissues**. Some plants have vascular tissue. The cells that make up vascular tissue work together to transport water, food, and minerals through tube-like structures in the plant. Plants with true vascular tissue are **vascular plants**.

Characteristics of Vascular Plants Vascular plants have vascular tissue, true roots, and a cuticle on their leaves. Vascular tissue carries important materials like water and nutrients to all the parts of a plant. Because of the way cells are grouped together, vascular tissue also strengthens the body of the plant. This support gives plants stability and allows plants to have height. The roots of vascular plants anchor the plant to the ground, but they also draw up water and nutrients from the soil. Vascular plants have a waxy waterproof layer called a cuticle that covers the leaves and stems. Since leaves have stomata for gas exchange, the cuticle inhibits water loss.

Vascular Tissue There are two types of vascular tissue that transport materials throughout vascular plants. Food moves through the vascular tissue called phloem (FLOH um). Once food is made in the leaves, it must travel through phloem to reach other parts of the plant that need food. Water and minerals, on the other hand, travel through the xylem (ZY lum). Roots absorb water and minerals from the soil and the xylem moves them up into the stem and leaves.

Nonvascular Plants The characteristics of nonvascular plants are different from those of vascular plants. The moss in **Figure 4** is a **nonvascular plant**, a low-growing plant that lacks vascular tissue for transporting materials. Most nonvascular plants live in moist areas and feel wet, because they obtain water and minerals from their surroundings. They are only a few cell layers thick, so water and minerals do not travel far or quickly. Nonvascular plants do not have true roots that take up water and nutrients from the soil. The function of their roots is to anchor them to the ground. Also, their cell walls are thin, which prevents them from gaining height.

✓ READING CHECK **Determine Central Ideas** Name three characteristics of vascular plants that make them different from nonvascular plants.

....

....

Plan It!

Plants need water, carbon dioxide, and sunlight to grow. You want to determine the impact of sunlight on plant growth. Consider how you could prove that sunlight is an important factor in plant growth.

Plan Your Investigation 🖊 Design a procedure to investigate how sunlight affects the growth of a plant. Include a sketch of your investigation.

Procedure:

....

....

....

....

....

Sketch:

Academic Vocabulary

In math class, how would you explain an object that had symmetry?

....

....

....

Characteristics of Animals

All organisms are classified according to how they are related to other organisms, by comparing DNA, body structure and development. All animals are classified based on whether or not they have a backbone. **Vertebrates** are animals with a backbone. Animals without a backbone are classified as **invertebrates**.

Structure of Animals
All animals are multicellular and most have several different types of tissue. Complex animals have organs and organ systems. An **organ** is a body structure composed of different kinds of tissues that work together. An organ performs a more complex task than each tissue could alone. For example, the eye is a specialized sense organ. It has about ten different tissues working together to enable sight. A group of different organs that work together to perform a task is called an organ system. The organization of cells, tissues, organs, and organ systems describes an animal's body structure.

Most organisms have a balance of body parts called **symmetry**. As you see in **Figure 5**, animals have different types of symmetry or no symmetry. Animals with no symmetry are asymmetrical and have simple body structures with specialized cells but no tissues.

Types of Symmetry

Figure 5 ✏ Symmetry occurs when the organism can be divided into two or more similar parts. Draw the lines of symmetry on the animals that have radial and bilateral symmetry.

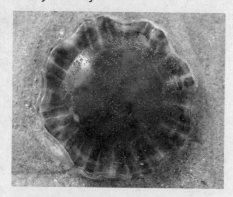

Asymmetrical Animals without symmetry, such as this sea sponge, are asymmetrical.

Radial Symetry Animals with radial symmetry, such as this jellyfish, live in water and have complex body plans with tissues and usually have organ systems. An animal has radial symmetry if many imaginary lines drawn through a central point divide the body into two mirror images.

Bilateral Symetry Most animals, such as this horseshoe crab, have bilateral symmetry. Only one line can be drawn to divide the body into halves that are mirror images.

Invertebrates Most animals are invertebrates. Scientists separate invertebrates into six main groups. **Figure 6** shows the different characteristics defining each group. While invertebrates do not have backbones, many have structures that support their bodies in a similar way. For example, arthropods have an exoskeleton, a tough waterproof outer covering that protects, supports, and helps prevent evaporation of water from the body. In contrast, echinoderms have an endoskeleton, a structural support system that is found within the animal.

✓ READING CHECK **Determine Meaning**
What is the difference between an exoskeleton and an endoskeleton?

....

....

....

👆 **INTERACTIVITY**

Determine how to use characteristics of an organism to identify it.

Echinoderms have a system of tubes to move and obtain food and oxygen.

Arthropods have jointed appendages and shed their exoskeleton as they grow.

Mollusks have one or two hard shells to protect internal organs.

Worms are simple animals but have a brain and digestive system.

Cnidarians have stinging cells and take food into a central body cavity.

Invertebrates

Figure 6 This diagram shows how scientists believe invertebrates evolved, starting with sponges and ending with echinoderms. Consider other characteristics that separate invertebrates into different groups.

Relate Structure and Function Starting at sponges and moving to echinoderms, what happens to the body structures of the invertebrates?

Sponges are made of specialized cells, adults are attached, and they take food into their bodies to get energy.

....

....

....

....

VIDEO

Explore the differences between plants and animals.

Vertebrates Most of the animals you see at an aquarium or zoo are members of the phylum Chordata and are called chordates. All chordates belong to Domain Eukaryota and Kingdom Anamalia and have a nerve cord. Most chordates, like you, have a backbone to protect the nerve cord. Some chordates, like sea squirts (**Figure 7**), do not have a backbone.

Common Structures All chordates have three structures in common: a notochord, a nerve cord, and pouches in the throat area. A notochord is a flexible rod that supports the chordate's back. The nerve cord runs down the back. It connects the brain to nerves. For most chordates, the throat pouches disappear before birth. In fish, they become gill slits.

Body Temperature Vertebrates must maintain their body temperature (**Figure 7**). Animals, such as amphibians and reptiles, that produce little internal body heat are ectotherms. Their body temperature changes with the environment. To stay warm, they go to a sunny spot and bask in sunlight. In contrast, endotherms control their internal heat and regulate their own temperature. Birds and mammals are endotherms. They have structures such as sweat glands, fur or feathers.

Vertebrate Groups **Figure 8** shows the five major groups of vertebrates: fish, amphibians, reptiles, birds, and mammals. Members of each group share unique characteristics. For example, a **mammal** is a vertebrate whose body temperature is regulated by its internal heat, and has skin covered with hair or fur and glands that produce milk to feed its young.

Animals Control Their Body Temperature

Figure 7 Animals control their body temperature one of two ways.

1. **Apply Scientific Reasoning** Determine whether each animal is an endotherm or ectotherm.

2. **Construct Explanations** Would it be more difficult for a hare to live in a tropical rainforest or a frog to live in the Arctic? Explain.

....

....

....

sea squirts

Monotremes are the only egg-laying mammals. Examples include: duck-billed platypus and spiny anteaters.

Marsupials carry their young in a pouch. Examples include: kangaroo, koalas, possums, and opossums.

Placentals have live births. While developing in the mother, the embryo receives nourishment from an organ that surrounds the embryo called a placenta. Examples include: rodents, whales, cattle, dogs, and humans.

Mammals have mammary glands to feed their young milk. They are further grouped into three types: monotremes, marsupials, and placentals.

Birds have wings, lightweight bones, and a 4-chambered heart.

Reptiles have scales, thick skin, and lay their eggs on land.

Amphibians have permeable skin; live their early life in water and adult life on land.

Fish live in water, have scales, and use gills to collect dissolved oxygen.

Vertebrates

Figure 8 This diagram shows how scientists believe vertebrates evolved, starting with fish and ending with mammals. Consider other differences among these five groups of vertebrates.

1. **Describe Patterns** What is one characteristic that amphibians, reptiles, birds, and mammals share?

....

2. **Determine Differences** How are amphibians different from fish?

....

481

Movement Adaptations

Figure 9 Animals display a wide range of adaptations for movement. ✏ Rate each movement adaptation from 1 (fastest) to 5 (slowest) in the circles. Explain your highest rank.

....

....

....

Wings Birds and insects have wings that allow them to fly, hover, dive, and soar.

Fins Fish and whales have fins, and their bodies are streamlined to help them move through water.

Tube Feet Echinoderms have several tiny tube feet under their body. Water moves from their vascular system to the tube feet. This water movement expands each foot, causing it to move.

Muscular Foot Mollusks have a foot that is made of several thin muscles. This foot is used for digging or creeping along the surface.

Jet Propulsion Octopuses take water into a muscular sac and quickly expel it out a narrow opening to move. They also elongate and contract their arms to move.

👆 **INTERACTIVITY**

Explain the organization of different organisms.

☑ READING CHECK

Draw Evidence What adaptations does the octopus have that would help it open a jar?

....

....

....

Traits Unique to Animals

All animals have unique traits. Characteristics that organisms inherit to help them survive in their environment are called adaptations. These adaptations may be used to separate animals into minor groups.

Adaptations for Movement Animals have a variety of adaptations for movement. Humans walk on two legs, while other animals use four. Animals are best adapted to the environment in which they live. As you see in **Figure 9**, adaptations vary greatly within the animal kingdom.

Adaptations for Conserving Water Obtaining fresh water from the salty ocean or dry desert is difficult for animals. Some animals, however, have adaptations that help them hold on to as much water as they can. A reptile's kidneys can remove solid material from its waste and then reabsorb the liquid material. Because they recycle the fluid part of their waste, reptiles do not need to take in as much water. Whales, seals, and dolphins also have specialized kidneys to conserve water. Their fresh water comes from the food they eat. Their waste first passes through a filter that removes the salt. It then passes through another tube that absorbs more water.

MS-LS1-1, MS-LS1-2, MS-LS1-3

1. **Determine Similarities** What are two characteristics that both plants and animals have in common?

....

....

2. **Analyze Properties** How do some animals protect themselves against water loss?

....

....

....

3. **Apply Concepts** What is the function of a backbone in vertebrates?

....

....

4. **Relate Structure and Function** What are the three functions of roots?

....

....

....

....

....

....

5. **Apply Scientific Reasoning** The tallest plants on Earth are redwood trees. They can grow to heights over 100 m. How are redwood trees able to transport water and nutrients from their roots to their leaves?

....

....

....

....

....

....

....

6. **Construct Explanations** Why are organisms that have organs classified as more complex than organisms without organs?

....

....

....

....

....

....

....

Quest CHECK-IN

In this lesson, you learned that plants and animals are classified into different groups based on their cell structures, presence of different tissue types, traits, and adaptations.

Classify When you create your field guide, what physical characteristics would you use to separate plants and animals?

....

....

....

....

👆 INTERACTIVITY

Multicellular Rainforest Organisms

Go online to to take a field trip to a rain forest. There, you will make observations and use them to classify various organisms.

☑TOPIC 10 Review and Assess

1 Living Things

MS-LS1-1

1. What are the basic building blocks of all living things?
A. food
B. energy
C. cells
D. water

2. Which is an example of homeostasis?
A. reproduction
B. controlling an experiment
C. growth and development
D. maintaining a steady temperature

3. The kind of reproduction that requires two parents is called _____.

4. Analyze Systems An oasis is a place in a sandy desert where water rises to the surface. Trees and plants often grow by the water and animals make their homes there. What would happen to the organisms living in an oasis if the water dried up?

....

....

....

5. Construct Explanations Design a controlled experiment to demonstrate that birds do not spontaneously generate on birdfeeders.

....

....

....

....

....

....

2 Classification Systems

MS-LS4-2

6. The mosquito *Aedes aegypti* is a carrier of the Zika virus. *Aedes* is the name of the mosquito's
A. order.
B. family.
C. genus.
D. species.

7. Which could happen through convergent evolution?
A. Two unrelated species could evolve into one species.
B. Two unrelated species could evolve similar features.
C. Two unrelated species could evolve very different features.
D. Two unrelated species could finish evolving.

8. Two organisms that share several classification levels will be _____

and have _____
in common.

9. Make Models ✏ Develop a taxonomic key that a person could use to identify the following animals: hawk, alligator, duck, snake.

hawk   alligator   duck   snake

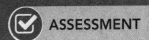
3 Viruses, Bacteria, Protists, and Fungi

MS-LS1-1

10. Which of the following groups is always heterotrophic?
A. Domain Archaea
B. Domain Bacteria
C. Kingdom Fungi
D. Kingdom Protista

11. Which of the following statements is true about viruses?
A. Viruses contain very small cells.
B. Viruses never eat any food.
C. Viruses can reproduce themselves quickly.
D. Viruses have hyphae that help them take up water.

12. Two ways that bacteria help people are
.... and
....

13. Explain Why is *diverse* a good word to use to describe protists?
....
....
....
....
....

14. Predict Describe three problems that could occur if all the fungi on Earth disappeared.
....
....
....
....

4 Plants and Animals

MS-LS1-1, MS-LS1-2, MS-LS1-3

15. Cause and Effect Explain why vascular plants can gain height, but nonvascular plants only grow close to the ground.
....
....
....
....
....
....
....
....
....
....
....

16. Compare and Contrast Explain how vertebrates and invertebrates are similar and different.
....
....
....
....
....
....
....
....
....

MS-LS1-1, MS-LS1-2, MS-LS1-3

Evidence-Based Assessment

Naya is using a microscope to investigate the similarities and differences between two organisms. One is an animal called a rotifer and the other is a protist called a paramecium. She records her observations about both organisms in a table.

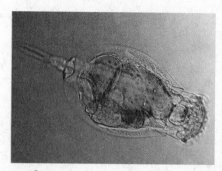

rotifer

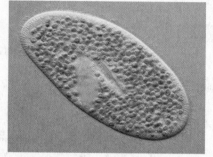

paramecium

Observations	Organism A	Organism B
Organization is more complex	X	
Injury to one cell does not affect ability of the organism to stay alive	X	
Organism's lifespan is relatively short		X
Contains substances such as water, proteins, and lipids	X	X
Creates offspring through sexual reproduction	X	X
Gets energy by using hair-like structures to move food into its mouth		X
Requires energy in order to survive	X	X
Can only be observed with microscope	X	X
Responds to surroundings		
No cell differentiation		
One cell carries out necessary functions for life		

1. **Analyze Data** Based on the data in the table, which statement is true?
   A. Organism A is multicellular.
   B. Organism B is multicellular.
   C. Both organisms are unicellular.
   D. Both organisms are multicellular.

2. Naya adds another row for the following observation: Can only be produced from other living cells. For which organism is this statement true?
   A. Organism A
   B. Organism B
   C. Both organisms
   D. Neither organism

3. **Use Scientific Reasoning** Which organism is Organism A? Which is Organism B? Explain how you classified the organisms as you did.

....

....

....

....

....

4. **Make Observations** Refer to the images and existing observations to complete the table for the last three observations. Write an X in the appropriate column(s).

5. **Apply Concepts** Suppose that Naya decides to observe a sample of quartz, a mineral found in Earth's crust. If Naya were to add quartz to the table, which observations could she check off for it? Explain.

....

....

....

....

....

6. **Construct Arguments** Explain why both the paramecium and rotifer are considered living things. Which organism is more complex, and which has better chances of survival?

....

....

....

....

....

....

....

....

Quest FINDINGS

Complete the Quest!

Phenomenon In a group, identify the criteria and constraints for your field guide. Then, create your guide for the nature center.

Identify Limitations What are some of the drawbacks or difficulties in using classification systems in your field guide? How else could you organize living things?

....

....

....

....

....

....

👆 **INTERACTIVITY**

Create Your Field Guide

It's Alive!

How can you **gather evidence** to **distinguish living** things from **nonliving** things?

Background

Phenomenon Before scientists could peer into microscopes, they had very different ideas about what living things were made of. It was a challenge to classify organisms when they couldn't even distinguish between living and nonliving things.

It may seem pretty obvious to you today that a flower is a living thing and a rock is a nonliving thing. But how could you explain this difference to a class of third-grade students in a way they would understand? In this investigation, you will observe samples of living and nonliving things. You will use the data you collect to develop an explanation of how living things can be distinguished from nonliving things.

Materials

(per pair)

- hand lens
- samples of living and nonliving things
- prepared slides or microscope pictures of living and nonliving things
- microscope

Safety

Be sure to follow all safety guidelines provided by your teacher. The Safety Appendix of your textbook provides more details about the safety icons.

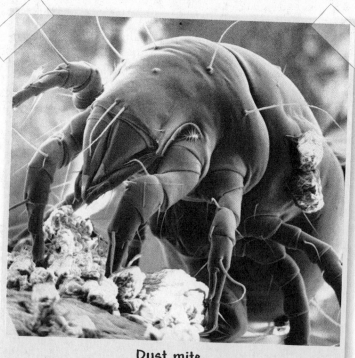

Dust mite

Procedure

1. Work with a partner. At your workstation, you should have a hand lens, a microscope, and paper and pencils for drawing.

2. Discuss with your partner what you should be looking for to help you determine whether your samples are living or nonliving. Then, from the class supplies, choose one sample and the microscope slide or microscope photograph that goes with it. Take them to your station to examine.

3. On a separate paper, make detailed observations of your sample, label it, note whether it is living or nonliving, and describe any structures you observe.

4. Return your sample and select a new one. Continue until you have examined five different samples. You should include three different organisms and two nonliving things, and include at least one fungus and one autotroph.

5. Based on your observations, complete the data table that follows. There may be some spaces that you are not sure how to fill out. If you have time, take another look at the sample(s) in question to gather more evidence.

HANDS-ON LAB

Demonstrate Go online for a downloadable worksheet of this lab.

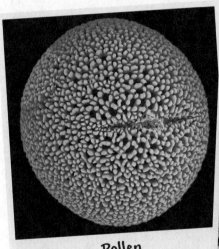

Pollen

Honey

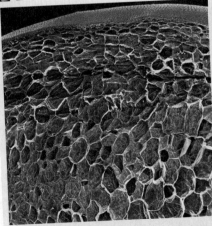

Cross-section of tomato

Observations

Which Samples Are Living or Nonliving?			
Sample Name	Living or Nonliving?	Observations	Sketches

Analyze and Interpret Data

1. **Evaluate Scale** Why is the microscope necessary for determining whether a sample is living or nonliving?

   ....

   ....

   ....

   ....

2. **Analyze Properties** Compare the appearance of the living samples to the appearance of the nonliving samples. How do you explain the differences in structures?

   ....

   ....

   ....

   ....

   ....

   ....

3. **Apply Concepts** Based on what you observed, what are some ways that the living things in this lab could be grouped or organized?

   ....

   ....

   ....

   ....

4. **Construct Explanations** How would you explain to a class of third-graders the difference between living things and nonliving things? What are some examples you would give to support your thinking?

   ....

   ....

   ....

   ....

   ....

SEP.1, SEP.8

The Meaning of Science

Science Skills

Reflect Think about a time you misplaced something and could not find it. Write a sentence defining the problem. What science skills could you use to solve the problem? Explain how you would use at least three of the skills in the table.

Science is a way of learning about the natural world. It involves asking questions, making predictions, and collecting information to see if the answer is right or wrong.

The table lists some of the skills that scientists use. You use some of these skills every day. For example, you may observe and evaluate your lunch options before choosing what to eat.

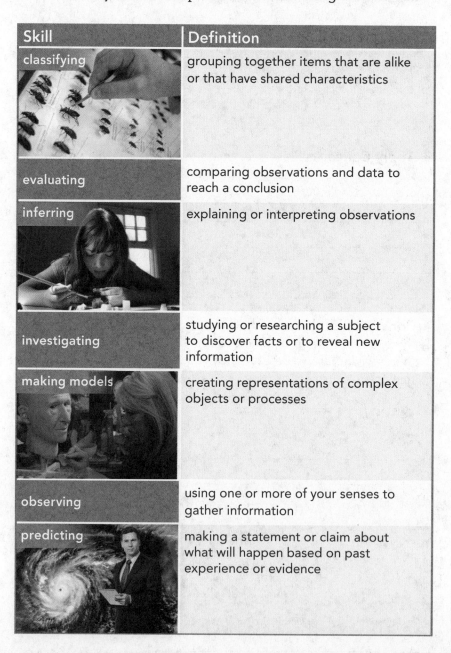

Skill	Definition
classifying	grouping together items that are alike or that have shared characteristics
evaluating	comparing observations and data to reach a conclusion
inferring	explaining or interpreting observations
investigating	studying or researching a subject to discover facts or to reveal new information
making models	creating representations of complex objects or processes
observing	using one or more of your senses to gather information
predicting	making a statement or claim about what will happen based on past experience or evidence

Scientific Attitudes

Curiosity often drives scientists to learn about the world around them. Creativity is useful for coming up with inventive ways to solve problems. Such qualities and attitudes, and the ability to keep an open mind, are essential for scientists.

When sharing results or findings, honesty and ethics are also essential. Ethics refers to rules for knowing right from wrong.

Being skeptical is also important. This means having doubts about things based on past experiences and evidence. Skepticism helps to prevent accepting data and results that may not be true.

Scientists must also avoid bias—likes or dislikes of people, ideas, or things. They must avoid experimental bias, which is a mistake that may make an experiment's preferred outcome more likely.

Scientific Reasoning

Scientific reasoning depends on being logical and objective. When you are objective, you use evidence and apply logic to draw conclusions. Being subjective means basing conclusions on personal feelings, biases, or opinions. Subjective reasoning can interfere with science and skew results. Objective reasoning helps scientists use observations to reach conclusions about the natural world.

Scientists use two types of objective reasoning: deductive and inductive. Deductive reasoning involves starting with a general idea or theory and applying it to a situation. For example, the theory of plate tectonics indicates that earthquakes happen mostly where tectonic plates meet. You could then draw the conclusion, or deduce, that California has many earthquakes because tectonic plates meet there.

In inductive reasoning, you make a generalization from a specific observation. When scientists collect data in an experiment and draw a conclusion based on that data, they use inductive reasoning. For example, if fertilizer causes one set of plants to grow faster than another, you might infer that the fertilizer promotes plant growth.

Make Meaning
Think about a bias the marine biologist in the photo could show that results in paying more or less attention to one kind of organism over others. Make a prediction about how that bias could affect the biologist's survey of the coral reef.

Write About It
Suppose it is raining when you go to sleep one night. When you wake up the next morning, you observe frozen puddles on the ground and icicles on tree branches. Use scientific reasoning to draw a conclusion about the air temperature outside. Support your conclusion using deductive or inductive reasoning.

493

SEP.1, SEP.2, SEP.3, SEP.4, CCC.4

Science Processes

Scientific Inquiry

Scientists contribute to scientific knowledge by conducting investigations and drawing conclusions. The process often begins with an observation that leads to a question, which is then followed by the development of a hypothesis. This is known as scientific inquiry.

One of the first steps in scientific inquiry is asking questions. However, it's important to make a question specific with a narrow focus so the investigation will not be too broad. A biologist may want to know all there is to know about wolves, for example. But a good, focused question for a specific inquiry might be "How many offspring does the average female wolf produce in her lifetime?"

A hypothesis is a possible answer to a scientific question. A hypothesis must be testable. For something to be testable, researchers must be able to carry out an investigation and gather evidence that will either support or disprove the hypothesis.

Scientific Models

Models are tools that scientists use to study phenomena indirectly. A model is any representation of an object or process. Illustrations, dioramas, globes, diagrams, computer programs, and mathematical equations are all examples of scientific models. For example, a diagram of Earth's crust and mantle can help you to picture layers deep below the surface and understand events such as volcanic eruptions.

Models also allow scientists to represent objects that are either very large, such as our solar system, or very small, such as a molecule of DNA. Models can also represent processes that occur over a long period of time, such as the changes that have occurred throughout Earth's history.

Models are helpful, but they have limitations. Physical models are not made of the same materials as the objects they represent. Most models of complex objects or processes show only major parts, stages, or relationships. Many details are left out. Therefore, you may not be able to learn as much from models as you would through direct observation.

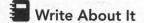 **Write About It** Describe a question that you posed, formally or informally, about an event in your life that you needed to investigate or resolve. Write the hypothesis you developed to answer your question, and describe how you tested the hypothesis.

Reflect Identify the benefits and limitations of using a plastic model of DNA, as shown here.

Science Experiments

An experiment or investigation must be well planned to produce valid results. In planning an experiment, you must identify the independent and dependent variables. You must also do as much as possible to remove the effects of other variables. A controlled experiment is one in which you test only one variable at a time.

For example, suppose you plan a controlled experiment to learn how the type of material affects the speed at which sound waves travel through it. The only variable that should change is the type of material. This way, if the speed of sound changes, you know that it is a result of a change in the material, not another variable such as the thickness of the material or the type of sound used.

You should also remove bias from any investigation. You may inadvertently introduce bias by selecting subjects you like and avoiding those you don't like. Scientists often conduct investigations by taking random samples to avoid ending up with biased results.

Once you plan your investigation and begin to collect data, it's important to record and organize the data. You may wish to use a graph to display and help you to interpret the data.

Write About It
List four ways you could communicate the results of a scientific study about the health of sea turtles in the Pacific Ocean.

Communicating is the sharing of ideas and results with others through writing and speaking. Communicating data and conclusions is a central part of science.

Scientists share knowledge, including new findings, theories, and techniques for collecting data. Conferences, journals, and websites help scientists to communicate with each other. Popular media, including newspapers, magazines, and social media sites, help scientists to share their knowledge with nonscientists. However, before the results of investigations are shared and published, other scientists should review the experiment for possible sources of error, such as bias and unsupported conclusions.

SEP.1, SEP.6, SEP.7, SEP.8

Scientific Knowledge

Scientific Explanations

Suppose you learn that adult flamingos are pink because of the food they eat. This statement is a scientific explanation—it describes how something in nature works or explains why it happens. Scientists from different fields use methods such as researching information, designing experiments, and making models to form scientific explanations. Scientific explanations often result from many years of work and multiple investigations conducted by many scientists.

Scientific Theories and Laws

A scientific law is a statement that describes what you can expect to occur every time under a particular set of conditions. A scientific law describes an observed pattern in nature, but it does not attempt to explain it. For example, the law of superposition describes what you can expect to find in terms of the ages of layers of rock. Geologists use this observed pattern to determine the relative ages of sedimentary rock layers. But the law does not explain why the pattern occurs.

By contrast, a scientific theory is a well-tested explanation for a wide range of observations or experimental results. It provides details and describes causes of observed patterns. Something is elevated to a theory only when there is a large body of evidence that supports it. However, a scientific theory can be changed or overturned when new evidence is found.

▮ Write About It
Choose two fields of science that interest you. Describe a method used to develop scientific explanations in each field.

Compare and Contrast Complete the table to compare and contrast a scientific theory and a scientific law.

	Scientific Theory	Scientific Law
Definition		
Does it attempt to explain a pattern observed in nature?		

Analyzing Scientific Explanations

To analyze scientific explanations that you hear on the news or read in a book such as this one, you need scientific literacy. Scientific literacy means understanding scientific terms and principles well enough to ask questions, evaluate information, and make decisions. Scientific reasoning gives you a process to apply. This includes looking for bias and errors in the research, evaluating data, and identifying faulty reasoning. For example, by evaluating how a survey was conducted, you may find a serious flaw in the researchers' methods.

Evidence and Opinions

The basis for scientific explanations is empirical evidence. Empirical evidence includes the data and observations that have been collected through scientific processes. Satellite images, photos, and maps of mountains and volcanoes are all examples of empirical evidence that support a scientific explanation about Earth's tectonic plates. Scientists look for patterns when they analyze this evidence. For example, they might see a pattern that mountains and volcanoes often occur near tectonic plate boundaries.

To evaluate scientific information, you must first distinguish between evidence and opinion. In science, evidence includes objective observations and conclusions that have been repeated. Evidence may or may not support a scientific claim. An opinion is a subjective idea that is formed from evidence, but it cannot be confirmed by evidence.

Write About It
Suppose the conservation committee of a town wants to gauge residents' opinions about a proposal to stock the local ponds with fish every spring. The committee pays for a survey to appear on a web site that is popular with people who like to fish. The results of the survey show 78 people in favor of the proposal and two against it. Do you think the survey's results are valid? Explain.

Make Meaning
Explain what empirical evidence the photograph reveals.

SEP.3, SEP.4

Tools of Science

Measurement

Making measurements using standard units is important in all fields of science. This allows scientists to repeat and reproduce other experiments, as well as to understand the precise meaning of the results of others. Scientists use a measurement system called the International System of Units, or SI.

For each type of measurement, there is a series of units that are greater or less than each other. The unit a scientist uses depends on what is being measured. For example, a geophysicist tracking the movements of tectonic plates may use centimeters, as plates tend to move small amounts each year. Meanwhile, a marine biologist might measure the movement of migrating bluefin tuna on the scale of kilometers.

Units for length, mass, volume, and density are based on powers of ten—a meter is equal to 100 centimeters or 1000 millimeters. Units of time do not follow that pattern. There are 60 seconds in a minute, 60 minutes in an hour, and 24 hours in a day. These units are based on patterns that humans perceived in nature. Units of temperature are based on scales that are set according to observations of nature. For example, 0°C is the temperature at which pure water freezes, and 100°C is the temperature at which it boils.

Write About It

Suppose you are planning an investigation in which you must measure the dimensions of several small mineral samples that fit in your hand. Which metric unit or units will you most likely use? Explain your answer.

Measurement	Metric units
Length or distance	meter (m), kilometer (km), centimeter (cm), millimeter (mm) 1 km = 1,000 m 1 cm = 10 mm 1 m = 100 cm
Mass	kilogram (kg), gram (g), milligram (mg) 1 kg = 1,000 g 1 g = 1,000 mg
Volume	cubic meter (m³), cubic centimeter (cm³) 1 m³ = 1,000,000 cm³
Density	kilogram per cubic meter (kg/m³), gram per cubic centimeter (g/cm³) 1,000 kg/m³ = 1 g/cm³
Temperature	degrees Celsius (°C), kelvin (K) 1°C = 273 K
Time	hour (h), minute (m), second (s)

Math Skills

Using numbers to collect and interpret data involves math skills that are essential in science. For example, you use math skills when you estimate the number of birds in an entire forest after counting the actual number of birds in ten trees.

Scientists evaluate measurements and estimates for their precision and accuracy. In science, an accurate measurement is very close to the actual value. Precise measurements are very close, or nearly equal, to each other. Reliable measurements are both accurate and precise. An imprecise value may be a sign of an error in data collection. This kind of anomalous data may be excluded to avoid skewing the data and harming the investigation.

Other math skills include performing specific calculations, such as finding the mean, or average, value in a data set. The mean can be calculated by adding up all of the values in the data set and then dividing that sum by the number of values.

Hour	Number of Ducks Observed at a Pond
1	12
2	10
3	2
4	14
5	13
6	10
7	11

Calculate The data table shows how many ducks were seen at a pond every hour over the course of seven hours. Is there a data point that seems anomalous? If so, cross out that data point. Then, calculate the mean number of ducks on the pond. Round the mean to the nearest whole number.

Graphs

Graphs help scientists to interpret data by helping them to find trends or patterns in the data. A line graph displays data that show how one variable (the dependent or outcome variable) changes in response to another (the independent or test variable). The slope and shape of a graph line can reveal patterns and help scientists to make predictions. For example, line graphs can help you to spot patterns of change over time.

Scientists use bar graphs to compare data across categories or subjects that may not affect each other. The heights of the bars make it easy to compare those quantities. A circle graph, also known as a pie chart, shows the proportions of different parts of a whole.

Write About It
You and a friend record the distance you travel every 15 minutes on a one-hour bike trip. Your friend wants to display the data as a circle graph. Explain whether or not this is the best type of graph to display your data. If not, suggest another graph to use.

SEP.1, SEP.2, SEP.3, SEP.6

The Engineering and Design Process

Engineers are builders and problem solvers. Chemical engineers experiment with new fuels made from algae. Civil engineers design roadways and bridges. Bioengineers develop medical devices and prosthetics. The common trait among engineers is an ability to identify problems and design solutions to solve them. Engineers use a creative process that relies on scientific methods to help guide them from a concept or idea all the way to the final product.

Define the Problem

To identify or define a problem, different questions need to be asked: *What are the effects of the problem? What are the likely causes? What other factors could be involved?* Sometimes the obvious, immediate cause of a problem may be the result of another problem that may not be immediately apparent. For example, climate change results in different weather patterns, which in turn can affect organisms that live in certain habitats. So engineers must be aware of all the possible effects of potential solutions. Engineers must also take into account how well different solutions deal with the different causes of the problem.

Reflect Write about a problem that you encountered in your life that had both immediate, obvious causes as well as less-obvious and less-immediate ones.

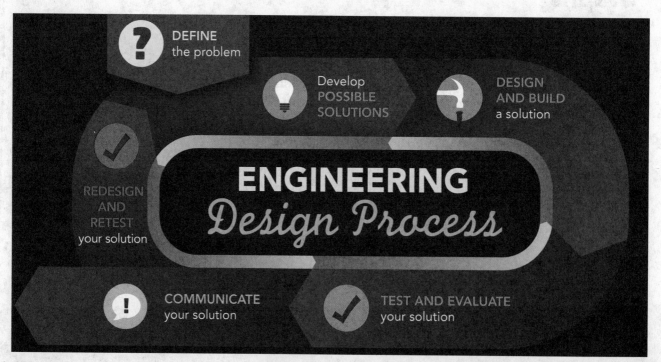

DEFINE the problem

Develop POSSIBLE SOLUTIONS

DESIGN AND BUILD a solution

REDESIGN AND RETEST your solution

ENGINEERING *Design Process*

COMMUNICATE your solution

TEST AND EVALUATE your solution

As engineers consider problems and design solutions, they must identify and categorize the criteria and constraints of the project.

Criteria are the factors that must be met or accomplished by the solution. For example, a gardener who wants to protect outdoor plants from deer and rabbits may say that the criteria for the solution are "plants are no longer eaten" and "plant growth is not inhibited in any way." The gardener then knows the plants cannot simply be sealed off from the environment, because the plants will not receive sunlight and water.

The same gardener will likely have constraints on his solution, such as budget for materials and time that is available for working on the project. By setting constraints, a solution can be designed that will be successful without introducing a new set of problems. No one wants to spend $500 on materials to protect $100 worth of tomatoes and cucumbers.

Develop Possible Solutions

After the problem has been identified, and the criteria and constraints identified, an engineer will consider possible solutions. This often involves working in teams with other engineers and designers to brainstorm ideas and research materials that can be used in the design.

It's important for engineers to think creatively and explore all potential solutions. If you wanted to design a bicycle that was safer and easier to ride than a traditional bicycle, then you would want more than just one or two solutions. Having multiple ideas to choose from increases the likelihood that you will develop a solution that meets the criteria and constraints. In addition, different ideas that result from brainstorming can often lead to new and better solutions to an existing problem.

Make Meaning
Using the example of a garden that is vulnerable to wild animals such as deer, make a list of likely constraints on an engineering solution to the problem you identified before. Determine if there are common traits among the constraints, and identify categories for them.

Design a Solution

Engineers then develop the idea that they feel best solves the problem. Once a solution has been chosen, engineers and designers get to work building a model or prototype of the solution. A model may involve sketching on paper or using computer software to construct a model of the solution. A prototype is a working model of the solution.

Building a model or prototype helps an engineer determine whether a solution meets the criteria and stays within the constraints. During this stage of the process, engineers must often deal with new problems and make any necessary adjustments to the model or prototype.

Test and Evaluate a Solution

Whether testing a model or a prototype, engineers use scientific processes to evaluate their solutions. Multiple experiments, tests, or trials are conducted, data are evaluated, and results and analyses are communicated. New criteria or constraints may emerge as a result of testing. In most cases, a solution will require some refinement or revision, even if it has been through successful testing. Refining a solution is necessary if there are new constraints, such as less money or available materials. Additional testing may be done to ensure that a solution satisfies local, state, or federal laws or standards.

Make Meaning Think about an aluminum beverage can. What would happen if the price or availability of aluminum changed so much that cans needed to be made of a new material? What would the criteria and constraints be on the development of a new can?

A naval architect sets up a model to test how the the hull's design responds to waves.

Communicate the Solution

Engineers need to communicate the final design to the people who will manufacture the product. This may include sketches, detailed drawings, computer simulations, and written text. Engineers often provide evidence that was collected during the testing stage. This evidence may include graphs and data tables that support the decisions made for the final design.

If there is feedback about the solution, then the engineers and designers must further refine the solution. This might involve making minor adjustments to the design, or it might mean bigger modifications to the design based on new criteria or constraints. Any changes in the design will require additional testing to make sure that the changes work as intended.

Redesign and Retest the Solution

At different steps in the engineering and design process, a solution usually must be revised and retested. Many designs fail to work perfectly, even after models and prototypes are built, tested, and evaluated. Engineers must be ready to analyze new results and deal with any new problems that arise. Troubleshooting, or fixing design problems, allows engineers to adjust the design to improve on how well the solution meets the need.

Communicate Suppose you are an engineer at an aerospace company. Your team is designing a rover to be used on a future NASA space mission. A family member doesn't understand why so much your team's time is taken up with testing and retesting the rover design. What are three things you would tell your relative to explain why testing and retesting are so important to the engineering and design process?

....

....

....

....

....

....

....

....

Safety Symbols

These symbols warn of possible dangers in the laboratory and remind you to work carefully.

 Safety Goggles Wear safety goggles to protect your eyes in any activity involving chemicals, flames or heating, or glassware.

 Lab Apron Wear a laboratory apron to protect your skin and clothing from damage.

 Breakage Handle breakable materials, such as glassware, with care. Do not touch broken glassware.

 Heat-Resistant Gloves Use an oven mitt or other hand protection when handling hot materials, such as hot plates or hot glassware.

 Plastic Gloves Wear disposable plastic gloves when working with harmful chemicals and organisms. Keep your hands away from your face, and dispose of the gloves according to your teacher's instructions.

 Heating Use a clamp or tongs to pick up hot glassware. Do not touch hot objects with your bare hands.

 Flames Before you work with flames, tie back loose hair and clothing. Follow your teacher's instructions about lighting and extinguishing flames.

 No Flames When using flammable materials, make sure there are no flames, sparks, or other exposed heat sources present.

 Corrosive Chemical Avoid getting acid or other corrosive chemicals on your skin or clothing or in your eyes. Do not inhale the vapors. Wash your hands after the activity.

 Poison Do not let any poisonous chemical come into contact with your skin, and do not inhale its vapors. Wash your hands when you are finished with the activity.

 Fumes Work in a well-ventilated area when harmful vapors may be involved. Avoid inhaling vapors directly. Test an odor only when directed to do so by your teacher, and use a wafting motion to direct the vapor toward your nose.

 Sharp Object Scissors, scalpels, knives, needles, pins, and tacks can cut your skin. Always direct a sharp edge or point away from yourself and others.

 Animal Safety Treat live or preserved animals or animal parts with care to avoid harming the animals or yourself. Wash your hands when you are finished with the activity.

 Plant Safety Handle plants only as directed by your teacher. If you are allergic to certain plants, tell your teacher; do not do an activity involving those plants. Avoid touching harmful plants such as poison ivy. Wash your hands when you are finished with the activity.

 Electric Shock To avoid electric shock, never use electrical equipment around water, when the equipment is wet, or when your hands are wet. Be sure cords are untangled and cannot trip anyone. Unplug equipment not in use.

 Physical Safety When an experiment involves physical activity, avoid injuring yourself or others. Alert your teacher if there is any reason you should not participate.

 Disposal Dispose of chemicals and other laboratory materials safely. Follow the instructions from your teacher.

 Hand Washing Wash your hands thoroughly when finished with an activity. Use soap and warm water. Rinse well.

 General Safety Awareness When this symbol appears, follow the instructions provided. When you are asked to develop your own procedure in a lab, have your teacher approve your plan.

Using a Laboratory Balance

The laboratory balance is an important tool in scientific investigations. Different kinds of balances are used in the laboratory to determine the masses and weights of objects. You can use a triple-beam balance to determine the masses of materials that you study or experiment with in the laboratory. An electronic balance, unlike a triple-beam balance, is used to measure the weights of materials.

The triple-beam balance that you may use in your science class is probably similar to the balance depicted in this Appendix. To use the balance properly, you should learn the name, location, and function of each part of the balance.

Triple-Beam Balance

The triple-beam balance is a single-pan balance with three beams calibrated in grams. The back, or 100-gram, beam is divided into ten units of 10 grams each. The middle, or 500-gram, beam is divided into five units of 100 grams each. The front, or 10-gram, beam is divided into ten units of 1 gram each. Each gram on the front beam is further divided into units of 0.1 gram.

Apply Concepts What is the greatest mass you could find with the triple-beam balance in the picture?

....

Calculate What is the mass of the apple in the picture?

....

The following procedure can be used to find the mass of an object with a triple-beam balance:

1. Place the object on the pan.

2. Move the rider on the middle beam notch by notch until the horizontal pointer on the right drops below zero. Move the rider back one notch.

3. Move the rider on the back beam notch by notch until the pointer again drops below zero. Move the rider back one notch.

4. Slowly slide the rider along the front beam until the pointer stops at the zero point.

5. The mass of the object is equal to the sum of the readings on the three beams.

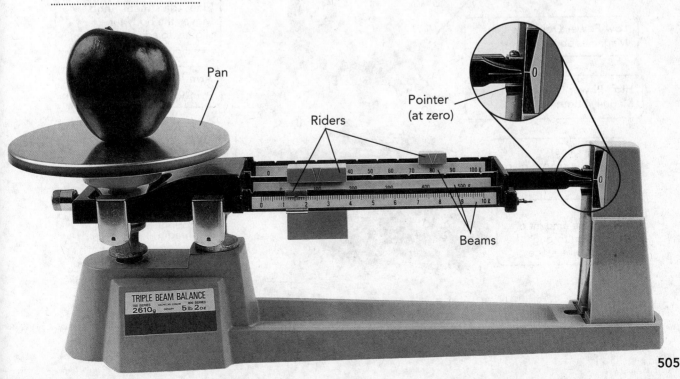

Pan

Riders

Pointer (at zero)

Beams

TRIPLE BEAM BALANCE
700 SERIES   800 SERIES
2610g   5 lb 2 oz

Using a Microscope

The microscope is an essential tool in the study of life science. It allows you to see things that are too small to be seen with the unaided eye.

You will probably use a compound microscope like the one you see here. The compound microscope has more than one lens that magnifies the object you view.

Typically, a compound microscope has one lens in the eyepiece (the part you look through). The eyepiece lens usually magnifies 10×. Any object you view through this lens will appear 10 times larger than it is.

A compound microscope may contain two or three other lenses called objective lenses. They are called the low-power and high-power objective lenses. The low-power objective lens usually magnifies 10×. The high-power objective lenses usually magnify 40× and 100×.

To calculate the total magnification with which you are viewing an object, multiply the magnification of the eyepiece lens by the magnification of the objective lens you are using. For example, the eyepiece's magnification of 10× multiplied by the low-power objective's magnification of 10× equals a total magnification of 100×.

Use the photo of the compound microscope to become familiar with the parts of the microscope and their functions.

The Parts of a Microscope

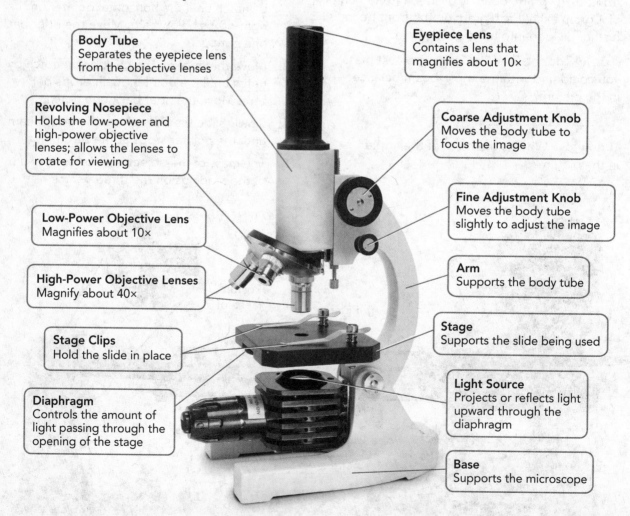

Body Tube
Separates the eyepiece lens from the objective lenses

Eyepiece Lens
Contains a lens that magnifies about 10×

Revolving Nosepiece
Holds the low-power and high-power objective lenses; allows the lenses to rotate for viewing

Coarse Adjustment Knob
Moves the body tube to focus the image

Low-Power Objective Lens
Magnifies about 10×

Fine Adjustment Knob
Moves the body tube slightly to adjust the image

High-Power Objective Lenses
Magnify about 40×

Arm
Supports the body tube

Stage Clips
Hold the slide in place

Stage
Supports the slide being used

Diaphragm
Controls the amount of light passing through the opening of the stage

Light Source
Projects or reflects light upward through the diaphragm

Base
Supports the microscope

Using the Microscope

Use the following procedures when you are working with a microscope.

1. To carry the microscope, grasp the microscope's arm with one hand. Place your other hand under the base.

2. Place the microscope on a table with the arm toward you.

3. Turn the coarse adjustment knob to raise the body tube.

4. Revolve the nosepiece until the low-power objective lens clicks into place.

5. Adjust the diaphragm. While looking through the eyepiece, adjust the mirror until you see a bright white circle of light. **CAUTION:** Never use direct sunlight as a light source.

6. Place a slide on the stage. Center the specimen over the opening on the stage. Use the stage clips to hold the slide in place. **CAUTION:** Glass slides are fragile.

7. Look at the stage from the side. Carefully turn the coarse adjustment knob to lower the body tube until the low-power objective almost touches the slide.

8. Looking through the eyepiece, very slowly turn the coarse adjustment knob until the specimen comes into focus.

9. To switch to the high-power objective lens, look at the microscope from the side. Carefully revolve the nosepiece until the high-power objective lens clicks into place. Make sure the lens does not hit the slide.

10. Looking through the eyepiece, turn the fine adjustment knob until the specimen comes into focus.

Making a Wet-Mount Slide

Use the following procedures to make a wet-mount slide of a specimen.

1. Obtain a clean microscope slide and a coverslip. **CAUTION:** Glass slides and coverslips are fragile.

2. Place the specimen on the center of the slide. The specimen must be thin enough for light to pass through it.

3. Using a plastic dropper, place a drop of water on the specimen.

4. Gently place one edge of the coverslip against the slide so that it touches the edge of the water drop at a 45° angle. Slowly lower the coverslip over the specimen. If you see air bubbles trapped beneath the coverslip, tap the coverslip gently with the eraser end of a pencil.

5. Remove any excess water at the edge of the coverslip with a paper towel.

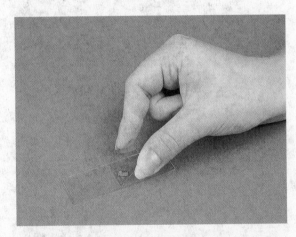

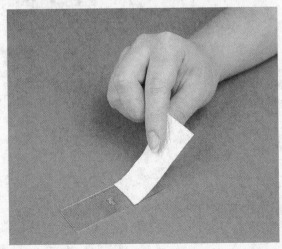

Periodic Table of Elements

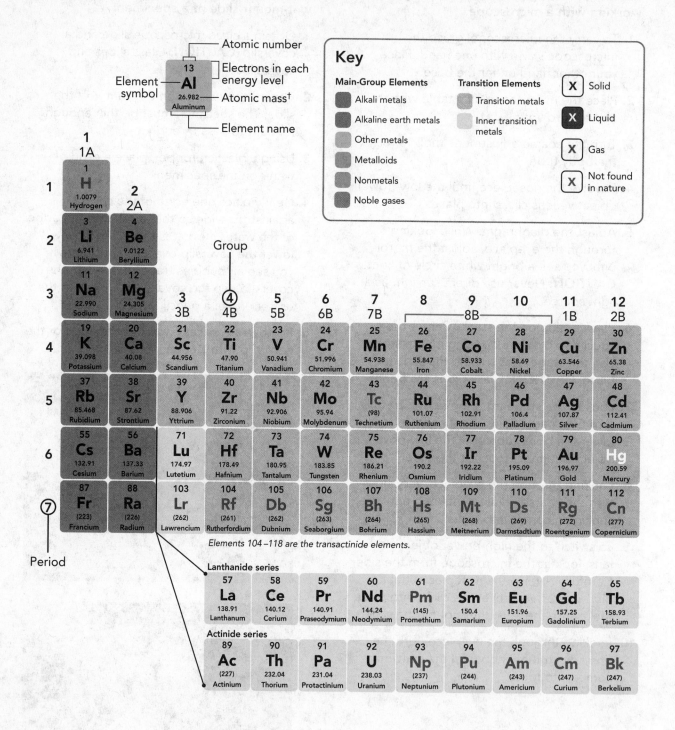

Atomic number
Electrons in each energy level
Element symbol — **Al** — Atomic mass†
13
26.982
Aluminum
Element name

Key

Main-Group Elements
- Alkali metals
- Alkaline earth metals
- Other metals
- Metalloids
- Nonmetals
- Noble gases

Transition Elements
- Transition metals
- Inner transition metals

- X Solid
- X Liquid
- X Gas
- X Not found in nature

Elements 104–118 are the transactinide elements.

Lanthanide series

| 57 La 138.91 Lanthanum | 58 Ce 140.12 Cerium | 59 Pr 140.91 Praseodymium | 60 Nd 144.24 Neodymium | 61 Pm (145) Promethium | 62 Sm 150.4 Samarium | 63 Eu 151.96 Europium | 64 Gd 157.25 Gadolinium | 65 Tb 158.93 Terbium |

Actinide series

| 89 Ac (227) Actinium | 90 Th 232.04 Thorium | 91 Pa 231.04 Protactinium | 92 U 238.03 Uranium | 93 Np (237) Neptunium | 94 Pu (244) Plutonium | 95 Am (243) Americium | 96 Cm (247) Curium | 97 Bk (247) Berkelium |

†The atomic masses in parentheses are the mass numbers of the longest-lived isotope of elements for which a standard atomic mass cannot be defined.

13 3A	14 4A	15 5A	16 6A	17 7A	18 8A
					2 **He** 4.0026 Helium
5 **B** 10.81 Boron	6 **C** 12.011 Carbon	7 **N** 14.007 Nitrogen	8 **O** 15.999 Oxygen	9 **F** 18.998 Fluorine	10 **Ne** 20.179 Neon
13 **Al** 26.982 Aluminum	14 **Si** 28.086 Silicon	15 **P** 30.974 Phosphorus	16 **S** 32.06 Sulfur	17 **Cl** 35.453 Chlorine	18 **Ar** 39.948 Argon
31 **Ga** 69.72 Gallium	32 **Ge** 72.59 Germanium	33 **As** 74.922 Arsenic	34 **Se** 78.96 Selenium	35 **Br** 79.904 Bromine	36 **Kr** 83.80 Krypton
49 **In** 114.82 Indium	50 **Sn** 118.69 Tin	51 **Sb** 121.75 Antimony	52 **Te** 127.60 Tellurium	53 **I** 126.90 Iodine	54 **Xe** 131.30 Xenon
81 **Tl** 204.37 Thallium	82 **Pb** 207.2 Lead	83 **Bi** 208.98 Bismuth	84 **Po** (209) Polonium	85 **At** (210) Astatine	86 **Rn** (222) Radon
113 **Nh** (284) Nihonium	114 **Fl** (289) Flerovium	115 **Mc** (288) Moscovium	116 **Lv** (292) Livermorium	117 **Ts** (294) Tennessine	118 **Og** (294) Oganesson

66 **Dy** 162.50 Dysprosium	67 **Ho** 164.93 Holmium	68 **Er** 167.26 Erbium	69 **Tm** 168.93 Thulium	70 **Yb** 173.04 Ytterbium

98 **Cf** (251) Californium	99 **Es** (252) Einsteinium	100 **Fm** (257) Fermium	101 **Md** (258) Mendelevium	102 **No** (259) Nobelium

GLOSSARY

A

air mass A huge body of air that has similar temperature, humidity, and air pressure at any given height. (241)

air pressure The pressure caused by the weight of a column of air pushing down on an area. (225)

alluvial fan A wide, sloping deposit of sediment formed where a stream leaves a mountain range. (409)

altitude Elevation above sea level. (225)

anticyclone A high-pressure center of dry air. (246)

aquifer An underground layer of rock or sediment that holds water. (204)

atmosphere The relatively thin layer of gases that form Earth's outermost layer. (180, 223)

atom The basic particle from which all elements are made; the smallest particle of an element that has the properties of that element. (8)

B

bacteria Single-celled organisms that lack a nucleus; prokaryotes. (464)

binomial nomenclature The classification system in which each organism is given a unique, two-part scientific name indicating its genus and species. (451)

biosphere The parts of Earth that contain living organisms. (180)

boiling point The temperature at which a liquid boils. (60)

Boyle's Law A principle that describes the relationship between the pressure and volume of a gas at constant temperature. (71)

C

cell The basic unit of structure and function in living things. (440)

Charles's Law A principle that describes the relationship between the temperature and volume of a gas at constant pressure. (69)

chemical change A change in which one or more substances combine or break apart to form new substances. (27)

chemical energy A form of potential energy that is stored in chemical bonds between atoms. (112)

chemical property A characteristic of a substance that describes its ability to change into different substances. (7)

chemical weathering The process that breaks down rock through chemical changes. (388)

classification The process of grouping things based on their similarities. (451)

coastline A line that forms the boundary between the land and the ocean or a lake. (191)

compound A substance made of two or more elements chemically combined in a specific ratio, or proportion. (10)

compression Stress that squeezes rock until it folds or breaks. (353)

condensation The change in state from a gas to a liquid. (62, 200, 232)

conduction The transfer of thermal energy from one particle of matter to another. (149)

conductor A material that conducts heat well. (159)

continental glacier A glacier that covers much of a continent or large island. (418)

convection The transfer of thermal energy by the movement of a fluid. (149)

convection current The movement of a fluid, caused by differences in temperature, that transfers heat from one part of the fluid to another. (149)

convergent boundary A plate boundary where two plates move toward each other. (345)

convergent evolution The process by which unrelated organisms evolve similar characteristics. (457)

crust The layer of rock that forms Earth's outer surface. (284)

cryosphere The portion of the hydrosphere that is frozen, including all the ice and snow on land, plus sea and lake ice. (180)

crystal A solid in which the atoms are arranged in a pattern that repeats again and again. (293)

crystallization The process by which atoms are arranged to form a material with a crystal structure. (297)

cyclone A swirling center of low air pressure. (246)

D

deflation The process by which wind removes surface materials. (400)

delta A landform made of sediment that is deposited where a river flows into an ocean or lake. (191, 409)

density The measurement of how much mass of a substance is contained in a given volume. (18)

deposition Process in which sediment is laid down in new locations. (397)

dew point The temperature at which condensation begins. (232)

divergent boundary A plate boundary where two plates move away from each other. (345)

domain The most basic level of organization in the classification of organisms. (452)

dormant Term used to describe a volcano that is not currently acrtive but able to become active in the future. (370)

drought A long period of low precipitation. (263)

dune A hill of sand piled up by the wind. (191)

E

earthquake The shaking that results from the movement of rock beneath Earth's surface. (357)

elastic potential energy The energy of stretched or compressed objects. (105)

electrical energy The energy of electric charges. (113)

electromagnetic radiation The energy transferred through space by electromagnetic waves. (113)

element A pure substance that cannot be broken down into other substances by chemical or physical means. (8)

energy The ability to do work or cause change. (91, 181)

erosion The process by which water, ice, wind, or gravity moves weathered particles of rock and soil. (387)

evaporation The process by which molecules at the surface of a liquid absorb enough energy to change to a gas. (60, 199, 231)

evolution Change over time; the process by which modern organisms have descended from ancient organisms. (456)

extinct Term used to describe a volcano that is no longer active and unlikely to erupt again. (370)

F

fault A break in Earth's crust along which rocks move. (354)

flood An overflowing of water in a normally dry area. (263)

flood plain The flat, wide area of land along a river. (407)

force A push or pull exerted on an object. (92)

freezing point The temperature at which a liquid freezes. (59)

front The boundary where unlike air masses meet but do not mix. (243)

GLOSSARY

G

gas A state of matter with no definite shape or volume. (53)

genus A taxonomic category that names a group of similar, closely-related organisms. (451)

geosphere The densest parts of Earth that include the crust, mantle, and core. (180)

glacier Any large mass of ice that moves slowly over land. (417)

gravitational potential energy Potential energy that depends on the height of an object. (104)

groundwater Water that fills the cracks and spaces in underground soil and rock layers. (411)

H

heat The transfer of thermal energy from a warmer object to a cooler object. (141)

homeostasis The condition in which an organism's internal environment is kept stable in spite of changes in the external environment. (446)

host An organism that provides a source of energy or a suitable environment for a parasite to live with, in, or on. (462)

hot spot An area where magma from deep within the mantle melts through the crust above it. (367)

humidity The amount of water vapor in a given volume of air. (233)

humus Dark-colored organic material in soil. (391)

hurricane A tropical storm that has winds of about 119 kilometers per hour or higher. (260)

hydrosphere The portion of Earth that consists of water in any of its forms, including oceans, glaciers, rivers, lakes, groundwater and water vapor. (180)

I

ice age Time in Earth's history during which glaciers covered large parts of the surface. (418)

igneous rock A type of rock that forms from the cooling of molten rock at or below the surface. (305)

inner core A dense sphere of solid iron and nickel at the center of Earth. (286)

insulator A material that does not conduct heat well. (159)

invertebrate An animal without a backbone. (478)

J

jet stream Band of high-speed winds about 10 kilometers above Earth's surface. (241)

K

kinetic energy Energy that an object has due to its motion. (101)

L

landform A feature on the surface of Earth, such as a coastline, dune, or mountain. (187)

lava Liquid magma that reaches the surface. (365)

law of conservation of energy The rule that energy cannot be created or destroyed. (122)

liquid A state of matter that has no definite shape but has a definite volume. (51)

loess A wind-formed deposit made of fine particles of clay and silt. (401)

longshore drift The movement of water and sediment down a beach caused by waves coming in to shore at an angle. (424)

M

magma A molten mixture of rock-forming substances, gases, and water from the mantle. (365)

magnitude The measurement of an earthquake's strength based on seismic waves and movement along faults. (359)

mammal A vertebrate whose body temperature is regulated by its internal heat, and that has skin covered with hair or fur and glands that produce milk to feed its young. (480)

mantle The layer of hot, solid material between Earth's crust and core. (285)

mass A measure of how much matter is in an object. (15)

mass movement Any one of several processes by which gravity moves sediment downhill. (398)

matter Anything that has mass and takes up space. (5)

mechanical energy Kinetic or potential energy associated with the motion or position of an object. (109)

mechanical weathering The type of weathering in which rock is physically broken into smaller pieces. (388)

medium The material through which a wave travels. (113)

melting point The temperature at which a substance changes from a solid to a liquid; the same as the freezing point, or temperature at which a liquid changes to a solid. (58)

metamorphic rock A type of rock that forms from an existing rock that is changed by heat, pressure, or chemical reactions. (307)

meteorologist A scientist who studies the causes of weather and tries to predict it. (249)

mid-ocean ridge An undersea mountain chain where new ocean floor is produced; a divergent plate boundary under the ocean. (334)

mineral A naturally occurring solid that can form by inorganic processes and that has a crystal structure and a definite chemical composition. (293)

mixture Two or more substances that are together in the same place but their atoms are not chemically bonded. (11)

molecule A neutral group of two or more atoms held together by covalent bonds. (9)

motion The state in which one object's distance from another is changing. (91)

mountain A landform with high elevation and high relief. (190)

multicellular Consisting of many cells. (440)

N

nonvascular plants A low-growing plant that lacks true vascular tissue for transporting materials. (477)

nuclear energy The potential energy stored in the nucleus of an atom. (110)

O

ocean trench An undersea valley that represents one of the deepest parts of the ocean. (336)

organ A body structure that is composed of different kinds of tissues that work together. (478)

organism A living thing. (439)

outer core A layer of molten iron and nickel that surrounds the inner core of Earth. (286)

P

parasite An organism that benefits by living with, on, or in a host in a parasitism interaction. (467)

physical change A change that alters the form or appearance of a material but does not make the material into another substance. (25)

physical property A characteristic of a pure substance that can be observed without changing it into another substance. (6)

plucking The process by which a glacier picks up rocks as it flows over the land. (419)

potential energy The energy an object has because of its position; also the internal stored energy of an object, such as energy stored in chemical bonds. (103)

power The rate at which one form of energy is transformed into another. (96)

precipitation Any form of water that falls from clouds and reaches Earth's surface as rain, snow, sleet, or hail. (200, 234)

pressure The force pushing on a surface divided by the area of that surface. (67)

protist A eukaryotic organism that cannot be classified as an animal, plant, or fungus. (467)

GLOSSARY

R

radiation The transfer of energy by electromagnetic waves. (149)

relative humidity The percentage of water vapor in the air compared to the maximum amount of water vapor that air can contain at a particular temperature. (233)

response An action or change in behavior that occurs as a result of a stimulus. (441)

river A natural stream of water that flows into another body of water, such as an ocean, lake, or another river. (191)

rock cycle A series of processes on the surface and inside Earth that slowly changes rocks from one kind to another. (311)

runoff Water that flows over the ground surface rather than soaking into the ground. (405)

revolution The movement of an object around another object. (442)

rotation The spinning motion of a planet on its axis. (441)

S

sand dune A deposit of wind-blown sand. (401)

sea-floor spreading The process by which molten material adds new oceanic crust to the ocean floor. (335)

sediment Small, solid pieces of material that come from rocks or the remains of organisms; earth materials deposited by erosion. (306, 397)

sedimentary rock A type of rock that forms when particles from other rocks or the remains of plants and animals are pressed and cemented together. (306)

seismic wave Vibrations that travel through Earth carrying the energy released during an earthquake. (282)

shearing Stress that pushes masses of rock in opposite directions, in a sideways movement. (353)

soil The loose, weathered material on Earth's surface in which plants can grow. (391)

solid A state of matter that has a definite shape and a definite volume. (48)

species A group of similar organisms that can mate with each other and produce offspring that can also mate and reproduce. (451)

specific heat The amount of heat required to raise the temperature of 1 kilogram of a material by 1 kelvin, which is equivalent to 1°C. (160)

spontaneous generation The mistaken idea that living things arise from nonliving sources. (442)

stimulus Any change or signal in the environment that can make an organism react in some way. (441)

storm A violent disturbance in the atmosphere. (257)

storm surge A "dome" of water that sweeps across the coast where a hurricane lands. (261)

stream A channel through which water is continually flowing downhill. (406)

stress A force that acts on rock to change its shape or volume. (353)

subduction The process by which oceanic crust sinks beneath a deep-ocean trench and back into the mantle at a convergent plate boundary. (336)

sublimation The change in state from a solid directly to a gas without passing through the liquid state. (63)

substance A single kind of matter that is pure and has a specific set of properties. (5)

surface tension The result of an inward pull among the molecules of a liquid that brings the molecules on the surface closer together; causes the surface to act as if it has a thin skin. (52)

surveying A process in which mapmakers determine distances and elevations using instruments and the principles of geometry. (192)

T

taxonomy The scientific study of how living things are classified. (452)

temperature How hot or cold something is; a measure of the average energy of motion of the particles of a substance; the measure of the average kinetic energy of the particles of a substance. (57, 142)

tension Stress that stretches rock so that it becomes thinner in the middle. (353)

thermal energy The total kinetic and potential energy of all the particles of an object. (57, 111, 141)

thermal expansion The expansion of matter when it is heated. (161)

thunderstorm A small storm often accompanied by heavy precipitation and frequent thunder and lightning. (259)

till The sediments deposited directly by a glacier. (420)

tissue A group of similar cells that perform a specific function. (476)

topography The shape of the land determined by elevation, relief, and landforms. (187)

tornado A rapidly whirling, funnel-shaped cloud that reaches down to touch Earth's surface. (262)

transform boundary A plate boundary where two plates move past each other in opposite directions. (345)

transpiration The process by which water is lost through a plant's leaves. (199)

tributary A stream or river that flows into a larger river. (406)

tsunami A giant wave usually caused by an earthquake beneath the ocean floor. (361)

U

unicellular Made of a single cell. (440)

uniformitarianism The geologic principle that the same geologic processes that operate today operated in the past to change Earth's surface. (387)

V

vaccine A substance used in a vaccination that consists of pathogens that have been weakened or killed but can still trigger the body to produce chemicals that destroy the pathogens. (462)

valley glacier A long, narrow glacier that forms when snow and ice build up in a mountain valley. (418)

vaporization The change of state from a liquid to a gas. (60)

vascular plants A plant that has true vascular tissue for transporting materials. (476)

vertebrate An animal with a backbone. (478)

virus A tiny, nonliving particle that enters and then reproduces inside a living cell. (462)

viscosity A liquid's resistance to flowing. (52)

volcano A weak spot in the crust where magma has come to the surface. (365)

volume The amount of space that matter occupies. (15)

W

water cycle The continual movement of water among Earth's atmosphere, oceans, and land surface through evaporation, condensation, and precipitation. (199, 231)

watershed The land area that supplies water to a river system. (202)

weight A measure of the force of gravity acting on an object. (15)

well A hole sunk into the ground to reach a supply of water. (204)

wind The horizontal movement of air from an area of high pressure to an area of lower pressure. (228)

work Force exerted on an object that causes it to move. (93)

INDEX
Page numbers for key terms are printed in boldface type.

452, 465, 469–471, 473–474,
479, 482–483, 487
Video, 2, 6, 13, 16, 26, 44, 50,
53, 61, 73, 88, 91, 104, 110,
117, 122, 138, 144, 152, 155,
176, 180, 190, 202, 204, 220,
236, 245, 251, 255, 262, 278,
328, 336, 346, 363, 366–367,
384, 403, 408, 436, 480
Virtual Activity, 233
Virtual Lab, 160, 258, 387
Vocabulary App, 4, 14, 24, 46,
56, 66, 90, 100, 108, 118, 140,
148, 158, 178, 186, 198, 222,
230, 240, 248, 256, 280, 292,
302, 310, 330, 340, 352, 364,
386, 396, 404, 416, 438, 450,
460, 472

Diorite, 305
Diseases
    bacterial, 464
    fungal, 469
    viral, 462
    viral treatment of, 471
Distillation, 11, 26
Divergent boundaries, 345, 346,
    366
Divides (water), 202
Domains, 452, 461
Dormant volcanoes, 370
Drainage basin, 406
Drinking water, 204, 239
    need for, 440, 444, 448–449
Droughts, 263
Dunes, 191

E

Earth. *See* **Minerals; Rocks**
Earth system
    atmosphere, 180, 223–228
    biosphere, 180–181
    cryosphere, 180, 182–183, 417
    distribution of water, 201–205
    elements of, 180–183
    feedback system, 182–185
    geosphere, 180, 187–195
    hydrosphere, 180–181,
    199–208
    rock cycle, 179, 311–317
    water cycle, 179, 199–200,
    230–239
Earthquakes, 345, 357–361
    and tsunamis, 360–361

Earth's layers, 280–289
    and convection currents,
    289, 342
    core, 286–287
    crust, 284, 353–356
    mantle, 285, 288–289
    and plate tectonics,
    353–356
    studying, 281–282, 291
Earthworms, 393
East African Rift System, 366
Echinoderms, 479
Ecological issues
    geothermal energy,
    156–157
    mining, 301
    oil exploration (Deepwater
    Horizon oil rig), 22–23
    rising sea levels, 185
    sinkholes, 414–415
    water management (Aral Sea),
    208–209
Ectotherms, 480
Elastic potential energy, 105
Electrical energy, 113
Electricity generation
    from geothermal energy,
    156–157
    from nuclear energy, 110
Electromagnetic energy, 113
Electronic balances, 505
Elements, 8–9
    in periodic table, 508–509
Elevation, 187
    mapping, 192–193
Endospore, 465
Endothermic reactions, 31
Endotherms, 480
Energy, 91, 181
    and atmosphere, 227
    and changes in matter,
    30–31
    chemical, 112
    electrical, 113
    electromagnetic, 113
    flow in Earth system, 181
    and force, 92
    kinetic, 57, 67–69, 101–102,
    141, 162
    law of conservation of, 152
    mechanical, 109
    and motion, 91
    nuclear, 110
    potential, 57, 103–105, 141
    and power, 96–98

    and temperature, 143–145, 160
    thermal, 111
    transformation of, 119-125, 152,
    162
    See also **Thermal energy**
**Energy conservation, law
    of, 122**–124
**Energy sources, U.S.
    consumption,** 126–127
Energy transformation, 119–125
    and conservation of energy,
    122–124
    and energy transfer, 121, 123
    and friction, 162
    and heat transfer, 152
    between kinetic and potential
    energy, 120, 123
    single and multiple, 119
Engineering
    Defining the Problem, 197,
    291, 395
    Designing Solutions, 55
    Impact on Society, 33, 471
    Prototype to Product,
    107, 155
    Sustainable Design, 239, 363
    See also **Science and
    Engineering Practices;
    uEngineer It!**
**Engineering and design
    process,** 500–503
    communicating solutions, 503
    defining problems, 500–501
    designing, testing, and
    evaluating solutions, 502
    developing solutions, 501
    identifying criteria and
    constraints, 501
    redesigning and retesting
    solutions, 503
    See also **Science practices**
Epicenter, 357–358
Epidemics, 463
Erosion, 312, 314, **387,**
    397–401
    and deposition, 306, 308, 397,
    401, 409–411, 420, 424
    by glacier, 417–421
    and mass movement, 398–399
    rate of, 388, 390, 397, 412, 419,
    423
    of rock, 306, 308
    by water, 405–412
    by waves, 422–424
    and weathering, 387–390

INDEX

CREDITS

Photographs

Photo locators denoted as follows: Top (T), Center (C), Bottom (B), Left (L), Right (R), Background (Bkgd)
Front Cover: Lava eruption, G. Brad Lewis/Aurora/Getty Images
Back Cover: blank notes and papers Marinello/DigitalVision Vectors/Getty Images

Front Matter

iv: Clari Massimiliano/Shutterstock; vi: Sokkajar/Fotolia; vii: Makieni/Fotolia; viii: David Jones/PA Images/Alamy Stock Photo; ix: Fabriziobalconi/Fotolia; x: Mark Whitt Photography/Getty Images; xi: Switas/Getty Images; xii: Demerzel21/Fotolia; xiii: AFP/Getty Images; xiv: Robert Harding/Alamy Stock Photo; xv: Martin Harvey/Getty Images; xvi: Brian J. Skerry/National Geographic/Getty Images; xvii: Steve Byland/Shutterstock

Topic 1

xviii: sokkajar/Fotolia 002: Stock_Colors/E+/Getty Images; 004: Sami Sarkis RM CC/Alamy Stock Photo; 006 Bkgd: Lazyllama/Shutterstock; 006 BL: Subinpumsom/Fotolia; 007 BL: Borroko72/Fotolia; 007 BR: Arpad NagyBagoly/Fotolia; 008 BR: Anyka/123RF; 008 C: James Steidl/Shutterstock; 010 TC: Smereka/Shutterstock; 010 TR: GIPhotoStock/Science Source; 011 TCR: Bert Folsom/123RF; 011 TR: Lepas2004/iStock/Getty Images; 013 BC: SuperStock; 013 Bkgd: Massimo Pizzotti/AGE Fotostock/SuperStock; 013 TR: David L. Ryan/The Boston Globe/Getty Images; 014: Michelle McMahon/Moment/Getty Images; 016 T: Martin Shields/Alamy Stock Photo; 016 TR: Martin Shields/Alamy Stock Photo; 017 BR: Leungchopan/Fotolia; 017 CR: GIPhotoStock/Science Source; 017 L: Hitandrun IKON Images/Newscom; 018: SchulteProductions/E+/Getty Images; 020 CR: RF Company/Alamy Stock Photo; 020 L: Denis Radovanovic/Shutterstock; 020 R: Siim Sepp/Alamy Stock Photo; 020 T: Victor21041958/Fotolia; 022: U.S. Coast Guard; 025: Fuse/Corbis/Getty Images; 026: Sergey Dobrydnev/Shutterstock; 027 BCL: Vinicef/Alamy Stock Photo; 027 BCR: Vinicef/Alamy Stock Photo; 027 BL: Stephanie Frey/Fotolia; 027 BR: Kzen/Shutterstock; 028 CL: Fuse/Corbis/Getty Images; 028 CR: Charles D. Winters/Science Source; 028 TL: Studio on line/Shutterstock; 028 TR: 123RF; 030 Bkgd: Peter Barritt/Alamy Stock Photo; 030 BL: Paul Souders/Alamy Stock Photo; 031: Byrdyak/123RF; 033: Kiyoshi Takahase Segundo/Alamy Stock Photo; 035: Shaiith/iStock/Getty Images; 038: Torontonian/Alamy Stock Photo; 039: USantos/Fotolia

Topic 2

042: Makieni/Fotolia; 044: Studio 8/Pearson Education Ltd.; 046: Kendall Rittenour/Shutterstock; 048: Dmytro Skorobogatov/Alamy Stock Photo; 049 BL: Marco Cavina/Shutterstock; 049 BR: CrackerClips Stock Media/Shutterstock; 049 T: Erika8213/Fotolia; 050 BCL: Robyn Mackenzie/Shutterstock; 050 BL: Fototrips/Fotolia; 051 BL: Kropic/Fotolia; 051 BR: Rony Zmiri/Fotolia; 052 BL: Wiklander/Shutterstock; 052 BR: Oriori/Fotolia; 053 T: Sutichak/Fotolia; 053 TL: Hudiemm/Getty Images; 055 BCR: Özgür Güvenç/Fotolia; 055 CR: Xiaoliangge/Fotolia; 056: WavebreakMediaMicro/Fotolia; 060 TC: PhotoAlto/Odilon Dimier/Getty Images; 060 TL: Petr Malyshev/Fotolia; 060 TR: Uygaar/Getty Images; 062 B: Michael Hare/Shutterstock; 062 CR: Cultura Creative (RF)/

Alamy Stock Photo; 063: Charles D. Winters/Science Source; 066: Ronstik/Fotolia; 068 T: Saap585/Shutterstock; 068 TC: Eric Audras/PhotoAlto/AGE Fotostock; 068 TL: Gudellaphoto/Fotolia; 068 TR: Peterspiro/iStock/Getty Images; 071: Cebas/Shutterstock; 073 B: Faded Beauty/Fotolia; 073 CL: Alexmit/iStock/Getty Images; 076 Bkgrd: Physicx/Shutterstock; 076 BL: Mara Zemgaliete/Fotolia; 076 TL: Denisfilm/Fotolia; 078 BC: Pakhnyushcha/Shutterstock; 078 C: Reika/Shutterstock; 078 CR: Richard Megna/Fundamental Photographs; 082: Mrallen/Fotolia; 083: Bestphotostudio/Fotolia

Topic 3

086: David Jones/PA Images/Alamy Stock Photo; 088: Jeffrey Coolidge/Getty Images; 090: Derek Watt/Alamy Stock Photo; 094: Hero Images/Getty Images; 095 BC: Steven May/Alamy Stock Photo; 095 BL: WavebreakMediaMicro/Fotolia; 095 BR: Monkey Business/Fotolia; 096 BL: Ben Schonewille/Shutterstock; 096 BR: Andrey Popov/Shutterstock; 097: Egmont Strigl/imageBROKER/Alamy Stock Photo; 098 TCL: Ariel Skelley/Blend Images/Getty Images; 098 TL: B Christopher/Alamy Stock Photo; 100: AFP/Getty Images; 103: Feng Yu/Fotolia; 104: Anatoliy Gleb/Fotolia; 107: Sportpoint/Fotolia; 108: Fhm/Moment/Getty Images; 109: Steve Byland/Shutterstock; 111: Paul Vinten/Fotolia; 112: Toa55/Shutterstock; 117 B: John Lund/Marc Romanelli/Blend Images/Getty Images; 117 TR: Hero Images/Alamy Stock Photo; 118: Holger Thalmann/Cultura RM/Alamy Stock Photo; 120 BL: Richard Megna/Fundamental Photographs; 120 BR: Kim Karpeles/Alamy Stock Photo; 122: Parkerphotography/Alamy Stock Photo; 124: Ian McDonnell/iStock/Getty Images; 126: Blackpixel/Shutterstock; 132: Stockbyte/Getty Images

Topic 4

136: Fabriziobalconi/Fotolia; 138: Ragnar Th Sigurdsson/Arctic Images/Alamy Stock Photo; 140: Andrew Cline/Alamy Stock Photo; 143: Yanika Panfilova/123RF; 147 B: Jim West/Alamy Stock Photo; 147 TR: Evgeny Itsikson/Shutterstock; 149: EduardSV/Fotolia; 153: Alextype/Fotolia; 158: Zavgsg/Fotolia; 161 BR: Tom Uhlman/Alamy Stock Photo; 161 T: Coffeemill/Shutterstock; 162: Juice Images/Getty Images; 163: NASA; 167 BL: Panther Media GmbH/Alamy Stock Photo; 167 CL: Jason Bazzano/Alamy Stock Photo; 167 TL: Halfpoint/Fotolia; 170: Hugo Felix/Shutterstock

Topic 5

174: Mark Whitt Photography/Getty Images; 176 Bkgrd: 123RF; 176 TR: Tfoxfoto/Getty Images; 178: Samuel Borges/Alamy Stock Photo; 180 BL: Marco Regalia/Alamy Stock Photo; 180 CL: Dorota Wasik/EyeEm/Getty; 181 BR: Panther Media GmbH/Alamy Stock Photo; 181 CR: Marco Regalia/Alamy Stock Photo; 185: Seafarer/Shuttesrstock; 188: David Pearson/Alamy Stock Photo; 189: Stocktrek Images, Inc./Alamy Stock Photo; 192: Charles Gurche/Danita Delimont/Alamy Stock Photo; 194 B: UniversalImagesGroup/Getty Images; 194 T: Tetra Images/Alamy Stock Photo; 197 BCR: Songquan Deng/Shutterstock; 197 CR: Everett Collection/Shutterstock; 198: Paul Prescott/Shutterstock; 202: Clint Farlinger/Alamy Stock Photo; 203 CR: Aurora Photos/Alamy Stock Photo; 203 TR: imageBROKER/Alamy Stock Photo; 208: NASA; 211: Westend61/Getty Images; 212: NASA; 214: Sergio Azenha/Alamy Stock Photo; 215: BW Folsom/Shutterstock

Topic 6

218: Switas/Getty Images; 220: A.T. Willett/Alamy Stock Photo; 222: Studio23/Shutterstock; 224: LukaKikina/Shutterstock; 230: Alexanderkorotun/Fotolia; 233 C: David J. Green Technology/ Alamy Stock Photo; 233 CR: GIPhotoStock/Science Source; 235 B: Mario Beauregard/Fotolia; 235 CL: Georgeion88/ Fotolia; 235 CR: Nebojsa/Fotolia; 235 TR: Tatiana Belova/ Fotolia; 239: Frans Lemmens/Alamy Stock Photo; 240: ValentinValkov/Fotolia; 243: Galyna Andrushko/Fotolia; 246: Harvepino/Fotolia; 248: GIS/Fotolia; 250 Bkgrd: Solarseven/ Shutterstock; 250 BR: Carolina K. Smith MD/Shutterstock; 250 CR: Chanelle/Fotolia; 250 TR: Karim Agabi/Science Source; 251: NOAA; 255 Bkgrd: Pavelk/Shutterstock; 255 BR: Science Source; 255 TR: David R. Frazier/Danita Delimont Photography/Newscom; 256: Smith Collection/Gado/Getty Images; 259: Stnazkul/123RF; 262: Carlo Allegri/Reuters; 263: Aram Boghosian/The Boston Globe/Getty Images; 266: Juanmonino/Getty Images; 267: Logan Bowles/AP Images; 272: Paul Aniszewski/Shutterstock; 273: 123RF

Topic 7

276: Demerzel21/Fotolia; 278: John Bryson/The LIFE Images Collection/Getty Images; 280: Wead/Shutterstock; 281: John Cancalosi/Getty Images; 289: Paul Silverman/Fundamental Photographs; 291: AOES Medialab/ESA; 301 B: PerAnders Pettersson/Getty Images; 301 TR: Eric Baccega/AGE Fotostock/Alamy Stock Photo; 302: Brian Jannsen/Alamy Stock Photo; 308: Wead/Shutterstock; 310: Michael Routh/Alamy Stock Photo; 312: Kmartin457/Getty Images; 313 C: Mark Yarchoan/Shutterstock; 313 CL: Joel Arem/Science Source; 313 CR: 123RF; 313 TCL: Tom Holt/Alamy Stock Photo; 313 TCR: Trevor Clifford/Pearson Education Ltd; 316 Bkgrd: Brandon B/ Shutterstock; 316 CL: Universal Images Group North America LLC/Alamy Stock Photo; 322: Jon Bilous/Shutterstock; 323 B: MM Studio/Fotolia; 323 CR: Pavlo Burdyak/123RF; 323 TR: Image/Shutterstock

Topic 8

326: AFP/Getty Images; 328: Christopher Boswell/ Shutterstock; 335 TL: Mr. Elliot Lim and Mr. Jesse Varner, CIRES & NOAA/NCEI; 335 TR: OAR/National Undersea Research Program/NOAA; 339: Sueddeutsche Zeitung Photo/Alamy Stock Photo; 340: MarkushaBLR/Fotolia; 346: Wildestanimal/ Moment Open/Getty Images; 347 B: Vadim Petrakov/ Shutterstock; 347 CR: David Burton/Alamy Stock Photo; 350: Travel Pictures/Alamy Stock Photo; 352: The Asahi Shimbun/ Getty Images; 361: JiJi Press/AFP/Getty Images; 363: Epa European Pressphoto Agency b.v./Alamy Stock Photo; 364: Pall Gudonsson/Getty Images; 370 TL: Siim Sepp/Alamy Stock Photo; 370 TR: Sandatlas/Shutterstock; 371: Hulton Archive/ Getty Images; 372 BR: Rosa Irene Betancourt 3/Alamy Stock Photo; 372 TL: Janet Babb/Hawaiian Volcano Observatory/U.S. Geological Survey; 379: Space_Expert/Fotolia

Topic 9

382: Robert Harding/Alamy Stock Photo; 384: Maggie Steber/ Getty Images; 385: Xu Jian/Getty Images; 386: Russ Bishop/ Alamy Stock Photo; 388 TL: Sean Kaufmann/Getty Images; 388 TR: Thomas Mitchell/Alamy Stock Photo; 389 TC: Mironov/ Shutterstock; 389 TL: IPics Photography/Alamy Stock Photo;

391: Madllen/123RF; 393 TCR: Sean Kaufmann/Getty Images; 393 TR: Vinicius Tupinamba/Shutterstock; 395: Alejandro Zepeda/EPA/Newcom; 396: Macduff Everton/National Geographic Magazines/Getty Images; 403 B: David Weintraub/ Science Source; 403 TR: Roman Kadarjan/Alamy Stock Photo; 404: Songquan Deng/Shutterstock; 409 CL: Totajla/ Shutterstock; 409 TL: Planet Observer/UIG/Getty Images; 411: Macduff Everton/Getty Images; 412: AP Images; 414 B: Cobalt88/Shutterstock; 414 BC: Spencer Grant/Getty Images; 416: Design Pics Inc/Alamy Stock Photo; 419: Pavel Svoboda Photography/Shutterstock; 423: Hemis/Alamy Stock Photo; 425: Mick Jack/Alamy Stock Photo

Topic 10

434: Martin Harvey/Getty Images; 436: Jutta Klee/Getty Images; 438: WonderfulEarth.Net/Alamy Stock Photo; 440 B: Edo Schmidt/Alamy Stock Photo; 440 CR: Cdascher/ Getty Images; 440 TL: Ed Reschke/Getty Images; 441 B: Edo Schmidt/Alamy Stock Photo; 441 CL: Science Pictures Limited/Science Photo Library/Getty Images; 441 TR: Tom Grill/Corbis/Glow Images; 446 B: Nature Picture Library/ Alamy Stock Photo; 446 BL: Gareth Codd/Getty Images; 448 BCL: Eye of Science/Science Source; 448 CL: Eye of Science/Science Source; 451: Antonio Camacho/Getty Images; 452: Holly Kuchera/Shutterstock; 454 C: Robert Wyatt/Alamy Stock Photo; 454 CL: JohnatAPW/Fotolia; 454 CR: Arco Images GmbH/Alamy Stock Photo; 455: James Jordan Photography/Getty Images; 457 C: Kirsanov Valeriy Vladimirovich/Shutterstock; 457 CL: Christopher Mills/Alamy Stock Photo; 457 T: Steve Bloom Images/Alamy Stock Photo; 459 B: WILDLIFE GmbH/Alamy Stock Photo; 459 BR: Joe Ravi/ Shutterstock; 460: M. I. Walker/Science Source; 462 BCL: Lee D. Simon/Science Source; 462 CL: Cultura RM/Alamy Stock Photo; 462 TL: James Cavallini/Science Source; 464 TCL: Chris Bjornberg/Science Source; 464 TL: VEM/Science Source; 465: B. Murton/Southampton Oceanography Centre/Science Source; 466: Andrew Syre/Science Source; 467 BC: Moment Open/Getty Images; 467 BL: Royaltystockphoto/123RF; 467 BR: Paul Glendell/Alamy Stock Photo; 469 BC: Jackan/Fotolia; 469 BR: Steve Gschmeissner/Science Photo Library/Getty Images; 469 CL: Domenico Tondini/Alamy Stock Photo; 469 CR: Unicusx/Fotolia; 469 TR: Eye of Science/Science Source; 472: Matthew Oldfield Underwater Photography/Alamy Stock Photo; 475 TL: Kateko/Shutterstock; 475 TR: Digital Paradise/ Shutterstock; 476 T: NigelSpiers/Shutterstock; 476 TC: Valzan/ Shutterstock; 476 TL: StudioByTheSea/Shutterstock; 476 TR: Guliveris/Shutterstock; 478 BC: Ashley Cooper/Getty Images; 478 BL: Silvia Iordache/Shutterstock; 478 BR: Andrew Burgess/Shutterstock; 479 BCR: Edgieus/Shutterstock; 479 BR: Stubblefield Photography/Shutterstock; 479 C: Igor Sirbu/Shutterstock; 479 CL: Royaltystockphoto/Shutterstock; 479 TCR: Harmonia101/123RF; 479 TR: 2009fotofriends/ Shutterstock; 480 BL: WaterFrame/Alamy Stock Photo; 480 BR: FotoRequest/Shutterstock; 480 C: Robert W. Ginn/Alamy Stock Photo; 480 CL: Dinda Yulianto/Shutterstock; 480 CR: Kathy Kay/Shutterstock; 481 BC: Audrey SniderBell/Shutterstock; 481 BCR: Jay Ondreicka/Shutterstock; 481 BR: Oleg Nekhaev/ Shutterstock; 481 CL: Jim Cumming/Shutterstock; 481 TC: BMCL/Shutterstock; 481 TCR: Redbrickstock/Alamy Stock Photo; 481 TL: Worldswildlifewonders/Shutterstock; 481 TR: Bernd Wolter/Shutterstock; 482 C: Rudmer Zwerver/

CREDITS

Shutterstock; 482 CL: Mark Boulton/Alamy Stock Photo; 482
CR: Vladimir Wrangel/Shutterstock; 482 TC: SuperStock/
Alamy Stock Photo; 482 TR: Julia Golosiy/Shutterstock; 486
TL: Marek Mis/Science Source; 486 TR: Lebendkulturen.de/
Shutterstock; 488: BSIP SA/Alamy Stock Photo; 489 BC: The
Natural History Museum/Alamy Stock Photo; 489 BL: Cultura
RM/Alamy Stock Photo; 489 BR: Zoonar GmbH/Alamy Stock
Photo

End Matter
492 BCL: Philippe Plailly & Elisabeth Daynes/Science
Source; 492 BL: EHStockphoto/Shutterstock; 492 TCL:
Cyndi Monaghan/Getty Images; 492 TL: Javier Larrea/AGE
Fotostock; 493: WaterFrame/Alamy Stock Photo; 494: Africa
Studio/Shutterstock; 495: Jeff Rotman/Alamy Stock Photo;
496: Grant Faint/Getty Images; 497: Ross Armstrong/Alamy
Stock Photo; 498: Geoz/Alamy Stock Photo; 501: Martin
Shields/Alamy Stock Photo; 502: Nicola Tree/Getty Images;
503: Regan Geeseman/NASA; 505: Pearson Education Ltd.;
506: Pearson Education Ltd.; 507 BR: Pearson Education Ltd.;
507 CR: Pearson Education Ltd.

Take Notes

Take Notes

Take Notes

Take Notes

Use this space for recording notes and sketching out ideas.

Take Notes

Use this space for recording notes and sketching out ideas.